Elisabeth Mann Borgese and the Law of the Sea

Legal History Library

VOLUME 59

Studies in the History of International Law

VOLUME 23

The titles published in this series are listed at *brill.com/shil*

Ocean wave during storm in the Atlantic ocean. Photo: iStock.com/DKart

Elisabeth Mann Borgese and the Law of the Sea

By

Tirza Meyer

BRILL
NIJHOFF

LEIDEN | BOSTON

This book has been funded by the Research Council of Norway (SAMKUL), Project name: The High Seas and the Deep Oceans: Representations, Resources and Regulatory Governance (3ROceans). Project number: 259419. Project period: 2016–2021.

Cover illustration: Elisabeth Mann Borgese Juli 1998 Weltausstellung der Meere, Lissabon, im Deutschen Pavillon vor Schaukasten/photo: Wolf Gaudlitz.

The Library of Congress Cataloging-in-Publication Data is available online at https://catalog.loc.gov
LC record available at https://lccn.loc.gov/2022001954

Typeface for the Latin, Greek, and Cyrillic scripts: "Brill". See and download: brill.com/brill-typeface.

ISSN 1874-1793
ISBN 978-90-04-50330-4 (hardback)
ISBN 978-90-04-51144-6 (e-book)

This book is printed on acid-free paper and produced in a sustainable manner.

Contents

PART 2
Preparing for the Law of the Sea Convention 1967–73

PART 3
Negotiating the Law of the Sea 1973–82

Foreword

Elisabeth Mann Borgese (1918–2002) proved courageous enough to peer into the future and imagine it in her own terms. An idealist dedicated to pursing economic justice, she found in the oceans a space that invited new, even radical concepts of just governance. In this welcome contribution to the history of international law and to ocean history, Tirza Meyer interweaves the story of Mann Borgese's remarkable life with an account of the negotiations that led to the United Nations Convention on the Law of the Sea, concluded in 1982. The daughter of the Nobel Prize-winning German author Thomas Mann and a mother, Katia, with Jewish ancestry, Mann Borgese was displaced with her family when the Nazi Party seized power, becoming first a citizen of Czechoslovakia in 1936, then of the United States in 1941, and finally of Canada in 1983 after she became a professor of political science at Dalhousie University.

Through her husband, Giuseppe Antonio Borgese, a professor of Romance literature and languages, Mann Borgese joined a group of academics at the University of Chicago, many political refugees, that drafted a "World Constitution" proposing to replace nation states with a single federal system. It was published in the *Bulletin of the Atomic Scientists* in 1948, reflecting concerns about strident nationalism and Cold War tensions leading to nuclear annihilation. Although politically unrealistic, the draft articulated principles that Mann Borgese worked to transform into reality for the rest of her life, including the idea that the life-giving resources of air, water, earth and energy were the common property of all humans. A 1964 opportunity to work in a new institution, the Center for the Study of Democratic Institutions in Santa Barbara, California, directed her attention to the possibility that the ocean might be a promising setting for the cultivation of internationalism and world governance. Meyer presents intriguing evidence that in 1967 Mann Borgese may have been attracted to on-going ocean governance negotiations by a vision of science and technology promising to tap new sources of wealth in the oceans that might be deployed to feed the hungry, aid underdeveloped nations, and enable effective international governance.

Such a vision was shortly thereafter presented to the UN General Assembly by the Maltese Ambassador, Arvid Pardo, in his famous November 1967 speech proposing that the ocean's resources in areas beyond national jurisdiction be declared the "Common Heritage of Mankind" (now referred to as the Common Heritage of Humankind). Pardo's proposal rekindled international law of the sea negotiations, begun with the first UN Conference on the Law of the Sea in 1958 and extended fairly unsuccessfully in a second conference in 1960. Mann

Borgese, newly following the events associated with Law of the Sea, lost no time in contacting Pardo after his speech and inviting him to Santa Barbara. Their initial meetings set the stage for the influential *Pacem in Maribus* conferences, which provided informal opportunities for those involved in Law of the Sea negotiations to discuss proposals in the hopes of incorporating internationalist ideals.

Mann Borgese worked tirelessly trying to insert idealistic elements into Law of the Sea, especially ones promoting world governance and economic justice, long after Pardo stepped away from the fray. Meyer argues that Mann Borgese's legacy includes the International Ocean Institute, which she founded in 1972, the same year that the Third UN Conference on Law of the Sea opened. The institute continues to carry forward her vision and work, although it did not, as she dreamed, become a UN institution to govern the world oceans or an implement for collecting wealth from newly accessible ocean resources to equalize an unequal world. While the UN Convention on the Law of the Sea, concluded in 1982, articulated the common heritage principle, that ideal was eroded by the provisions negotiated between then and 1994 to persuade the United States and other industrialized nations to accept the treaty. Nevertheless, Meyer presents Mann Borgese as an exemplar of determination, a quality she balanced with flexibility in shifting strategies as needed to pursue her goals. Her precise influence on Law of the Sea is debatable as many of her ideals failed to be incorporated into it and she herself could be a polarizing figure, but her story draws attention to the importance of paying attention to individuals as well as non-governmental institutions and other non-state actors in this history. It also demonstrates the value of accounts of Law of the Sea written by historians drawing upon extensive archival research to complement the many works penned by participants in the negotiations and by legal scholars, both of which tend to offer teleological accounts documenting the path to final outcomes rather than telling a fuller story.

Concluding the Law of the Sea Treaty required international cooperation and assent. It involved as well a collective imagining of the future in terms of anticipated technological advancements that might draw wealth from oceans, predicted geopolitical conflicts and alliances, and also idealized hopes for greater justice, equality, and peace. Meyer rightly points out that, in the present moment with the ocean's heightened environmental and geopolitical importance, Mann Borgese's attention to questions of justice and injustice, and to the promise of internationalism, render her writings and her life a resource for the present and future.

Helen M. Rozwadowski

Preface

Before diving into the story of Elisabeth Mann Borgese and the Law of the Sea, it is important to clarify the use of terminology in this book. The attentive reader will find several terms that are today either outdated or debated. These include the term *common heritage of mankind,* along with references to *developed, developing, industrialised* and *third world* countries. For some of these terms, researchers and the international community at the United Nations have not yet agreed universal modern alternatives.

The term *third world* has been abolished because it suggests a global hierarchy of first, second and third-class countries. It appears just once in this book followed by an explanatory footnote. However, the division of countries into *developing* and *developed* is still widely used both in this book and in general. For instance, the UN has the 'United Nations Office of the High Representative for the Least Developed Countries, Landlocked Developing Countries and Small Island Developing States (UN-OHRLLS)'.[1] Some countries that fall into the *developing* category may also like to use the term because it has financial implications for them. However, this way of dividing up the world is problematic because it suggests that there is only one narrow type of development: that of the industrialised western societies that are mainly in the global north and often have colonial pasts. But who is to say that there is only one kind of 'good' development? In 2015, the World Bank announced that it was phasing out the terms in favour of dealing with regions and income groups,[2] but I could not make the same choice in this book for a variety of reasons.

The book's main events took place between the 1960s and 1980s, and this is reflected in the language used in the archival material and other sources. For those living at the time, the world was very much divided into a 'communist' east, a 'developing' south and an 'industrialised' north-west. This affected how people spoke to each other and what kinds of challenges they felt needed to be solved. During the UNCLOS negotiations, the issue of justice for less industrially developed former colonies was keenly debated. UN delegates and the public used these terms to describe the differences between world regions, and

---

1 United Nations Office of the High Representative for the Least Developed Countries, Landlocked Developing Countries and Small Island Developing States (UN-OHRLLS). https://www.un.org/ohrlls/.

2 Tariq Khokhar, Umar Serajuddin, 'Should we continue to use the term "developing world"?', World Bank Blogs, 16 November 2015, available at: https://blogs.worldbank.org/opendata/should-we-continue-use-term-developing-world.

for the sake of clarity and readability I have made the conscious choice to stick to the established terms. There are also no widely agreed alternatives, as shown by the fact that the UN still uses these terms.

In the case of the *common heritage of mankind*, I had the option of using the more gender-neutral term, 'common heritage of humankind' which many recent scholars have begun to favour. However, this book follows the evolution of the Law of the Sea, and the language and terminology of the law text is a key part of this. Who 'mankind' is and who this 'common heritage' applies to are very interesting questions, and it's important to note that to this day the term *common heritage of mankind* is the one inscribed in the Law of the Sea. In any discussion about the modern meaning of the common heritage principle, I would have used the gender neutral version, but since this book is a history, I have stuck to the historically used term for the sake of readability and clarity. Finally, we need to keep in mind that – gender neutral or not – the term is loaded with ambiguous meaning and symbolism. What implications does it have for humankind's action on this planet if we see ourselves as the sole heirs to every being and everything on Earth? In the future, we will have to find answers to this question.

Acknowledgments

This book is a refined version of my dissertation that was the result of my PhD project at the Norwegian University of Science and Technology (NTNU) in Trondheim. The research was made possible through the generous funding by the Norwegian University of Science and Technology Strategic Research Area – NTNU Oceans with director Siri Granum Carson and the Faculty of Humanities.

I would like to express my great appreciation to my former supervisors Håkon With Andersen and Thomas Brandt for their steady support, great advice and patient guidance. Your expertise has been invaluable. I also wish to express my gratitude towards Helen M. Rozwadowski and Peder Roberts who were on the evaluation committee of my doctoral thesis. I thank you for encouraging me to turn my dissertation into a book and for your assistance in the process. A special thanks is due to Helen, who gratiously agreed to write the foreword to this book.

All my colleagues and friends at the 3ROceans project group at NTNU deserve special thanks for their encouragement and support. The group has been an inexhaustible source of inspiration and joy. I would like to thank Mats Ingulstad and Gard Paulsen, Knut Ove Eliassen, Kim Ménage, Christopher Messelt and Widar Aalrust Kristoffersen. My grateful thanks are extended to all my former colleagues at the Department of Historical and Classical Studies and the Department of Modern History and Society at the Norwegian University of Science and Technology for their support. The Division of History of Science, Technology and Environment at KTH in Stockholm deserves my gratitude for warmly welcoming me and giving me a space to continue my work on ocean related questions that are inspired by this book.

Rosemary Rayfuse and Lucas Lixinski have offered me the great opportunity to visit the Faculty of Law at the University of New South Wales. Thank you for your guidance and hospitality. I also want to thank Shirley Scott from UNSW Canberra for her useful and constructive recommendations on my project.

I want to extend my gratitude to the Deep Sea Mining Pilot project group at NTNU Oceans for giving me the great opportunity to contribute a humanistic approach to an interdisciplinary project. I would also like to thank my colleagues at the Reading Group of the Oslo School of Environmental Humanities for helping me to polish the framework of this book to make it accessible for a wider audience.

I am particular thankful for the assistance given by the staff of the International Ocean Institute in Halifax and the International Ocean Institute Headquarters in Malta for connecting me with important interview partners, helping me to find research material and offering me to use their workspaces for interviews and reading during my visits in Malta and Halifax. I would like to offer my special thanks to Madeleine Coffen-Smout from the IOI in Halifax for her speedy help and guidance. Thank you for sharing with me your profound knowledge about Elisabeth Mann Borgese's network and connecting me with important people. I also wish to acknowledge the help provided by Antonella Vassallo, at the IOI in Malta, who has been likewise resourceful in finding the right people and providing me with valuable material from the IOI library.

Very special thanks is due to my interviewees and informants, who have been generous with their time and open and willingly shared with me important and valuable information about the life of Elisabeth Mann Borgese and UNCLOS III. I would like to thank Francois Bailet, Nica Borgese, H. E. Saviour Borg, Aldo Chircop, Anita Coady, Catherine Enright, Nikolaus Gelpke, Tommy Koh, Ian McAllister and Hugh Williamson.

My special thanks are extended to the staff at Dalhousie University Archives in Halifax for their resourcefulness, helpful advice and for extending their opening hours in order for me to be able to view all the materials I had on my list. I would also like to thank David Attard for making me aware of the International Maritime Law Institute – Pardo Archives, where I could find some essential information about Arvid Pardo that was not available elsewhere. I would also like to thank the staff of the United-Nations Archive, in New York City, the staff of the Literaturarchiv der Monacensia in Munich and the Thomas-Mann-Archive in Zürich for providing me with speedy information, access and excellent help and guidance whenever I could not find a dearly needed document. My grateful thanks are extended to Nica Borgese, who has been so kind to invite me into her home and provide me with documents of her mother that were not available elsewhere.

I would like to thank photographer and film maker Wolf Gaudlitz for allowing me to use one of his famous portraits of Elisabeth Mann Borgese for the cover of this book. I am grateful for the support and guidance I received by the publishing team at Brill/Martinus Nijhoff. My proofreader Joly Braime deserves my gratitude. All remaining errors are mine.Finally, I want to thank my family and partner, who have encouraged me whenever I needed support.

Oslo, October 2021

Figures

Introduction

When Elisabeth Mann Borgese (1918–2002) – professor of law and political science, activist and world citizen – stepped up to the speaker's desk to give the Nexus Lecture in 1999, she said, 'The idealists of today are the realists of tomorrow. The realists of today are dead tomorrow'.[1] Those two sentences encapsulated her core values. Elisabeth Mann Borgese was an idealist at heart and she believed in the power of ideas. At the time she was over eighty years old with no plans to retire. She had worked with the oceans for almost half a century, had travelled the world attending countless meetings, had fought with politicians and argued with United Nations delegates, pushing on through disagreements and setbacks. For the numerous people who have followed her work and who are familiar with the Law of the Sea, she had become '*the mother of the oceans*'.[2]

This book is both about her personal and professional life and about one of history's largest international efforts to govern the oceans: The United Nations Law of the Sea Convention (1958–94), often shortened to UNCLOS. While it may seem unusual to set one person's life story alongside a history of intergovernmental United Nations processes, it is only through this double-lens that we can examine how ideas for political improvement change through time and travel through an institution, and how social, political, governmental and environmental events shape the ideas and ideals of individuals. This gives us a unique insight into the way individual people, ideas and institutions can come together to leave lasting legacies.

In this book, there are two separate legacies to account for. First, there is the legacy of the Law of the Sea Convention itself, in the form of the Law of the Sea Treaty – sometimes called the 'Constitution of the Ocean'.[3] This contains rules and regulations that the international community has agreed shall apply

1 Elisabeth Mann Borgese, 'The Years of my Life. The Nexus Lecture' (1999), in *Elisabeth Mann Borgese und das Drama der Meere*, exhibition catalogue, eds. Holger Pils and Karolina Kühn (Hamburg: mareverlag, 2012), 206–226.

2 Awni Benham, 'Whither IOI? (2): Ten Years beyond the Loss of Elisabeth Mann Borgese', in *Ocean Yearbook* 26 (1): 7. doi:10.1163/22116001-92600100.

3 Shirley Scott argues that viewing the Law of the Sea Convention treaty as constitutional would strengthen its legitimacy and international recognition, despite the inherent disagreements around certain portions of the treaty that have kept the US from ratifying it. Scott argues that '[…] a constitution cannot help but play a symbolic role, representing respect for the rules of law within that society'. *Cf.* Shirley V. Scott, 'The LOS Convention as a Constitutional Regime for the Oceans', in *Stability and Change in the Law of the Sea: The role of the LOS Convention,* ed. Alex G. Oude Elferink (Leiden: Martinus Nijhoff Publishers, 2005), 38.

to the ocean, including transport on its surface, fishing in its waters and how borders are drawn.[4] Second, there is Elisabeth Mann Borgese's own legacy, and this is a bit more complicated, since the outcome of her work and the meaning of her life are less linear and quantifiable than a successful intergovernmental convention with a ratification date and a treaty at the finish line. From 1967 until the end of her life, Elisabeth Mann Borgese worked for a better ocean order – for fair and just rules and regulations governing the use of the oceans. As I researched this book, tracing her ideas and actions, I concluded that her legacy was two-fold. Firstly, she founded an institution that continues to carry forward her work: the International Ocean Institute that still operates in locations including Malta and Halifax, Nova Scotia. But her legacy also lies in how relevant her proposals and ideas still are today. Although the story of Elisabeth Mann Borgese and UNCLOS unfolded in the second half of the last century, questions of justice, injustice and international collaboration in the context of the ocean environment remain challenging to this day. Anyone interested in intergovernmental ocean issues – including scholars, activists, diplomats and state officials alike – would benefit from investigating Elisabeth Mann Borgese's radical vision for a just world ocean order.[5]

4 There is some disagreement about the success of UNCLOS and the effectiveness of the rules that were adopted and that are still valid today. Scott is partly contradicted by the findings of scholars studying the way developing countries engaged with the Law of the Sea. Peter Bautista Payoyo, for instance, argues in his 1997 book, *Cries of the Sea*, that not all states were equally served by the outcome. Landlocked developing states in particular were 'effectively marginalized from the global sharing arrangements […]'. *See* Payoyo, *Cries of the Sea*, 151. *See also* Stephen Charles Vasciannie, *Land-Locked and Geographically Disadvantaged States in the International Law of the Sea* (Oxford: Clarendon Press, 1990), 221.

5 The Law of the Sea is as important today as it was in the 1970s. Its rules and regulations are constantly probed, tested and filled out with practical meaning. Therefore, a lot of the discussions that were ongoing during UNCLOS are still relevant. For instance, in order to keep up with accelerating developments in technology, along with political circumstances and legal context, Friedheim calls for a 'sort of universal ocean institution that can help bring ocean law continuously up to date'. *See* Robert L. Friedheim, 'A Proper Order for the Oceans: An Agenda for the New Century', in *Order for the Oceans at the Turn of the Century,* eds. Davor Vidas and Willy Østreng (The Hague: Kluwer Law International, 1999), 555. David Freestone's article compilation, *The 1982 Law of the Sea Convention at 30: Successes, Challenges and New Agendas*, published in 2013, makes similar points about rethinking a functioning Law of the Sea. The work advocates considering the ramifications of the treaty in the light of today's challenges from climate change, and addressing issues of environmental protection in areas outside national jurisdiction. *See* Alan Boyle, 'Law of the Sea Perspective on Climate Change', in *The 1982 Law of the Sea Convention at 30: Successes, Challenges and New Agendas,* ed., David Freestone (Leiden/Boston: Martinus Nijhoff Publishers, 2013), 157–164. *See also* Christina M. Gjerde, 'Challenges to Protecting the Marine Environment beyond National Jurisdiction',

1 World Traveller, Oyster Farmer and Dog Lover

When I started interviewing people about Elisabeth Mann Borgese's life, work and personality, I began to hear a lot of stories. Once, after an interview at the International Ocean Institute (IOI) in Halifax, one of her former colleagues kept on telling anecdotes even after the audio recorder was turned off and buried in my pocket. Standing in the small hallway of the IOI, he recalled how Elisabeth had once nearly capsized a dinghy off the coast of Jamaica, tilting the boat perilously as she made a sudden, enthusiastic move to get a closer look at some dolphins. The other passengers were horrified since they had passed a group of sharks just minutes earlier, but he told me she had giggled the whole incident off afterwards. Elisabeth Mann Borgese was never afraid to rock the boat.

There were so many other stories too – of the family of dogs that slept in her bed (all five or six of them) and of her house by the sea in Halifax, Nova Scotia – where neighbours who were invited round for dinner might find themselves rubbing shoulders with visiting diplomats. The Maltese ambassador, Arvid Pardo, could sometimes be spotted relaxing on her wooden deckchairs, while a former student and dog-sitter recalled seeing the honourable ambassador of Singapore, Tommy Koh, doing push-ups on the deck dressed in a white singlet. There was the time Elisabeth and her neighbour, Catherine – who had a diving certificate and an interest in ocean farming – started a business planting and harvesting oysters in their local waters. The oysters, a foreign species, flourished – perhaps too well since their descendants can still be found on the coast of Crystal Crescent beach a mile or so from the house. There are memories of the chic, all-black outfits she wore for her extensive travels, and photographs of her sat at her desk in a kaftan, looking out from her A-frame house across the lagoon to the ocean beyond. People told me of visitors who came and went, of travels to far-off places, of encounters with diplomats and state officials and of the spirit of adventure and hard work that went into everything she did (not just the oyster-farming business). But it was in the development of ocean governance that she cut an even more remarkable figure.

Elisabeth Mann Borgese wanted a new order for the oceans at a time when there were almost no rules governing them. A time when the extent of a nation state's sovereignty over its coastal waters was still measured by the distance of a cannon shot[6] (about four nautical miles) and fishing and transport rights

in *The 1982 Law of the Sea Convention at 30: Successes, Challenges and New Agendas*, ed., David Freestone (Leiden/Boston: Martinus Nijhoff Publishers, 2013), 165–173.

6 On the origin of the cannon shot rule see 'The Three-Mile Limit as a Rule of International Law', *Columbia Law Review* 23, no. 5 (1923): 473, doi:10.2307/1112336.

FIGURE 1 Elisabeth Mann Borgese in New York in front of the United Nations Building
MONACENSIA LITERATURARCHIV UND BIBLIOTHEK, EMB F 179
PHOTO: UNKNOWN

were negotiated bilaterally.[7] In fact, Mann Borgese's ambitions went beyond even this – she wanted a fairer system of governance not just for the oceans but for the entire world. The personal stories about her life are a testament to her enthusiasm for everything she engaged with – that same enthusiasm that almost capsized the dinghy in Jamaica and sometimes had a similar effect on discussions at the United Nations.

7 David Anderson writes about the status of ocean governance prior to UNCLOS: 'During the early decades of the twentieth century, maritime law was stable and could be summarized as follows. Coastal states had territorial waters extending to three nautical miles (nm), subject to insignificant exceptions, and measured in a belt around the coast. Beyond that limit, the seas and oceans had the status of high seas. Maritime law was based upon relatively simple foundations: international custom derived from the practice of States, among which maritime powers loomed large; a few conventions on technical matters; the writing of professors; and a few arbitral decisions. No inter-governmental organizations with maritime mandates existed and there was no forum for discussing maritime questions. Maritime disputes were justiciable only with the consent of the States concerned'. *See* David Anderson, ed., *Modern Law of the Sea. Selected Essays,* Publications on Ocean Development Volume 59 (Leiden/Boston: Martinus Nijhoff Publishers, 2008), 6.

2 The Potential of Uncharted Territory in the Ocean

When Elisabeth Mann Borgese threw herself into ocean governance discussions at the United Nations, she understood that it was one of the greatest opportunities of the century. For years, despite the disruption of two world wars, the international community had recognised that discussing ocean governance needed to be made a priority.[8] In 1958, the United Nations called for a Convention on the Law of the Sea (UNCLOS), hoping to resolve the ever-increasing number of governance issues. The convention would become one of the largest ever attempts to agree on an international treaty.[9] In the end, it took three decades and three attempts (UNCLOS I in 1958, UNCLOS II in 1960, and UNCLOS III in 1973–82) to finalise the convention, plus countless meetings at the United Nations. Each group or delegation involved had their own interests in the oceans depending on their geographical location, state of industrial development, political ties, colonial past and military interests.

The Law of the Sea Convention was a mammoth endeavour, with complicated logistics not unlike those of space exploration. Without international cooperation, it would be impossible to achieve anything, since dividing the ocean into zones and regions relied on the will to collaborate across national borders. The challenges went beyond international relations, though, and many were tied to the uncertain nature of the ocean itself. Much like space scientists, the delegates had to try and foresee future developments in technology and underwater activity, set within an environment that was largely unexplored and hostile to human life. There were numerous dilemmas tied into the renegotiation of the Law of the Sea. How far offshore could coastal states claim territory? What would happen to free passage on the high seas if territorial claims exceeded the cannon shot rule? What should be done with areas that were not yet under national jurisdiction? Should the oceans be claimed like territory on dry land? Or could there be another way?

---

8 Edward L Miles discusses the question of why the international community worked its way towards a new ocean order at the start of the new century in Edward L. Miles, 'Preparations for UNCLOS IV?', *Ocean Development and International Law* 19, no. 5 (1988): 422–423, https://doi.org/10.1080/00908328809545870.

9 In terms of international law-making processes, the Law of the Sea – especially UNCLOS III – has been perceived as 'the most important multilateral conference of the 1970s'. *See* Gabriele Goettsche-Wanli, 'The United Nations Convention on the Law of the Sea: Multilateral Diplomacy at Work', *Conference Diplomacy 1815–2015, UN Chronicle,* 51, no. 3 (2014), https://www.un.org/en/chronicle/article/united-nations-convention-law-sea-multilateral-diplomacy-work.

The biggest obstacle during UNCLOS III remained the question of how to govern the area of the seafloor that was outside national jurisdiction.[10] This aspect of ocean governance – and world governance in general – was uncharted territory. No space on Earth was outside national jurisdiction in the same way as the deep seafloor, and it also contained potential wealth in the form of deep sea minerals that could be harvested in the future.[11]

In 1967, the Maltese diplomat Arvid Pardo – that same man who during the 1970s and 80s was occasionally observed sunning himself in a deckchair on Elisabeth Mann Borgese's porch – officially proposed a radical solution.[12] He suggested applying the principle of 'common heritage of mankind'[13] to the seafloor outside national jurisdiction and its resources. The central idea of this was simple: that the seafloor should belong to everyone and that everyone should be able to access it and benefit from its mineral wealth. Pardo's suggestion accelerated but also complicated the negotiations. Delegates at UNCLOS III

---

10 Some of the reasons for the difficulties in agreeing on a seabed regime are examined in Markus G Schmidt's 1989 work, *Common Heritage or Common Burden?*. Schmidt attempts to explain the United States' reservations about applying the common heritage principle to the seafloor, arguing that the hesitation was of a more 'ideological nature, directed against the creation of an "unaccountable and self-perpetuating world bureaucracy" [...]'. *See* Markus G. Schmidt, *Common Heritage or Common Burden? The United States position on the development of a regime for deap [sic: deep] sea-bed mining in the Law of the Sea Convention* (Oxford: Clarendon Press, 1989), 307.

11 *See generally* for future perspectives on the current state of deep sea mining: David Anderson, ed., *Modern Law of the Sea. Selected Essays,* Publications on Ocean Development Volume 59 (Leiden/Boston: Martinus Nijhoff Publishers, 2008). Donald R. Rothwell et. al., *The Oxford Handbook of the Law of the Sea* (Oxford/New York: Oxford University Press, 2015). Seoung-Yong Hong and Jon M. Van Dyke, eds., *Maritime Boundary Disputes, Settlement Processes, and the Law of the Sea,* Publications on Ocean Development Volume 65 (Leiden/Boston: Martinus Nijhoff Publishers, 2009). James Harrison, *Making the Law of the Sea. A Study in the Development of International Law* (Cambridge: Cambridge University Press, 2011). Alex G. Oude Elferink, ed., *Stability and Change in the Law of the Sea: The role of the LOS Convention* (Leiden: Martinus Nijhoff Publishers, 2005). Davor Vidas, ed., *Law, Technology and Science for Oceans in Globalisation. Iuu Fishing, Oil Pollution, Bioprospecting, Outer Continental Shelf* (Leiden: Martinus Nijhoff Publishers, 2010).

12 *See* Arvid Pardo's speech in A/C.1/PV.1515; A/C.1/PV.1516.

13 The concept of the 'common heritage of mankind' has been discussed in several publications. The term 'mankind' is used by Kemal Baslar in Kemal Baslar, *The Concept of the Common Heritage of Mankind in International Law* (Dordrecht, The Netherlands: Martinus Nijhoff, 1998). Peter Bautista Payoyo uses 'common heritage of humanity', In Peter Bautista Payoyo, *Cries of the Sea: World Inequality, Sustainable Development and the Common Heritage of Humanity* (Dordrecht, The Netherlands: Martinus Nijhoff, 1997). In this book, the concept will be referred to as 'common heritage of mankind', since the work does not aspire to discuss the philosophical and theoretical origins of the concept or to develop the principle further.

seriously disagreed over what to do with those areas of the oceans that were not controlled by nation states, and the international community was divided into several camps with differing interests.[14]

The industrialised states, predominantly in the geographical north, had been working to develop technologies that might soon make it possible to dive into deep sea areas and extract minerals. These states were mostly interested in bringing about arrangements that would make it easy for them to access the area outside national jurisdiction, and to utilise the resources they found there. On the other hand, developing states – often former colonies in the southern hemisphere – were much more in favour of the common heritage approach, which would make it possible for them to partake in the 'prospects of rich harvests and mineral wealth'[15] of the sea despite not possessing the advanced technology of the industrialised states.[16]

To complicate things further, the UNCLOS negotiations were held during the Cold War, in a diplomatic environment that was sometimes hostile and prone to all kinds of disagreements. Because discussions spanned more than thirty years, the political backdrop and diplomatic climate shifted several times, making the negotiations even more difficult. The convention was also the first to allow non-governmental organisations (NGOs) to contribute to the negotiations, and the combination of NGOs and nation states made for an interesting mix, as the different stakeholders lobbied for a variety of aims. Elisabeth Mann Borgese was one of those who recognised that the ocean floor was a sort of blank space that could be filled with new concepts and ideas of governance.[17]

14 *Cf.* Payoyo, *Cries of the Sea*, 151.

15 Lyndon B. Johnson, 'Remarks at the Commissioning of the Research Ship – Oceanographer', (speech, Washington, DC, July 13, 1966), The American Presidency Project, http://www.presidency.ucsb.edu/ws/index.php?pid=27711.

16 *The Law of Deep Sea-Bed Mining* by Said Mahmoudi examines whether the seabed regime succeeded in balancing the needs of both the industrialised states and the developing world. The study was written in light of the absence of ratification by the US, Great Britain and the German Federal Republic in 1987, but Mahmoudi argues that '[…] even though the Convention has not yet achieved universality *stricto sensu*, it certainly has acquired something very close to that'. *See* Said Mahmoudi, *The Law of Deep Sea-Bed Mining. A Study of the Progressive Development of International Law Concerning the Management of the Polymetallic Nodules of the Deep Sea-Bed* (Stockholm: Almqvist & Wiksell International, 1987), 341.

17 In 1992, Monica Allen published *An Intellectual History of the Common Heritage of Mankind as Applied to the Oceans*. She examines the idea of common heritage, and how states, groups and individuals tried to apply it to the ocean floor. She also includes the efforts of Arvid Pardo and Elisabeth Mann Borgese. Allen, like many others, focuses on Arvid Pardo and uses him as the main carrier of the idea. She argues that developing nations and other individual actors used the concept of common heritage as a vehicle for

3 Life History – Why People Matter

During Elisabeth Mann Borgese's years working with the Law of the Sea, she became an influential activist who built institutions of lasting importance for ocean governance. Like other activists affiliated with non-governmental organisations, she was mostly interested in the seafloor outside national jurisdiction, and for one simple reason – it held the greatest potential for developing and introducing new principles and ways of governance into international law.[18] But why would a person develop such a burning enthusiasm for ocean governance?

Elisabeth Mann Borgese was not a diplomat in the conventional sense. Unlike Arvid Pardo, she had not aimed at a career in the United Nations system, nor had any nation state appointed her to serve permanently on their mission to the United Nations. In 1967, when she first became involved with preparations for UNCLOS, she was working as a researcher at the Center for the Study of Democratic Institutions in Santa Barbara. Being an outsider meant that she had to find alternative ways into the convention, first through founding her own NGO, the International Ocean Institute, and later by joining the Austrian delegation as an adviser. In the grand scheme of intergovernmental collaboration, Elisabeth Mann Borgese's position was unusual, and her powerful motivation to effect change perhaps distinguished her work from that of a career diplomat.[19] But why was she so keen to be there in the first place? This is where her biography, upbringing, background and personal relations

---

their own purposes. *See* Monica Allen, 'An Intellectual History of the Common Heritage of Mankind as Applied to the Oceans' (Master thesis, University of Rhode Island, 1992).

18 The diplomatic historian Ralph B Levering and his mother Miriam Lindsay Levering (a member of the Neptune Group NGO at UNCLOS) published a study that homed in on individual actors. The Leverings limited their focus to one group of activists: The Neptune Group. The book *Citizen Action for Global Change: The Neptune Group and Law of the Sea* is especially interesting in regard to the way the Leverings worked. *See* Ralph B. Levering and Miriam L. Levering, *Citizen Action for Global Change. The Neptune Group and Law of the Sea* (New York: Syracuse University Press, 1999). *See also* John Hannigan, *The Geopolitics of Deep Oceans* (Cambridge: Polity Press, 2016), 62. Hannigan refers to Levering and Levering, *Citizen Action*, 33.

19 The Leverings (see note above) were interested in change too, and this book reveals some striking similarities between the activism of individuals like Mann Borgese and the Levering family. The Leverings had no legal training, but ended up trying to shape and influence the Law of the Sea at a high level. They also allied themselves with developing countries, and saw the convention as an opportunity to influence discussions on world governance, although the exact impact of their activism and diplomatic skills is hard to quantify.

are important for this book. To understand her activism and her vision, we need first to understand what drove her.[20]

During my research I travelled to some of the places that were central to Mann Borgese's work – Halifax, New York and Malta – and I interviewed people who knew her. I wanted to get to know 'the mother of the oceans' on more than one level. Although her papers, speeches and reports about UNCLOS III are important sources for understanding her ideas and vision, other aspects of her life also deserve examination. I spent a long time going through letters she wrote to colleagues, family and friends, and as I charted her personal relationships I discovered that her working and personal lives were very much intertwined and that the ideas and visions she took to UNCLOS sprung out of some of those personal relations.

Although following Mann Borgese's path is an integral part of this book, it should not be read as a biography. I have used elements of biographical writing to illuminate the origins of her internationalism and her ideal vision for a just world order. We need to explore her background to understand her ideals and what her efforts ultimately meant for the negotiations and the outcome of UNCLOS, but there is no need to follow every detail of Mann Borgese's life all the way through from birth to death. The biographical approach in this book follows a historical tradition that Judith M Brown calls 'life histories'.[21] Like Brown, who has written Gandhi and Nehru's biographies, I see myself more as 'a historian of time and region […] who uses the medium of "life histories," of individuals and groups of individuals, to seek for evidence to probe many

20 In 2012, Betsy Baker published the article 'Uncommon Heritage: Elisabeth Mann Borgese, Pacem in Maribus, the International Ocean Institute and Preparations for UNCLOS III'. The article presents the findings of a limited archival case study on the possible impact or influence Elisabeth Mann Borgese and her peers could have had on negotiations at UNCLOS through their preparation conferences, *Pacem in Maribus*. In her study, Baker states that the efforts of the International Ocean Institute, which Mann Borgese founded in 1972, were think tank activity, but that a more detailed account of Elisabeth Mann Borgese's influence would 'require further study'. *See* Betsy Baker, 'Uncommon Heritage: Elisabeth Mann Borgese, Pacem in Maribus, the International Ocean Institute and Preparations for UNCLOS III'. In *Ocean Yearbook Online*, Vol. 26 (Brill 2012): 11–34. https://doi.org/10.1163/22116001-92600099. There is also an article collection in an exhibition catalogue about EMB's life. The catalogue gives an overview of Mann Borgese's life and work, and the origins of her ideals. The articles in the catalogue range from personal memories to the discussion of Mann Borgese's literary works, and this spread reflects the general state of research about Mann Borgese and her work with the ocean, much of which is fragmented. *See* Holger Pils and Karolina Kühn, eds., *Elisabeth Mann Borgese und das Drama der Meere*, exhibition catalogue, (Hamburg: mareverlag, 2012).

21 Judith M. Brown, '"Life Histories" and the History of Modern South Asia', *The American Historical Review* 114, nr. 3 (June 2009): 587–95, https://doi.org/10.1086/ahr.114.3.587.

key historical issues'.[22] I have chosen to follow Elisabeth Mann Borgese's work because she makes a good model for an individual operating in international negotiations. She can give us a unique understanding of how major international agreements can be controlled by a small number of key players, how individual people's ideas travel through time, how they evolve and how they adapt to political and institutional change.[23] Her story might even hint at what could be done today to counter the environmental and political challenges faced by the world's oceans.

In this book, I have tried to explore how Elisabeth Mann Borgese's motivations, ideas and strategies evolved within the wider climate of twentieth-century global politics, and how they affected the institutions and processes she worked with. I have chosen to study proposals, reports and articles from different periods of her work in the context of the time when they were produced rather than in the light of the convention's eventual outcomes – and in doing so I hope to present a history of time and region understood through the personal background of one individual actor

4 Elisabeth Mann Borgese Fonds and Other Archives

Most of the material I examined for this book stems from the Elisabeth Mann Borgese Fonds,[24] held by the Dalhousie University Archives in Halifax, Nova Scotia. The fifth floor of the concrete building at Lemarchant Street, not far from Elisabeth Mann Borgese's former headquarters – the IOI – holds most of her private and work-related correspondence, as well as academic articles, research documents, newspaper articles, and other hand-written and typed material. The full archive far exceeds the material used in this book, and I have concentrated on UNCLOS-related correspondence with key actors at the convention, with a special focus on her allies and collaborators. I have also reviewed Mann Borgese's academic documents – including lectures, reports,

22 Brown, '"Life Histories"', 587.

23 Mann Borgese was not the only interesting character at the convention, and other works have shed some light on individual participants or groups operating during UNCLOS. One example is a book by Canadian journalist Clyde Sanger called *Ordering the Oceans*. Sanger was present during the negotiations, and reported about the negotiation process, its challenges and the key actors involved. He gives some interesting character descriptions of key actors at the Convention. *See* Clyde Sanger, *Ordering the Oceans – The Making of the Law of the Sea* (London: Zed Books Ltd., 1986).

24 Elisabeth Mann Borgese Fonds, MS-2-744, Dalhousie University Archives and Special Collections, Halifax, Canada.

articles, memorandums and books – and I have occasionally incorporated newspaper articles that give an outsider's perspective of particular issues.

For biographical information about Mann Borgese's upbringing, her family and her young adult life, I viewed material from the Monacensia Archive[25] in Munich and the Thomas Mann Archive[26] in Zürich. A small proportion of the material on her personal life was retrieved from the house of her daughter, Nica Borgese,[27] in Milan. This mostly consisted of private and professional correspondence from the 1940s and 50s.

For access to official records of the UNCLOS III negotiations, I supplemented the extensive collection of official UN documents at the Dalhousie University Archives by visiting the United Nations Archives[28] in New York – where Mann Borgese spent a good deal of her time during the negotiation phase at UNCLOS.

To explore Mann Borgese's relations with Arvid Pardo and the Maltese government, I visited the Pardo Archive[29] at the International Maritime Law Institute in Malta, which contains a small amount of personal correspondence, newspaper articles and academic work. Unfortunately, material about Arvid Pardo is very limited – especially compared to the abundance of material about Mann Borgese – and most of the personal correspondence between Pardo and Mann Borgese is also available at the Dalhousie University Archives. There is one classified folder on Arvid Pardo at the United Nations Archive in New York,[30] which if declassified might contain interesting information on his work. The scope of this book means that the lack of material on Arvid Pardo is not necessarily a problem. Although Arvid Pardo was an important ally and friend to Elisabeth Mann Borgese, my focus lies on her ideals, ideas and strategy before, during and after UNCLOS. Pardo's main relevance to the book relates to his role in the development of Mann Borgese's ideas and their collaboration in the 1970s.

---

25 Nachl. Elisabeth Mann Borgese, EMB, Monacensia Literaturarchiv, München, Germany.

26 Ergänzter Nachlass Thomas Mann, B-III Briefe von Familienmitgliedern (direkte Nachkommen Thomas und Katia Manns, deren Ehepartner sowie Katia Mann), Thomas-Mann- Archiv, Zürich, Switzerland.

27 Nica Borgese, Private Collection, Milano, Italy.

28 Office of the Secretary-General Law of the Sea Conference Records 1973–1983, United Nations Archives & Record Management Section, New York City, United States of America.

29 Pardo Archive, International Maritime Law Institute, Msida, Malta.

30 *See* S-0289-0009-36 Office of the Chef de Cabinet, Personnel case files, Arvid Pardo, 01.10. 1964-30.04.1972. (strictly confidential).

Finally, for further insights into Elisabeth Mann Borgese's personality, I conducted ten interviews with colleagues, friends and a family member.[31] I treated the content from these interviews as background information, and they provided clues that prompted further investigation into specific issues around Mann Borgese's thought processes, her way into the Law of the Sea and her personal history. The interviews also gave me an understanding of her extraordinary personality and how it might have helped her negotiate in favour of a new ocean order.

5 An Overview – Elisabeth Mann Borgese and the Law of the Sea from 1918–94

This book is divided into four main parts. The first part (1918–67) deals with Elisabeth Mann Borgese's earlier life, her route into academia and how her ideal of internationalism first evolved. The second part (1967–73) looks into her work before UNCLOS III and charts how she developed ideas to try and promote her internationalist ideals. The third part (1973–82) explores Mann Borgese's attempts to try and push her ideas through during the hot negotiation phase of UNCLOS III, while the final part (1982–94) briefly examines the aftermath of the convention and how Mann Borgese tried to rescue her ideas during the implementation period.

31 Bailet, Francois. (Senior Legal Officer, United Nations DOALOS), telephone interview with the author, 11 November 2016. New York – Trondheim. USA/Norway. Borgese, Nica. (Professor CNR Institute of Neuroscience, Milano), interview with the author, 26 October 2015. Milano, Italy. Borg, H. E. Saviour F. (Ambassador of Malta to Switzerland, Ministry of Foreign Affairs), interview with the author, 15 March 2017. Valetta, Malta. Chircop, Aldo. (Professor of Law, Canada Research Chair (Tier 1), in Maritime Law and Policy), interview with the author, 6 March 2016. Oslo, Norway. Coady, Anita. (Member of the International Ocean Institute Governing Board), interview with the author, 25 May 2017. Halifax/NS, Canada. Enright, Catherine. (Retired associate Professor, Nova Scotia Agricultural College), interview with the author, 25 May 2017. Sambro Head/NS, Canada. Gelpke, Nikolaus. (Editor and head of Mareverlag publishing house; president of the International Ocean Institute), telephone interview with the author, 12 September 2016. Trondheim – Hamburg. Norway/Germany. Koh, Tommy. (Ambassador-at-Large Singapore Ministry of Foreign Affairs; Professor and rector of Tembusu College, Faculty of Law), e-mail to the author, 8 September 2016. McAllister, Ian. (Professor Emeritus, Department of Economics, Dalhousie University), interview with the author, 26 May 2017. Halifax/ , Canada. Williamson, Hugh. (Adjunct Professor: Marine Affairs Program, Dalhousie University), interview with the author, 29 April 2016. Halifax/NS, Canada.

Part 1 begins by sketching the background of the book's two main subjects, Elisabeth Mann Borgese and the Law of the Sea. We will follow Mann Borgese through the first forty years of her life, tracing her unconventional route into academia and the development of her internationalist ideals through influences such as her husband, her work on the Committee to Frame a World Constitution and her fellowship at the Center for the Study of Democratic Institutions in Santa Barbara. Having explored Mann Borgese's own history, we will move onto that of the Law of the Sea, beginning with the fundamental principles of ocean governance that were first developed in 1600. We will track the early attempts to codify the Law of the Sea, examine how the Truman Proclamation of 1945 made things suddenly more urgent, and investigate how the outcomes of the first two UNCLOS conventions laid the groundwork for UNCLOS III.

Part 2 follows Elizabeth Mann Borgese's actions and evolving ideas during the preparation period prior to UNCLOS III, and particularly her collaboration with Arvid Pardo, the Maltese ambassador. We will explore how Pardo's own vision for ocean governance compared with Mann Borgese's even more ambitious ideals, their deteriorating relations with the Maltese government, and Mann Borgese's creation of the International Ocean Institute – an NGO that gave her a way into the UNCLOS III negotiations.

Part 3 deals with the action of UNCLOS III, beginning with the extreme tension between developing and industrial states and the complicated web of alliances and interests that Mann Borgese had to navigate as she joined the negotiations. We will examine Mann Borgese's suggestions for a fair mode of ocean governance and her attempts to promote them and will follow her transition from NGO representative to a more influential role in the Austrian delegation. The section closes with the stalemate caused by the Reagan administration, the final vote in 1982 and Mann Borgese's last ditch attempts to make the deep seafloor the 'common heritage of mankind'.

Finally, the last section summarises the outcomes of the convention in the context of Mann Borgese's internationalist ideals. We will see how her ideas were ultimately defeated when the 1994 Implementation Agreement was adopted, leaving her nevertheless determined 'to pick up the pieces and see what we can do with them'.

PART 1

Elisabeth Mann Borgese's Introduction to World and Ocean Governance 1918–67

CHAPTER 1

Elisabeth Mann Borgese's Introduction to World Governance

1 Elisabeth Mann Borgese's Life in Time-Lapse

Elisabeth Mann Borgese spent much of her professional life between places. She was always on the move, travelling from one conference, session or gathering to another. Several times during her life she moved home between countries and even continents. Depending on where she lived and worked she changed citizenship on various occasions, seemingly without any great sentiment. Who was this woman and how did she get into ocean governance?

Elisabeth Veronika Mann was born in Munich on 24 April 1918. She was the fifth child in the intellectual Mann family,[1] but succeeded in making enough of an impression on the world to rise above simply being 'Thomas Mann's daughter'. In academic and diplomatic circles there was often little interest in her family background.[2]

By her teenage years, the travelling and movement that would characterise her life had already begun. Germany had become a hostile place for families with Jewish heritage and Elisabeth Mann's mother, Katia, had Jewish ancestry, so the family left the country in 1933.[3] At first, they moved to neighbouring Switzerland, where Elisabeth Mann lived with her family in Zürich and

1 Several CV versions exist. For detailed information from 1918–1982, *see* MS-2-744, Box 16, Folder 19. Shorter version *see* MS-2-744, Box 362, Folder 6.

2 For more information on the Mann family, several studies are available. Memoirs of family members: Monika Mann, *Vergangenes und Gegenwärtiges. Erinnerungen* (München: Kindle Verlag, 1956); Klaus Mann, *Der Wendepunkt. Ein Lebensbericht* (Reinbek: Rowohlt 2006, first edition 1952); Elisabeth Plessen and Michael Mann, eds., *Meine ungeschriebenen Memoiren* (Frankfurt am Main: Fischer Verlag, 1974). Biographies about family members: Inge Jens and Walter Jens, *Frau Thomas Mann: Das Leben der Katharina Pringsheim* (Reinbek: Rowohlt, 2004). Karin Andert, *Monika Mann. Eine Biographie* (Hamburg: mareverlag, 2010); Klaus Harpprecht, *Thomas Mann: Eine Biographie* (Reinbek: Rowohlt, 1995).

3 *Cf.* Irmela von der Lühe, '"Ich gehöre doch zu den Kleinen" Elisabeth Mann Borgese als Chronistin ihrer "amazing family"', in *Elisabeth Mann Borgese und das Drama der Meere*, exhibition catalogue, eds. Holger Pils and Karolina Kühn (Hamburg: mareverlag, 2012), 20. *See also* Thomas Sprecher, 'Eine Jugend in Zürich. Elisabeth Mann in den Jahren 1933–1938', in *Elisabeth Mann Borgese und das Drama der Meere*, exhibition catalogue, eds. Holger Pils and Karolina Kühn (Hamburg: mareverlag, 2012), 34.

 | DOI:10.1163/9789004511446_003

attended the Freie Gymnasium Zürich, graduating in 1935 at seventeen years old. When she was nineteen, she finished her training as a concert pianist,[4] though she did not pursue this career path further. In 1936, the family obtained Czech citizenship.[5] Together with their two youngest children, Elisabeth and Michael, the Manns moved to Italy for a short while. This may have been because they wanted to reassess the European political situation, or because Thomas Mann was reluctant to completely abandon his home region.[6] Finally, in 1938, like many other European intellectuals, the family turned away from Europe and made their way across the Atlantic to the United States.[7] The Manns found a new home in Princeton, where they were surrounded by other European emigrees. At one point during their time there, Albert Einstein lived in the neighbourhood.[8]

In Princeton, Elisabeth Mann met her future husband, the famous writer and scholar Giuseppe Antonio Borgese, who was thirty-six years her senior. One year later, in 1939, the couple married. In 1940, when Elisabeth Mann was twenty-two, her first daughter, Angelica, was born in Chicago. She obtained citizenship of the United States in 1941, four years after her arrival in Princeton, and her second daughter, Nica, was born in Chicago in 1944.[9] From 1946–52, Elisabeth Mann Borgese and her husband worked on formulating a 'World Constitution' in Chicago.[10] In September 1952, the couple returned to Europe and settled in Fiesole, outside Florence in Italy. Just two months later, on 4 December 1952, Giuseppe Antonio Borgese died there.[11] From 1953–64, Elisabeth Mann Borgese lived with her daughters in Italy and worked on several different projects. According to her Curriculum Vitae, she was employed as an editor for 'international publications'[12] affiliated with the Ford Foundation. One was a magazine about culture called *Perspectives*, while another was a UNESCO-funded magazine called *Diogenes*.[13] She also 'wrote short stories,

4 *Cf.* MS-2-744, Box 362, Folder 6. *See* Sprecher, 'Eine Jugend in Zürich', 43.

5 Sprecher, 'Eine Jugend in Zürich', 43. Sprecher refers to Thomas Mann Tagebücher: 1935–1936, 396 [10.03.1937].

6 *Cf.* Holzer, *Elisabeth Mann Borgese*, 69–70.

7 *Cf.* Sprecher, 'Eine Jugend in Zürich', 45.

8 *See* Holzer referring to Einstein in Holzer, *Elisabeth Mann Borgese*, 94. Elisabeth Mann Borgese wrote a letter to Albert Einstein in 1951. *See* B-III.17.EINS-1, 24.03.1951.

9 *Cf.* Giovanni di Stefano, 'Giuseppe Antonio Borgese. Porträt eines unruhigen Weltenbürgers', in *Elisabeth Mann Borgese und das Drama der Meere*, exhibition catalogue, eds. Holger Pils and Karolina Kühn (Hamburg: mareverlag, 2012), 60.

10 *Cf.* MS-2-744, Box 362, Folder 6.

11 *Cf.* Stefano, 'Giuseppe Antonio Borgese', 62.

12 MS-2-744, Box 16, Folder 19.

13 *Cf.* Holzer, *Elisabeth Mann Borgese*, 146–147.

essays and plays'.[14] In 1964, she returned to the United States to take up a senior fellowship at the Center for the Study of Democratic Institutions in Santa Barbara.[15]

We have fast-forwarded through forty-six years of Elisabeth's life. In that time, she had changed citizenship three times and lived in four different countries – Germany, Switzerland, the United States and Italy. She had married a much older man, borne two children, been widowed at just thirty-four years old, and managed to get the family through some rough years after Borgese's death. Before we continue with her life and start looking into how she got involved with the oceans, we should linger for a while over her relationship with Giuseppe Antonio Borgese and the work she did for the Committee to Frame a World Constitution. Did associating with the intellectuals in the Chicago circle influence her thoughts, and would this be reflected in her later career as she moved towards shaping the Law of the Sea?

2 Making Connections – An Intellectual Love with Giuseppe Antonio Borgese

Whenever Elisabeth Mann Borgese was asked about her late husband, the anti-fascist novelist and academic Giuseppe Antonio Borgese, she always talked about him with respect and pride,[16] often choosing to emphasise the effect he had on her intellectual education.[17] He gave her books he wanted her to read, introduced her to people he thought she would find interesting, and made her his close confidante, secretary and later research assistant.[18]

Elisabeth Mann was only twenty years old when she met Borgese for the first time at her parents' home in Princeton. Borgese was fifty-six.[19] Throughout her

14 A first extensive collection of Mann Borgese's publications can be found in Pils and Kühn, eds., *Elisabeth Mann Borgese*, 246–255.

15 NB-Folder 5, May 20, 1964.

16 *See* Holzer, *Elisabeth Mann Borgese*, 129: ' "Er war ein Gentleman, ehrenhaft und hochanständig", betont sie, "und ich habe ihn sehr verehrt. Aber er war eben unerträglich." '

17 Holzer described this in Holzer, *Elisabeth Mann Borgese*, 112–114. Mann Borgese refers to his influence on her in a letter to her daughters in 1982. *Cf.* EMB B4 Mann Borgese, 15.10.1982.

18 *Cf.* Baker, 'Elisabeth Mann Borgese', 91.

19 For a more detailed account of their first meeting *see* Holzer, *Elisabeth Mann Borgese*, 96–110.

life, she always told the same story about how they met and fell in love.[20] She had been reading his book, *Goliath – The March of Fascism*,[21] which was published in 1937 and was the first of Borgese's literary works to be written and published in exile.[22] He, like Thomas Mann, had left Europe because of the rising threat of fascism, moving to the University of California in 1931 after several incidents where his lectures at the University of Milan were disrupted by fascists.[23] Initially, the visit was only planned to last six months, but he decided to stay in the United States after receiving a letter from the Italian government stating that all university lecturers were requested to take an oath of loyalty to the nationalist regime.[24] By 1937, he had become a vocal advocate of anti-fascism in exile.[25] This was the man Elisabeth Mann decided she wanted to marry, based on having read his book.[26] She never said exactly what it was that fascinated her so much about his writing, but perhaps she thought it was obvious: Borgese's powerful call for anti-fascism and his accurate assessment of the global political situation in the lead-up to World War II. *Goliath – The March of Fascism* was undoubtedly a precursor to Giuseppe Antonio Borgese's involvement with the world constitution from 1945 onwards. At the moral heart of his work was the conviction that nation states had served their purpose, and that a new era of international cooperation was to come.[27]

As luck would have it, Elisabeth Mann met the author of this prophetic book when he came to meet Thomas Mann at their home in Princeton in 1938.[28] In an interview about her life, she said that her older sister Erika had helped arrange the meet-cute.[29] Elisabeth Mann was instructed to pick Borgese up from the train station, and as she later told her biographer Kerstin Holzer, the reality of the man lived up to her image of him. Over the ensuing month, her

20 For instance, at the Nexus Lecture in 1999. *See* Elisabeth Mann Borgese, 'The Years of my Life. The Nexus Lecture' (1999), in *Elisabeth Mann Borgese und das Drama der Meere*, exhibition catalogue, eds. Holger Pils and Karolina Kühn (Hamburg: mareverlag, 2012), 211.

21 Giuseppe Antonio Borgese, *Goliath – The March of Fascism* (New York: Viking Press, 1937).

22 *Cf.* Stefano, 'Giuseppe Antonio Borgese', 55.

23 He held several chair positions from 1931–1936 also in New York. *Cf.* Hannibal S. Noce, "Giuseppe Antonio Borgese", in *Modern Philology* 50, no. 4, (May, 1953): 218, https://www.jstor.org/stable/pdf/434830.pdf?refreqid=excelsior%3A4c0966418150857 9e876d414c219c14f.

24 *Cf.* Stefano, 'Giuseppe Antonio Borgese', 54–55.

25 *Cf.* Stefano, 'Giuseppe Antonio Borgese', 55.

26 *Cf.* EMB B4 Mann Borgese, 15.10.1982.

27 *Cf.* Stefano, 'Giuseppe Antonio Borgese', 56.

28 *Cf.* Holzer, *Elisabeth Mann Borgese*, 101.

29 *See* Ingo Hermann, ed., 'Elisabeth Mann Borgese. Die Meer Frau. Gespräch mit Amadou Seitz' in der Reihe "Zeugen des Jahrhunderts" (Göttingen: Lamuv Verlag GmbH, 1993), 27.

siblings arranged further meetings, and the pair quickly became a couple.[30] This seemingly chance romance might have been more of a deliberate arrangement and her own family may even have been hoping for it. Neither Elisabeth Mann Borgese herself nor any member of the Mann family ever contradicted this version of events, so we cannot know whether her fantastic love story was the absolute truth or a romanticised version of it. Giovanni di Stefano, who mentioned Elisabeth Mann Borgese's story in an article about her husband, suggested that she might have perpetuated this version of their meeting to emphasise their intellectual connection.[31]

Elisabeth Mann was fascinated by the older and more experienced man, and she had a clear sense of purpose in this, as she confided to her biographer Kerstin Holzer. Holzer reported that Elisabeth Mann 'wanted to learn, and she wanted to look up to someone. She was able to do that as a student of her husband'.[32] The urge to learn – and maybe even to admire – were traits that she would display throughout her life, and Borgese was not the only man she would look up to. He was the second – after her father[33] – in a series of important men in her life with whom she felt an intellectual connection and in some cases a romantic one too. That those people she admired were men was perhaps due to the fact that not many women in the 1950s could aspire to much beyond being a housewife. It might be more correct to suggest that Elisabeth Mann Borgese in general admired people who pursued their goals by using their wit and intellect, and that in 1950, those people were mostly men.[34]

The question of the relationship between men and women interested Elisabeth Mann even before she met Borgese. For many years, she worked on a

---

30 *Cf.* Holzer, *Elisabeth Mann Borgese*, 103.

31 Stefano, 'Giuseppe Antonio Borgese', 46.

32 Holzer, *Elisabeth Mann Borgese*, 112. 'Elisabeth wollte lernen, und sie wollte zu jemandem aufblicken. Als Schülerin ihres Mannes konnte sie das'.

33 *Cf.* Peter Serracino Inglott, 'Elisabeth Mann Borgese: A Metaphysician by Birth', *Ocean Yearbook* 18 (2004): 22–74, quoted in Wolfgang U. Eckert, 'Das "Utopia" der Meer-Frau. Elisabeth Mann Borgese und der "Aufstieg der Frau" (1963–1965)', in *Elisabeth Mann Borgese und das Drama der Meere*, exhibition catalogue, eds. Holger Pils and Karolina Kühn (Hamburg: mareverlag, 2012), 67.

34 Her daughter emphasised in an interview that Mann Borgese was not a feminist. Borgese, Nica. (Professor CNR Institute of Neuroscience, Milano), interview with the author, October 26, 2015. Milano, Italy. Elisabeth Mann Borgese has recently been studied from a feminist research perspective in a series about Gender and the Law of the Sea in Mallia, Patricia, and David Testa, 'Elisabeth Mann Borgese, Gender and the Law of the Sea', in *Gender and the Law of the Sea*, (Leiden: Brill | Nijhoff, 2019) https://doi.org/10.1163/9789004375178_005.

short book about the subject, eventually published as *Ascent of Woman*.[35] The book was first published in 1963, but she had been working on it for years.[36] In a letter to her husband in 1951, she reported on her progress: 'I have worked myself again into the old Blaustrümpfli; now called "The Ascent of Woman" which would go so very well with "The Descent of Man." I like that title, although it might be to some extent misleading since, as you know, the book is not feminist at all'.[37]

Indeed, the book is far from the feminist pamphlet its title suggests. Wolfgang U Eckert, who wrote an article about *Ascent of Woman*, supports this view.[38] But while the book is therefore not suited to a study of early feminism, it can, however, give us some insights into Mann Borgese's understanding of the male-dominated society she lived in. In the book, Mann Borgese lays out a utopian theory in which women first rise through the ranks of society, but in the end are dominated by older, wiser patriarchs from whom they are supposed to learn. When the society of women has been perfected, families are built that are led by older, mature men 'between forty-five and seventy-five years, from whom the "young, beautiful, receptive, sacrificial, loyal, committed women" learn wisdom and virtue'.[39] Finally, women actually turn into men and reach a kind of higher wisdom.[40]

According to Wolfgang Eckert's reading of the theory, 'Elisabeth's *Ascent of Woman* is not about this ascent, or even the "descent of the man", but solely about the rise of Elisabeth Mann Borgese to male acceptance in a male-dominated family'.[41] A male-dominated society too, we might add. Elisabeth Mann Borgese's theories in *Ascent of Woman* might also have been an attempt to explore her own life choices in marrying Borgese and learning from him. Perhaps she felt this was her only chance at finding a way to greater 'wisdom' or a deeper purpose beyond domestic life.

35 Elisabeth Mann Borgese, *Ascent of Woman* (New York: George Braziller, 1963).

36 *Cf.* Hermann, ed., *Die Meer Frau*, 40. Mann Borgese said she started becoming interested in this topic when she was fourteen or fifteen years old.

37 EMB B3 Mann Borgese, 26.09.1951.

38 *See* Eckert, 'Das "Utopia" ', 64–71.

39 Eckert, 'Das "Utopia" ', 71. '[…] zwischen fünfundvierzig und fünfundsiebzig Jahren, von denen die "jungen, schönen, aufnahmefähigen, opferwilligen, loyalen, dienstfertigen Frauen" Weisheit und Tugend erlernen'.

40 *Cf.* Eckert, 'Das "Utopia" ', 71.

41 Eckert, 'Das "Utopia" ', 71. 'Letztlich geht es in EMBs Aufstieg der Frau gar nicht um eben diesen Aufstieg, oder gar um den 'Abstieg des Mannes', sondern alleine um den Aufstieg der Elisabeth Mann Borgese zur männlichen Akzeptanz in einer männlich dominierten Familie'.

Decades later, she wrote a letter to her daughters saying that 'He [sic: Borgese] taught me most of the things I know'.[42] She then explained what she had perhaps been attempting to articulate through *Ascent of Woman*:

> You may be surprised that I mention all those "intellectual" things first, but when you are 20, and marry a man 56, and you fell in love with his intellectual work, that was all very important. We spent long, long evenings, over a bottle of wine, talking and talking and talking (he did most of the talking, but I did some too), and there were very happy evenings. Inspite for [sic: in spite of] some storminess, it was, for many years, a very successful and happy marriage.[43]

Maybe *Ascent of Woman* is a reflection on their early years of marriage, during which Elisabeth Mann Borgese's husband influenced her intellectual development. We have to bear in mind that, although she had travelled and moved around a lot, she had lived with her parents for most of her life. Her marriage to Borgese was the first time she had moved outside her parents' sphere of influence.[44] During their marriage, Giuseppe Antonio Borgese enhanced Elisabeth Mann's interest in discussions on fascism, politics and world governance. In an early letter to Borgese before their marriage, she wrote: 'Concerning Lehr- und Wanderjahre I am not yet content. My opinion is one has to lernen und zu wander all one's life'.[45] This was a reference to Goethe's classic *Wilhelm Meister's Journeyman Years* and perhaps referred back to a previous discussion between them. The assertion that 'one has to lernen und zu wander all one's life' is something Elisabeth Mann Borgese truly put into action throughout her own life. Even at this early stage, the learning and wandering had already started, and through her marriage to Giuseppe Antonio Borgese she would be given a direction.

Elisabeth Mann went from being the youngest daughter in an expat-German intellectual household, safeguarded by the ties of her family and her status as the youngest female member, to being the spouse of a well-respected man who had built himself a reputation based on decades of publishing and teaching success. Elisabeth Mann had just finished her 'Matura' in Zurich and completed her concert pianist training in Switzerland a year before they met.

---

42 EMB B4 Mann Borgese, 15.10.1982.

43 EMB B4 Mann Borgese, 15.10.1982.

44 *See* Holzer, *Elisabeth Mann Borgese*, 110. She was the only one of the six children to live with her parents until her marriage.

45 EMB B3 Mann Borgese, Tuesday [no date].

FIGURE 2 Elisabeth Mann Borgese with her husband in Chicago 1943
MONACENSIA LITERATURARCHIV UND BIBLIOTHEK MÜNCHEN, EMB F 203PHOTO: UNKNOWN

Now, instead of starting a career as a concert pianist, she began her new life as newlywed, taking care of the household, learning to cook and doing some typing work for her husband.[46]

Starting out as a personal secretary – in much the same way that her mother, Katia Mann, carried out secretarial functions for Thomas Mann – Elisabeth Mann Borgese became familiar with her husband's academic work. Unlike her mother, though, she soon had higher aspirations. She was eager to learn and to contribute to her husband's research for the Committee to Frame a World Constitution in Chicago.[47]

3 The Chicago Committee to Frame a World Constitution

When Elisabeth Mann Borgese came to Chicago in 1939, two people were going to be of great importance for her further career. One was her husband,

46 *Cf.* Holzer, *Elisabeth Mann Borgese*, 110–114.

47 *Cf.* Holzer, *Elisabeth Mann Borgese*, 121.

who introduced her to the Chicago circle, and the other was Robert Maynard Hutchins. Hutchins was the president and later chancellor of the University of Chicago from 1929–51.[48] When he came to office in 1929 at just thirty years old[49] he was the youngest ever university president in the United States. Under Hutchins's presidency, the University of Chicago took a central role in the administration and organisation of the Manhattan Project.[50] Hutchins failed to foresee that the project would lead to the discovery of nuclear energy and ring in the 'Atomic Age', saying later that he simply thought 'it couldn't be done'.[51] From his point of view, this misconception not only caused the sudden death of about 100,000 civilians when 'Little Boy' and 'Fat Man' were dropped on Hiroshima and Nagasaki in August 1945, but also marked the end of World War II and the start of a new, conflict-ridden era: the Atomic Age.

Hutchins was conscience-stricken about his participation in the project, feeling that he had contributed to the horror that the bomb inflicted not only on the Japanese but also on the whole world.[52] In a radio programme called 'The University of Chicago Roundtable', broadcast on 12 August 1945, Hutchins argued that 'all the evidence points to the fact that the use of the bomb was unnecessary. [...] Therefore, the United States has lost its moral prestige!'[53] Prior to the bombing of Hiroshima, Hutchins and physicists from Chicago had attempted to convince President Truman to drop the bomb on rural Japan, thus allowing the United States to demonstrate its power without actually harming large numbers of civilians. Leo Szilard, a Jewish-Hungarian physicist who was part of the Manhattan Project and had conceived the nuclear chain reaction, drafted a petition against the use of the atomic bomb after the Trinity test in July 1945. The petition was supported by Hutchins and signed by some sixty-five of the engineers and physicists involved in the project, mainly those

48 *See* Mann Borgese, 'The Years of my Life', 212. *See also* Robert A. McCaughey, 'Shaking things up in Chicago', *The New York Times*, 1989. https://www.nytimes.com/1989/09/03/books/shaking-things-up-at-chicago.html.

49 Edward, Shils, 'Robert Maynard Hutchins', *The American Scholar* 59, no. 2 (1990), 218 http://www.jstor.org/stable/41211779.

50 *Cf.* Milton Mayer, *Robert Maynard Hutchins. A Memoir*, (Berkley: University California Press, 1993), 275.

51 Mayer, *Robert Maynard Hutchins,* 275.

52 *Cf.* Mann Borgese, 'The Years of my Life', 214.

53 'The Chicago University Roundtable – 8/12/45 – Gordon Skene Sound Collection', accessed 30 September 2021, https://pastdaily.com/2015/08/13/the-atomic-bomb-now-what-august-12-1945/.

located in Chicago.[54] However, the scientists' petition was stopped by the Secretary of State, Jimmy Byrnes, and never reached Truman.[55] The first order to drop the bomb was issued on 6 August 1945.[56]

No-one realised at the time that the enormously potent weapon the Truman administration had unleashed would backfire so spectacularly, ringing in an infinity echo of horror and paranoia that persists right up to the present day. The US had sole possession of the weapon for just four short years, and apparently President Truman's only strategy was to rely on the belief that no other country could ever uncover the 'engineering secrets' of the weapon.[57] What a misconception. By 1949, the Soviet Union had managed to create her first nuclear bomb, the US responded by developing the super hydrogen bomb, and the Soviet hydrogen bomb followed shortly after. Just five years later, the bombs dropped on Hiroshima and Nagasaki had already been superseded by much more destructive weapons.[58]

With the University of Chicago at the forefront of atomic sciences, Hutchins decided to use his remaining years in office to educate scientists and ordinary Americans about nuclear energy. Perhaps as an act of reparation, he threw all his efforts into sourcing funding for three nuclear energy research institutes at the University of Chicago.[59] At around the same time, the *Bulletin of the Atomic Scientists*[60] started up. The *Bulletin* was a non-technical journal that was founded in 1945 to educate both scientists and the wider public about the Atomic Age, the dangers of the atomic bomb, and the impact that scientific discoveries such as nuclear fission could have in political and social spheres.[61] The *Bulletin* was very much connected to what Hutchins was doing at the University of Chicago, and several pieces that appeared in the *Bulletin* were in fact written by researchers involved in Hutchins's education efforts at the

54 *Cf.* Mayer, *Robert Maynard Hutchins,* 264.

55 *Cf.* Mayer, *Robert Maynard Hutchins,* 264.

56 For the public announcement, *see* Press release by the White House. 'Immediate Release. Statement by the President of the United States'. August 6, 1945, available at: https://www.trumanlibrary.gov/library/research-files/press-release-white-house.

57 *Cf.* Mayer, *Robert Maynard Hutchins,* 376.

58 *Cf.* Mayer, *Robert Maynard Hutchins,* 376.

59 *Cf.* Mayer, *Robert Maynard Hutchins,* 270.

60 *See* Bulletin of the Atomic Scientists, 'Background and Mission: 1945–2018', https://thebulletin.org/background-and-mission-1945-2018.

61 *Cf.* Bulletin of the Atomic Scientists, 'Background and Mission: 1945–2018', https://thebulletin.org/background-and-mission-1945-2018.

institutes.[62] The *Bulletin* still exists today, and 2017 marked the seventieth anniversary of the Doomsday Clock – which was the first cover image of the *Bulletin* in 1947. It was supposed to illustrate the urgency of the approaching catastrophe that came with the Atomic Age, and when it first appeared it was set at seven minutes to midnight. Over the years, the hands of the clock have hopped back and forth, sometimes closer to twelve, sometimes several minutes back, all depending on the world's current situation.

The *Bulletin's* January 2020 statement reported that the Doomsday Clock countdown was 'closer than ever: It is 100 seconds to midnight'.[63] Editor-in-chief John Mecklin stated that 'Civilization-ending nuclear war – whether started by design, blunder, or simple miscommunication – is a genuine possibility. Climate change that could devastate the planet is undeniably happening'.[64] The scientists, politicians and academics who allowed the Manhattan Project to come to fruition in 1945 undoubtedly wound up the Doomsday Clock and it is still ticking away today. Hutchins was one of those who regretted his involvement deeply and wanted to make amends. He founded institutes researching nuclear energy and also supported the foundation of the Chicago Committee to Frame a World Constitution in 1945.[65]

4 A New World Constitution

While Hutchins was grappling with the organisation and later the outcomes of the Manhattan Project, Giuseppe Antonio Borgese had been working as a professor of Romance literature and languages at the University of Chicago since 1936.[66] In 1945, together with Richard P McKeon, Borgese suggested founding the Committee to Frame a World Constitution. Hutchins, who by

---

62 *See* for example Robert M. Hutchins et al., 'Preliminary Draft of a World Constitution', *Bulletin of the Atomic Scientists* 4, no. 5 (1948): 145–150. The other authors were the members of the Committee to Frame a World Constitution: G. A. Borgese, Albert Guérard, Harold A. Innis, Erich Kahler, Wilber G. Katz, Charles H. McIlwain, Robert Redfield, Rexford G. Tugwell, Stringfellow Barr, Mortimer J. Adler.

63 John Mecklin eds., 'It is a 100 seconds to midnight – 2020 Doomsday Clock Statement', *Bulletin of the Atomic Scientists* (2020), https://thebulletin.org/wp-content/uploads/2020/01/2020-Doomsday-Clock-statement.pdf, 3.

64 John Mecklin eds., 'It is a 100 seconds to midnight – 2020 Doomsday Clock Statement', *Bulletin of the Atomic Scientists* (2020), https://thebulletin.org/wp-content/uploads/2020/01/2020-Doomsday-Clock-statement.pdf, 4.

65 *See* Mann Borgese, 'The Years of my Life', 240. *See* Mayer, *Robert Maynard Hutchins*, 327.

66 *Cf.* Noce, 'Giuseppe Antonio Borgese', 218.

then had become chancellor of the university, supported the suggestion. Other members of the committee were Mortimer J Adler, Stringfellow Barr, Albert Guérard, Harold Innis, Erich Kahler, Wilbur O Katz, Charles H McIlwain, Robert Redfield, and Rexford G Tugwell.[67] All were well-educated academics, scientists and thinkers who were keen to make a difference in the world. Some of them, like Borgese and Erich Kahler, were Europeans who had been directly affected by the horrors of World War II, and who were now worried about the looming Cold War and the beginning of the Atomic Age.

In 1946 – the year in which the Manhattan project finished its work as its horrendous consequences became apparent – Elisabeth Mann Borgese started getting involved with her husband and Robert Maynard Hutchins's work on the Committee to Frame a World Constitution.[68] The goal was to write a 'world constitution' – a holistic ideal of governing the world as one federal system by abolishing nation states. The University of Chicago was not the only place where this endeavour was pursued.[69] In fact, at the time there was a wide movement for promoting world governance and world citizenship,[70] including the World Federalist Movement and many other large and small attempts to unite the world's citizens.[71] The outcome of the committee's work, apart from a monthly journal called *Common Cause*[72] in which other world constitutions were presented and reviewed,[73] was a drafted world constitution that was published in the *Bulletin of the Atomic Scientists* in 1948, and was dedicated to Gandhi.[74]

That the drafted world constitution was printed in the fifth issue of the *Bulletin of the Atomic Scientists* was hardly a coincidence. Hutchins was in contact with the *Bulletin* because part of its purpose was to educate Americans

---

67 Robert M. Hutchins et al., *Preliminary Draft of a World Constitution* (Chicago: The University of Chicago Press, 1947/1948), ii.

68 *Cf.* MS-2-744, Box 362, Folder 6.

69 *Cf.* Mann Borgese, 'The Years of my Life', 216.

70 Mann Borgese worked on a platform for world citizenship. *See* MS-2-744, Box 135, Folder 22.

71 *Cf.* Mann Borgese, 'The Years of my Life', 114–116.

72 A complete collection of the publication *Common Cause* can be accessed at: University of Chicago Library, the Committee to Frame a World Constitution. Records, 1945–1951, (Special Collections Research Center University of Chicago Library 1100 East 57th Street Chicago, Illinois 60637 U.S.A.), in 'Series III: Common Cause and the Preliminary Draft Files', https://www.lib.uchicago.edu/e/scrc/findingaids/view.php?eadid=ICU.SPCL.CFWC. The collection has not been accessed for this study.

73 *Cf.* Mann Borgese, 'The Years of my Life', 216.

74 *Cf.* Hutchins et al., 'Preliminary Draft', 145–150. *See* the committee's publication of the draft: Robert M. Hutchins et al., *Preliminary Draft of a World Constitution* (Chicago: The University of Chicago Press, 1947/1948).

and scholars about the Atomic Age – a matter close to his own heart. What is more, the draft world constitution was a valuable contribution to addressing exactly those questions posed by the *Bulletin*: how to deal with the combination of the nuclear threat and the growing differences between nation states in the east and west. One sentence in the preamble of the constitution draft states that 'the age of nations must end, and the era of humanity begin'.[75]

The committee designed the constitution as follows: The world constitution should provide for a president who would be the 'protector of peace' in the Federal Republic of the World.[76] This president would be elected by delegates, each delegate representing 'the people of all states'[77] at a rate of one delegate per million people.[78] These delegates, together with the elected president, would constitute the world government. Furthermore, the committee allocated several 'grants of powers' to the world government. One which was especially important in the context of the Atomic Age was the 'limitation or control of weapons and domestic militias [...]'.[79] Others included 'the maintenance of peace'[80] and the 'judgment of conflict'[81] – all-in-all, the kinds of tasks a democratic, constitutional government of a nation state would carry out. However, in the constitution's 'declaration of duties and rights' section there was a key passage which revealed a relatively new way of thinking. The committee proclaimed that 'The four elements of life – earth, water, air, energy – are the common property of the human race'.[82] To dedicate elemental resources to the whole human race – instead of to specific nation states, stakeholders or other 'owners' – was not necessarily well-received by the (probably quite limited) audience who read and discussed the draft of the world constitution.

In a review published in 1949 by Ely Culbertson, a member of the Citizens Committee of the United Nations Reform,[83] the draft constitution was criticised harshly. That all resources could be shared without the supervision of nation states seemed unthinkable – Marxist, in fact – and inevitably

75 Hutchins et al., 'Preliminary Draft', 145.
76 *Cf.* Hutchins et al., 'Preliminary Draft', 146, 149.
77 Hutchins et al., 'Preliminary Draft', 146.
78 *Cf.* Hutchins et al., 'Preliminary Draft', 146.
79 Hutchins et al., 'Preliminary Draft', 146.
80 Hutchins et al., 'Preliminary Draft', 145.
81 Hutchins et al., 'Preliminary Draft', 145.
82 Hutchins et al., 'Preliminary Draft', 145.
83 For more information on the early UN reform attempts, *see* Joseph Preston Baratts, *The Politics of World Federation: United Nations, UN Reform, Atomic Control* (Westport, Conn.: Praeger Publishing, 2004).

destructive.[84] What unsettled the author of the review even more was the fact that if each delegate was elected by a million people, Asians and Africans would be 'overrepresented' in the world government. This, so the gloomy prediction went on, would lead to a so-called 'rabbit system'.[85] He argued that:

> it is true that the life and dignity of any human is a sacred trust of society. It is not true that China with its 400,000,000 is ten times more valuable than France with its 40,000,000. It is not true that 150,000,000 Americans who have created the greatest democracy of all times should sit humbly in the back rows of the world arena and surrender their sovereignties to a billion proliferating Asiatics.[86]

Culbertson concluded with the diagnosis that the 'disease of internationalism, such as the Communist internationalism, can be as monstrous as the disease of nationalism'.[87] Such attitudes among the opponents of world governance show how unlikely it was that the 'utopian ideals' of the Chicago draft (or any idealistic vision of a world constitution) had any chance of being implemented in the 1940s.

At the Nexus Lecture many decades later, Elisabeth Mann Borgese talked about her involvement with the Chicago committee, saying that they had known the constitution was not 'realistic', but had meant it to be a 'blueprint pointing in the direction of a desirable or probably ineluctable future'.[88] This blueprint was, in fact, later used for the Law of the Sea. By the 1940s, earth had been nationalised and remained hotly contested; air had been largely nationalised; energy had been nationalised, but (sea) water remained untouched beyond the coastlines of each nation state. In her work with the Chicago committee, Elisabeth Mann Borgese had reviewed several drafts of world constitutions and had been present as they discussed their own draft. While ultimately the committee's work was neither finalised nor implemented, Elisabeth Mann Borgese took some of it with her when she started working on the Law of the Sea Convention. If earth, air and energy were not going to be the common

84 *Cf.* Ely Culbertson, 'The preliminary Draft of a World Constitution, by the Committee to Frame A World Constitution', *Indiana Law Journal* 24, no. 3, (1949): 477, http://www.repository.law.indiana.edu/ilj/vol24/iss3/20.

85 Culbertson, 'The preliminary Draft', 481.

86 Culbertson, 'The preliminary Draft', 481.

87 Culbertson, 'The preliminary Draft', 474.

88 Mann Borgese, 'The Years of my Life', 215.

property of the human race, she wanted to make sure that water would be the common heritage of mankind – at least on paper.

It is difficult to gauge the extent of Elisabeth Mann Borgese's involvement in designing this first draft constitution. One thing for certain is that during her years with the committee, her role went far beyond that of a secretary, and her participation might shed some light on her deepening involvement with world governance issues.

5 From Secretary to Academic

How exactly Elisabeth Mann Borgese made her way into academia through the committee is somewhat blurry. Her Curriculum Vitae, dated December 1982, lists some of her activities from 1948 onwards. The document mentions her having 'helped Borgese and Hutchins (Chancellor of U. of Chicago) found "The Committee to Frame a World Constitution," [and] Contributed research papers on Comparative Constitutional Law, some 12 of which were subsequently published in *The Bulletin of Atomic Scientists* and *Common Cause*. [...]'.[89] Furthermore, it says that she was the editor of *Common Cause*, a monthly journal published by the Chicago committee from 1948–52.[90]

It is unclear whether she composed this CV herself or for what purpose it was written. The University of Chicago Library, where the records of the Committee to Frame a World Constitution are stored, lists her as 'research assistant for the Committee and later editor of the journal *Common Cause*',[91] not as a founding member of the committee. It seems odd to believe that she would have been deeply involved in founding the Committee to Frame a World Constitution, bearing in mind her young age and the fact that she had given birth to her second daughter the previous year.[92] It is also questionable whether her husband, Giuseppe Antonio Borgese, would have accepted this view. In Elisabeth Mann Borgese's biography, Kerstin Holzer notes his struggle with her growing professional independence in 1949.[93]

89 MS-2-744, Box 16, Folder 19.

90 *Cf.* MS 16–19.

91 *See* The guide to the Committee to Frame a World Constitution. Records, 1945–1951, (Special Collections Research Center University of Chicago Library 1100 East 57th Street Chicago, Illinois 60637 U.S.A.), https://www.lib.uchicago.edu/e/scrc/findingaids/view.php?eadid=ICU.SPCL.CFWC. *Compare* MS 16–19.

92 Nica Borgese was born in Chicago in 1944. *See* Stefano, 'Giuseppe Antonio Borgese', 60.

93 *See* Holzer, *Elisabeth Mann Borgese*, 129.

Another peculiar side-note is her involvement in the council of the World Federalist Movement. Kerstin Holzer claims in her biography that Elisabeth Mann Borgese was elected chairman in 1950,[94] but this is not listed in either of the two CVs from her archive in Halifax.[95] The records of the World Movement for World Federal Government (WMWFG) suggest that her involvement stemmed from her affiliation with the Committee to Frame a World Constitution. These records reveal that the committee had joined the movement in 1947, and that she was listed as the chairman of the Executive Committee of the Council from 1948–50. Her husband was close by, listed as the co-chairman of a special 'group of scholars mandated by the Congress [of the WMWFG] with the task of preparing some research material for world congresses of the WMWFG in the future for their consideration'.[96]

Although the exact circumstances are difficult to reconstruct, all evidence suggests that Elisabeth Mann Borgese made her way into academia without a degree or an academic publishing record, mainly by taking on a growing role in her husband's academic work. Borgese introduced her to Robert Maynard Hutchins, who in turn became an important partner in her further career, and her involvement with the Committee to Frame a World Constitution would lay the foundation for her later work with the oceans.[97]

In a 1951 letter to George Kennan at the Institute for Advanced Studies at Princeton University, Elisabeth Mann Borgese described the nature of her work with the Chicago committee. She recounted that she had written 'about

94 *Cf.* Holzer, *Elisabeth Mann Borgese*, 124–125.

95 MS-2-744, Box 16, Folder 19. Also not mentioned in Mann Borgese, 'The Years of my Life', 214.

96 *See* 'Historical note', The guide to the Committee to Frame a World Constitution. Records, 1945–1951, (Special Collections Research Center University of Chicago Library 1100 East 57th Street Chicago, Illinois 60637 U.S.A.), https://www.lib.uchicago.edu/e/scrc/findingaids/view.php?eadid=ICU.SPCL.CFWC. Read: 'In 1947, the Committee to Frame a World Constitution became a member of the World Movement for World Federal Government (WMWFG); at this time Mrs. Borgese, a member of the CFWC secretariat, was elected one of the Committee's delegates to the WMWFG. From the fall of 1947 to the fall of 1948 she was a member of the WMWFG Council. From the fall of 1948 to the winter of 1950 she was the Chairman of the Executive Committee of the Council of the WMWFG. Until June 1951, Mr. G. A. Borgese was Co-Chairman of the Commission Constitutionelle Mondiale, "a group of scholars mandated by the Congress [of the WMWFG] with the task of preparing some research material" for world congresses of the WMWFG in the future for their consideration. [The papers come to an end on June 30, 1951 with the dissolution of the Committee to Frame a World Constitution and the cessation of its publication, *Common Cause.*]'

97 Baker comes to a similar conclusion. *See* Baker, 'Uncommon Heritage', 14.

a dozen papers',[98] and that these largely examined constitutions, such as analyses of 'the Russian, the Chinese, Spanish, Swedish and Indian constitutions, insofar as their consideration was useful for the drafting of a constitution for the world'.[99] In addition, she had written three history papers: one about 'the history of functional representation',[100] one about 'the history of changing appearances of the Tribune of the People; and a brief paper on the problem of languages in plurilingual states'.[101] She had also written 'the draft on which the present Statutes of the World Movement are based, as well as the Movement's by-laws (rules of procedure) and most of its publicity and fund raising material'.[102] She claimed that her articles were 'mainly concerned with political action for world unity and European unity'.[103]

Clearly, by 1951 her tasks in the committee had far exceeded those of a regular secretary. She must, however, have started her deeper academic involvement later than 1945, since she wrote: 'during the two years of research for the Committee [...]',[104] meaning that she had spent at least three years doing more standard secretarial duties. Though she probably spent only two years researching, she managed to write twelve articles, all of which were closely related to the committee's core work. She became familiar with various drafts for a world constitution, wrote and discussed her own ideas around those drafts, and in general practised writing papers on 'world unity' and 'European unity'.

Apart from telling us about Mann Borgese's growing professional expertise, paired with her ability to work herself into institutional settings through informal or unconventional channels, the letter to Kennan also reveals that in March 1951 she was looking for a job. She wrote, 'Mr. Hutchins tells me that you might have an opening for me to work on your staff in Princeton'.[105] Apparently things were not going well for the Chicago committee. That Hutchins was helping them find new positions suggests that it was not a lack of effort or expertise on the part of Mann Borgese or her husband that was making them look for new jobs. Rather, external circumstances threatened the committee's existence.

98 B-III.17-KENN-1, 29.03.1951.
99 B-III.17-KENN-1, 29.03.1951.
100 B-III.17-KENN-1, 29.03.1951.
101 B-III.17-KENN-1, 29.03.1951.
102 B-III.17-KENN-1, 29.03.1951.
103 B-III.17-KENN-1, 29.03.1951.
104 B-III.17-KENN-1, 29.03.1951.
105 B-III.17-KENN-1, 29.03.1951.

The committee was negatively affected by the general atmosphere that came with the rise of the McCarthy era in the United States, when 'Peace became a dirty word'[106] and a number of academics were fired from their positions when their research was perceived to be communist or in other ways hostile to the United States. Consequently, many 'blacklisted' exiles returned to their home countries – among them Mann Borgese's own parents, Thomas Mann and his wife Katia.[107]

The peculiar distaste for the 'disease of Communist internationalism'[108] also affected the Committee to Frame a World Constitution at the University of Chicago. Though the committee was probably not seen to be directly communist or pursuing communist goals, there was little appetite for peace-seeking activities with the Eastern Bloc. Efforts to design a world constitution had gone out of fashion, lectures were forbidden, people were fired, and the whole enterprise was shut down in 1952,[109] when Hutchins left the University of Chicago to take a job as director of the Ford Foundation.[110] The committee members, including the Mann Borgeses, had to find new employment.

6 Retreat to Italy

In September 1952, Elisabeth Mann Borgese returned to Europe. Her husband had been offered a job at the University of Milan,[111] and she followed together with her two daughters. The couple agreed to find a house in San Domenico in Fiesole and, according to Katrin Holzer, Elisabeth Mann Borgese declined a job offer at an American cultural journal called *Perspectives*, opting to settle into life as a mother to her daughters and a caring wife for her husband.[112] Just two months later, she would have to rethink this decision. Giuseppe Antonio died unexpectedly at the age of seventy on 4 December 1952,[113] leaving Elisabeth Mann Borgese and her two daughters alone in Italy. The family had not even had a chance to take up residence in their new house. Instead, Elisabeth Mann

106 Mann Borgese, 'The Years of my Life', 216.
107 *Cf.* Mann Borgese, 'The Years of my Life', 216.
108 Culbertson, 'The preliminary Draft', 474.
109 *Cf.* Mann Borgese, 'The Years of my Life', 216.
110 *Cf.* Shils, 'Robert Maynard Hutchins', 234.
111 *Cf.* Noce, 'Giuseppe Antonio Borgese', 218.
112 *Cf.* Holzer, *Elisabeth Mann Borgese*, 142.
113 *Cf.* Holzer, *Elisabeth Mann Borgese*, 145. *See also* Stefano, 'Giuseppe Antonio Borgese', 62.

Borgese moved in as a widow, and she would go on to live there with Nica and Angelica for fourteen turbulent years.[114]

Her time in Italy could be described as a period of varied jobs, interesting involvements, writing and experimental living.[115] She did everything from teaching German to political science students at the University of Florence[116] to more adventurous work like travelling to India to interview Nehru and conduct behavioural experiments on elephants.[117] First of all, she reconsidered the job offer she had so recently declined, taking up employment as editor of *Perspectives*.[118] Another job she took to make a living was at a UNESCO-financed magazine called *Diogenes*, where she also got to know her second life partner, Corrado Tumiati.[119] Tumiati was a former psychologist who had written a book about his work in a closed institution, and he was supposed to help Mann Borgese with her editing jobs. At the time, he worked at a magazine called *Il Ponte*.[120] Once again, Elisabeth Mann Borgese picked a man much older than herself, and Tumiati would live in the villa in Fiesole until his death in 1967.[121] During the years in Italy, Mann Borgese also published several smaller tales and novels, one of which was *To Whom It May Concern*[122] – a collection of peculiar stories about futuristic freak scenarios, published in 1960.

There seems to be a kind of veil draped over Elisabeth Mann Borgese's years in Italy.[123] Although she was occupied with a variety of different smaller jobs, she always kept in contact with Hutchins – who now worked at the Ford Foundation – and with the American circle she had been part of in Chicago. She also started to develop an increasing interest in behavioural studies of

---

114 *Cf.* Holzer, *Elisabeth Mann Borgese*, 146.

115 More on Mann Borgese's years in Italy, *see* Baker, 'Uncommon Heritage', 14–15.

116 *Cf.* Holzer, *Elisabeth Mann Borgese*, 146.

117 For letters in which Mann Borgese reports about her travels, *see* B-III.17-MANN-106, B-III.17-MANN-106, B-III.17-MANN-107, B-III.17-MANN-108, B-III.17-MANN-109, B-III.17-MANN-110. *See also* Holzer, *Elisabeth Mann Borgese*, 167–168. Her 1964 trip to India has been described by Peter K. Wehrli, '"Überall ist alles anders!" Mit Elisabeth auf dem Landweg nach Indien', in *Elisabeth Mann Borgese und das Drama der Meere*, exhibition catalogue, eds. Holger Pils and Karolina Kühn (Hamburg: mareverlag, 2012), 142–175.

118 *Cf.* Holzer, *Elisabeth Mann Borgese*, 146–147.

119 *Cf.* Holzer, *Elisabeth Mann Borgese*, 147.

120 *Cf.* Holzer, *Elisabeth Mann Borgese*, 147.

121 Katrin Holzer has discussed Mann Borgese's relations with older men. *See* Holzer, *Elisabeth Mann Borgese*, 158. Mann Borgese's relations with men or her feminist theories in *Ascent of Woman* will not be discussed any further in this book.

122 Elisabeth Mann Borgese, *To Whom it May Concern* (New York: George Braziller, 1960).

123 Katrin Holzer deals with the years in Italy under the title 'Krisenjahre' (years of crises) in Holzer, *Elisabeth Mann Borgese*, 125.

animals, starting with her famous typewriting dogs.[124] She could not resist entertaining her associates with her animal stunts, and in a letter dated September 1963, Hutchins wrote, 'In the meantime, we thank you for the pictures. We are both perfectly positive that you have faked the one with the dog doing the typewriting'.[125]

By 1964, Hutchins had started a new project in the United States, and having maintained contact with Mann Borgese throughout her years in Italy, he now asked her to join him. At this point, the pieces of her unusual career path started to fall into place.

7 The Center for the Study of Democratic Institutions in Santa Barbara

Elisabeth Mann Borgese had been sending Hutchins more than just funny pictures of typewriting dogs. Their correspondence had revolved around the Encyclopaedia Britannica[126] – a reference work that had been donated to the University of Chicago – and other projects. These included at least one conference that Mann Borgese apparently took a role in organising, although it is not quite clear what it was about or for whom.[127] From their correspondence in January 1964 we can glean only that the conference would deal with 'nothing less than the future of man'[128]and that Mann Borgese was interested in merging it with another conference that Hutchins had mentioned at Christmas.

Robert Hutchins had been working as the head of the Ford Foundation, after leaving the University of Chicago amid political upheavals and the animosities brought about by McCarthyism.[129] In 1959, he had set up the Center for the Study of Democratic Institutions in Santa Barbara, using money from 'The Fund for the Republic' – a fund established by the Ford Foundation while he was at its head.[130] Having returned to academia, Hutchins now reached out

124 In her new job in Santa Barbara she would eventually keep a monkey for a couple of years. *See* Holzer, *Elisabeth Mann Borgese* 169–170.

125 NB-Folder 5, September 30, 1963.

126 The Britannica was donated to the University of Chicago in 1943. William Benton, then vice President, became the Chairmen of the Board. He and Hutchins were friends. *See* Mayer, *Robert Maynard Hutchins*, 197.

127 NB Folder 5, January 16, 1964.

128 NB Folder 5, January 16, 1964.

129 *See* Mayer, *Robert Maynard Hutchins*, 396 -397, 400.

130 *Cf.* Mayer, *Robert Maynard Hutchins*, 470–471. About foundation of the centre, *see* Baker, 'Elisabeth Mann Borgese', 93.

to former colleagues from Chicago to see if they would become involved with this newly founded centre.

Mann Borgese's correspondence shows that she was already working for Hutchins before she was invited to join the centre in Santa Barbara.[131] However, in May 1964 she wrote to Mortimer J Adler – a former colleague from Chicago who had worked on the Encyclopaedia Britannica project – asking for advice about a new job offer 'Bob'[132] had made her. She wrote: 'I am doing a whole lot of work for Bob [...]',[133] and went on to say that he had 'sent my head spinning'[134] with a 'wonderful'[135] job offer at the Center for the Study of Democratic Institutions in Santa Barbara. Mann Borgese found this 'terribly attractive',[136] though she had some concerns since she felt he could find other people better suited for the position, while she thought she could be 'more useful to the Britannica in its foreign designs and relations [...]'.[137] Judging by Adler's reply, it seems Hutchins had been recruiting for some time. He wrote:

> Bob has asked me to come to Santa Barbara a good many times and every time I have thought about it, I have had a deep revulsion against doing so. I like Bob, as you know, and I like being with him; but my habits of work are so different from the way things are done in Santa Barbara that I know that I would be miserable in that environment. My hunch is that your habits of work are very much like mine and that you would be equally out of place there.[138]

Elisabeth Mann Borgese did not take Adler's advice. Instead, she took the job offer. In a letter Hutchins wrote to her in May after she had accepted, he informed her about her tasks and how she could split her life between Santa Barbara and Florence.[139] Elisabeth Mann Borgese was about to embark on a new adventure in Santa Barbara where, according to Hutchins, 'we need you in our discussions. We are beginning to think, once more, about a world

131 Betsy Baker writes that she was in touch with her colleagues from Chicago. *See* Baker, 'Uncommon Heritage', 15.
132 NB Folder 5, May 17, 1964.
133 NB Folder 5, May 17, 1964.
134 NB Folder 5, May 17, 1964.
135 NB Folder 5, May 17, 1964.
136 NB Folder 5, May 17, 1964.
137 NB Folder 5, May 17, 1964.
138 NB Folder 5, May 20, 1964.
139 *Cf.* NB Folder 5, May 26, 1964.

constitution'.[140] When Hutchins wrote 'we need you in our discussions', he meant it literally. He had built the centre around the principle of discourse, and had been quite ambitious in trying to recruit star researchers, but had not managed to attract the right kind of scholars to commit to a permanent fellowship.[141] Milton Meyers describes the centre's procedures in *Robert Maynard Hutchins: A Memoir*. According to Meyers, the day would unfold as follows:

> Hutchins called the Fellows to the conference table by ringing an old school bell three or four mornings a week – occasionally five – at 11 A.M. The twenty to twenty-five persons assembled as often as not included whoever happened to be on the premises, invited or uninvited.[142]

Before the meeting started, the paper that was on the agenda that day had to be handed out to the participants, and they were expected to study it before the bell called them to the discussion room.[143] According to Meyers, the discourse was often unfocused and fluid, and the effect and importance of the centre's activity was questionable. As the Vietnam War raged, Kennedy was shot and world politics generally went up in flames, the fellows explored abstract futuristic questions on governance or world order, many of which were detached from reality and inaccessible to a broader audience.[144]

The centre's most significant efforts, Meyers writes, were four conferences organised between 1965 and 1975 called *Pacem in Terris*.[145] The first conference, set in New York in 1965, was concerned with questions of world peace, and the hosts themselves billed it as 'an attempt to see whether the understanding and

---

140 NB Folder 5, May 26, 1964.

141 *See* Mayer, *Robert Maynard Hutchins*, 472. Mayer writes of the fellows: 'Over the next ten years there were a few academics who became attached as Fellows: Wheeler, a political scientist; Rexford Guy Tugwell, the one-time Chicago economist and Roosevelt Brain Truster; John Wilkinson and William Gorman, young philosophers; Stanley Sheinbaum, a young economist; sociologist John Seeley; none of them, however, of the caliber that Hutchins had originally tried to get. An ailing Scott Buchanan – who was of that caliber – came out for a few years preceding his death, as did his St. John's associate, historian Stringfellow Barr. Another of the Fellows was Elizabeth Mann Borgese, nonacademic daughter of Thomas Mann and widow of Hutchins's old associate, G.A. Borgese. Nobel Prize-winning chemist and peace activist Linus Pauling and the controversial Episcopal bishop James A. Pike accepted fellowships but were more often than not away'.

142 Mayer, *Robert Maynard Hutchins*, 474.

143 *Cf.* Mayer, *Robert Maynard Hutchins*, 474.

144 *Cf.* Mayer, *Robert Maynard Hutchins*, 480.

145 *Cf.* Mayer, *Robert Maynard Hutchins*, 481.

interchange advocated by Pope John XXIII is possible'.[146] What had the Pope meant by understanding and interchange? The conference was named after an encyclical that had addressed the challenges facing society due to changes in living standards, rights and regulations, and technology that could seriously interfere with the natural order on Earth. The Pope had gone on to assert that the equality of all human beings – not just Catholics – was a natural order that should be promoted by states and governments without using the power of weaponry.[147] Through the *Pacem in Terris* conferences, the Center for the Study of Democratic Institutions attempted to take the Pope's suggestions seriously. The four conferences differed in terms of size and importance. The second conference in Geneva in 1967 was distinctly smaller than the first huge gathering, which saw more than a thousand participants attend. The third and fourth conferences, which took place in Washington in 1973 and 1975, were even larger than the first, with two and three thousand participants respectively.[148]

When Elisabeth Mann Borgese joined the centre in 1964, preparations for the first mammoth conference were probably ongoing. How much she was involved in organising the first two conferences is hard to determine, but in her holdings at the Dalhousie University Archives there is at least one folder containing a report on the *Pacem in Terris* II Convocation.[149] The centre's interest in organising conferences would come in handy for Mann Borgese's later work, and thematically the *Pacem in Terris* conferences were of interest to her. Documents from her first year in Santa Barbara show that she was once again involved in discussions about a world constitution.[150]

Her involvement with the world constitution in Chicago in the early years of her marriage with Borgese meant she slipped easily back into to the circle of academics and intellectuals that were now gathered once again in Santa Barbara. Here she would be able to rethink and refine her understanding of world governance, after a twelve-year detour in Italy. On a practical level, the centre also made a good training ground for learning about organisational skills, networking and funding. Organising large-scale international conferences was not always simple. Over the years, conflict arose at the centre – often

146 Mayer, *Robert Maynard Hutchins*, 481. For the encyclical, *see* Pope John XXIII, 'Pacem in Terris – Peace on Earth', (1963), Papal Encyclicals online, last modified February 20, 2017, http://www.papalencyclicals.net/john23/j23pacem.htm.

147 Pope John XXIII, 'Pacem in Terris'.

148 Cf. Mayer, *Robert Maynard Hutchins*, 482.

149 *See* MS-2-744, Box 145, Folder 11.

150 *See* MS-2-744, Box 43, Folder 54. Mann Borgese also worked on 'World Communities'. *See* MS-2-744, Box 147, Folder 1.

in connection with the *Pacem in Terris* conferences, but also around other issues. The fellows were critical towards spending money on certain causes, and Hutchins was constantly looking for funds.[151]

When Adler told Mann Borgese that he was unsure whether she was suited to a position at the centre, perhaps he was referring to Hutchins's particular method of discourse-based research. But despite Adler's grave predictions, Elisabeth Mann Borgese was not 'miserable'[152] during her first years at the centre, and she thrived on the opportunity to work on world governance once more. Meanwhile, over at the United Nations in New York, discussions on ocean governance were already on the agenda and were about to accelerate.

151 Mayer, *Robert Maynard Hutchins*, 484.

152 NB Folder 5, May 20, 1964.

CHAPTER 2

Reordering the Oceans

1 How Free Are the Oceans?

In the 1940s and 50s, while the Borgeses were busy working on world governance with the Committee to Frame a World Constitution, the international community was already beginning to explore questions of international cooperation and negotiation in relation to the deeper parts of the world. As Elisabeth Mann Borgese and her colleagues in Chicago and Santa Barbara investigated new principles of world governance, others were looking into governance that extended beyond the boundaries of dry land and into the oceans.

Interestingly, the idea of governing 'water' was not an alien concept to the Chicago committee. Mann Borgese and her colleagues had already touched upon the issue of ocean governance in the 1948 draft world constitution, where water had been declared one of four elements that were the common property of the human race.[1] During the 1950s, the wider world community would discover that the potential of the ocean exceeded the traditional rules that governed it. These regulations were based on two rival principles that had existed since the fifteenth century. The principles were '*Mare Clausum* vs *Mare Liberum*'.[2] Directly translated, *mare clausum* means 'closed sea' and *mare liberum* means 'free sea', so it is easy to see why these principles contradicted each other. One principle promoted freedom, while the other promoted restriction. Ocean governance before the twentieth century was mostly a matter for seafaring powers or nations that possessed a coastline, and which principle one favoured depended largely on what one wanted with the ocean.[3]

The *Mare Liberum* principle dates back to a fifteenth-century quarrel between Spain and Portugal over who had the right to rule the oceans between their respective colonies in America and the East Indies.[4] At that time, trade

1 *See* Hutchins et al., *Preliminary Draft,* 6.
2 *Cf.* Leary, *International Law,* 80.
3 For the original publication (English translation): *see* Hugo Grotius, *The Free Sea, trans. Richard Hakluyt, with William Welwod's Critique and Grotius's Reply,* ed. David Armitage (Indianapolis: Liberty Fund, 2004), http://oll.libertyfund.org/titles/859.
4 *Cf.* Leary, *International Law,* 80. Leary points out in a footnote that the division of the sea between the Spanish and Portuguese was not the first in history. *See* Leary, *International Law,* 81: 'For detailed account of these claims see T.W. Fulton; The Sovereignty of the Sea. An historical Account of the Claims of England to the Dominion of the British Seas, and

and transport were extremely important for the two naval powers to maintain control over their colonies, and these factors could also be a source of conflict when it came to who controlled which passage. In 1494, the dispute was settled by the Treaty of Tordesillas,[5] in which each power took one section of the ocean to rule over.[6] The Dutch and English were not very happy about this division, and in 1609 a Dutch jurist called Hugo Grotius published a book called *Mare Liberum*,[7] in which he argued that the sea should be 'public gifts',[8] not 'private property'.[9] Grotius asserted that all passage and trade should be free, and that no nation or naval power should be able to control or restrict it.[10]

In 1635, the British scholar and diplomat John Selden[11] published a treaties on the closed sea called '*Mare Clausum, seu de dominio maris libri duo*',[12] in which he argued that states should be able to claim control over parts of the sea if they could dominate those parts with their military power.[13] Selden was one of many who joined the conversation.[14] Still, in the following centuries in legal practise Grotius's principle of *Mare Liberum* was applied to the high seas.[15] The international rule of thumb up until the early twentieth century

---

of the Evolution of the Territorial Waters: with special reference to the Rights of Fishing and the Naval Salute (1911)'.

5 *Cf.* Leary, *International Law*, 80. For information on the original treaty, *see* Duve, Thomas, 'Treaty of Tordesillas', *Max Planck Encyclopedia of Public International Law*, January 2013, 30 September 2021, http://opil.ouplaw.com/view/10.1093/law:epil/9780199231690/law-9780199231690-e2088#.

6 *See* R.P. Anand, *Origin and Development of the Law of the Sea.* (1983), 42, quoted in Leary, *International Law*, 80. 'On May 4, 1493 Pope Alexander VI divided the world between Spain and Portugal and "defined a line of demarcation running 100 leagues west of the Azores and Cape Verde Islands and granted Spain all lands west of it, and to Portugal all lands of its east" '.

7 *See* Grotius, *The Free Sea.*

8 Anand, *Origin and Development, 82,* quoted in Leary *International Law,* 81.

9 Grotius, *The Free Sea*, 108.

10 *See* Leary, *International Law*, 81.

11 For a discussion of the *mare clausum* principle *see* Randall Leaffer, 'Mare clausum (The Closure of the Sea or The Ownership of the Sea) 1635 John Selden (1584–1654)', in, *The Formation and Transmission of Western Legal Culture. 150 Books that Made the Law in the Age of Printing* (Studies in the History of Law and Justice 7), eds. Serge Dauchy, Georges Martyn, Anthony Musson, Heikki Pihlajamäki and Alain Wijffels (Cham: Springer Verlag, 2016), 190–194.

12 Tullio Treves, 'Historical Development of the Law of the Sea', in Donald R. Rothwell et. al., *The Oxford Handbook of the Law of the Sea* (Oxford/New York: Oxford University Press, 2015), 4.

13 *Cf.* Leary, *International Law,* 81.

14 William Wellwood was another of Grotius opponents. *See* Treves, 'Historical Development', 4.

15 *Cf.* Treves, 'Historical Development', 4: '[...] in his treatise on 'The Law of War and Peace' (De Jure Belli a Pacis, published in 1625), Grotius made more explicit some of the above

was that territorial waters reached 'as far as a cannon could shoot' from the shore,[16] while the rest of the sea was free for transport and passage.

In terms of the uses of the sea, these two principles demonstrate the tension between sovereign claims and communal freedom.[17] As technology evolved – including even the simple fact that cannon range increased – the necessity to establish exactly how far territorial waters reached had become a pressing legal issue by the early twentieth century.[18]

2 Moving towards a New Law of the Sea

Back in 1907, the international community had begun trying to resolve some of the issues around the use of the oceans. At that time, attempting to identify international problems and solve them through universal agreements developed by an international community was all very new.[19] The first attempts to identify these kinds of international community issues were made at The Hague Peace Conference in 1907,[20] and this was followed by the Hague Codification Conference of 1930.[21] Neither conference was principally concerned with

points, and clearly held that occupation of small parts of the seas, such as in bays and straits, was possible for the coastal State through the presence of military fleets and by exercising coercion from the shore in the same was as on land'.

16 Michael P. Scharf, 'Seizing the Grotian Moment: Accelerated Formation of Customary International Law During Times of Fundamental Change', *Faculty Publications,* 18 (2010), 108, http://scholarlycommons.law.case.edu/faculty_publications/18. For the origin of the principle of the cannon shot rule by Cornelius an Bynkershoeck, *see also* Treves, 'Historical Development', 5.

17 *See* Leary, *International Law,* 79.

18 *Cf.* Anderson, *Modern Law,* 6. Anderson writes: 'During the early decades of the twentieth century, maritime law was stable and could be summarized as follows. Coastal states had territorial waters extending to three nautical miles (nm), subject to insignificant exceptions, and measured in a belt around the coast. Beyond that limit, the seas and oceans had the status of high seas. Maritime law was based upon relatively simple foundations: international custom derived from the practice of States, among which maritime powers loomed large; a few conventions on technical matters; the writing of professors; and a few arbitral decisions. No inter-governmental organizations with maritime mandates existed and there was no forum for discussing maritime questions. Maritime disputes were justiciable only with the consent of the States concerned'.

19 Edward L Miles discusses the question on why codification was pressing at the time in Edward L. Miles, 'Preparations for UNCLOS IV?', *Ocean Development and International Law* 19, no. 5 (1988): 422–423, https://doi.org/10.1080/00908328809545870.

20 *Cf.* Harrison, *Making the Law,* 28.

21 *Cf.* Sanger, *Ordering the Oceans,* 13.

ocean governance, rather aiming to explore general practices with which the international community could develop treaties and law-making that transcended state borders.[22]

The main point of ocean governance to come out of the 1907 and 1930 conferences was that three nautical miles defined a kind of 'territorial zone'. Beyond that zone, the waters had the status of the high seas, while any conflict that arose within the territorial zones was handled between the states concerned.[23] According to David Anderson in his 2007 essay collection, *Modern Law of the Sea*, 'Maritime Law was based upon relatively simple foundations: international custom derived from the practice of States [...], a few conventions on technical matters; the writings of professors; and a few arbitral decisions'.[24]

Beginning in the aftermath of World War I, serious efforts were made to identify or codify issues that needed international regulation. In this context, codification meant not only recording and collecting existing agreements, but also 'clarifying state practice and [...] making suggestions about how ambiguities or disagreement could be overcome'.[25] This burgeoning interest in inscribing state practice into transnational treaties was not just because the ocean was becoming more accessible. It was also the first time in history that there was an international organisation that could ask such questions: the League of Nations. Therefore, 'In 1924 the Council of the League of Nations [...] established a Committee of Experts for the Progressive Codification of International Law [...]'.[26] This committee aimed to identify international state practices that needed clarification and to present them at the Hague Codification Conference in 1930.[27] The Law of the Sea was one of the issues that the committee picked out right from the start of its work in 1924.[28]

---

22 For a contemporary witness account of the conference, *see* Hunter Miller, 'The Hague Codification Conference', *The American Journal of International Law* 24, no. 4 (October 1930): 674–693, http://www.jstor.org/stable/2190056.

23 *Cf.* Anderson, *Modern Law*, 6.

24 Anderson, *Modern Law*, 6.

25 Harrison, *Making the Law,* 29.

26 Harrison, *Making the Law,* 29.

27 *See* First Report Submitted to the Council by the Preparatory Committee for the Codification Conference, *The American Journal of International Law* 24, no. 1, Supplement: Official Documents (January 1930): 1–3 http://www.jstor.org/stable/2213295.

28 *Cf.* Harrison, *Making the Law,* 29–30. Read page 29: 'The initial list of subjects identified by the Committee of Experts for potential codification included the status of territorial waters, the status of government ships engaged in commerce, the suppression of piracy and the exploitation of the products of the sea'. Harrison refers to: Rosenne, *Committee of Experts for the Progressive Codification of International Law* (1925–1928), at lxi.

It was apparent that renegotiating a new Law of the Sea beyond the simple *Mare Clausum/Mare Liberum* principles was going to be a very complicated task. This became evident as early as 1930, when despite the efforts of the Committee of Experts for the Progressive Codification of International Law, the issue of how to handle territorial waters was perceived as too difficult and overarching. The Hague Codification Conference came to no conclusions on the matter, though several draft Articles were presented.[29] Although the conference was inconclusive, the committee's efforts were not entirely in vain. According to James Harrison in *Making the Law of the Sea*, fragments of these early draft Articles can be found in today's Law of the Sea. With this in mind, Harrison asserts that the Articles presented at the Hague Codification Conference laid the foundations for the further development of the Law of the Sea, even though no concrete conclusions were reached in 1930.[30] Shortly afterwards, the escalating international conflict that peaked with World War II would put the codification efforts on hold.

3 Nation States Reach Out for Territory in the Oceans

Shortly after World War II, unilateral action by the United States catapulted the question of maritime boundaries to the top of the agenda of outstanding international issues. On 28 September 1945, the president of the United States, Harry S Truman, made a presidential proclamation that would trigger a chain reaction of unexpected dimensions. President Truman made it clear that the United States was ready to claim territory beyond its coastal waters, stating that:

> the Government of the United States regards the natural resources of the subsoil and sea bed of the continental shelf beneath the high seas but contiguous to the coasts of the United States as appertaining to the United States, subject to its jurisdiction and control [...].[31]

29 *Cf.* Harrison, *Making the Law,* 30–31.

30 *Cf. Making the Law,* 30–31. *See also* Sanger, *Ordering the Oceans,* 13: 'A main purpose of the conference was to reach agreement on some standard limits to territorial water. The 'cannon-shot' rule was always a vague measure. The United States and Britain had settled on a three-mile limit, but this was by no means universally adopted. Scandinavian countries had a four-mile limit, France claimed six and Czarist Russia had proclaimed a 12-mile territorial sea'.

31 Harry S. Truman, 'Proclamation 2667: Policy Of The United States With Respect To The Natural Resources Of The Subsoil And Sea Bed Of The Continental Shelf (1)', September

Truman also announced that the US would seek agreements with other coastal states if the continental shelf – meaning the seafloor that stretched from the US out into the sea – touched their coastlines. He made assurances that the principle of free navigation and passage – the underlying concept of the high seas – would not be affected by US claims on the seabed.[32]

Truman's proclamation had serious consequences for maritime law and the way it had been practised before 1945. Other coastal states, starting with the Latin American nations, formulated their own proclamations and responded with similar claims.[33] By the end of this chain reaction, the US found itself in conflict with 'every Pacific coast state of southern and central America and with most of the then independent states of the Caribbean'.[34] The list also included its neighbour, Canada, plus several European states, the USSR, coastal states in the east Mediterranean region, and some coastal and archipelagic states in the Asia-Pacific region.[35] This huge reaction left no doubt that maritime boundaries had to be defined and renegotiated. It has been a common consensus in research that the Truman proclamation kick-started the first serious international efforts to settle agreements on new ocean borders.[36] Ultimately, these efforts resulted in the three United Nations Law of the Sea Conventions that lasted from 1958–82.[37]

Although a lot of research has examined the aftermath of the Truman proclamation, its origins were not explored until Donald Cameron Watt investigated them in an article in 1979.[38] Watt wrote that 'Until recently, it was difficult

28, 1945. https://www.trumanlibrary.gov/library/proclamations/2667/policy-united-states-respect-natural-resources-subsoil-and-sea-bed.

32 *Cf.* Truman Proclamation, 28. Sept 1945.

33 The chain reaction started in Mexico. *Cf.* Watt, Donald Cameron,'First steps in the enclosure of the oceans. The origins of Truman's proclamation on the resources of the continental shelf, 28 September 1945', *Marine Policy*, 3 (1979): 221, doi: 10.1016/0308-597X(79)90053-8.

34 Watt, 'First steps', 222.

35 *Cf.* Watt, 'First steps', 222. The states involved were: Argentine, Chile, Peru, Ecuador, Columbia, Panama, Costa Rica, Nicaragua, Honduras, El Salvador, Mexico, Cuba, Canada, Iceland, Norway, Denmark, Portugal, USSR, Saudi Arabia, Philippines, Korea, China.

36 *See* Helmut Tuerk, *Reflections on the Contemporary Law of the Sea* (Boston: Martinus Nijhoff Publishers, 2012), 9: 'Ironically, the first major challenge to the freedom-of-the-seas doctrine came from the power that has the utmost interest in maintaining it-The United States of America'. *See also* Scharf, 'Seizing the Grotian Moment', 109: 'Although the Truman Proclamation is widely viewed as a singular turning point, long before 1945 coastal states had made legal claims to the resources of the seabed and subsoil beyond the territorial sea'.

37 *Cf.* Watt, 'First steps', 211: 'Commonly agreed'.

38 Watt, 'First steps'.

to say anything about the origins of the proclamation. It was obviously not considered of any great importance by those who were involved in this issue'.[39] In the article, he describes the developments that lead up to the proclamation.

During World War II, the United States was worried about its future supply of raw materials – especially oil.[40] Therefore, in 1943 a state committee was set up to study the fish stocks and resources in the sea adjacent to the US coast, because they foresaw that this would be a matter for negotiation after the war.[41] Also, 'the US was concerned to enjoy the exclusive access to the oil and gas in the seabed situated just beyond its three mile limit in the Gulf of Mexico and off California'.[42] The state secretary of the interior, Harold Ickes, sent a letter to Roosevelt – Truman's predecessor as president – expressing his concerns about the US's future supply of raw materials unless alternative sources could be explored. In this letter, he referred to the continental shelf as a 'storehouse of natural resources',[43] and recommended that they 'evolve new concepts of maritime territorial limits beyond three miles [...]'.[44] Roosevelt acknowledged Ickes's concerns, and replied with a letter encouraging him to investigate the matter further.[45] This resulted in several proposed unilateral proclamations devised by state officials over the following two years. Finally, under-secretary of state Joseph C Grew and Ickes sent two memorandums to Roosevelt, proposing regulations to deal with areas of the high seas and the continental shelf. Their aim was to:

> assert jurisdiction and control over the natural resources under the seabed and the continental shelf and to assert a policy of establishing conservation zones for the protection of coastal fishery resources.[46]

39 Watt, 'First steps', 211: 'President Truman does not mention it in his memoirs. It does not rate a mention in the memoirs of his Secretary of State, James Byrnes, or those of his predecessors, Edward R. Stettinius, or Cordell Hull, who clearly had something to do with its formulation'.

40 *Cf.* Anderson, *Modern Law*, 8: 'During the Second World War, demand for oil increased and the industry developed technology so that it was able to work in shallow waters just off the coast'.

41 *Cf.* Watt 'First steps', 212.

42 Anderson, *Modern Law*, 8. For more information on the various proclamations Anderson refers to Ann Hollick, *U.S. Foreign Policy and the Law of the Sea* (Princeton: Princeton University Press, 1981). *See also* Scharf, 'Seizing the Grotian Moment', 110–111.

43 Watt, 'First steps', 212.

44 Watt, 'First steps', 212.

45 *Cf.* Watt, 'First steps', 212.

46 Watt, 'First steps', 215.

As a precaution, Ickes and Grew also advised distributing the memorandums beforehand to the representatives of states that would be affected by the proclamation. In fact, only Canada, Mexico, the United Kingdom and the Soviet Union were handed the memorandums.[47] Modern-day legal analyst Michael P Scharf argues that 'the communications were more in the nature of advanced notification than actual consultations'.[48] Additionally, Watt notes that nowhere was it stated that any negative or hostile reactions from these nations should be taken into account.[49]

In fact, criticism from those state officials who were handed the preliminary memorandums – of whom only the UK expressed reservations[50] – was met by the US with arguments based on national interest, like the need to feed the nation and secure supplies of raw materials.[51] According to Watt, this paid 'lip-service'[52] to all other nation states, encouraging them to follow the US's example and base their claims on their own national interests. Michael P Scharf shares this view, and concludes that 'the legal rationale was based on geological reality, technological development, national security, economic necessity, conservation, and the efficacy of coastal state regulation'. He adds that this justification for US claims on ocean resources would 'render the action easier to accept and replicate by other states'.[53]

President Roosevelt approved the 2267th proclamation on 31 March 1945, but died shortly afterwards on 12 April. The former vice-president, Harry S Truman, came into office immediately, and his new cabinet continued where Roosevelt and his state officials had left off.[54] Bilateral agreements – which had been suggested by the UK – were briefly considered as an alternative to a unilateral proclamation, but were rejected by the new secretary of state, James Byrnes, in summer 1945.[55] Shortly after this, on 28 September 1945, President Truman made the two proclamations, 'and the first long step towards fencing-in of the common land of the oceans had begun'.[56] A month later, the first reaction came from Mexico, which was something

47 *Cf.* Scharf, 'Seizing the Grotian Moment', 115.
48 Scharf, 'Seizing the Grotian Moment', 115.
49 *Cf.* Watt, 'First steps', 215.
50 Cf. Scharf, 'Seizing the Grotian Moment', 155. For the UK's reaction, *see* Hollick, *U.S. Foreign Policy*.
51 *Cf.* Scharf, 'Seizing the Grotian Moment', 218, 220.
52 Watt, 'First steps', 219.
53 Scharf, 'Seizing the Grotian Moment', 114.
54 *Cf.* Scharf, 'Seizing the Grotian Moment', 112–113.
55 *Cf.* Watt, 'First steps', 221.
56 Watt, 'First steps', 221.

of a surprise. According to Watt, the US had been confident of Mexico's support, and was puzzled when its neighbour to the south answered with a similar claim, followed closely by other South Pacific coastal states.[57] Claims and counterclaims continued to trickle in until the US found itself in conflict[58] with a large number of coastal states from all around the world. Some of the claims made by other states far exceeded those of the Truman proclamation. In 1947, Iceland put forward a 'long-term national policy aim to equate fisheries jurisdiction with the outer limits of the continental shelf'.[59] And in 1952, Chile, Ecuador and Peru went even further, demanding a '200 mile zone of sovereignty and jurisdiction'[60] – a claim that endangered free passage on the high seas because it implied the expansion of territorial waters from 3 to 200 miles.[61]

Faced with these developments, by 1950 the US had already begun to backpedal, stating that 'the presidential proclamation of September 1945 did not represent a new concept in international law nor alter the pre-existing regime of the high seas'.[62] According to Watt, the US finally arrived at a point where they were open to the proposals the UK had made in 1943 and again in 1945 – to seek international agreement instead of making unilateral proclamations.[63] In the following years, the US managed to arrive at international agreements with states that had been affected by their earlier claims. There was a treaty with Canada concerning salmon and halibut conservation, a convention with Mexico and Costa Rica about tuna, and finally the North West Atlantic Fisheries Convention (NWAFC).[64] An immediate crisis was averted, but the incident had made it very apparent that the international community needed to seek agreement and negotiation.

---

57 *Cf.* Watt, 'First steps', 222: 'The Mexican example, in extending its jurisdiction over the continental shelf was outdone by other Caribbean and Latin American states, the Argentine (11 October 1946), Chile (23 June 1947), Peru (1 August 1947) and Costa Rica (July 1948) all claiming to extend their sovereignty up to two hundred miles from low-water mark'.

58 There was actually a 'lack of protest' instead of counter claims. *Cf.* Scharf, 'Seizing the Grotian Moment', 116.

59 Anderson, *Modern Law*, 8.

60 Anderson, *Modern Law*, 8–9.

61 *Cf.* Anderson, *Modern Law*, 9.

62 Watt, 'First steps', 223.

63 *Cf.* Watt, 'First steps', 224.

64 *Cf.* Watt, 'First steps', 223. Today the NAFO. The organization was called ICNAF in 1950. More about the organisation *see* Hollick, *U.S. Foreign Policy*, 64 – 65.

4 Access to Resources Makes Ocean Governance a Pressing Issue Post-War

While Truman had made a big splash with his 1945 proclamation, diplomats had in fact been working towards trying to solve the very same issue for decades. However, the chain reaction caused by Truman's proclamation, and the subsequent wrangling over maritime boundaries, showed that it was time to seek more ambitious international agreements. Analysing the reasons for the US's reluctance to seek international agreements in the 1940s, Watt sees 'one of those periodic failures of nerve, lapses into panic and evocations of exhaustion of US national resources [...]'.[65] This interpretation that the US government had lapsed into an episode of hysteria over their maritime boundaries seems plausible, especially when we consider the political, historical and technological context in which the incident unfolded. A great deal of literature concerned with the Law of the Sea Convention attributes this international movement towards a new ocean order to a combination of technological progress and political circumstance.[66]

One factor involved was the experience nations had gained from World War II. More than ever before, states had become aware of the severe consequences that shortages of raw materials could have. Watt mentions US fears of a potential oil shortage in 1943, when they were worried that the UK would persuade Saudi Arabia to cut US concessions in favour of their own oil supply.[67] Meanwhile, technological progress heralded the feasibility of offshore mining, starting with the continental shelf in the 1950s.[68] It is difficult to pinpoint which cause was uppermost – progress in technological and scientific knowledge, or the need for solutions spurred by political circumstances. Most likely, both factors fed off each other.

---

65 Watt, 'First steps', 224.

66 Anderson, *Modern Law,* 7: 'The state of law, including the question of national limits, remained largely unchanged until 1945 when the first major changes (not directly connected with the end of the Second World War) were witnessed. Pressure for the acceptance of wider limits so as to meet the growing need for resources was ever-increasing. Further significant changes followed throughout the second half of the century as mankind's involvement with the seas intensified'. *See also* before technology development kicked off Vidas, *Law, Technology*, 27: 'Due to the technology available, human impacts on the sea and its resources were limited; and humans were also limited in number, since the global population in the early 17th century was around 500 million – some 14 times less than today'.

67 *Cf.* Watt, 'First steps', 213.

68 *Cf.* Schmidt, *Common Heritage*, 18'. *See also* Bernaerts, *Bernaerts' Guide,* 3.

The fact that Harold Ickes called the continental shelf off the American coast a 'storehouse of natural resources'[69] suggests that the US was not necessarily looking to exploit them in the immediate future.[70] If he had wanted to imply that the resources were to be used there and then, he might have used words like 'source' or 'pit'. The term 'storehouse' evokes images of a dusty stockroom, filled with goods reserved for hard times. One reason for Ickes's use of the word 'storehouse' over a term implying immediate accessibility could have been the fact that technology – although it was advancing – was still a long way off being able to exploit the 'hidden goods' scientists had found on the seafloor. Another reason might have been the looming Cold War, and the still-fresh memories of the First and Second World Wars[71] that kept America in a state of constant worry over how to provide for its own needs if yet another catastrophe struck. Securing future stores of natural resources was an insurance policy for lean times – not just in terms of raw materials from the seafloor, but also in the form of food from fish stocks in the coastal waters.[72]

The chain reaction caused by Truman's proclamation in 1945 proves that the US was not alone in these worries. They were not the only state to have experienced shortages of natural resources during the war, nor were they the only ones to observe the increasing tensions between east and west with a great

69 Watt, 'First steps', 212. Watt cites from a letter from Ickes to Roosevelt, 5 June 1943.

70 We know today that this would in fact not be a possibility until recently. *Cf.* Japan's first successful attempt to extract minerals: METI Ministry of Economy, Trade and Industry, *World's First Success in Continuous Ore Lifting test for Seafloor Polymetallic Sulphides, Pilot test of excavating and ore lifting conducted for seafloor polymetallic sulphides under the sea area near Okinawa Prefecture* (METI, 2017), http://www.meti.go.jp/english/press/2017/0926_004.html. For a recent historical overview over the development of deep sea mining from 1965 until 2019, *see* Ole Sparenberg, 'A historical perspective on deep-sea mining for manganese nodules, 1965–2019', *The Extractive Industries and Society* 6, nr. 3 (2019), 842–854, https://doi.org/10.1016/j.exis.2019.04.001.

71 *See* Watt, 'First steps', 224. Watt traces this even further back, writing: 'This psychology, rooted in images of the dust-bowl and the ghost-town, made the USA one of the earliest pioneers in the movement for conservation by government, a movement whose origins lie within a decade of the announcement by the Superintendent of the Census in 1890 that there was no longer a US frontier. But the traumas of the boom and bust years of the last three decades of the nineteenth century, reinforced as they were by the experiences of 1929–1936, the years between the crash of the Big Bull market and the agricultural depression so vividly depicted in Steinbeck's Grapes of Wrath, have driven this recurrent fear deep into the psyche of a nation which by 1945 was so powerful and dominant that its action echoed throughout world politics'.

72 The conservation zone was one of the US's worries to secure food for the population. *Cf.* Watt, 'First steps', 216.

deal of concern. One solution was to invest in finding and securing alternative deposits of natural resources, and the seabed was a prime source – especially in terms of raw materials.

5 Preparing for the First Convention on Ocean Governance

The founding of the United Nations after World War II was central to the further development of international agreements and law,[73] including the Law of the Sea. A new committee was set up to study international issues – this time under the auspices of the United Nations General Assembly. In 1947, the International Law Commission (ILC) was founded, replacing the committee of experts that had been set up for the Hague Codification Conference in 1930.[74] Once again, the Law of the Sea was pinpointed as one of the matters to be addressed, and this time the territorial waters and high seas were 'identified as key issues'.[75] Finally, the General Assembly decided that a large convention should examine the Law of the Sea at some point in the upcoming years, and that the ILC should lay the groundwork for this conference by scoping out the various questions that needed to be addressed.[76]

The ILC's preparatory work took six years. Part of this preparation was to incorporate the work of other international conferences on related issues. These included the Food and Agriculture Organization (FAO) International Technical Conference on the Conservation of the Living Resources of the Sea (Rome, 1955), and the Conference of Marine Resources (Ciudad Trujillo, 1956), sponsored by the Organization of American States (OAS).[77] The ILC drafted Articles about issues concerning the continental shelf and fisheries, and presented them to the General Assembly in 1953. However, the General Assembly refused to handle the items addressed in these Articles, stating that 'it would not deal with any aspects of the regime of the high seas or of the

73 *Cf.* Harrison, *Making the Law,* 31. *See also* Anderson, *Modern Law,* 7: 'From the standpoint of 2006, the Law of the Sea can now be seen to have been first codified and developed and later substantially reformed during the period between 1945 and the end of the century, a period that also saw many diplomatic controversies and disputes over maritime limits, mainly about fishing'.

74 *Cf.* Harrison, *Making the Law,* 29.

75 Harrison, *Making the Law,* 32.

76 *Cf.* Anderson, *Modern Law,* 9.

77 *Cf.* Hollick, *U.S. Foreign Policy,* 128.

regime of territorial waters until all problems involved have been studied by the Commission and reported by it to the General Assembly'.[78]

In 1956, the ILC handed in a 'single set of draft articles' to the General Assembly that would become the 'basis for discussions at the First Law of the Sea Conference'.[79] In February 1957, the General Assembly released a resolution stating that:

> an international conference of plenipotentiaries should be convoked to examine the law of the sea, taking account not only of the legal but also of the technical, biological, economic and political aspects of the problem, and to embody the results of its work in one or more international conventions or such other instruments as it might seem appropriate […].[80]

The resolution showed that there had been a change in the strategies used to negotiate international law between the first codification attempts in 1907 and the presentation of the ILC's draft Articles in 1956. With this resolution, the General Assembly recognised that negotiation processes had to look beyond the purely legal aspects of an issue. Therefore, the resolution included the requirement for a broader examination of relevant issues like politics, biology and technology during the international conference that was to come.

6 UNCLOS I – Defining Legal Concepts, 1958

Renegotiating ocean governance would see the world community entangled in discussion for most of the second half of the twentieth century. The Law of the Sea was a gargantuan task, and even just identifying some of the core issues had already taken almost half a decade. In 1958, the international community was finally ready to delve into the material that the International Law Commission had provided. The first major task would be to agree on defining terms and concepts of maritime boundaries, and this was done during the first two Conventions on the Law of the Sea.

---

78 Regime of the High Seas, UNGA Resolution 798(VIII), December 7, 1953, quoted in Harrison, *Making the Law*, 33.

79 Harrison, *Making the Law*, 33–34.

80 UN General Assembly, International conference of plenipotentiaries to examine the law of the sea, 21 February 1957, A/RES/1105, available at: http://www.refworld.org/docid/3b00f06d4.html, accessed 30 September 2021.

The first conference was held in Geneva from 24 February to 27 April 1958.[81] Eighty-six countries were party to it, and seventy-five Articles drafted by the International Law Commission over the course of six years[82] were discussed.[83] Five main committees were set up to handle the different topics that the ILC had submitted as drafts.[84] These committees succeeded in adopting four respective conventions over the course of the negotiation period: the Convention on the High Seas,[85] the Conventions on Fishing and Conservation of the Living Resources of the High Seas,[86] the Convention on the Territorial Sea[87] and the Convention on the Continental Shelf.[88] In addition to the committees, a plenary was set up, and the conventions adopted by the committees had to pass the plenary as well. This proved a challenge for two of the conventions – those dealing with fishing limits in the territorial sea, and the outer limits of the continental shelf.[89] These conventions failed to pass at the plenary because it had different rules of procedure. Instead of the simple majority rule of the committees, conventions could only be passed in the plenary by a two-thirds majority.[90]

---

81 For an overview over the history, procedure and documents, *see* Tullio Treves, '1958 Geneva Conventions on the Law of the Sea', United Nations Audivisual Library of International Law, (2008), http://legal.un.org/avl/ha/gclos/gclos.html.

82 *Cf.* Hollick, *U.S. Foreign Policy,* 128. The ILC was set the task of preparing documents for the first convention.

83 *Cf.* Sanger, *Ordering the Oceans,* 15.

84 Treves, '1958 Geneva Conventions', 1.

85 1958 Convention on the High Seas, opened for signature 29 April 1958. 450 UNTS 11 (entered into force 30 September 1962).

86 1958 Conventions on Fishing and Conservation of the Living Resources of the High Seas, opened for signature 29 April 1958. 559 UNTS 285, (entered into force 20 March 1966).

87 1958 Convention on the Territorial Sea and the Contiguous Zone, opened for signature 29 April 1958. 516 UNTS 205, (entered into force 10 September 1964).

88 1958 Convention on the Continental Shelf, Geneva, 29 April 1958. 499 UNTS 311, (entered into force 10 June 1964), *Cf.* Sanger, *Ordering the Oceans,* 14–15. *See also* United Nations, The Work of the International Law Commission, at 42, quoted in Harrison, *Making the Law,* 35: 'The Continental Shelf Convention was adopted by 57 votes to 3, with 8 abstentions. The Fisheries Conventions was adopted by 45 votes to 1, with 18 abstentions. THE High Seas Conventions was adopted by 65 votes to none, with 2 abstentions. The Territorial Sea Convention was adopted by 61 votes to none, with 2 abstentions'.

89 *See* Anderson, *Modern Law*, 9–10.

90 *Cf.* Treves, '1958 Geneva Conventions', 2. The voting issue is also discussed in Anderson, *Modern Law*, 9: 'A simple majority sufficed in Committee and a two-thirds majority in Plenary. This was not an entirely satisfactory method of working on this particular topic, mainly because some significant minorities were left empty handed: a rule requiring the seeking of consensus would have required, of course, a far longer conference'.

The first committee worked on a list of the four freedoms of the high seas,[91] which was relatively straightforward to agree on. The committee defined the 'high seas' as 'all parts of the sea that are not included in the territorial sea or in the internal waters of a State'.[92] Article 2 of the convention stated that the area of the high seas was to be 'open to all nations'[93] and that no state could claim sovereignty over this area.[94] Freedom was an important part of Article 2 and it was granted to coastal and non-coastal states alike:

(1) Freedom of navigation;
(2) Freedom of fishing;
(3) Freedom to lay submarine cables and pipelines;
(4) Freedom to fly over the high seas.[95]

This meant that the high seas were an area of the ocean that all states could use, regardless of whether they had a coastline or not. The high seas therefore became important for the entire international community and there was a collective will to agree on practicable rules.

The second committee worked on fishing and conservation of the living resources of the high seas, and they managed to agree on some rules of cooperative conservation.[96] The committee stated in their preamble that 'the need of the world's expanding population for food, has exposed some of these resources to the danger of being over-exploited […]',[97] and further that this had caused problems for the conservation of 'living resources' – meaning fish and other biological resources for consumption and other human use. The committee went on to say that 'there is a clear necessity that [these problems] be solved, whenever possible, on the basis of international co-operation through the concerted action of all the States concerned'.[98]

---

91 *Cf.* Sanger, *Ordering the Oceans,* 16.

92 *1958 Convention on the High Seas*, Geneva, 29 April 1958. 450 UNTS 11 (entered into force 30 September 1962). United Nations, *Treaty Series,* vol. 450, p. 11, article 1. available at: https://treaties.un.org/doc/Treaties/1964/06/19640610%2002-10%20AM/Ch_XXI_01_2_3_4_5p.pdf.

93 *1958 Convention on the High Seas*, article 2.

94 *Cf. 1958 Convention on the High Seas*, article 2.

95 *1958 Convention on the High Seas*, article 2.

96 *Cf.* Sanger, *Ordering the Oceans,* 16.

97 *1958 Conventions on Fishing and Conservation of the Living Resources of the High Seas,* Geneva, 29 April 1958. 559 UNTS 285, (entered into force 20 March 1966). United Nations, *Treaty Series,* vol. 559, p. 285, available at: https://www.gc.noaa.gov/documents/8_1_1958_fishing.pdf.

98 *1958 Conventions on Fishing and Conservation of the Living Resources of the High Seas*, preamble p. 258.

Another reason the second committee met with success was because it left the really tricky question of the contiguous zone – a transition area between the high seas and the territorial sea of coastal states – to the third committee, which was concerned with the limits of the territorial sea.[99] This was indicated in Article 6.3 (and following) of the convention, which states that:

> A State whose nationals are engaged in fishing in any area of the high seas adjacent to the territorial sea of a State shall, at the request of that coastal State, enter into negotiations with a view to prescribing by agreement the measures necessary for the conservation of the living resources of the high seas in that area.[100]

How to agree on fishing rules for 'the area adjacent to the high seas' – meaning the contiguous zone – was left to the third committee. This committee had to deal with one of the most complicated questions about the limits of the territorial sea, and they ultimately failed to solve it. However, they did manage to agree on straight baselines for the territorial sea, as set out in Section II Article 3: 'the normal baseline for measuring the breadth of the territorial sea is the low-water line along the coast as marked on large-scale charts officially recognized by the coastal State'.[101] Another point the committee succeeded in settling was the 'innocent passage' of ships through international straits.[102]

The fourth committee was concerned with the continental shelf, and managed to settle two legal points of issue: the rights of coastal states and the delimitation of the shelf.[103] The committee succeeded in defining the concept of the continental shelf as:

> referring (a) to the seabed and subsoil of the submarine areas adjacent to the coast but outside the area of the territorial sea, to a depth of 200 metres or, beyond that limit, to where the depth of the superjacent waters admits of the exploitation of the natural resources of the said areas; (b) to

99 *Cf.* Sanger, *Ordering the Oceans*, 16. *See also* Treves, '1958 Geneva Conventions', 2.

100 *1958 Conventions on Fishing and Conservation of the Living Resources of the High Seas*, Article 6.3.

101 *1958 Convention on the Territorial Sea and the Contiguous Zone*, Geneva, 29 April 1958. 516 UNTS 205, (entered into force 10 September 1964). United Nations, *Treaty Series*, vol. 516, p. 205, section II article 3, available at: https://treaties.un.org/doc/Treaties/1964/06/19640610%2002-10%20AM/Ch_XXI_01_2_3_4_5p.pdf.

102 *Cf.* Sanger, *Ordering the Oceans*, 16.

103 *Cf.* Sanger, *Ordering the Oceans*, 16.

> the seabed and subsoil of similar submarine areas adjacent to the coasts of islands.[104]

In Article 6.1, the convention states that coastal states whose continental shelves are adjacent to one another are encouraged to agree on the respective limits of their continental shelves,[105] and the rights of each nation state to utilise the resources of the continental shelf are listed in several Articles.[106] In *Modern Law of the Sea,* David Anderson writes that the success of UNCLOS I was 'qualified by the failure to reach agreement on the maximum breadth of the territorial sea and the question of introducing an exclusive fishery zone'.[107] He also notes other shortcomings, pointing out that agreements concerning the continental shelf were expressed

> in terms of depth and exploitability, two criteria that proved in practice to be unsatisfactory as a result of technological advances. The rapid movement of the offshore oil and gas industry into deeper and remoter waters was not anticipated in 1958.[108]

7 UNCLOS II – Failing to Fill Out Legal Concepts, 1960

During the first convention, it became apparent that outstanding issues concerning the limits of the territorial sea and fisheries would not be agreed upon. Therefore, the Australian delegation proposed a second convention in Geneva. The Australians had chaired the difficult third committee on the territorial sea and were well aware of the issues that had still to be resolved.[109] As a result, the General Assembly released a resolution on convening the conference, stating that 'a second international conference of plenipotentiaries on the law of the

---

104 *1958 Convention on the Continental Shelf,* Geneva, 29 April 1958. 499 UNTS 311, (entered into force 10 June 1964). United Nations, *Treaty Series,* vol. 499, p. 311, article 1, available at: https://treaties.un.org/doc/Treaties/1964/06/19640610%2002-10%20AM/Ch_XXI_01_2_3_4_5p.pdf.

105 *Cf.* 1958 Convention on the Continental Shelf, article 6. 1,2.

106 Too many to mention here. *See* 1958 Convention on the Continental Shelf. There is an ongoing discussion about what kind of resources were meant by 'natural resources'. More about the discussion in Leary, *International Law,* 88.

107 Anderson, *Modern Law,* 9–10.

108 Anderson, *Modern Law,* 9–10.

109 *Cf.* Sanger, *Ordering the Oceans,* 17.

sea should be called for the purpose of considering further the questions of the breadth of the territorial sea and fishery limits […]'.[110]

The second Conference on the Law of The Sea convened in 1960, and was held in Geneva from 16 March to 26 April.[111] This time, eighty-eight states were involved in the discussions. Three committees were set up: the 'General Committee', the 'Committee of the Whole' and the 'Credentials Committee'.[112] Although the conference had identified two specific issues that needed resolving – the limits of the territorial sea and fisheries – no agreement was reached this time round either. The United States and Canada presented a proposal of a six-mile fishing zone and six-mile territorial zone,[113] but it failed by one vote.[114]

Ultimately, the conference adopted two resolutions. One was concerned with making the discussions among the participants and the records public.[115] The second was to recognise 'that the development of international law affecting fishing may lead to changes in the practices and requirements of many States, […]'.[116] This was followed by a list of information and action initiatives to aid states who wanted to follow up the development. In other words, there was no significant agreement other than that the discussions on the Law of the Sea were still ongoing and that the questions around fisheries and the limits of the territorial sea remained to be resolved.

Tullio Treves, who was a legal expert during UNCLOS III, wrote of UNCLOS I and II that since no final agreements were reached concerning the most pressing questions, their importance was 'mostly historical'.[117] He added that though the conferences failed to find any answers to the major issues, they did lay the groundwork on which UNCLOS III would be built.[118] Obviously, the outcomes of the first two conventions were not very satisfactory. However, UNCLOS I and II had succeeded in defining legal concepts for negotiating the Law of the Sea. Another conference would be needed to fill out those concepts with specific definitions, from the limits of territorial seas to the exact measurements of the

110 General Assembly resolution 1307 (XIII), *Convening of a second conference on the Law of the Sea*, (10 December 1958). (To see the resolution of the Conference concerning the issue: Official Records of the United Nations Conference on the Law of the Sea, vol. II, annexes, document A/CONF.13/L.56, resolution VIII).

111 *Cf.* Treves, '1958 Geneva Conventions', 2.

112 A/CONF.19/L.15.

113 A/CONF.19/C.1/L.4.

114 *Cf.* Anderson, *Modern Law*, 10, and Sanger, *Ordering the Oceans*, 17.

115 A/CONF.19/L.15 annex I.

116 A/CONF.19/L.15 annex II.

117 Treves, '1958 Geneva Conventions', 3.

118 *Cf.* Treves, '1958 Geneva Conventions', 3.

continental shelves. In hindsight, the Canadian journalist Clyde Sanger wrote about the fragmented aftermath of UNCLOS I and II that 'it required a person of rare vision to raise the possibility of pulling the fragments together and making a thorough attempt to create a framework for the management of the world's oceans'.[119]

119 Sanger, *Ordering the Oceans*, 1.

PART 2

Preparing for the Law of the Sea Convention 1967–73

CHAPTER 3

The Maltese Initiative Changes Ocean Governance

1 Dipping into the Oceans – A Letter to Santa Barbara

In the first week of October 1967, a handwritten letter appeared in the in-tray at the Center for the Study of Democratic Institutions. The letter was formally addressed to 'Dr Hutchins', and was from a Mr Aubrey H Whitelaw of North Stonington, Connecticut.[1] Rather than Hutchins, it was Elisabeth Mann Borgese who replied to the letter. Perhaps the letter arrived on Hutchins's desk at a busy time; he may have had a quick look at it and passed it on to her. We will never know the full story, but the follow-up letter from Whitelaw was addressed directly to Elisabeth Mann Borgese, thanking her for her reply in October.[2]

This correspondence is significant because there has been some uncertainty about where, when and how Elisabeth Mann Borgese was introduced to the discussions about ocean governance that had been going on at the United Nations since the International Law Commission (ILC) had identified questions around the Law of the Sea as 'key issues'[3] in 1947.[4] Did the first two Conventions on the Law of the Sea – UNCLOS I in 1958 and UNCLOS II in 1960 – pass unnoticed by Mann Borgese and her colleagues in Chicago and Santa Barbara? And what was it about the preparations for UNCLOS III that made it so appealing for an 'internationalist' who had worked on world governance and the *Pacem in Terris* conferences to engage with the discussions in the late 60s?

The correspondence with Whitelaw might give us a hint. In the letter that appeared on Mann Borgese's desk in early October 1967, Whitelaw wrote that he had 'recently become intrigued by the proposal that the U.N. might gain financial independence of its sovereign national members'.[5] He added that he

1 MS-2-744, Box 43, Folder 17, 28. September 1967.

2 MS-2-744, Box 43, Folder 17, 02. November 1967.

3 *Cf.* Harrison, *Making the Law,* 32.

4 *See* MS-2-744, Box 43, Folder 17. *See* Baker, 'Uncommon Heritage', 16. I found out later that Baker had already discussed the letter in her 2011 article.

5 MS-2-744, Box 43, Folder 17, 28. September 1967: 'Resolution 15 adopted July 13. 1967, by Geneva World Peace Through Law Conference [...] is to me a tremendous significance – for reasons as yet, apparently, not publicized'.

believed 'the U.N. must very soon play a much more effective peace-keeping role in world affairs than the major national sovereign members are likely to permit or encourage'.[6] Whitelaw reported that he had been looking into the field of 'oceanography', and had started to become aware of 'the many promising aspects of exploiting the ocean depths (70% of the Earth's surface which belong to no nation) [...]'.[7] He could not help 'relating the significance of these new sources of wealth to a possible solution to some of the world's most pressing problems, such as: famine conditions, industrial resources for undersupplied and underdeveloped nations [...]'.[8]

Whitelaw's proposal was mostly about financing the United Nations with revenues from seabed exploitation, and possibly extending this source of funding to other 'pressing problems' that the international community would face during the twentieth century and in the more distant future. What must have made his suggestions particularly interesting for Mann Borgese was that he believed problem-solving needed to be internationalised, and that nation states were less suited to the challenges that lay ahead. This must have resonated with Mann Borgese's own ideas of world governance. In his letter, Whitelaw pointed out that potential sources of wealth existed in the oceans, and that these had not been appropriated by any nation state – meaning they could be used to solve world problems. He had made a connection between what Elisabeth Mann Borgese's work at the Center for the Study of Democratic Institutions stood for – experimenting with internationalism and world governance – and possible future developments in the form of peace-keeping through international organisations and using marine resources to achieve economic equity.[9] The only missing link, assuming that the centre was not yet aware of it, was his remark about the 'promising aspects of exploiting the ocean depths'.[10]

The discussions that preceded UNCLOS III were fuelled by the widely recognised fact that marine minerals and other resources existed and could soon be utilised. Even back in 1945, President Truman had already understood that

6 MS-2-744, Box 43, Folder 17, 28. September 1967.

7 MS-2-744, Box 43, Folder 17, 28. September 1967.

8 MS-2-744, Box 43, Folder 17, 28. September 1967.

9 *See* Richard Samuel Deese, 'From World War to World Law: Elisabeth Mann Borgese and the Law of the Sea', *World History Bulletin* 32, no. 2, (2016): 5–8, https://www.researchgate.net/publication/311707074_From_World_War_to_World_Law_Elisabeth_Mann_Borgese_and_the_Law_of_the_Sea. Deese argues that the world committee had already sown the seeds of Mann Borgese's engagement with UNCLOS.

10 MS-2-744, Box 43, Folder 17, 28. September 1967.

the continental shelf might harbour resources worth claiming, and it was with this in mind that the state secretary of the interior, Harold Ickes, had called the US continental shelf a 'storehouse of resources'.[11] What had changed between 1945 and 1967 was the state of technological development, and the possibilities that came with this. In 1945, the resources on and underneath the seafloor had been largely out of reach, hence Ickes's storehouse metaphor. In 1967, on the other hand, there was an optimistic view that technological development would make these resources accessible in the near future.[12] This meant that in the minds of many of those working on ocean governance questions, the seafloor had shifted from being a 'storehouse' to an actual deposit.

In 1999, Mann Borgese said of Whitelaw (who she called an 'unknown gentleman from Connecticut')[13] that his letter had drawn her attention to 'the growing importance of the issues involved in the Law of the Sea, including various proposals to declare the oceans to be Common Heritage of Mankind'.[14] Whitelaw's suggestions reminded her of the proposal in the old draft world constitution to apply the concept of common property to the world, and she immediately set about convincing Hutchins to sanction a three-year project examining the Law of the Sea. For Mann Borgese, 'the prospect of seeing at least one of the "four elements of life" declared to be the common heritage of mankind was indeed exciting [...]',[15] and she believed that the project would be a 'worthwhile undertaking, enabling us to bring the utopian ideals of the World Constitutions into the arena of real politics'.[16] Having convinced Hutchins, Mann Borgese started to work on a project proposal with international law expert, Wolfgang Friedmann.[17] Shortly after this, a speech at the First Committee of the United Nations General Assembly addressed exactly the same issue, and 'struck like lightning'.[18]

---

11 Watt, 'First steps', 212.

12 Sam Robinson discusses the optimism for new technological solutions that would shape ocean governance in the decades to come in Sam Robinson, 'Scientific imaginaries and science diplomacy: The case of ocean exploitation', *Centaurus* (2020), 1– 21, https://doi.org/10.1111/1600-0498.12342.

13 MS-2-744, Box 345, Folder 4, Arvid Pardo, Retrospect and Prospects, 1999.

14 MS-2-744, Box 345, Folder 4, Arvid Pardo, Retrospect and Prospects, 1999. Obituary written 1999 after Arvid Pardo's passing.

15 MS-2-744, Box 345, Folder 4, Arvid Pardo, Retrospect and Prospects, 1999.

16 MS-2-744, Box 345, Folder 4, Arvid Pardo, Retrospect and Prospects, 1999.

17 *Cf.* MS-2-744, Box 345, Folder 4, Arvid Pardo, Retrospect and Prospects, 1999. Friedmann published 'The Changing Structure of International Law'.

18 MS-2-744, Box 345, Folder 4, Arvid Pardo, Retrospect and Prospects, 1999.

2 A Person of Rare Vision?

On 1 November 1967, a tall, middle-aged man with a vanishing hairline and a slight belly took his place behind the speaker's desk at the First Committee of the United Nations General Assembly. He might have placed a bundle of papers carefully upon the speaker's desk or adjusted his thick black glasses before taking a deep breath and starting to speak.[19] It was an ordinary Wednesday in November, and there were surprisingly few people there to witness what was about to happen.[20] The man who had ascended to the speaker's desk proceeded to deliver a two-hour speech that those present would continue to talk about for decades. It was a 'you should have been there' kind of moment.[21]

That man was Arvid Pardo. In 1964, he had been appointed Malta's first ambassador to the United Nations.[22] The tiny archipelagic state had recently gained independence from Great Britain, and was eager to make a splash in the only arena available to small states: the United Nations. The speech was about humanity's ventures into the deep oceans and the possibilities that lay ahead.[23] Arvid Pardo compared the air on Earth to the water in the sea. The air, he said, was the 'atmosphere of land',[24] while water was the 'atmosphere of submerged land'.[25] He made a connection between the space inhabited by humanity – namely the Earth and the airspace above it – and the underwater space that humanity was about to infiltrate.

Pardo went on to talk about the origins of humanity's interest in the deep sea, which had been inaccessible for most of history. The first attempts to utilise the seafloor, he said, had been the efforts to lay the first transatlantic cable.[26] He continued by outlining various existing possibilities for extracting resources from the oceans, such as the attempts to get gold and silver out of

---

19 Picture in *Commemoration of the 30th Anniversary of the United Nations Convention on the Law of the Sea and the Common Heritage of Mankind* (Malta: Ministry of Foreign Affairs; IMO International Maritime Law Institute), 11.

20 In conversation with: Williamson, Hugh. (Adjunct Professor: Marine Affairs Program, Dalhousie University), interview with the auhtor, April 29, 2016. Halifax/NS, Canada. Hugh Williamson.

21 In conversation with: Williamson, Hugh. (Adjunct Professor: Marine Affairs Program, Dalhousie University), interview with the author, April 29, 2016. Halifax/NS, Canada. Hugh Williamson.

22 *See* the letter of appointing Pardo in *Commemoration of the 30th Anniversary*, 9.

23 For the entire speech *see*: Statement of Arvid Pardo, 1 November 1967, First Committee 1515th & 1516th Meeting, A/C.1/PV.1515/; A/C.1/PV.1516.

24 A/C.1/PV.1515, 8.

25 A/C.1/PV.1515, 8.

26 A/C.1/PV.1515, 8.

seawater – which he claimed the German government had already tried in the interwar period but had found too expensive.[27] Pardo also mentioned humanity's long-standing interest in the hunt for 'sunken treasures'[28] and 'archaeological treasures'.[29] He went on to cover the penetration of the seafloor through 'sub-bottom mining'[30] and noted the extraction of oil[31] and gas.[32] All these he used as examples of resources that humans knew about and had tried to exploit.

Having established the current state of humanity's knowledge and capabilities, Pardo moved on to what he thought lay ahead: the extraction of polymetallic nodules from the seafloor.[33] He described the nodules as 'irregularly spherical in shape, like potatoes, ranging from 0.5 to 25 cm in diameter'.[34] Pardo asserted that there was an 'abundance'[35] of these resources, and that in some places they were found in a 'concentration of 50 kg per square metre'.[36] According to Pardo, these figures were taken from John Mero's book, *The Mineral Resources of the Sea*,[37] in which Mero had attempted to estimate the deposits of nodules on the seafloor.

That the seabed held potential as a new source of raw materials was not breaking news. To understand Pardo's enthusiasm for these potato-shaped stones on the seafloor, we need to go back to their initial discovery. The first attempt to research marine manganese nodules was the HMS *Challenger* expedition from 1872–6.[38] GP Glasby, a geologist from New Zealand, mentioned this expedition in the historical preface of a book he edited in the 1970s that was concerned with marine manganese deposits in the world's oceans.[39] 'The results of this cruise', Glasby stated, 'were unique in as much as they were to dominate thinking on manganese nodules for over 80 years'.[40] This takes us

27 *Cf.* A/C.1/PV.1515, 16.
28 *Cf.* A/C.1/PV.1515, 19.
29 A/C.1/PV.1515, 20.
30 A/C.1/PV.1515, 21.
31 A/C.1/PV.1515, 22.
32 A/C.1/PV.1515, 23.
33 *Cf.* A/C.1/PV.1515, 26.
34 A/C.1/PV.1515, 26.
35 A/C.1/PV.1515, 26.
36 A/C.1/PV.1515, 26.
37 John L. Mero, *The Mineral Resources of the Sea*, (New York: Elsevier Oceanography Scientific Publishing Company, 1964), quoted in A/C.1/PV.1515, 26.
38 G.P. Glasby, 'Historical Introduction', in *Marine Manganese Deposits*, (New York: Elsevier Oceanography Scientific Publishing Company, 1977), 1.
39 *See* Glasby, 'Historical Introduction'.
40 Glasby, 'Historical Introduction', 1.

up to the 1950s when new studies were conducted – most likely prompted by increasing demand for new sources of raw materials after a period of instability and international conflict. It was this same climate that would dominate international relations and policy-making during UNCLOS.

According to Glasby, there were 'sporadic' follow-ups to the *Challenger* expedition's research. Expeditions were conducted by the *Albatross* from 1899–1900 and 1904–5 in the North Pacific, while other research trips included the *Carnegie* expedition in 1928–9 and the *John Murray* expedition in 1933–4 where nodules were collected. Apart from these, little was done to investigate deep sea nodules until after World War II.[41] A Swedish expedition in 1947–8 carried out pioneering research assembling an extensive collection of 'deep sea sediment cores',[42] but it was only in 1965 that John Mero first managed to collect 'data on the regional variation of nodule composition throughout the Pacific [...]'.[43] In terms of the economic value of deep sea nodules, Mero had already published a relevant study in 1958.[44] It was the same year UNCLOS I took place in Geneva, but at that time deep sea minerals were not specifically on the agenda. It took Arvid Pardo's 1967 speech to officially bring them into the negotiations on ocean governance.

Despite the existence of other resources, polymetallic nodules would become the resource that was most discussed in connection with UNCLOS III in the following years. It is difficult to work out exactly why the nodules remained so persistently on the agenda for the delegates at the United Nations. One explanation could be that Mero's study meant there was a very optimistic (and incorrect)[45] estimate of their commercial value. Another could be that

41 *Cf.* Glasby, 'Historical Introduction', 7.

42 Glasby, 'Historical Introduction', 8.

43 Glasby, 'Historical Introduction', 8.

44 *See* John L. Mero, 'Economic Aspect of Nodule Mining', in G.P. Glasby ed., *Marine Manganese Deposits* (New York: Elsevier Oceanography Scientific Publishing Company, 1977), 372: '[...] a study was initiated by the Institute of Marine Resources of the University of California to determine if it might be economic to mine and process their nodules for their cobalt, nickel and copper contents. The economic factors involved in mining and processing nodules. All the research and development in this matter dates from the release of the report describing the result of that study (Mero, 1958)'.

45 Mero's study was too optimistic at the time. *See* Sanger, *Ordering the Oceans*, 17. Lately this issue has been referred to by Secretary-General of the ISA, Michael Lodge. *See* Michael Lodge, 'The International Seabed Authority and Deep Seabed Mining', *UN Chronicle* 54, no.1&2 (2017), https://unchronicle.un.org/article/international-seabed-authority-and-deep-seabed-mining. *See also* Payoyo, *Cries of the Sea*, 220.

they were the resources that had been explored and studied most extensively since the first *Challenger* expedition way back in 1872–6.[46]

Polymetallic nodules, however, were not the only minerals known to scientists in 1967, and Arvid Pardo's speech ranged much more widely. He was clearly interested in a variety of marine resources such as 'phosphorite nodules',[47] 'calcareous ooze'[48] in sediments and 'pelagic clays'.[49] And having listed the potential mineral resources available, Pardo went even further, extending his scope to what today we would call 'genetic resources'[50] – a general term for all potential resources in the oceans that could be farmed or otherwise utilised for food supply or biotechnological purposes.[51] He even suggested that dolphins might be used as sheepdogs[52] in futuristic fish farms.[53]

Pardo made predictions about when each method of using these marine resources might be possible, based on the existing state of technological development. He drew a distinction between farming – as a way to utilise the genetic resources – and the exploitation of mineral resources. The latter, according to Pardo, was 'imminent',[54] while farming and other forms of utilisation were 'in the future'.[55] Although Arvid Pardo recognised that the vehicles used to extract nodules could have high operating costs, he was enthusiastic about the imminent exploitation of marine minerals, due to the development of technology

46 Helen Rozwadowski notes in a recent study of oceanic history that the interest in the ocean environment was not solely marked by the Challenger expedition *see* Helen M. Rozwadowski, *Vast Expanses A History of the Oceans* (London: Reaktion Books LTD, 2018), 118: 'Long considered the foundational event for oceanography, the circumnavigation voyage by the *Challenger* (1872 to 1876) instead represents the culmination of scientific interest in the ocean from many sources'.

47 A/C.1/PV.1515, 30.

48 A/C.1/PV.1515, 31.

49 A/C.1/PV.1515, 32.

50 Discussed recently in Leary, *International Law*.

51 *Cf.* A/C.1/PV.1515, 37. In hindsight, Pardo has been accused of having exaggerated the abundance of mineral resources on the seafloor. Mann Borgese defends his vision claiming that Pardo was interested in more than just the polymetallic nodules. *See* MS-2–744, Box 345, Folder 4, Arvid Pardo, Retrospect and Prospects, 1999.

52 A/C.1/PV.1515, 33.

53 Although this sounds peculiar, it is not that far-fetched if we consider that the US navy began using dolphins and other marine mammals as minesweepers in the 1960s. *See* Wood, Forrest G., Naval Oceans Systems Center San Diego, 'Annotated Bibliography of Publications from the U.S. Navy's Marine Mammal Program'. Update November 1987, available at: https://apps.dtic.mil/sti/citations/ADA188266.

54 A/C.1/PV.1515, 34.

55 A/C.1/PV.1515, 34.

that would make this exploitation less costly.[56] Pardo's speech reveals that he was well-informed about the technology that was already on the market or in development. He seemed positive that effective mining equipment was right around the corner. For instance, he reported that 'A prototype submersible for commercial mining of the rich manganese-nodule deposits [...] is under construction now, and others are planned'.[57] As for the extraction technology, he informed his listeners that: 'The nodules will be raked from the ocean floor and pumped into the vessel [...]',[58] and that from there they would be 'transferred easily to an accompanying cargo-ship by means of a floating conduit'.[59]

This must have been exciting news for the delegates listening to the speech. Pardo made it seem like the exploitation of marine minerals was within reach, and so it was only reasonable that he should also warn of an imminent and unfair race to the seafloor.[60] Pardo noted the lack of a worldwide overarching 'institutional framework'[61] that could grapple with ocean issues and prevent this from happening. He argued that many United Nations agencies were involved with the oceans in one way or another,[62] and that this made dealing with the ocean on an international basis a difficult and compromised affair. Another of Pardo's worries was that the seafloor could be used for warfare. He warned that sovereign states might start installing weaponry stations on the seafloor as soon as the technology to do so was in place.[63] To prevent this, he suggested making the seafloor outside national jurisdiction into a zone in which warfare was off-limits. He also warned of the hazards of dumping atomic waste, and in general of what he called 'the wider problem of marine pollution'.[64] In engaging with the question of pollution, Pardo was picking up a thread that had been touched on briefly by only one of the four conventions that had been negotiated during UNCLOS I and II – the Convention on the High Seas. Articles 24 and 25 are concerned with the pollution of the high seas through dumping of atomic waste or – and this is interesting – pollution through exploration for exploitation of the seabed.[65]

---

56 *Cf.* A/C.1/PV.1515, 42.
57 A/C.1/PV.1515, 34.
58 A/C.1/PV.1515, 34.
59 A/C.1/PV.1515, 34.
60 A/C.1/PV.1515, 91.
61 A/C.1/PV.1515, 103.
62 Some of Pardo's examples: A/C.1/PV.1515, 94: International Labour Organisation (ILO), FAO, IMCO and UNCTAD.
63 A/C.1/PV.1515, 45.
64 A/C.1/PV.1515, 87.
65 *See* 1958 Convention on the High Seas. *See also* Tuerk, 'The Thirtieth Anniversary', 22: 'It should be recalled that already the 1958 Geneva Convention on the High Seas prohibits any occupation of the high seas, including the respective seabed'.

By this point, Arvid Pardo had spoken for such a long time that he had to break off and resume his talk in the afternoon session.[66] Back at the speaker's desk, he made some final remarks in summary. He called for an 'effective international régime',[67] which would be accepted by 'rich and poor countries, strong and weak, coastal and landlocked states'.[68] Thus far, Pardo had mainly talked about the various possibilities that existing and future technologies brought to the deep seas. He had cautioned of the hazards that were intrinsic to humanity's ventures into this area, and now he had a suggestion to manage both the possibilities and the dangers. To this end, Arvid Pardo suggested applying the concept of common heritage of mankind to the ocean floor outside national jurisdiction, stating that 'the seabed and the ocean floor are a common heritage of mankind and should be used and exploited for peaceful purposes and for the exclusive benefit of mankind as a whole'.[69]

Otherwise, Pardo warned, technologically superior nation states would soon quarrel as they attempted to dominate the resources of the world's oceans, and this would:

> lead to a competitive scramble for sovereign rights over the land underlying the world's seas and oceans, surpassing in magnitude and in its implication last century's colonial scramble for territory in Asia and Africa.[70]

To achieve a sense of order in the oceans that would avoid such a chaotic race, he asked the international community to establish a kind of 'trustee'[71] of the ocean floor. An agency that would have everyone's approval. Pardo was very clear that this could not be achieved by giving all countries the same voting power,[72] and to some extent this was quite prophetic, since the question of how to reach agreement during UNCLOS III would be the first of many stumbling blocks. In order to establish such a 'trustee' or 'agency' for a new Law of the Sea, Pardo suggested putting together a collection of representatives who would start working on the question of ocean governance.[73]

---

66 A/C.1/PV.1516.

67 A/C.1/PV.1516, 3.

68 A/C.1/PV.1516, 4.

69 A/C.1/PV.1516, 13.

70 A/C.1/PV.1516, 91.

71 A/C.1/PV.1516, 8.

72 *Cf.* A/C.1/PV.1516, 8. This would later ring through also in his suggestion for an ocean space treaty.

73 *Cf.* A/C.1/PV.1516, 15.

Pardo's speech shows clearly what was the driving force behind the urge to renegotiate ocean governance after UNCLOS I and UNCLOS II had failed to close the deal. Together with the exact definition of maritime boundaries, two other issues had surfaced: the exploitation of natural resources and the potential to place weaponry stations on the seafloor outside national jurisdiction. Pardo had tried to address both these issues. He suggested an overarching agency for the ocean floor that could govern the resources in a way that would ensure access and benefit to all mankind. And he wanted to reserve this same space for peaceful purposes only, thereby preventing anyone from installing weaponry on the seafloor.

The need to renegotiate ocean governance had been foreshadowed both by the Truman proclamation and its ensuing chain reaction of ocean territory claims, and also by the first two UNCLOS conferences, in which the possibilities and shape of maritime boundaries had been discussed for the first time. Arvid Pardo compounded these developments with another one – the exploration of marine mineral resources – and united them all under a new concept: the common heritage of mankind. Arvid Pardo's speech has been celebrated as a starting point – as the initial idea that would spark decades of diplomatic uproar at the United Nations and revolutionise the Law of the Sea. The story usually goes on to celebrate Arvid Pardo as the 'father of the Law of the Sea'.[74] But who was the Maltese ambassador? Where did he come from? How did he end up behind the speaker's desk? And why did his speech have such dramatic consequences?

3 Arvid Pardo – From Political Prisoner to Diplomat

Arvid Pardo did not appear out of nowhere to take the podium at the United Nations – and nor did his suggestions for ocean governance. Both the man and his ideas had a back story. Pardo was born in Rome on 12 February 1914, the child of an international marriage. His father, Guido Pardo, was born in Valetta in 1874, while his mother, Dagmar Julin, was a Swede born in Gothenburg in 1878. Pardo was half Swedish and half Maltese, but was born in Italy and attended kindergarten in London and Geneva. He became an orphan in 1922 at just eight years old. His father died from typhus caught on a mission for the International Labour Organization in Russia and his mother followed shortly afterwards from complications caused by surgery for appendicitis. His brother

74 *Cf.* MS-2-744, Box 345, Folder 4, Arvid Pardo, Retrospect and Prospects, 1999.

had died the year before in a motorcycle accident.[75] Bernardo Attolicio – who was an Italian ambassador to Brazil, the Soviet Union and Germany – became Arvid Pardo's guardian until he was twenty-one years old.[76]

Pardo's bad luck would continue until the end of World War II. Although he managed to gain a doctoral degree in international law at the University of Rome in 1933 and a degree in diplomatic history at the University of Tours in 1938–9,[77] he was arrested in Rome in 1940 for underground activities.[78] The exact nature of his offences remains uncertain, other than that he was 'organizing groups to aid the Allies'.[79] He was sentenced to eighteen years in prison by an Italian court, and was detained in Regina Coeli prison in Rome.[80] From a letter Pardo wrote to the Ministry of Foreign Affairs in Malta in 1968, many years later, we learn that his sentence was annulled after World War II.[81]

In the same letter, he reported further that he had been deported to Germany in 1943, together with Ruggero Zangrandi, an Italian journalist and author. Pardo claimed that Zangrandi mentioned him under a pseudonym in his book, *A Train to the Brenner*,[82] an account of their deportation and hazardous journey through German prison camps and back to Rome. If we believe Pardo that he is portrayed in the book, we can only guess at which character he is. Most likely, he is one of the two Italian 'intellectuals',[83] Aldo and Paolo, who are deported together in a bus and taken to the Alexanderplatz prison in Berlin. Since Paolo is the main character in the book – and must therefore

75 PR-Box: Tributes, Feature, 47, 1990. *See also* Raymond Daniell, 'Malta Assigns a Rare Diplomat to U.N.', *New York Times*, 24 January 1965, reprinted in *Commemoration of the 30th Anniversary of the United Nations Convention on the Law of the Sea and the Common Heritage of Mankind* (Malta: Ministry of Foreign Affairs; IMO International Maritime Law Institute), 30.

76 PR-Box: Tributes, Feature, 47, 1990. *See also* PR-Box: Personal Correspondences & Materials, letter from Arvid Pardo to Secretary Ministry of Commonwealth, 18. October 1968, appendix 'D'. Pardo's CV can be found in MS-2-744, Box 108, Folder 1.

77 MS-2-744, Box 108, Folder 1, Curriculum Vitae of Dr. Arvid Pardo. 'Educated at Collegio Modragone, Frascati, Italy (1926–33)'. Also more about his positions at the United Nations before he became Ambassador.

78 *Cf.* PR-Box: Tributes, Feature, 47, 1990. *See also* PR-Box: Personal Correspondences & Materials, letter from Arvid Pardo to Secretary Ministry of Commonwealth, 18. October 1968.

79 MS-2-744, Box 186, Folder 4, Ambassador Arvid Pardo.

80 MS-2-744, Box 186, Folder 4, Ambassador Arvid Pardo.

81 PR-Box: Personal Correspondences & Materials, letter from Arvid Pardo to Secretary Ministry of Commonwealth, 18. October 1968.

82 Ruggero Zangrandi, *A Train to the Brenner* (London: GALLERY PRESS LTD, 1963).

83 Zangrandi, *Train to the Brenner*, 15.

be Zangrandi himself – it is likely that the other Italian on the bus, 'a lawyer named Aldo',[84] represents Arvid Pardo.

Although identifying Pardo's fictional counterpart is mainly guesswork, Zangrandi's book can give us a real idea of what Pardo and his companions experienced in Germany. For instance, Zangrandi describes the condition of the prison, which was:

> characterized by the brilliance of metal, the smell of disinfectant and a frightening lay-out. All day long squads of Kalfakter washed the floors and walls, polished the gates, railings, pipes, taps and bolts. In spite of such scrupulous cleansing the prison was nearly always in quarantine, because of the epidemics of petechial typhus which broke out at frequent intervals.[85]

Zangrandi reports the death of cell-mates, hunger and envy among the prisoners, and the shell-shocking experience of the bombing of Berlin as witnessed by the inmates. He paints a picture of an existence endured under life-threatening conditions, of endless harassment by the guards – especially towards Italians – and of the hard labour the prisoners had to carry out in order to be fed.

This corresponds with many of the other reports about conditions in German prisons, and we can assume that Zangrandi's experiences were the same as those of his fellow inmates – including Arvid Pardo. When he was sentenced and imprisoned in Italy, Pardo was just twenty-six years old. He would spend five years of his life in prison before he was freed by the Red Cross in 1945 and was able to make for the border in southern Germany – on foot, according to some sources.[86] During that time, he was moved from the prison in Rome to the forced labour camp at Grossbeeren, then to Alexanderplatz prison, and was briefly arrested by the Russians before he could make his journey home.[87]

Arvid Pardo's ingrained interest in peacekeeping and justice could be partly explained through his personal history, especially the war years spent in prison. Soon after returning to Rome, he took up a modest administrative position at the United Nations as the chief of the archives[88] (1946–7)[89] and started to

---

84 Zangrandi, *Train to the Brenner,* 128.

85 Zangrandi, *Train to the Brenner,* 42.

86 *Cf.* MS-2-744, Box 186, Folder 4, Ambassador Arvid Pardo.

87 MS-2-744, Box 186, Folder 4, Ambassador Arvid Pardo.

88 *See* Letter of appointment to chief librarian: PR-Box: Personal Correspondences & Materials, letter of appointment, 15. August 1946.

89 *Cf.* MS-2-744, Box 186, Folder 4, Ambassador Arvid Pardo.

climb the ranks. He served as social affairs officer (1947–60), represented the UN Development Program in Nigeria and Ecuador (1961–3 and 1963–4) and became Malta's permanent representative to the UN in 1964,[90] while also being the Maltese ambassador to the United States and the Soviet Union (1966 and 1968–71).[91] It was in his capacity as Malta's ambassador to the United Nations that Pardo gave his speech about the world's oceans. It would earn him the title of 'father of the Law of the Sea'.

4 The Maltese Initiative – Did Pardo Really Do It Single-Handedly?

Naturally, Arvid Pardo's November 1967 speech at the United Nations did not occur out of the blue and without prior discussion. Back in August, the Maltese had already asked to put the seabed on the agenda, and had thereby announced the Maltese initiative.[92] It was no secret – either to the United Nations officials or to Mann Borgese and her colleagues at the Center for the Study of Democratic Institutions – that something was about to happen in the United Nations concerning the Law of the Sea and the seafloor. Some UN member states were already critical towards Malta's initiative even before Arvid Pardo took the podium, to the extent that the Maltese government felt that their ambassador had to begin his speech by responding to scepticism from the United States. Pardo started out by making it clear that 'I can categorically state that we are not a sounding-board for any State, and nobody, "put the Maltese Government up to it" '.[93]

Apparently there were suspicions that the Maltese were acting as a puppet for Great Britain's maritime interests. This suspicion was not too far-fetched, since Malta had gained independence in 1964, only two years earlier. In that same year, when Arvid Pardo was first made Maltese representative to the United Nations, he had said in an interview for the *New York Times* that his government 'still had ties to Britain'.[94] However, in 1967 the Maltese were adamant that Arvid Pardo's speech was entirely their own initiative, and that it was

90 *See* letter from Prime Minister G. George Olivier 23: PR-Box: Personal Correspondences & Materials, letter from G. George Olivier to Arvid Pardo, 23. November 1964.

91 MS-2-744, Box 186, Folder 4, Ambassador Arvid Pardo. *See also* MS-2-744, Box 108, Folder 1, Curriculum Vitae of Dr. Arvid Pardo.

92 For the seabed proposal on 6 October 1967 *see* A/PV.1582, 123.

93 A/C.1/PV.1515, 5.

94 Daniell, 'Malta Assigns Rare Diplomat', 30.

simply an attempt to put the tiny archipelagic state on the map.[95] Considering that Malta was the smallest member of the United Nations by area, making the proposal was certainly a bold step.[96]

Arvid Pardo's appearance in the General Assembly is often referred to as a pivotal moment in the history of the Law of the Sea. Sometimes the appreciation of its significance goes so far as to suggest that Pardo did this 'single-handedly'.[97] However, more recent studies have started to question the notion that Malta and Arvid Pardo were the first to introduce the common heritage concept to the international community. Surabhi Ranganathan attempts to put Pardo's speech into context, stating that it is 'often (if wrongly) recalled as the world's first introduction to the concept of CHM, entailing the international administration of the deep seabed'.[98]

There were a number of ongoing discussions about the Law of the Sea – both at the United Nations and in other arenas – and several versions of the common heritage approach had already been presented.[99] One such example, of course, was the Chicago committee's proposal to declare 'the four elements of life' as common property.[100] It is questionable whether a wider audience had encountered the Chicago circle's 1948 draft of a world constitution, but Arvid Pardo had almost certainly not heard about it. Instead, he mentioned a July 1966 speech by Lyndon B Johnson, the United States president, at the commissioning of the research vessel *Oceanographer*. Johnson had said that:

> under no circumstances, we believe, must we ever allow the prospects of rich harvests and mineral wealth to create a new form of colonial competition among the maritime nations. We must be careful to avoid a race

---

95 *Cf.* Surabhi Ranganathan, 'Global Commons', *European Journal of International Law* 27, no. 3 (August 2016): 709, https://doi.org/10.1093/ejil/chw037.

96 *Cf.* Daniell, 'Malta Assigns Rare Diplomat', 30.

97 Salvino Busuttil, 'Ocean affairs', *Times of Malta*, November 6, 2007, https://www.timesofmalta.com/articles/view/20071106/opinion/ocean-affairs.181476.
Salvino Busuttil reports that the Swedish king had said this to him.

98 Ranganathan, 'Global Commons', 704.

99 *See* for a historical overview: Ingo Klaus Heidbrink, 'The Oceans as the Common Property of Mankind from Early Modern Period to Today', *History Compass* 6, no. 2 (February 2008): 659–672, https://doi.org/10.1111/j.1478-0542.2007.00504.x. *See also* from a legal perspective: Prue Taylor, 'The Common Heritage of Mankind: A Bold Doctrine Kept Within Strict Boundaries', in *The Wealth of the Commons. A World Beyond Market & State,* David Bollier and Silke Helfrich, eds., (Amherst: Levellers Press, 2013), http://wealthofthecommons.org/essay/common-heritage-mankind-bold-doctrine-kept-within-strict-boundaries.

100 *Cf.* Hutchins et al., *Preliminary Draft,* 6.

> to grab and to hold the lands under the high seas. We must ensure that the deep seas and the ocean bottoms are, and remain, the legacy of all human beings.[101]

Clearly, different terms were in circulation to describe ownership or entitlement relating to the resources in the uncharted territory of the ocean floor. Johnson chose to label this right 'the legacy of all human beings', while Pardo opted to talk about 'the common heritage of mankind'. He had considered using the term 'common property' as the Chicago committee had done, but he rejected the thought quickly, since 'property' might imply a particular sense of entitlement that could lead to a race to grab the resources on the seafloor.[102]

Setting aside for a moment the details of terms and phrases and the question of who was first to come up with the common heritage concept, the United States' suspicions concerning Malta's initiative were still legitimate. Why would the Maltese ambassador, of all people, be interested in talking about resources on the ocean floor? There are several possible ways to explain this. One is from Arvid Pardo's own perspective, of which we have some knowledge from letters and explanatory articles in the aftermath of the convention. But it could also be explained through the various political and diplomatic climates in Malta, the US Senate and the United Nations, where different proposals were brought forward and discussed openly throughout 1967.

5 Arvid Pardo's Interest in Ocean Governance

We will start with Pardo's own story of how he became interested in the seabed and its resources. Perhaps the most straightforward explanation available is in a letter Arvid Pardo wrote to a Maltese Ministry of Foreign Affairs member called Salvino Busuttil.[103] Unfortunately, the letter is undated, but Pardo refers

101 Lyndon B. Johnson, 'Remarks at the Commissioning of the Research Ship – Oceanographer', (speech, Washington, DC, July 13, 1966), The American Presidency Project, http://www.presidency.ucsb.edu/ws/index.php?pid=27711.

102 *Cf.* Jean Buttigieg, 'Arvid Pardo: a diplomat with a mission', *Symposia Melitensia*, no 12(2016): 17, https://www.um.edu.mt/library/oar//handle/123456789/14918.

103 The letter is available at: PR-Box: Personal Correspondences & Materials, undated letter from Dr. Arvid Pardo to Salvino Busuttil (handwritten note on the right corner). CC: Joe Friggieri, Fr Peter Serracino Inglott, Freddie Amato Gauci, ~~Victor Gauci~~, Charlie Vella, Elizabeth Mann Borgese, ~~Victor Ragonesi~~.

to the book *Interfaces: Essays in Honour of Peter Serracino Inglott,*[104] which was published in 1997 with an introduction by Busuttil. We can thus assume that the letter must have been written sometime between 1997 and 1999, the year of Pardo's death. The date is of some interest, since it informs us that this is the letter of an old man reminiscing about his career. This becomes even clearer when we learn the reason for the letter: Although framed in friendly words and respectful phrases, Pardo is criticising the introduction of the book for crediting Fr Peter Serracino Inglott – a Maltese priest, philosopher and former rector of the University of Malta[105] – with responsibility for Malta's proposal at the General Assembly in 1967. Arvid Pardo refers to the following passage:

> On the international scene, Father Peter was behind most of Malta's initiatives for peace and the rational use of the world's resources. With Arvid Pardo, he was responsible for Malta's proposal, presented to the UN General Assembly and accepted in 1967, of putting the resources of the seabed beyond the jurisdiction of nation states and under global management and control.[106]

According to Pardo, this version of the story needed rectifying. He argued that, although Inglott had been active in the Law of the Sea question in later years, he had not been part of the preparations prior to the General Assembly speech in 1967. Pardo was probably justified in his criticism, since Inglott does not appear to have been on the scene until later.[107] A biography about Inglott suggests otherwise, but seems to be based on Inglott's own memories.[108] The letter

104 Joe Friggieri and Salvino Busuttil, eds., *Interfaces: essays in philosophy and bordering areas in honour of Peter Serracino Inglott* (Malta: University of Malta, 1997).

105 *Interfaces: essays in philosophy and bordering areas in honour of Peter Serracino Inglott* has a short biography of Inglott. *See* Joe Friggieri and Salvino Busuttil, 'Preface', in *Interfaces: essays in philosophy and bordering areas in honour of Peter Serracino Inglott*, eds., Joe Friggieri and Salvino Busuttil (Malta: University of Malta, 1997): xii.

106 Friggieri and Busuttil, 'Preface', xii.

107 There might be earlier dated letters between Inglott and the IOI in the Dalhousie Archives.

108 *See* Buttigieg, 'Arvid Pardo', 15: 'According to Daniel Massa, in his book PSI KINGMAKER, Dr George Borg Olivier, prime minister of Malta, had asked Fr Peter Serracino Inglott who was teaching philosophy at the University of Malta, what kind of peace initiative Malta could take in the United Nations, to promote peace. Fr. Peter found it very difficult to come up with any concrete proposal but things changed when Pardo, charged with a prophetic vision to make the undersea resources a common heritage of mankind, began sending to Malta, draft proposals, memos and other dossiers for Borg Olivier to see'. Buttigieg refers to the biography: Daniel Massa, *PSI Kingmaker: Life, Thought and Adventures of Peter Serracino Inglott* (Valetta: Allied Newspapers Ltd, 2013), 292. The same story is also retold in, Salvino Busuttil, 'Foreword', in Prue Taylor and Lucy Stroud, eds.,

gives us a fairly direct explanation of how Arvid Pardo, according to his own recollections, became involved with the question of ocean floor governance. He writes about what provoked his interest:

> A proposal by Ambassador Roosevelt (USA) in November 1966 requesting a UN secretariat study on the mineral resources of the seabed.
>
> 2. A dream which I had in January 1967. After this dream I studied the question very hard for several months. I consulted Victor Gauci on the best way to draft a memorandum to the Ministry of Commonwealth and Foreign Affairs requesting permission to present the question to the United Nations. I also asked Victor to test the interest of some poor countries (but not the major powers) in the sea.[109]

There is a hint of esotericism and a tendency towards mystical explanations when the origins of 'great ideas' are revisited. We cannot know whether Pardo really dreamed about the seafloor, but parts of his speech at the United Nations have a dreamy, mystical quality, quite at odds with the character of a hard-headed, stoic diplomat. Maybe this was part of Pardo's personality. At any rate, this is how he remembered the story towards the end of his life.[110]

From the perspective of content, his first point about the USA's seabed study proposal from 1966 is rather more interesting.[111] So far, only references

---

Common Heritage of Mankind. A Bibliography of Legal Writing (Valetta: Foundation de Malta, 2012), xii. A different reading of the events can be found in Rijk Van Doorn, *Legal implications of the 'common heritage' principle for Atlantic bluefin tuna* (Berlin: Duncker & Humblot, forthcoming), 91. Van Doorn supports the version in which Inglott was the first one to mention the principle.

109 PR-Box: Personal Correspondences & Materials, undated letter from Dr. Arvid Pardo to Salvino Busuttil (handwritten note on the right corner). CC: Joe Friggieri, Fr Peter Serracino Inglott, Freddie Amato Gauci, ~~Victor Gauci~~, Charlie Vella, Elizabeth Mann Borgese, ~~Victor Ragonesi~~.

110 Others refer to the dream too – *see* Christopher Grima, 'Special Tribute to the late Ambassador Arvid Pardo of Malta on the occasion of the Thirtieth Anniversary of the United Nations Convention on the Law of the Sea', in *Commemoration of the 30th Anniversary of the United Nations Convention on the Law of the Sea and the Common Heritage of Mankind*, 5–7 (Malta: Ministry of Foreign Affairs; IMO International Maritime Law Institute).

111 *See* the report: ST/ESA/107/Add.1 This UN report from 1982 on the status of seabed minerals hints at the older report that was most likely the outcome of the US request in 1966 for a seabed survey "Sea-Bed Mineral Resource Development: Recent Activities of the International Consortia" (United Nations publications, A/CN.9/SER.A/1978). *See also*: GA Resolution 2172 (XXI), *Resources of the sea* (1485th plenary meeting, 6 December 1966): '[…] the effective exploitation and development of these resources can raise the

to the study have been found,[112] pointing to a discussion item at the United Nations.[113] We can assume that after Truman's 1945 proclamation on the resources of the sea, seabed resources were discussed in different circles both in the United States and at the United Nations. In fact, Ranganathan addresses this issue when she writes that Pardo's initiative was 'only one among numbers of initiatives of the time, many connected to the UN in some way, and some with more comprehensive subject matter, taking in the seabed and the high seas'.[114] Furthermore, she points out that 'As early as 1963, a corporate executive suggested the UN assume title to the international seabed and allocate exploitation rights generating revenue for itself'.[115]

It is likely, therefore, that countries like the US would have requested studies on seabed resources, and that they also conducted studies themselves. Since UNCLOS II had left several questions on how to govern the oceans outside national jurisdiction unanswered, there is little doubt that politicians all over the world sought to explore these issues. Clearly, so did Malta. Apart from Pardo's personal reminiscences about how he became interested in the seafloor and the questions of seabed governance, there is a bigger picture surrounding the Maltese initiative. We must consider the political and historical context of the newly independent archipelagic state, and how the Maltese initiative got to the United Nations.

6 Malta Prepares the Seabed Proposal

If we are to believe Arvid Pardo, he contacted Victor Gauci[116] – a diplomat who worked for the government of Malta – to help him discuss ideas on seabed governance with the Ministry of Commonwealth and Foreign Affairs.

economic level of peoples throughout the world, and in particular of the developing countries, [...]'.

112 *See* Ranganathan, 'Global Commons', 707: in footnote 80 Ranganathan refers to the survey citing S. Nandan et al., *The Development of the Regime for Deep Sea Mining* (2002). Buttigieg also refers to the survey in Buttigieg, 'Arvid Pardo', 17. He mentions the year 1965.

113 *See* Arvid Pardo, 'The Origins of the 1967 Malta Initiative', *International Insights* 9, no.2 (1993): 65, 66.

114 Ranganathan, 'Global Commons', 707.

115 Ranganathan, 'Global Commons', 707.

116 Gauci was permanent representative to the United Nations from 1978 onwards. *See* Michael Testa, 'An insider's look at foreign policy', *Times of Malta,* November 13, 2004, https://www.timesofmalta.com/articles/view/20041113/local/an-insiders-look-at-foreign-policy.107258.

Unfortunately, the exact content of the earlier drafts of his speech is uncertain, since they cannot be found in his material. It is likely that the common heritage of mankind principle was central. He reported in his later letter to Busuttil that he had 'asked Victor to test the interest of some poor countries (but not the major powers) in the sea'.[117] How Victor Gauci tested this interest is unknown, but since he worked as a diplomat, we can only guess that he may have had contacts at the United Nations.[118] Ranganathan goes so far as to suggest that Arvid Pardo was 'headhunted'[119] for the job to 'establish a voice in international affairs'.[120]

Pardo himself wrote in a 1993 article entitled 'The Origins of the 1967 Maltese Initiative' that he had not been aware of subsea resources before he became familiar with the US proposal, after which he started studying the subject.[121] Leaving aside the exact circumstances in which he came across the idea, the proposal – which arose out of the initiatives of Pardo and others – reached the United Nations on 17 August 1967 in the form of a 'note verbale' from the permanent mission of Malta to the United Nations, asking for:

> the inclusion of the following item in the agenda of the twenty-second session of the General Assembly: Declaration and treaty concerning the reservation to exclusively for peaceful purposes of the sea-bed and the ocean floor, underlying the seas beyond the limits of present national jurisdiction, and the use of their resources in the interest of mankind.[122]

The proposal was followed by a memorandum in which the unregulated use of the seabed resources was problematised and an international agency was proposed as one possible solution to oversee seabed activity.[123]

From a subsequent report of the First Committee under the General Assembly (which was responsible for disarmament and international

117 PR-Box: Personal Correspondences & Materials, undated letter from Dr. Arvid Pardo to Salvino Busuttil (handwritten note on the right corner). CC: Joe Friggieri, Fr Peter Serracino Inglott, Freddie Amato Gauci, ~~Victor Gauci~~, Charlie Vella, Elizabeth Mann Borgese, ~~Victor Ragonesi~~.

118 Gauci has written about this. *See* Victor J. Gauci, *Genesis of Malta's Foreign Policy: A Personal Account* (Luqa: Agenda, 2005).

119 Ranganathan, 'Global Commons', 708.

120 Ranganathan, 'Global Commons', 708.

121 *Cf.* Ranganathan, 'Global Commons', 708, about the proposal in Pardo, 'The Origins', 65.

122 A/6695.

123 *See* memorandum in A/6695.

security),[124] we learn that the General Committee recommended the inclusion of Malta's proposal on 21 September 1967[125] and approved the inclusion on 23 September.[126] This meant that the General Committee had seen the need to address the question of how to govern the seabed and ocean floor, and that they were willing to put the issue up for discussion. This did not pass unnoticed. Even before the item had been assigned its final title, the United States reacted by discussing Malta's initiative in Congress under the headline 'The Maltese Welfare Proposal'.[127] One delegate, Mr Hall, voiced his concern, worried that 'ocean floor resources are to be turned over to the United Nations or some nebulous international organization for administration. The revenues from exploration and exploitation are to be turned over to the developing nations of the world'.[128] He further expressed his surprise over the fact that:

> The tiny country of Malta on August 17, 1967[...], made such a proposal to the United Nations, rushing its proposal as an agenda item for the 22nd session even before studies to formulate proposals for expanded international cooperation were completed. [...] The Maltese proposal looks forward to a treaty which would reserve the ocean for peaceful purpose, establish an international agency to assume jurisdiction over the deep ocean floor [...].[129]

While the Senate was discussing Malta's intentions in 'rushing its proposal',[130] Olivier Borg, the prime minister of Malta, got permission to put forward a proposal at the United Nations. On 6 October 1967, he spoke at a plenary meeting about the seabed proposal put forward by his government. In his speech, he stated that:

> a determined search must be made for new major sources of development capital that do not imply increased burdens on the rich countries.

124 *See* United Nations, *Disarmament and International Security* (*first Committee*), accessed 30 September 2021, http://www.un.org/en/ga/first/.

125 A/6840.

126 A/6964.

127 113 CONG. REC. H12681 (daily ed. Sept. 28, 1967) (statement of Rep. Hall).

128 113 CONG. REC. H12681 (daily ed. Sept. 28, 1967) (statement of Rep. Hall).

129 113 CONG. REC. H12681 (daily ed. Sept. 28, 1967) (statement of Rep. Hall).

130 More on US position *see* Shigeru Oda, *Fifty Years of the Law of the Sea: With a Special Section on the International Courts of Justice* (Leiden/Boston: Martinus Nijhoff, 2003), 148 ff.

> It is felt that one such source could (be [sic]) the exploitation of the resources of an internationalized sea-bed and ocean floor.[131]

In reply to his proposal, the plenary put the seabed question on the agenda and promised to put it forward to the General Assembly.[132] And as we already know, the next step in the seabed proposal quarrel was Arvid Pardo's speech at the First Committee Meeting of the UN General Assembly on 1 November 1967.

7 The Seabed Committee Is Born

As an immediate reaction to the speech and the ongoing discussions about seafloor resources, the General Assembly decided to set up the Ad Hoc Seabed Committee.[133] This was what Arvid Pardo had asked for – a collective of representatives to review and organise an overarching global agency responsible for ocean governance.[134] The Seabed Committee would look into:

> Examination of the question of the reservation exclusively for peaceful purposes of the seabed and the ocean floor, and the subsoil thereof, underlying the high seas beyond the limits of present national jurisdiction, and the use of their resources in the interest of mankind.[135]

The establishment and preparation of the committee was somewhat complicated. It started with twenty-seven states, who prepared a draft resolution on how the ad hoc committee might look and what tasks it might have. The resolution was then presented by Belgium.[136] The ad hoc committee ended up having thirty-five member states, with Malta being one of them.[137] The

131 A/PV.1582, 123. The proposal was put forward on Friday 6 October.

132 *Cf.* A/PV.1582, 125.

133 *See* A/RES/22/2340.

134 *Cf.* Arvid Pardo's speech: A/C.1/PV.1516, 15.

135 A/RES/22/2340.

136 *Cf.* A/6964, 6. Refers to A/C.1/L.410. For more information and a document collection on the establishment and preparation of the Ad Hoc Seabed Committee *see* Shigeru Oda, ed., *The Law of the Sea in our Time – II The United Nations Seabed Committee 1968- 1973* (Leiden: Nijhoff, 1977), 3–10.

137 The other members were: Kenya, Liberia, Libya, Senegal, Somalia, Tanzania, United Arab Republic, Ceylon, India, Japan, Pakistan, Thailand, Bulgaria, Czechoslovakia, Poland, Romania, USSR, Yugoslavia, Argentina, Brazil, Chile, Ecuador, El Salvador, Peru; Australia, Austria, Belgium, France, Island, Italy, Malta, Norway, UK, USA. *Cf.* Oda, *Law of the Sea,* 13.

committee's task was to collect together all existing knowledge about the governance of the ocean floor and the evolving technological possibilities that could arise in this area, and to prepare for an international convocation.

This process was similar to previous attempts to prepare for a new Law of the Sea. The League of Nations had set up a comparable 'Committee of Experts' back in 1924, with the brief of gathering information about the Law of the Sea.[138] After World War II, this task had been taken over by the International Law Commission (ILC), which was instructed by the General Assembly to work up a list of issues to be addressed at the first Law of the Sea Convention in 1958.[139] Now, after two semi-successful conferences (UNCLOS I and UNCLOS II), the Ad Hoc Seabed Committee was set up to handle similar tasks to those undertaken before them by the Committee of Experts and the ILC. The job of the ad hoc committee was to collect information in preparation for a third United Nations Convention on the Law of the Sea.

In 1969, the committee went from being an ad hoc committee to being officially called the Seabed Committee. It now had forty-two member states, with some changes in membership.[140] In the book *The Law of the Sea in our Time – II The United Nations Seabed Committee 1968–1973*, Shigeru Oda, who was the committee's Japanese representative, provides a detailed run-through of all committee meetings from 1968–73. Although the book is written from the Japanese perspective, it gives us an in-depth report of the Seabed Committee's business, from the minutiae of rescheduled meetings to the matters that were discussed and the proposals put forward by various representatives.

In 1969, after a great deal of discussion, the Seabed Committee arrived at a resolution that would finally lead to UNCLOS III. Shigeru Oda wrote of the agreement that:

> The gist of the resolution was that the Secretary General should ascertain the views of Member States on the desirability of convening at an early date a conference of the law of the sea to review particularly the régimes of the high seas, the continental shelf, the territorial sea and contiguous zone, fishing and conservation of the living resources of the high seas, in order to clarify the definition of the area of the seabed and ocean floor beyond the limits of national jurisdiction, in the light of an international régime for that.[141]

---

138 *Cf.* Harrison, *Making the Law,* 29.

139 *Cf.* Harrison, *Making the Law,* 29. *See also* Hollick, *U.S. Foreign Policy,* 128.

140 *See* Oda, ed., *Law of the Sea,* 51. Refers to U.N. Doc. A/RES/2467 (XXIII), 21 December 1968.

141 Oda, ed., *Law of the Sea,* 86.

It was also decided that the committee would handle the preparations for the impending convention. This task made the Seabed Committee an interesting prospect for people who wanted to shape or influence future discussions on the Law of the Sea.

CHAPTER 4

Pacem in Maribus – A Think Tank for Ocean Questions

1 Can Santa Barbara Become a Think Tank for Ocean Questions?

Elisabeth Mann Borgese realised that Arvid Pardo was becoming an important advocate of the common heritage principle, and that he could play a key role in shaping the Law of the Sea. She contacted him 'immediately'[1] after his speech, and invited him to the Center for the Study of Democratic Institutions in Santa Barbara. Pardo made visits to the centre between 1968 and 1970,[2] during which they worked on three planning meetings that convened in February, May and June of 1968.[3] These meetings would lead to the first of several *Pacem in Maribus* (PIM) conferences, held in 1970.[4]

The name of the conference, *Pacem in Maribus* – which means 'peace in the oceans' – must surely have been an adaption of the *Pacem in Terris* convocations of 1965 and 1967. These two earlier conferences meant that the Center for the Study of Democratic Institutions in Santa Barbara already had considerable experience convening far-reaching international conferences on peace and world order by the time Pardo and Mann Borgese organised their first ocean conference in 1970. The *Pacem in Terris* convocations gave them the perfect model to develop further with the backing and help of the centre.[5]

For Arvid Pardo and Elisabeth Mann Borgese, their new collaboration was the first step towards attempting to influence the development of the Law of the Sea.[6] In organising the PIM conferences, they were creating an arena in which they could discuss proposals and designs for the upcoming Law of the Sea Convention. There was the potential for delegates of the Ad Hoc Seabed

1 MS-2-744, Box 345, Folder 4, Arvid Pardo, Retrospect and Prospects, 1999.
2 MS-2-744, Box 345, Folder 4, Arvid Pardo, Retrospect and Prospects, 1999.
3 *Cf.* Baker, 'Uncommon Heritage', 17. Baker refers to *The Ocean Regime.*
4 *Cf.* MS-2-744, Box 345, Folder 4, Arvid Pardo, Retrospect and Prospects, 1999. For all past PIM Conferences, see IOI overview: The International Ocean Institute, *Pacem in Maribus (PIM) Conferences – Past Conferences: (1970–2013)*, accessed 30 September 2021, https://www.ioinst.org/about-1/pacem-in-maribus-pim-conferences/.
5 Milton Mayer about Pacem in Terris: Mayer, *Robert Maynard Hutchins,* 484.
6 Later in this chapter we see that the group said specifically to the magazine *Saturday Review* that their aim was to influence the law-making process.

© TIRZA MEYER, 2022 | DOI:10.1163/9789004511446_006

Committee to gather their thoughts and air their interests with a broader audience present than was the case in their own meetings.[7] In order for this to work, the conference had to attract the right delegates, and Mann Borgese and Pardo succeeded in achieving this. Since Pardo himself was on the Seabed Committee on behalf of the Maltese government, he had direct access to colleagues on the committee, some of whom might become key actors in the forthcoming negotiations. If we take a look at the board of the ad hoc committee (which would later become the Seabed Committee), we can see the same names gracing the guest lists of the *Pacem in Maribus* convocations.[8] For instance, the chairman, Hamilton Shirley Amerasinghe from Ceylon, the vice-chairman, Alexander Yankov from Bulgaria, and of course a Maltese delegate, Victor J Gauci, who functioned as rapporteur.[9] Naturally, some of the names would change over the years. For instance, in 1969 another Maltese diplomat, Charles Vella, took over from Gauci as rapporteur of the Seabed Committee.[10] The role of chair, however, would be held by Amerasinghe right up until he was elected president of UNCLOS III in 1973.[11]

Pacem in Maribus I was held on Malta in 1970, under the headline 'Quiet Enjoyment: Arms Control and Police Forces for the Oceans'.[12] Amerasinghe agreed to chair PIM I, and Mann Borgese argued that this fact underlined PIM's closeness with the Seabed Committee.[13] In an interview given many years later in 1991, Elisabeth Mann Borgese said that the first conference was 'a great success'.[14]

---

7 Baker, 'Uncommon Heritage', 18. Baker about PIM I: 'The February planning meeting attracted enough members of the UN Sea-Bed Committee, and evidently offered enough worthwhile substance, that relatively high-level participation at subsequent meetings was assured. This meant in turn that at least some of the ideas discussed had a chance of finding their way into the deliberations of the committee itself – a rough measure for determining influence and flow of ideas, but worth noting'.

8 *See* MS-2-744, Folder 218, Box 33, Summary of Discussions, Planning Session on the Law of the Seas, February 24–26, 1968.

9 *See* Oda, ed., *Law of the Sea*, 14.

10 *See* Oda, ed., *Law of the Sea*, 97.

11 *See Statement by Mr. Hamilton Shirley Amerasinghe* (*Sri Lanka*), elected President, Third United Nations Conference on the Law of the Sea, 1st meeting. United Nations Headquarters, New York: Codification Division, Office of Legal Affairs. (3 December 1973), available at http://legal.un.org/avl/ha/uncls/video01.2.html.

12 MS-2-744, Box 345, Folder 4, Arvid Pardo, Retrospect and Prospects, 1999.

13 Baker, 'Uncommon heritage', 22. Baker refers to MS-2-744, Box 63, Folder 1, EMB to Forrest Murdon, 25 May 1973.

14 Hermann, ed., *Die Meer Frau*, 89.

Looking back on it, there is the impression that the journey from Mann Borgese's first encounter with questions of ocean governance to *Pacem in Maribus* and finally into the United Nations went relatively smoothly. However, at the time not everyone at the Center for the Study of Democratic Institutions in Santa Barbara was initially delighted with her proposal to concentrate on ocean-related matters in the forthcoming years – although she claimed to have 'easily convinced Hutchins'[15] with the prospect of applying some of their ideas on international world governance to the issue of ocean governance.[16]

Elisabeth Mann Borgese may have been enthusiastic, but the same could not be said for all her colleagues at the centre. The fellows had a practice of sending so-called 'memorandums'[17] back and forth between them, discussing issues like the focus of their work and other important matters. Various memorandums from 1968–9 – when *Pacem in Maribus* was in preparation and Mann Borgese was pushing the centre to take on a bigger role in the ocean discussions – reveal that some fellows had their concerns. Memorandums with titles like 'The Institutional Practice of Good in the World (Malta and similar undertakings)'[18] discussed issues such as how to engage in the activities that Malta was driving. Questions were raised about whether too many staff members would be tied up in the work, and whether other commitments would be undermined if the centre focused too much on ocean governance. Even the 'Practice of Good'[19] in the title was perhaps an ironic sideswipe at Mann Borgese and Pardo's enthusiastic – even idealistic – engagement with the common heritage principle.

Since Pardo's first visit to the Center for the Study of Democratic Institutions, he and Mann Borgese had organised several planning workshops centred around specific questions to do with the oceans.[20] Some of these took place in Malta, others in Santa Barbara. In a letter to Pardo, Mann Borgese wrote that the first *Pacem in Maribus* conference would be a more ambitious attempt to collect together the ideas they had been working on in these workshops, and to rehearse her concept of a 'Maritime Assembly'.[21] The government of Malta, prompted in this case by Pardo, was very interested in hosting the conference,

15 MS-2-744, Box 345, Folder 4, Arvid Pardo, Retrospect and Prospects, 1999.
16 *Cf.* MS-2-744, Box 345, Folder 4, Arvid Pardo, Retrospect and Prospects, 1999.
17 For a collection of memorandums concerning PIM, *see* MS-2-744, Box 47, Folder 6 and MS-2-744, Box 125, Folder 3.
18 MS-2-744, Box 47, Folder 6MS 47-6, Center Memorandum, 19 February 1969.
19 MS-2-744, Box 47, Folder 6MS 47-6, Center Memorandum, 19 February 1969.
20 *See* Chircop, 'Elisabeth Mann Borgese's humanist conception', 122–124.
21 MS-2-744, Box 108, Folder 1, EMB to Arvid Pardo, 22 September 1969.

and in January 1969 they sent out an official invitation to the Center for the Study of Democratic Institutions.[22] In March 1969, the centre accepted,[23] though memorandums reveal that this decision was not taken without some internal wrangling.

One fellow at the centre, P Ferry, wrote a memorandum to the 'Malta Committee' – meaning the fellows at the centre who were working with Arvid Pardo and the Maltese proposal. These were Elisabeth Mann Borgese, Harvey Wheeler and William Goreman.[24] Ferry asserted in his memorandum that 'a Conference at Malta is not a good idea'.[25] He feared that other projects would suffer if they became too heavily engaged in the Malta issue, and he was also worried about the political implications that could go hand-in-hand with such a project.[26] Elisabeth Mann Borgese replied to Ferry's concerns by explaining that all the experts and leaders present would be invited 'in a private and personal capacity',[27] and that they would 'not speak for their governments in any way, but make the kind of contribution to the Convocation, that active members of Government have made to the Pacem in Terris Convocations or to other conferences at the Center'.[28] She was backed up by Harvey Wheeler, who stressed the ultimate aim of the gathering. Wheeler wrote that 'it must not be permitted to assume the character of an informal diplomatic gathering, the essential purpose of which is to draft the treaty for the regime of the seas'.[29] P Ferry was not satisfied with the explanation, and in his reply a week later he queried why the ocean project had become:

> such a big and urgent issue, merely because we received an invitation from the government of Malta. I have not seen the invitation (it would be nice to know exactly what the Maltese have in mind) but this is surely not enough reason to commit the energies of the Center for a year and a half to a project no-one ever thought of three weeks ago.[30]

22 *Cf.* MS-2-744, Box 47, Folder 6, UN 1/7/14 (B) 8127.

23 *Cf.* MS-2-744, Box 108, Folder 1, Robert M. Hutchins to Arvid Pardo, 4 March 1969.

24 Most likely this is fellow William Gorman, the 'young philosopher' *Cf.* Mayer, *Robert Maynard Hutchins*, 472.

25 MS-2-744, Box 47, Folder, Center Memorandum, 20 February 1969.

26 *Cf.* MS-2-744, Box 47, Folder 6, Center Memorandum, 20 February 1969.

27 MS-2-744, Box 47, Folder 6, Center Memorandum, 3 February 1969.

28 MS-2-744, Box 47, Folder 6, Center Memorandum, 3 February 1969.

29 MS-2-744, Box 47, Folder 6, Center Memorandum, 11 February 1969.

30 MS-2-744, Box 47, Folder 6, Center Memorandum, 19 February 1969.

It seemed that for Ferry, Mann Borgese's sudden enthusiasm for a project 'no-one ever thought of three weeks ago' was too rash, especially if there was the possibility it might hinder other activity at the Center for the Study of Democratic Institutions. There were probably other reasons for Ferry's reservations too. In 1968, the centre – which was constantly on the search for funding – was in crisis, and was about to be restructured.[31]

Milton Mayer, Hutchins's colleague, friend and biographer wrote that 'As big-name conferences and convocations flourished and dialogue faltered, bickering and backbiting became the order of the day [...]'.[32] The Pardo-Borgese convocation initiative, together with *Pacem in Terris*, marked a changing trend from dialogue towards large conferences, which not only tied up other fellows at the centre but also strained the centre's funds.[33] Despite Ferry's concerns, though, the fellows accepted the conference invitation in March 1969, and the 'Malta Committee' could get on with planning the forthcoming event.

2 *Pacem in Maribus* – An Ambitious Undertaking

P Ferry was right when he suspected that Elisabeth Mann Borgese had grand plans for the ocean project. In a subsequent memorandum about organising the first *Pacem in Maribus* conference, she wrote that she hoped:

> the conference could be organised so that it would facilitate the beginning of an Ocean Regime through the establishment of a forerunner nonprofit corporation with a three year program of research, planning and communication financed by foundations, multinational firms (and governments?).[34]

31 *Cf.* Mayer, *Robert Maynard Hutchins,* 487.

32 Mayer, *Robert Maynard Hutchins,* 486.

33 Mayer on funds, *see* Mayer, *Robert Maynard Hutchins,* 487.

34 MS-2-744, Box 125, Folder 3, Center Memorandum, 5 November 1970. And further MS-2-744, Box 125, Folder 3, *Pacem in Maribus*. A proposed International Convocation on 'Frontiers of the Deep Seas' to Explore Peaceful Uses of The High Seas and the Sea-Bed Beyond the Limits of National Jurisdiction: 'The Center feels that the planning and carrying out of such activities must be based upon a new kind of dialogue among national governments, the international community and the public and private organizations engaged directly in development of living and non-living ocean resources and the scientific community'. There is also an advertisement of Convocation. *See* MS-2-744, Box 125, Folder 3, newspaper article, New Peril for Mankind, 2 April 1970.

From correspondence between Mann Borgese and Arvid Pardo, we can glean two things: firstly, their intended outcome for the conference, which was to kick-start negotiations on something they referred to as the 'Ocean Regime'.[35] That they used the term 'regime' suggests that Pardo and Mann Borgese were thinking about the governance of the oceans in a holistic way, rather than as a collection of separate elements. Their intention was not to examine different areas of ocean governance separately, but rather to look at them as parts of a whole. A Law of the Sea Treaty, in which the oceans were treated holistically, would consequently be an 'Ocean Regime'. Secondly, the memorandums discussing the first PIM conference underline how important they thought this gathering was. Elisabeth Mann Borgese had very specific ideas about how the conference should be framed, and stressed that it had to be as official and celebratory as possible. When she learned that the Governor's Palace in Malta was not available for the opening and afternoon session,[36] she wrote to Pardo:

> It is sad news that we cannot have the Governor's Palace. I don't want the Hilton (or Corinthia Palace) Convention halls. They are very nice and beautifully equipped, but if we wanted a businessmen's convention at a Hilton Hotel, we could have it at Beverly Hills [...]. We do want this rehearsal for the "Maritime Assembly" as official and solemnly housed and as closely and specifically tied to Malta as possible.[37]

The plan for the conference was ambitious: 'We are hoping that the opening banquet will be addressed by your Prime Minister, followed by U Thant [Sic: Secretary-General of the United Nations], and Mr Hutchins for the Center. [...] the closing session will be addressed by your Prime Minister'.[38] Mann Borgese and Pardo invited experts from the fields of research and science, the political arena, industry and the Seabed Committee, and as Mann Borgese reported in a letter to Pardo:

> We have lined up the 85 experts who will constitute the "core" of the Convocation, and are just in the process of sending out invitations to all the fishery organizations. Invitations have gone out, as you know, to the Mission of all Members of the Sea-bed Committee. I know that a number

35 MS-2-744, Box 125, Folder 3, Center Memorandum, 5 November 1970.
36 *See* MS-2-744, Box 108, Folder 1, Arvid Pardo to EMB, 12 September 1969.
37 MS-2-744, Box 108, Folder 1, EMB to Arvid Pardo, 22 September 1969.
38 MS-2-744, Box 108, Folder 1, Madeline C. Marina to Arvid Pardo, 6 February 1969.

> of them will accept. It might be very useful if you or your Government could send out concurrent invitations. This might be good practice also in the case of the fishery organizations: Many of whom might be more interested in Malta than in the Center for the Study of Democratic Institutions [...].[39]

Obviously, Elisabeth Mann Borgese suspected that important contacts in politics and industry would only attend if they were assured of the importance of the gathering, and that this would mean getting help from the Maltese government in some cases. In several letters that shuttled back and forth between Malta and Santa Barbara, she reported on which delegates had confirmed their attendance and asked Pardo for help with the invitations where she suspected invitees might have reservations.[40]

In terms of international organisations, she tried to get the International Atomic Energy Agency to attend, after having already secured the presence of the Inter-Governmental Maritime Consultative Organization, the World Meteorological Organization and the Food and Agriculture Organization.[41] She could also report that she was 'still working on ILO [sic: International Labour Organization] and a few others[...]',[42] and found it 'very important that this agency whose activities have such a bearing on maritime pollution, should be present at the Convocation. Do you think your Government could send a strongly-worded invitation?'[43] Apart from encouraging the Maltese government to write 'strongly-worded invitations' (whatever that meant – unfortunately there is no such invitation found in the archives), Mann Borgese also made a last-minute suggestion of producing *Pacem in Maribus* postage stamps, perhaps to add an official note of importance to the undertaking. Pardo replied to her idea saying it was 'excellent',[44] but while he did pass it on to his government, he also pointed out that 'The difficulty is time'.[45] Mann Borgese had sprung this idea on him in March 1970, and the convocation was to be held in June of the same year.

39 MS-2-744, Box 108, Folder 1, EMB to Arvid Pardo, 18 February 1969.

40 *See* MS-2-744, Box 108, Folder 1, EMB to Arvid Pardo, 8 April 1970. EMB enclosed a list of fishery representatives to contact.

41 *See* MS-2-744, Box 108, Folder 1, EMB to Arvid Pardo, 14 April 1970. The IMCO was renamed the International Maritime Organization in 1982.

42 MS-2-744, Box 108, Folder 1, EMB to Arvid Pardo, 14 April 1970.

43 MS-2-744, Box 108, Folder 1, EMB to Arvid Pardo, 14 April 1970.

44 MS-2-744, Box 108, Folder 1, Arvid Pardo to EMB, 11 March 1970.

45 MS-2-744, Box 108, Folder 1, Arvid Pardo to EMB, 11 March 1970.

3 Reaching Out to the Seabed Committee

After the first convocation, an extended feature article about *Pacem in Maribus* was published in the *Saturday Review* in September 1970. The *Saturday Review* was an American weekly magazine that had been founded in 1924. In its early years, the magazine focused on literature, but from the 1940s onwards it broadened its thematic scope.[46] Norman Cousins, who was editor-in-chief of the magazine from 1942–72, had a broad interest in the United Nations and world governance.[47] Under Cousins's leadership, the *Saturday Review* became more focused on politics, and the *New York Times* wrote of his magazine that it became a 'reflection of his own wide-ranging tastes and curiosities, exploring such topics as disarmament and environmental protection long before they became fashionable causes'.[48] This made the *Saturday Review* an ideal platform for presenting the efforts of *Pacem in Maribus* to a well-informed readership that was interested in evolving questions around world governance and the United Nations. Hutchins had met Cousins at least once in 1967 at a fundraising dinner in New York after the first *Pacem in Terris* convocation, when the Center for the Study of Democratic Institutions was running short of money.[49]

The report on ocean governance for the *Saturday Review* was put together by the Center for the Study of Democratic Institutions. It was mainly written by Elisabeth Mann Borgese, who had documented the outcomes of PIM in a larger report. Having undergone some 'surgery'[50] (meaning that it was heavily shortened and de-Germanised) courtesy of Harry Ashmore, the centre's president at that time, this report gives us the essentials of the convocation.[51] The *Saturday Review* publication was a way to reach out to the Seabed Committee in Geneva as well as to the general public, and a letter from Harry Ashmore to Mann Borgese sent just prior to the publication of the *Saturday Review* piece tells us a bit about the ambitions the PIM organisers had for the article. They wanted to make public what they had been doing at *Pacem in Maribus* and

46 *See Encyclopaedia Britannica*, s.v. 'History of Publishing – The United States – Saturday Review', accessed 30 September 2021, https://www.britannica.com/topic/Saturday-Review-American-magazine.

47 *Cf.* Eric Pace, 'Norman Cousins, 75, Dies; Edited The Saturday Review', *New York Times*, December 1, 1990, https://www.nytimes.com/1990/12/01/obituaries/norman-cousins-75-dies-edited-the-saturday-review.html.

48 Jonathan Friendly, 'Saturday Review Shuts down', *New York Times*, August 17, 1982, https://www.nytimes.com/1982/08/17/business/saturday-review-shuts-down.html.

49 *Cf.* Mayer, *Robert Maynard Hutchins*, 485.

50 MS-2-744, Box 125, Folder 2, Robert M. Hutchins to Norman Cousins, 17 August 1970.

51 For the material the fellows put together, *see* MS-2-744, Box 125, Folder 2.

hoped especially to reach the people working at the United Nations on the Seabed Committee.

Harry Ashmore wrote to Mann Borgese, 'As you are aware, time is of the essence if we are to get this stuff in general circulation in time to be of influence at Geneva. I hope, therefore, that you will be able to cable your clearance immediately'.[52] With regards to the platform afforded by the magazine, he added that 'I think this is probably the best exposure we could possibly have in the United States, since the *Review* is heavily United Nations oriented'.[53] Ashmore's assessment of the *Saturday Review's* readership was quite accurate. With Cousins at the helm, the magazine reached more than 600,000 readers.[54] According to Cousins, his readers were like a 'second family',[55] interested in the same issues as he was – namely world peace, disarmament and the nuclear threat.[56] If Cousins was right about his own readers, then this kinship was not just between him and his readership, but also with Mann Borgese, Arvid Pardo, and all the others who had been involved in the preparation period and were interested in renegotiating ocean governance under the common heritage of mankind principle.

That the article was aimed at a very specific audience becomes even more apparent from a letter sent by Ashmore to Cousins about the timing of publication: 'We are assuming that the 42-nations U.N. Committee on Peaceful Uses of the Seabed will still be in session at the time all of this is published'.[57] This implies the fellows in Santa Barbara hoped the report would be noticed by United Nations officials and that it would be regarded as a contribution to the discourse. Some days later, Ashmore wrote to Cousins again, stating that he was 'anxious to attract as much attention as possible around the world while the Seabed Committee is still sitting in Geneva'.[58] Ashmore also expressed a desire to publish the same or similar reports in 'England, France, Germany, Italy, Japan and anywhere else [...]'.[59] It is difficult to assess how much attention the report garnered, but it was published in the *Saturday Review* in September 1970, with the following preface from the editors:

---

52 MS-2-744, Box 125, Folder 2, Robert M. Hutchins to EMB, 18 August 1970.

53 MS-2-744, Box 125, Folder 2, Robert M. Hutchins to EMB, 18 August 1970.

54 *See* Pace, 'Norman Cousins'

55 Harvard Square Library, *Cousins, Norman (1915–1990)*, accessed 30 September 2021, http://www.harvardsquarelibrary.org/biographies/norman-cousins-2/.

56 *Cf.* Harvard Square Library, *Cousins.*

57 MS-2-744, Box 125, Folder 2, Robert M. Hutchins to Norman Cousins, 17 August 1970.

58 MS-2-744, Box 125, Folder 2, Harry Ashmore to Norman Cousins, 19 August 1970.

59 MS-2-744, Box 125, Folder 2, Robert M. Hutchins to EMB, 18 August 1970.

> *Saturday Review* presents the following summary report by Mrs. Borgese, and excerpts from the more significant contributions, in the belief that they represent a major contribution to the international dialogue.[60]

The report was accompanied by a handful of brief articles, probably in box-out style, featuring short contributions from several of the convention's attendees. In total, there were seven contributors,[61] and some of the headlines were quite eye-catching: 'Appeal to all nations, to all men and women of the planet',[62] 'Savannahs of the blue',[63] and 'The issue is survival'.[64] The headlines alone delivered the essence of what PIM was about: a plea for immediate action, a hint towards the possibilities in the uncharted territory of the 'blue Savannah' and a reminder of the life-and-death urgency of solving questions of ocean governance.

The 'appeal to all nations'[65] was a summary of a speech made by the former Romanian ambassador to the United States and the United Nations, Silviu Brucan. At the time, he was a professor of sociology at the University of Bucharest, and he gave his audience a choice:

> The oceans, with their pure water and sunny beaches can be a source of unmitigated joy or they can become the victim of unleashed technology. They can become a source of new bounty or they can become a vast graveyard for fish and other living species annihilated by pollution.[66]

The picture he painted of the worst-case scenario for the future of the oceans was dramatic. Who could possibly want 'unleashed technology' running wild in a 'vast graveyard for fish'? To deliver the oceans from this eventuality, he stressed that the aim had to be to reserve the seafloor outside national jurisdiction for

---

60 MS-2-744, Box 125, Folder 2, Revised 8/28/70 (Prefatory material to introduce *Pacem in Maribus* takeout).

61 The reports by Richi Kalder and Alva Myrdal are not included because they were more factual.

62 MS-2-744, Box 125, Folder 2, Revised 8/28/70 (Prefatory material to introduce *Pacem in Maribus* takeout).

63 MS-2-744, Box 125, Folder 2, Revised 8/28/70 (Prefatory material to introduce *Pacem in Maribus* takeout).

64 MS-2-744, Box 125, Folder 2, Revised 8/28/70 (Prefatory material to introduce *Pacem in Maribus* takeout).

65 MS-2-744, Box 125, Folder 2, Revised 8/28/70 (Prefatory material to introduce *Pacem in Maribus* takeout).

66 MS-2-744, Box 125, Folder 2, Brucan Save the Seas and the Oceans for Mankind.

peaceful purposes only, 'in order to remove the abysman [sic: abysmal] gap between the haves and the have-nots of this planet'.[67] By the 'haves', Brucan was referring to the developed nations, such as the United States or European nations like Germany, France and the United Kingdom. When he talked about the 'have-nots', he meant the developing countries, some of them former colonies which had only recently gained independence. These countries still had to catch up with the technological development of a rapidly advancing world.

Clare Luke,[68] an attendee at PIM, wrote about the ocean future that might lie before humanity if the speeches of the Maltese Ambassador were to be believed. In Luke's portrayal, Pardo is presented as an almost prophetic figure:

> Here on the Island of Malta there was a man who dreamed an impossible dream and reached for an unreachable star. His dream was of an ocean regime which would rule the great unclaimed savannahs of the blue and develop them and fructify them for the benefit of all mankind.[69]

There is the image of 'the dream', reaching for 'the stars' and the ability to 'fructify'. What more could one want from the father of the Law of the Sea? According to Luke, Pardo's speech at the United Nations had the impact 'of a tidal wave'.[70] The man behind this alleged tidal wave, Arvid Pardo, made some contributions of his own to the *Saturday Review* feature. His article addressed the urgency of what they were trying to achieve, and according to him it was a question of life and death. Like Brucan, he presented his readers with the various potential effects of recent technological development: 'Technology can unite and it can divide. It can elevate and it can degrade. It can create a new civilization of abundance, it may destroy all civilization and life on this globe'.[71] Pardo's core message was that the path for the future of the oceans had to be chosen wisely, and he concluded his piece with a powerful warning: 'At stake is the survival of man himself'.[72]

The florid language, dramatic tone and almost poetic elements of these various smaller articles must have made entertaining reading, but despite this, the report as a whole had a very serious side to it. The tranquility and

67 MS-2-744, Box 125, Folder 2, Brucan Save the Seas and the Oceans for Mankind.

68 Former Ambassador to Italy. *See* MS-2-744, Box 125, Folder 2, Participants in the *Pacem in Maribus* Convocation.

69 MS-2-744, Box 125, Folder 2, Luke, Savannah of the Blue.

70 MS-2-744, Box 125, Folder 2, Luke, Savannah of the Blue.

71 MS-2-744, Box 125, Folder 2, Pardo, The Issue is Survival.

72 MS-2-744, Box 125, Folder 2, Pardo, The Issue is Survival.

mystery of the ocean have inspired all kinds of texts over the years, but the PIM article connected this poetic aspect of the oceans with a much more practical call to action. In fact, the poetic tone that permeates the *Saturday Review* article seems to be a recurring element in discussions about the Law of the Sea in the 1960s and 70s. This was perhaps most strikingly illustrated in Pardo's first speech at the United Nations, where he talked about the oceans as the 'womb of life'.[73] The entire speech had a lyrical quality that would be reflected in the way others subsequently talked about the Law of the Sea. Perhaps Arvid Pardo's choice of tone inspired others to speak about the subject in a similar fashion, but nevertheless, however poetic his contribution there was a concrete purpose behind it: to influence the Seabed Committee's work.

4 Discussions and Achievements of *Pacem in Maribus*

The short pieces that accompanied Elisabeth Mann Borgese's larger review of PIM can give us an overview of the central themes and motivations of the convocation. The purposes of the conference were to prompt action, to call for the preservation of the oceans, and to influence members of the Seabed Committee. About 180 participants from 51 states were present at the gathering in Malta.[74] The list of participants included famous names like the 'Oceanographer [and] Explorer'[75] Jacques Piccard and sitting members of the Seabed Committee such as Hamilton Shirley Amerasinghe of Ceylon, along with a large number of United Nations ambassadors and industry representatives from all over the world.[76] The list of influential participants alone suggests that the convocation was a huge undertaking. Apparently, Malta's 'strongly-worded' invitations had fulfilled their purpose. Even without the attention from the *Saturday Review,* it is reasonable to suppose that the gathering would have had some impact on those important United Nations ambassadors who

73 A/C.1/PV.1515, 7.

74 All participants are listed in MS-2-744, Box 125, Folder 2, Participants in the *Pacem in Maribus* Convocation.

75 MS-2-744, Box 125, Folder 2, Participants in the *Pacem in Maribus* Convocation.

76 For the complete list *see* MS-2-744, Box 125, Folder 2, Participants in the *Pacem in Maribus* Convocation. Norwegian delegate Jens Evensen participated too. This information will be important in Chapter 7, which deals with unofficial groups and key players at the conference. Evensen was one of these.

attended the convention and later the gatherings of the Seabed Committee.[77] Of those who attended PIM I or the subsequent conferences, several would go on to be deeply involved in the Law of the Sea Convention in various capacities over the coming years.

In a letter to Aurelio Peccei – co-founder and president of the newly established Club of Rome[78] – Mann Borgese was clear about the purpose of the conference. The *Pacem in Maribus* convocation was about bringing together scientists, political leaders and industry to represent 'the internationalization of research & development',[79] 'the world community of science'[80] and 'the world community of production'.[81] Their task was to discuss the use of resources, the ecology of the ocean and the role of scientists.[82]

From the *Saturday Review* report, we learn that the gathering revolved around five major topics: 'The Scientific Dilemma',[83] 'The Harvest of the Seas',[84] 'The Ocean Enterprise',[85] 'The Underwater Arms Race'[86] and 'The Nixon Proposal'.[87] Having gathered together such a wide group of experts from different fields, it was inevitable that interests would differ tremendously on many aspects of ocean governance. It must have been challenging – if not impossible – to channel and unite all these points of view, but the conference gave a fairly accurate indication of the differing interests that would be present 'in the field'. Meaning, of course, in the United Nations, where each country had agendas and preferences that were influenced by their geographical location, their political system, their state of technological development, their industrial background, and their international alliances and agreements. Planning a conference like this would indeed be a 'rehearsal for the "Maritime Assembly" ',[88] just as Elisabeth Mann Borgese had envisioned it.

77 This is also in line with Baker, 'Uncommon Heritage', 17–18. Baker argues that the pre-conferences had already attracted attention.

78 The Club of Rome was founded by Aurelio Peccei and Alexander King in 1968 to tackle global issues. In 1972 the 'Limits to Growth' was published, which became the most famous and controversial contribution of the group. *See* The Club of Rome, Timeline, https://www.clubofrome.org/about-us/history/.

79 MS-2-744, Box 43, Folder 49, EMB to Dr. Aurelio Peccei, May 15, 1969.

80 MS-2-744, Box 43, Folder 49, EMB to Dr. Aurelio Peccei, May 15, 1969.

81 MS-2-744, Box 43, Folder 49, EMB to Dr. Aurelio Peccei, May 15, 1969.

82 *Cf.* MS-2-744, Box 43, Folder 49, EMB to Dr. Aurelio Peccei, May 15, 1969.

83 MS-2-744, Box 125, Folder 2, Pacem in Maribus: A Report and Some Reflections by EMB.

84 MS-2-744, Box 125, Folder 2, Pacem in Maribus: A Report and Some Reflections by EMB.

85 MS-2-744, Box 125, Folder 2, Pacem in Maribus: A Report and Some Reflections by EMB.

86 MS-2-744, Box 125, Folder 2, Pacem in Maribus: A Report and Some Reflections by EMB.

87 MS-2-744, Box 125, Folder 2, Pacem in Maribus: A Report and Some Reflections by EMB.

88 MS-2-744, Box 108, Folder 1, EMB to Arvid Pardo, 22 September 1969.

While Mann Borgese's report made the undertaking seem promising, the planning committee had in fact run into problems even at the invitation stage. Afterwards, Mann Borgese admitted that 'The major American and allied European oil producers were unrepresented at Pacem in Maribus, in response to a de facto boycott called by the American Petroleum Institute […]'.[89] As a consequence, only smaller enterprises had attended the conference, while the big players – those with the real power and influence – had stayed away. One participant at PIM, Dr Robin Murray of Great Britain from the London Graduate School of Business Studies,[90] was concerned at the control exerted by these big companies. He reported that, despite the boycott, 'one of the major oil companies, while declining to be represented at Malta, put pressure on one or two of the convocation's participants to see that this particular aspect of their operations was not aired at all'.[91] Unfortunately, we do not know which oil company this was, or which conference participants they supposedly tried to manipulate. Still, Murray's allegations can tell us two things: Firstly, that the oil industry made sure its interests were taken into account, regardless of the boycott, and secondly, that these companies must have recognised that PIM was a reasonably important platform – since they took the trouble not only to boycott it but at the same time to try and put someone on the case to watch out for their interests.

Despite the hiccup of the oil company boycott, the report shows that the conference participants managed to articulate some essential elements of what should later be negotiated during the Law of the Sea Convention. Several delegates argued in favour of a new approach to governing the oceans, instead of applying 'terrestrial thinking'[92] to ocean governance. Ambassador Mojsov of Yugoslavia said, 'we often follow the analogy of arguments used in the delimitation of national boundaries among different states and powers. […] If we continue along this line we shall, in the end, arrive at the proclamation of seabed colonies or seabed states'.[93] General Said Uddin Khan of Pakistan, a former head of UN peace-keeping missions,[94] pointed out that the essentially different nature of ocean boundaries had to be considered when it came to

89 MS-2-744, Box 125, Folder 2, Pacem in Maribus: A Report and Some Reflections by EMB.

90 *See* List of Participants MS-2-744, Box 125, Folder 2, Participants in the *Pacem in Maribus* Convocation.

91 MS-2-744, Box 125, Folder 2, Pacem in Maribus: A Report and Some Reflections by EMB.

92 MS-2-744, Box 125, Folder 2, Pacem in Maribus: A Report and Some Reflections by EMB.

93 MS-2-744, Box 125, Folder 2, Pacem in Maribus: A Report and Some Reflections by EMB.

94 *See* List of Participants MS-2-744, Box 125, Folder 2, Participants in the *Pacem in Maribus* Convocation.

addressing the concept of peace-keeping operations in such an environment. 'You have to invent something quite new', said General Khan. 'People in blue hats in boats will be quite helpless'.[95]

5 Defining Pressing Ocean Governance Problems

One of the first things that Elisabeth Mann Borgese mentioned in her report was the 'crisis of science'.[96] Having spoken to several scientists and researchers who were in attendance, she found that many of them reported challenges surrounding the difference between accumulating knowledge and utilising it. Mann Borgese wrote that 'scientists whose speculations and research spawned the Marine Revolution are appalled by many of the results that followed once technologists began to convert their theories into hardware'.[97] This quote has distinct overtones of the Manhattan Project, and we should bear in mind that the founder of the Center for the Study of Democratic Institutions was Robert Maynard Hutchins. Elisabeth Mann Borgese had worked with him for more than a decade, and she was familiar with his background in the Manhattan Project and his reasons for establishing the Committee to Frame a World Constitution – much of which had carried over to the centre in Santa Barbara. That Hutchins was founding father of the centre makes it likely that they were acutely aware of the 'hazards' of scientific innovation.

Although Mann Borgese does not mention the Manhattan Project in the report, we can make the connection between what had been observed during the Manhattan Project and the concerns around maritime issues reported by researchers. Once any research results were published, governmental, military or industrial bodies could exploit them without the researcher having control over what was done with their findings.[98] As a consequence, Mann Borgese reported that some researchers and scientists among her representatives had concluded that science was in an 'acute professional crisis'.[99] She noted that researchers 'who have freely roamed the seas since Darwin's day, now encounter severe restrictions arising from growing nationalism compounded by the fear that scientific investigation in the most remote waters might lead to exploitations by foreign commercial interests'.[100]

95 MS-2-744, Box 125, Folder 2, Pacem in Maribus: A Report and Some Reflections by EMB.
96 MS-2-744, Box 125, Folder 2, Pacem in Maribus: A Report and Some Reflections by EMB.
97 MS-2-744, Box 125, Folder 2, Pacem in Maribus: A Report and Some Reflections by EMB.
98 *Cf.* MS-2-744, Box 125, Folder 2, Pacem in Maribus: A Report and Some Reflections by EMB.
99 MS-2-744, Box 125, Folder 2, Pacem in Maribus: A Report and Some Reflections by EMB.
100 MS-2-744, Box 125, Folder 2, Pacem in Maribus: A Report and Some Reflections by EMB.

Not everyone at the gathering thought this was a negative thing. According to Mann Borgese's report, some considered that the freedom to explore science in the oceans could be a source of opportunity. Professor Milner Schaefer predicted that the 'United States will soon declare, unilaterally, freedom of scientific research on the seas and seabed adjacent to its own shores, even within the limits of national jurisdiction'.[101] Despite some differing opinions as to how far freedom of research would be an advantage or disadvantage for scientists and their results, Mann Borgese could report that:

> All agreed [...] it is no longer possible to cling blindly to the old concept of science as confined to passively observing and describing nature. Under modern conditions this creates a catastrophic gap between knowledge and action, and constructive impulses die away in a proliferating bureaucracy.[102]

The discussion then turned to the 'harvest of the sea' – in other words, the question of how to govern the way ocean resources were utilised in areas both within and outside of national jurisdiction. One topic was the living resources, meaning the fishing industry, which had representatives at the convocation.[103] In the case of marine minerals, Elisabeth Mann Borgese reported that:

> Representatives of the developing nations see their interests best served by a strong, effective international organization. Only this could enable them to participate at the essential stage of planning, when decisions must be made as to the allocation of resources and the setting of priorities for technological development.[104]

The issue of how resources on the ocean floor could be governed was discussed under the headline 'The Ocean Enterprises',[105] by which Mann Borgese meant to encompass all entities (private or public) that would in the future engage in industrial activities in the oceans, along with questions of how these activities should be governed. Mann Borgese wrote that US oil companies and their supporters in Congress 'seek to apply the traditional doctrine of freedom of the seas to the sea bottom as "first come, first served" [... .] there can be no doubt

101 MS-2-744, Box 125, Folder 2, Pacem in Maribus: A Report and Some Reflections by EMB.
102 MS-2-744, Box 125, Folder 2, Pacem in Maribus: A Report and Some Reflections by EMB.
103 *See* list of participants.
104 MS-2-744, Box 125, Folder 2, Pacem in Maribus: A Report and Some Reflections by EMB.
105 MS-2-744, Box 125, Folder 2, Pacem in Maribus: A Report and Some Reflections by EMB.

that they would enjoy a head start in any race to the undersea oil fields and mineral deposits'.[106] This comment emphasised the technology gap between industrialised and developing nations – an issue that was becoming increasingly visible in the early discussions surrounding marine resources and minerals prior to UNCLOS III. The freedom of the seas doctrine proposed by the US would favour those who possessed the necessary technological knowledge to exploit ocean resources. Therefore, even at PIM I in 1970, delegates were already airing the idea of internationally governed forms of 'Ocean Enterprises' that would be tasked with administering the differing interests of developing and industrial states.[107]

Another major topic of the conference – and one that affected all ocean governance questions – was the underwater arms race. The Ad Hoc Seabed Committee had been set up to look into the potential use of the seafloor for peaceful purposes as a result of Pardo's speech in 1967, and at PIM I, Arvid Pardo again spoke about the challenges that would face those negotiating the new Law of the Sea Treaty. According to Pardo, there were several interlinked issues connected to military action on the seafloor: 'Environmental reality',[108] 'Military reality',[109] 'Technical reality',[110] 'Legal reality'[111] and 'Political reality'.[112] Pardo expressed that, for the time being 'the only hope is a limited treaty, such as the one being negotiated in Geneva, [sic: In the Geneva Disarmament Committee[113]] dealing with relatively peripheral issues'. According to Mann Borgese, he further noted that the treaty of the Disarmament Committee could set an 'important precedent [...]'.[114]

Mann Borgese mentioned another participant who proposed a solution to the arms race problem. 'By pushing peaceful, industrial uses of the oceans [...]',[115] said Dr V Pavicevic of Yugoslavia's Mission to the UN, 'it may be possible to advance a peace system in which the arms race simply would have no place'.[116] The idea was that enhanced industrial use of the oceans could replace

106 MS-2-744, Box 125, Folder 2, Pacem in Maribus: A Report and Some Reflections by EMB.
107 *Cf.* MS-2-744, Box 125, Folder 2, Pacem in Maribus: A Report and Some Reflections by EMB.
108 MS-2-744, Box 125, Folder 2, Pacem in Maribus: A Report and Some Reflections by EMB.
109 MS-2-744, Box 125, Folder 2, Pacem in Maribus: A Report and Some Reflections by EMB.
110 MS-2-744, Box 125, Folder 2, Pacem in Maribus: A Report and Some Reflections by EMB.
111 MS-2-744, Box 125, Folder 2, Pacem in Maribus: A Report and Some Reflections by EMB.
112 MS-2-744, Box 125, Folder 2, Pacem in Maribus: A Report and Some Reflections by EMB.
113 *See* report MS-2-744, Box 125, Folder 2, Pacem in Maribus: A Report and Some Reflections by EMB.
114 MS-2-744, Box 125, Folder 2, Pacem in Maribus: A Report and Some Reflections by EMB.
115 MS-2-744, Box 125, Folder 2, Pacem in Maribus: A Report and Some Reflections by EMB.
116 MS-2-744, Box 125, Folder 2, Pacem in Maribus: A Report and Some Reflections by EMB.

FIGURE 3 Elisabeth Mann Borgese at Pacem in Maribus V in Malta 1974 with the topic: the common heritage of mankind
DALHOUSIE UNIVERSITY ARCHIVES MS-2-744 BOX 178 FOLDER 28
PHOTO: UNKNOWN

military activity because states would be motivated to decrease military activity in order not to disrupt the economic benefits of industrial activities.

The first 'Maritime Assembly', as Mann Borgese had envisioned the *Pacem in Maribus* conference, concluded with a statement from Elisabeth Mann Borgese herself: 'Either there will be no ocean regime at all – with chaotic revolutionary consequences – or there will be a comprehensive structure shaped to political reality'.[117] Mann Borgese called for international cooperation, new thinking and action to design a treaty that would incorporate and administer the needs of not just all states, but also entities within the states that were in some way or other concerned with the oceans. A selection of industry representatives, scientists, researchers and policy-makers had all been present at the conference, and had contributed to working up ideas around the outstanding issues

117 MS-2-744, Box 125, Folder 2, Pacem in Maribus: A Report and Some Reflections by EMB.

of ocean governance. What they had arrived at, according to Mann Borgese's report, was that in order to achieve a functioning ocean regime, something new had to be invented and old concepts had to be remodelled – whether those concepts related to research, property rights, ownership or military uses of the oceans.

CHAPTER 5

'The Ocean Regime' and the 'Draft Ocean Space Treaty'

1 A Holistic Treaty – Elisabeth Mann Borgese's 'The Ocean Regime'

In December 1970, the United Nations General Assembly released a resolution commissioning the Seabed Committee to 'prepare for the conference on the law of the sea draft treaty articles embodying the international regime – including an international machinery – for the area and the resources of the sea-bed and the ocean floor, and the subsoil thereof, beyond the limits of national jurisdiction'.[1] The Geneva sessions were scheduled for March, July and August 1971.

As it happened, Elisabeth Mann Borgese and Arvid Pardo were already working on proposals for an 'international regime' and its 'international machinery'. At *Pacem in Maribus* I, the participants were handed a draft paper entitled 'The Ocean Regime',[2] which was intended to be used as a basis for the discussion. (In a letter from Harry Ashmore concerning the *Saturday Review* article, we learn that Mann Borgese would have liked to see 'The Ocean Regime' printed in the *Saturday Review*, but Ashmore had to turn down her request due to limited space in the publication).[3]

In 1999, long after those first discussions on ocean governance at the United Nations, Arvid Pardo wrote a letter to Salvino Busuttil. The letter is important in several ways, and we have already referred to parts of it where Pardo talks about the origins of the Maltese initiative. The letter also tells us where, and most likely when, Elisabeth Mann Borgese and Arvid Pardo met for the first time. But closer investigation reveals that there is even more to the letter than this. In his letter to Busuttil, Arvid Pardo makes clear the truly radical nature of Mann Borgese's ideas, even at such an early stage in the preparation period prior to UNCLOS III. Pardo writes that 'During the period when I was

1 GA RES 2750 (XXV). B. 17 December 1970.

2 MS-2-744, Box 175, Folder 21, The Ocean Regime, December 1970.

3 MS-2-744, Box 125, Folder 2, Harry Ashmore to EMB, 18 August 1970: 'Your model got squeezed out by space requirements, but you will note that we are offering a free copy of The Ocean Regime to anyone who writes in'.

representative of Malta I was reluctant to support Prof. Borgese's enthusiasm […]'.[4] He outlines three reasons for his reluctance:

> 1. My dream had been limited to the seabed and oceans. 2. I was afraid that publicizing the broader implications of the common heritage concept would impact adversely ongoing treaty negotiations. 3. I believed that serious action to broaden the concept of common heritage in the sense desired by Prof. Borgese should take place only after a reasonably satisfactory ocean space (not seabed) treaty was safely in place.[5]

Initially, it might come as something of a surprise that Mann Borgese had an even broader understanding of the common heritage concept and its applications than Pardo. After all, Arvid Pardo is generally recognised as the initiator of the common heritage concept. However, when we consider the circles in which Mann Borgese moved, her work at the Committee to Frame a World Constitution in Chicago and the purpose of her employment at the Center for the Study of Democratic Institutions, it is not so very surprising that she tried to use the question of ocean governance to implement a broader application of the common heritage principle. In fact, one could go so far as to suggest that her first draft of 'The Ocean Regime' was an attempt to extend ocean governance to world governance.[6] To understand this, we must look further into the background of the draft that she presented to the participants at *Pacem in Maribus* I.

Before the draft of 'The Ocean Regime' was presented at PIM in 1970, Elisabeth Mann Borgese held a lecture,[7] dated 1969, in which she presented her ideas about the ocean regime. Unfortunately, the draft lecture does not tell us where or for what purpose the lecture was held, but it may have been prepared for one of the centre's planning meetings in the run-up to PIM I. Although the circumstances of the lecture are unclear, it can be treated as a precursor to

4 PR-Box: Personal Correspondences & Materials, undated letter from Dr. Arvid Pardo to Salvino Busuttil (handwritten note on the right corner). CC: Joe Friggieri, Fr Peter Serracino Inglott, Freddie Amato Gauci, ~~Victor Gauci~~, Charlie Vella, Elizabeth Mann Borgese, ~~Victor Ragonesi~~.

5 PR-Box: Personal Correspondences & Materials, undated letter from Dr. Arvid Pardo to Salvino Busuttil (handwritten note on the right corner). CC: Joe Friggieri, Fr Peter Serracino Inglott, Freddie Amato Gauci, ~~Victor Gauci~~, Charlie Vella, Elizabeth Mann Borgese, ~~Victor Ragonesi.~~.

6 Baker comes to the same conclusion in Baker, 'Uncommon Heritage'.

7 Place, date and time unfortunately unknown. For the lecture *see* MS-2-744, Box 139, Folder 16, Lecture on the Ocean Regime by Elisabeth Mann Borgese.

the 1970 draft. Apart from a detailed explanation of how 'The Ocean Regime' should be constructed, the lecture also sketches its background. Since it is a lecture, the tone is personal, and the various explanations of how the ideas behind 'The Ocean Regime' were formed give us insights into Mann Borgese's philosophies and personal beliefs. This information is missing from the more straight-laced draft of 1970, but is crucial to understanding where the draft stemmed from and where she intended it to go.

She started her lecture with the following words: 'The Oceans are free. The mere thought that they could be "appropriated" by any ruler, however mighty, by any nation, no matter how vast its empire, has something blasphemous'.[8] Several aspects of this introductory sentence are striking. Mann Borgese chose to emphasise that the oceans were free and should not be 'appropriated', while at the same time repeatedly using the phrase 'common property of mankind'[9] elsewhere in the lecture. We now know that the term 'property' was intentionally replaced by the term 'heritage' in later drafts. This was a deliberate decision, and in his 1967 speech to the UN, Pardo too had chosen to avoid the term 'property' in order not to give the false impression that he was emphasising the potential utilisation of the seabed and its resources.[10] Mann Borgese's main point – it seems reasonable to suppose – was that ocean resources should not be viewed as property that could only be owned by a finite number of nation states or companies who had the capabilities to use them. She also introduced an important spiritual note to the issue by using the term 'blasphemous'.[11] This gave the impression that the ocean was a god-like creature or mysterious natural power with the potential to be insulted.

Mann Borgese launched into her lecture with a historical overview of the period when the oceans were 'extra-human, superhuman, indomitable'.[12] She painted a colourful picture of what the oceans meant to humankind back in the days when they were mystical and inaccessible.

---

8 MS-2-744, Box 139, Folder 16, Lecture on the Ocean Regime by Elisabeth Mann Borgese.

9 MS-2-744, Box 139, Folder 16, Lecture on the Ocean Regime by Elisabeth Mann Borgese. EMB writes: ' – that the ocean floor and its resources beyond the present limits of national jurisdiction is to be considered the common property of mankind'.

10 *Cf.* Buttigieg, 'Arvid Pardo', 17: 'Arvid Pardo, in his speech to the General Assembly, specifically avoided referring to these natural resources as belonging to the whole of mankind. What Pardo had in mind, and it was in this formulation that he was prophetic, was a new concept of the use of property that was not in any way related to appropriation'.

11 MS-2-744, Box 139, Folder 16, Lecture on the Ocean Regime by Elisabeth Mann Borgese.

12 MS-2-744, Box 139, Folder 16, Lecture on the Ocean Regime by Elisabeth Mann Borgese.

> The air above, […], was for the birds, not for man; and the depth below, hiding sunken cities or continents, treasures, monsters and mermaids, was a dream world unfathomable as man's unconscious or the Milky Way.[13]

With this talk of treasures, monsters and mermaids, Mann Borgese's lecture once again emphasises the mystical nature of the ocean – a common theme across so many of the speeches, lectures and articles that were delivered on the subject in the 1960s and 70s. Such language reminds us of the florid prose some PIM participants used in their *Saturday Review* pieces in 1970.[14] Mann Borgese continued her lecture by outlining how human progress had added dimensions to the ocean. First, the invention of the submarine had added depth. Then the installation of underwater cables for telecommunications via the ocean floor had imparted a new principle of freedom. Finally, the airspace above the surface of the water was added to the domain of humanity with the invention of aeroplanes.[15] These new dimensions had caused humanity to view the ocean as a complex space. According to Mann Borgese, under-sea cables had made it necessary to study the seafloor, which in turn had prompted humans to realise the wealth that lay upon and under it.[16] This discovery of wealth posed a new challenge – the question of what to do with it – and Mann Borgese presented her listeners with two options:

> Two courses are open to mankind. One is to extend the law of the land to the submarine lands. That is, as technology develops, the developed nations would appropriate even larger portions of the submarine lands and subject them to their national sovereignty. The other course is to extend the law of the seas to the ocean floor, adding a fifth freedom to those embodied in the Conventions on the High Seas, by declaring that the ocean floor and its resources belong to mankind as a whole, are God's road, and cannot be appropriated by any Nation.[17]

In the face of technological development, Mann Borgese feared the rise of what she called 'neo-imperialism'[18] and warned that 'The colonial occupation

13 MS-2-744, Box 139, Folder 16, Lecture on the Ocean Regime by Elisabeth Mann Borgese.

14 *Cf.* MS-2-744, Box 125, Folder 2, Luke, Savannah of the Blue. *See also* MS-2-744, Box 125, Folder 2,
Brucan Save the Seas and the Oceans for Mankind.

15 *Cf.* MS-2-744, Box 139, Folder 16, Lecture on the Ocean Regime by Elisabeth Mann Borgese.

16 *Cf.* MS-2-744, Box 139, Folder 16, Lecture on the Ocean Regime by Elisabeth Mann Borgese.

17 MS-2-744, Box 139, Folder 16, Lecture on the Ocean Regime by Elisabeth Mann Borgese.

18 MS-2-744, Box 139, Folder 16, Lecture on the Ocean Regime by Elisabeth Mann Borgese.

of the ocean floor would be the death of the oceans, bringing us closer, by one giant step, to the death of the planet as a whole'.[19] Therefore, she stated, the seafloor must be the 'property of mankind'.[20] The purpose of the lecture, Mann Borgese explained to her audience, was to examine the Maltese seabed proposal,[21] to tease out its shortcomings or challenges, and then to present a solution to these problems, all of which would be comprised in the draft of the 'The Ocean Regime'. Mann Borgese identified two main challenges inherent in the Maltese proposal. First, that it was difficult to apply the common heritage of mankind concept to just one part of the ocean, meaning the seafloor.[22] The complexity of ocean space, she pointed out, meant that its governance had to be handled as a whole, or as she put it, in a 'systemic'[23] way rather than a fractured one. This lead on to her second point, which was that ocean governance should be independent or different from the existing United Nations system, since such a system, in her view, was not designed to handle issues in a holistic way.[24]

Reading further into her lecture, it soon becomes clear that this criticism of the Maltese proposal was Mann Borgese's way of preparing her audience for her own more holistic solution to ocean governance. She wanted to stress that innovation was essential. Not only did she intend to revolutionise ocean governance, she also wanted to revolutionise the whole system within which the United Nations operated, making ocean governance the starting point for this revolution. Her vision for the new system was that:

> It must be administratively efficient. It must be the trustee for all mankind. It must give maximum opportunity for participation. It must accommodate socialist and nonsocialist economies [..] and, the Regime must serve the interests both of developed and developing, of maritime and of land locked nations.[25]

The system Elisabeth Mann Borgese had in mind needed to be efficient, include all mankind, rely on participation, unite different economic systems,

19 MS-2-744, Box 139, Folder 16, Lecture on the Ocean Regime by Elisabeth Mann Borgese.

20 MS-2-744, Box 139, Folder 16, Lecture on the Ocean Regime by Elisabeth Mann Borgese.

21 Referring to Arvid Pardo's 1967 speech and perhaps an unpublished earlier version of the 'Draft Ocean Space Treaty'. Arvid Pardo and Mann Borgese worked closely together in 1970 and might have exchanged proposals.

22 *Cf.* MS-2-744, Box 139, Folder 16, Lecture on the Ocean Regime by Elisabeth Mann Borgese.

23 MS-2-744, Box 139, Folder 16, Lecture on the Ocean Regime by Elisabeth Mann Borgese.

24 *Cf.* MS-2-744, Box 139, Folder 16, Lecture on the Ocean Regime by Elisabeth Mann Borgese.

25 MS-2-744, Box 139, Folder 16, Lecture on the Ocean Regime by Elisabeth Mann Borgese.

and combine the interests of developed and developing countries. It was an ambitious brief. But Mann Borgese was not going to leave it at that. Her contribution went beyond simply making the case for an interesting sounding vision of idealism. She had actually prepared a detailed description of what 'The Ocean Regime' might look like, along with thoughts on what would have to be changed in the United Nations system to make it work. In the years following the 1969 lecture, she would elaborate on these ideas. In December 1970, she drafted a statute for the new ocean regime, [26] and in 1971 she developed this into a twenty-eight page document in which the various bodies of the new regime and their functions and tasks were laid out.[27] Both these draft statutes were most likely improved after having been discussed at the *Pacem in Maribus* conference in 1970.

Before Elisabeth Mann Borgese outlined the specific details of her proposed ocean regime, she pointed towards examples of similar undertakings in recent history. The most obvious one was the Outer Space Treaty.[28] She identified several resemblances, relating to the different 'zones' or areas one was faced with in both spaces. Territorial waters were comparable to the atmosphere, outer space to the high seas, and the seabed and ocean floor to the moon and other celestial bodies.[29] The difference, she pointed out, was that the issue of accessibility would pose more challenges in the case of the seafloor, arguing that it was 'considerably easier to keep the Moon and Other Celestial Bodies demilitarised than to keep the ocean floor demilitarised'.[30]

There were also examples closer to home, like the European Coal and Steel Community (ECSC).[31] The difference in this case, according to Mann Borgese, was that Europe was 'closely knit',[32] and the world's nation states as a whole were not. On the other hand, 'Coal and steel were thought to constitute the major war making potential of the European nations'.[33] In this respect, the potential value of the ocean floor was very similar to what was at stake when

26 *See* MS-2-744, Box 175, Folder 21, The Ocean Regime, December 1970.

27 *See* MS-2-744, Box 132, Folder 1, The Ocean Regime Draft Statute (Revised, February 1971).

28 *Treaty on Principles Governing the Activities of States in the Exploration and Use of Outer Space, including the Moon and Other Celestial Bodies*, Adopted by the General Assembly in its resolution 2222 (XXI), opened for signature on 27 January 1967, entered into force on 10 October 1967.

29 *Cf.* MS-2-744, Box 139, Folder 16, Lecture on the Ocean Regime by EMB. There are parallels to Pardo's speech in 1967.

30 MS-2-744, Box 139, Folder 16, Lecture on the Ocean Regime by EMB.

31 *Cf.* MS-2-744, Box 139, Folder 16, Lecture on the Ocean Regime by EMB.

32 MS-2-744, Box 139, Folder 16, Lecture on the Ocean Regime by EMB.

33 MS-2-744, Box 139, Folder 16, Lecture on the Ocean Regime by EMB.

the European Coal and Steel Community was negotiated. The possibility of using the ocean floor for stationary weapon systems had been a point of concern both in Pardo's speech in 1967 and also during the PIM I discussions, and it was clearly a driving force behind the need for renegotiation that Mann Borgese also recognised in her draft of 'The Ocean Regime'. Mann Borgese would compare the European Coal and Steel Community's efforts for unity to the potential ocean negotiations by stating that 'Coal and steel are, more or less, of yesterday. The ocean, the ocean floor, and outer space are essential for war and peace tomorrow. The Soviet Union and the United States are playing approximately the role in the world at large that France and Germany played in Europe'.[34]

Another example Mann Borgese drew some parallels to was the Euratom Treaty.[35] The important point here was the 'common property'[36] aspect of Euratom. She claimed that 'Under the Euratom Treaty, all fissionable material is the property of the Community, and there is a set of elaborate provisions that spell out this concept'.[37] Mann Borgese understood that the principle of the Euratom Treaty as a concept of 'common property' by material sharing was similar to the common property idea that she herself intended to apply to seabed resources in the early drafts of 'The Ocean Regime'. The intention of this historical overview of comparable transnational collaborations was most likely to prepare Mann Borgese's audience to be convinced of the possibility of an even larger cooperative venture: a regime for the oceans with a possible outlook for a new world regime.

2 An Ocean Regime through Participation

The new aspect Elisabeth Mann Borgese introduced to the question of ocean governance – and one for which there was no precedent or similar attempt on a smaller scale – was an International Assembly based on participation. She argued that it was essential to introduce an innovative new participation aspect to 'The Ocean Regime', and that in designing an International Assembly, 'drafters of the statute for an Ocean Regime must take a bold new step […]'.[38] Mann Borgese pointed out that Arvid Pardo had acknowledged in his speech

34 MS-2-744, Box 139, Folder 16, Lecture on the Ocean Regime by EMB.
35 *Cf.* MS-2-744, Box 139, Folder 16, Lecture on the Ocean Regime by EMB.
36 MS-2-744, Box 139, Folder 16, Lecture on the Ocean Regime by EMB.
37 MS-2-744, Box 139, Folder 16, Lecture on the Ocean Regime by EMB.
38 MS-2-744, Box 139, Folder 16, Lecture on the Ocean Regime by EMB.

before the General Assembly that developed countries would be unlikely to take part in a regime where they had a similar or lesser degree of power than the developing countries.[39]

With this in mind, Mann Borgese presented three different alternatives for the creation of an assembly. The first was to run it as a 'business corporation',[40] meaning that it would be organised solely for the governance and organisation needed to utilise the resources of the ocean floor. This, however, would mean the 'triumph of technocracy over democracy'.[41] The second option would be to 'adapt the national democratic parliamentary process somehow to the international scene'.[42] The problem in this case would be to work out a vote-weighting system that would be acceptable for all countries, and Mann Borgese deemed this so time-consuming that it would never be worked out in the foreseeable future.[43] The third option she offered was 'to recognize that parliamentary representative democracy has reached a dead end and that new principles have to be discovered'.[44] The existing system was direct and representative democracy, but Mann Borgese's new idea would go beyond that. She proposed to introduce 'participational democracy',[45] and perhaps to go even further.

What would this mean for 'The Ocean Regime'? Mann Borgese explained that the idea of participation was that 'workers must participate not only in the profits but in the decision-making processes of enterprises, students in the management of universities, tenants in the administration of housing projects etc [...]'.[46] She added further 'that participation, responsibility and initiatives are more important incentives than profits, that cooperation today is more productive than competition, that consensus is more important than coercion'.[47] This passage is very interesting because it reveals some of Mann Borgese's most deeply rooted beliefs about the effectiveness of internationalism. Cooperation instead of competition, consensus instead of coercion. In that sense, her initial idea – although it was altered in the course of the negotiations at UNCLOS – was embedded in internationalist ideology and clearly visible in her proposal for an ocean regime as presented in 1969.

39 *Cf.* MS-2-744, Box 139, Folder 16, Lecture on the Ocean Regime by EMB. For the passage in Pardo's speech, *see* A/C.1/PV.1516, 8.
40 MS-2-744, Box 139, Folder 16, Lecture on the Ocean Regime by EMB.
41 MS-2-744, Box 139, Folder 16, Lecture on the Ocean Regime by EMB.
42 MS-2-744, Box 139, Folder 16, Lecture on the Ocean Regime by EMB.
43 *Cf.* MS-2-744, Box 139, Folder 16, Lecture on the Ocean Regime by EMB.
44 MS-2-744, Box 139, Folder 16, Lecture on the Ocean Regime by EMB.
45 MS-2-744, Box 139, Folder 16, Lecture on the Ocean Regime by EMB.
46 MS-2-744, Box 139, Folder 16, Lecture on the Ocean Regime by EMB.
47 MS-2-744, Box 139, Folder 16, Lecture on the Ocean Regime by EMB.

Mann Borgese continued her lecture by explaining how she believed this principle could be applied to the ocean regime. She envisioned a Maritime Commission or Governing Board that would be responsible to an International Maritime Assembly. This Maritime Assembly would be made up of four chambers or houses. One would represent the nations and would be composed of delegates from the United Nations General Assembly, who would be appointed by the General Assembly. The second chamber would represent the experts and technocrats who would be involved in any kind of seabed mining or resource extraction activity. All non-governmental organisations (NGOs), governmental and intergovernmental organisations working in this field would be part of this second chamber too. The third chamber would represent the fisheries, assembled in the same way as the second. Finally, the fourth chamber would be made up of scientists working on ocean-related matters.[48] As we can see, these chambers represent pretty much the same assortment of diplomats, scientists and technological experts that Mann Borgese and Pardo had invited to *Pacem in Maribus*. In fact, Mann Borgese wrote in a letter to Pardo that PIM would be the rehearsal for a 'Maritime Assembly'.[49] This was her intention as early as 1969 when the letter was sent, and as we can see from the report in the *Saturday Review*, it ended up genuinely being the case.

In 1971, after PIM I, Mann Borgese revised her draft of 'The Ocean Regime', adding a fifth chamber that would represent shipping and cable companies.[50] We can assume that the chamber was added after the draft was discussed at PIM and the representatives of shipping and cable companies expressed their right to a chamber of their own in which they could represent their interests. The essential advantage of a chamber system comprised of experts in different fields was that it would be possible to add an unlimited number of new chambers for new and emerging fields. And this represented the first opening into a wider world constitution. Because if ocean matters could be discussed this way, why not any other matters? Why not add together an unlimited number of chambers for an unlimited number of matters and gather them under an International Assembly?[51] Any issue that had to be decided upon would be voted for in the first chamber, along with whichever chamber represented the issue that was being discussed. So for instance if a matter concerning deep sea mining regulations was to be voted on, the first chamber – representing all

48 *Cf.* MS-2-744, Box 139, Folder 16, Lecture on the Ocean Regime by EMB.

49 MS-2-744, Box 108, Folder 1, EMB to Arvid Pardo, 22 September 1969.

50 *See* MS-2-744, Box 132, Folder 1, The Ocean Regime Draft Statute (Revised, February 1971). The fourth chamber.

51 *See* MS-2-744, Box 139, Folder 16, Lecture on the Ocean Regime by EMB.

nations – would vote, together with the second chamber that represented the extraction of minerals. In Mann Borgese's system, the decision-making would require a simple majority of the first chamber plus the specialist secondary chamber.

Mann Borgese also introduced the concept of a maritime court before which nations and nation states – but also non-governmental and intergovernmental agencies and businesses – would be able to stand.[52] With the Maritime Assembly, the Maritime Commission and the Maritime Court, executive, legislative and judiciary powers were taken care of. Mann Borgese then added a twist to the traditional branches of governance by introducing something she called a Maritime Planning Agency.[53] This agency would 'take care of the problem of coordinating all the activities of the U.N. that are now dispersed'.[54] In her lecture, Mann Borgese did not explain the specific function of the Planning Agency any further, but its purpose and function are outlined in detail in the 1971 draft statute. In Article X, Section C. the agency's responsibilities and task are specified, saying that it shall:

> coordinate all efforts and projects presently undertaken by all organizations, within the U.N. system and outside, in the sphere of its competence; to prepare plans to maximize development and exploitation of living and non-living ocean resources and to ensure their conservation; to prepare a budget for the Regime; to redistribute revenue accruing to the Regime from fees, royalties, taxes or grants, and to take appropriate measures to protect developing Nations against the fluctuation of prices of minerals and metals, and in general, maximize the creation of wealth from the oceans while minimizing harmful interference with the interests of land-based industries and economies.[55]

Clearly 'The Ocean Regime' was not meant to divide up the different disciplines, to fracture management and coordination tasks, or to distribute responsibility between a number of different organisations. The goal was a holistic approach to ocean governance through the participation principle, held together by a 'Planning Agency'. In Mann Borgese's system, anyone who wanted to utilise ocean space would also take part in the governance of it. Hence the four, five or

52 *See* MS-2-744, Box 139, Folder 16, Lecture on the Ocean Regime by EMB.

53 *See* MS-2-744, Box 139, Folder 16, Lecture on the Ocean Regime by EMB.

54 MS-2-744, Box 139, Folder 16, Lecture on the Ocean Regime by EMB.

55 MS-2-744, Box 132, Folder 1, The Ocean Regime Draft Statute (Revised, February 1971), (Article X, C.).

eventually limitless number of chambers that would undertake the decision-making processes together with the first chamber of the nations. At the same time, the system was kept flexible by distributing responsibilities for different fields in ocean matters to different chambers. This meant it would be possible to let the relevant chamber of experts for a specific issue take part in the decision-making process, and that Mann Borgese's ocean regime would be flexible without being fragmented.

Elisabeth Mann Borgese concluded her lecture by pointing out four key advantages of her draft. First, that the 'Planning Agency' – specially designed for the ocean space – would 'solve functional problems',[56] and furthermore that:

> It would create a considerable amount of new wealth, by giving to enterprises a security for their investments without which technological development would inevitably slow down; and it would facilitate the redistribution of this wealth.[57]

Second, that the concept of 'nations' and all their sovereignty or whatever they had claimed sovereignty over would be preserved. No territorial or governing rights would have to be given up, since ocean space was uncharted territory. 'No iota of national sovereignty would be surrendered, but a new sovereignty would be created in a geographic and functional sphere which does not belong to any nation now'.[58] Her third point was that there would not need to be any revision of the UN Charter or other bodies of the UN. Instead, the ocean regime could shape new bodies of the UN member states. Mann Borgese argued that 'Their respective charters and statutes already contain enabling clauses under which they may set up committees, commissions, new organizations, and cooperate with these as the circumstances and the purpose set forth in these statutes or charters may require'.[59] Without this, the ocean regime would be 'utopian',[60] because changing the UN Charter would be too laborious to ever work out. Lastly, her fourth and final point was that the ocean regime would 'open new ways for the evolutionary transformation of the United Nations'.[61]

56 MS-2-744, Box 139, Folder 16, Lecture on the Ocean Regime by EMB.
57 MS-2-744, Box 139, Folder 16, Lecture on the Ocean Regime by EMB.
58 MS-2-744, Box 139, Folder 16, Lecture on the Ocean Regime by EMB.
59 MS-2-744, Box 139, Folder 16, Lecture on the Ocean Regime by EMB.
60 MS-2-744, Box 139, Folder 16, Lecture on the Ocean Regime by EMB.
61 MS-2-744, Box 139, Folder 16, Lecture on the Ocean Regime by EMB.

3 From Ocean Regime to World Regime?

Those present at *Pacem in Maribus* must have discussed the draft, and the various scientists, industry representatives, politicians and diplomats will have come up with amendments to Mann Borgese's ocean regime. Her revised 1971 draft statute is likely to have been the initial outcome of this. The point of the *Pacem in Maribus* convocation and the papers prepared for it – including 'The Ocean Regime' – was to somehow transport the concepts discussed at PIM to the United Nations. The question is, how did they make their way from one to the other? One matter that was discussed in the opening meeting of UNCLOS in Caracas in 1974 was the 'Draft Ocean Space Treaty'.[62] Officially, this was submitted by the Maltese delegation, but how much of it came from Elisabeth Mann Borgese's proposed ocean regime? Or was it a totally independent draft, developed by Arvid Pardo alone?

It is unlikely that this draft evolved entirely independently of Mann Borgese's work. Though handed in as a Maltese working paper, it was mostly written by Arvid Pardo, and was based on the ideas he had developed during 1967–8. By the time the draft was presented, he and Mann Borgese had already collaborated for three years, holding several workshops and four *Pacem in Maribus* conventions. Although we lack any correspondence between them showing how the discussions of different drafts and ideas unfolded,[63] we can nonetheless compare the Maltese proposal for an ocean space treaty with Mann Borgese's ocean regime paper. We can also assume that Pardo's proposed ocean space treaty must have been influenced by the *Pacem in Maribus* gatherings and their outcomes.

Arvid Pardo's letter to Salvino Busuttil in the late 1990s has already hinted at Pardo's take on Mann Borgese's ideas. He found her suggestion of applying the common heritage principle to the entire ocean space too radical. As we have seen, Mann Borgese's ultimate aim was to design an ocean regime that could eventually be expanded into a world regime, while Pardo was more focused on applying the principle of common heritage to the seafloor outside national jurisdiction. His hesitation to agree completely with Mann Borgese was also partly due to the fact that he was still working for the Maltese government. As a representative of Malta, Pardo was not acting in a personal capacity, and

62 United Nations General Assembly, 'Draft Ocean Space Treaty. Working paper submitted by Malta', A/AC.138/3. (23. August 1971), available at http://repository.un.org/handle/11176/167474.

63 To date no letters concerning their early collaboration could be found in either of the archives. It is likely they actually sat down together and discussed these things in person.

thus – as might be expected – the 'Draft Ocean Space Treaty' is more toned-down than Mann Borgese's 'The Ocean Regime'.

4 Arvid Pardo's Convictions and Visions for the Future

Prior to the *Pacem in Maribus* gatherings, Arvid Pardo had been vocal about his ideas concerning ocean governance. In October 1968, he published an article in the policy magazine *Foreign Affairs* with the title 'Who Will Control the Seabed'.[64] Just as Elisabeth Mann Borgese's 1969 lecture gives us deeper insights into her thoughts and intentions than those afforded by her draft of 'The Ocean Regime', so this article tells us more about Pardo's beliefs than the dry and technical 'Draft Ocean Space Treaty' can.

In the article, Pardo attempted to resolve the question posed in the headline, concluding with two possible answers as to who might control the seabed in the future. One was that 'only coastal States have the right to exploit the ocean floor [...]',[65] while the alternative, in Pardo's view, was that 'an international regime'[66] would be established. This, he thought, was only possible if the international community was willing to negotiate an appropriate treaty. Unlike Mann Borgese, who explored the composition of 'The Ocean Regime' in detail, Pardo did not drill down into how the regime he had in mind should be organised, but he did put forward a very detailed analysis of why ocean governance was both necessary and urgent. These arguments, as set out in the 1968 article, tell us a lot about Pardo's beliefs. It seems that Pardo's sense of urgency was fuelled by big adjectives concerning technological progress and invention. For example, he wrote that 'rapid technological progress has resulted in the discovery of vast mineral resources on and under the ocean floor [...]',[67] and that 'immense, untapped mineral resources exist on and under the ocean floor, [sic: though] some are likely to remain unexploited for the foreseeable future [...]'.[68] Pardo anticipated huge and possibly unforeseeable potential in these resources.

Although Pardo was careful not to sound too optimistic about technological progress – deliberately referring to conservative estimates that the Ad Hoc

64 Arvid Pardo, 'Who Will Control the Seabed?', *Foreign Affairs* 47, no. 1 (October 1968): pp.123–137.

65 Pardo, 'Who Will', 134.

66 Pardo, 'Who Will', 134.

67 Pardo, 'Who Will', 123.

68 Pardo, 'Who Will', 125.

Seabed Committee had made[69] – he pointed out that there were 'several indications that major breakthroughs may be imminent'.[70] This prediction was followed by a list of technological leaps made in recent years, like the increase in drilling depth from 359 feet (109 metres) to over 600 feet (183 metres),[71] or the construction of underwater vessels that could now reach down to 9,000 feet (2,740 metres) below sea level.[72] Clearly, Pardo had great confidence in the human ability to adapt, construct and invent. Which was made very clear by his next example – namely that 'it has been confidently predicted that by 1975 there will be colonies of aquanauts living and working on the ocean floor at depths in the neighborhood of 1,500 feet'.[73] Notions of these 'aquanauts', along with his idea of using dolphins as sheepdogs for fish,[74] neatly illustrate Pardo's ability to conjure up futuristic scenarios with a sense of imminence. While it was impossible to make such predictions with any degree of accuracy, nevertheless, put Pardo in front of an audience and he could inspire people with his florid language and futuristic optimism – as demonstrated during his 1967 speech, where he had already discussed much of what he wrote in the 1968 article. Even today, many of his scenarios remain to be realised. The sheepdog dolphins have not yet appeared and we are still waiting for hordes of aquanauts to colonise the plains of the seafloor.

Years later, in his obituary, Elisabeth Mann Borgese touched on Pardo's fascination with technological development – but also his clear-sightedness concerning the increasing importance of the utilisation of ocean space. Writing about how he had been criticised for his optimistic predictions, she asserted that 'his estimate was totally realistic. He was not talking about manganese nodules, to which UNCLOS III and the International Sea-bed Authority erroneously limited their attention. He was speaking of all known resources of the ocean floor […]'.[75] She also reported that 'During his later years, Pardo avidly followed every discovery, and every new technological development, all of which corroborated his earlier vision'.[76]

In his article, Pardo addressed another concern which could be solved by utilising marine and seafloor resources: that of the world's growing population

69 *Cf.* Pardo, 'Who Will', 125.

70 Pardo, 'Who Will', 125.

71 *Cf.* Pardo, 'Who Will', 125.

72 *Cf.* Pardo, 'Who Will', 126.

73 Pardo, 'Who Will', 126.

74 *See* A/C.1/PV.1515, 33.

75 MS-2-744, Box 345, Folder 4, Arvid Pardo, Retrospect and Prospects, 1999. Which is true, *see* Pardo, 'Who Will', 125.

76 MS-2-744, Box 345, Folder 4, Arvid Pardo, Retrospect and Prospects, 1999.

and its demand for resources of all kinds. He wrote that 'It is unlikely that the land alone will be able to provide for all the needs of mankind at acceptable cost; hence the vital importance of oceanic and suboceanic resources'.[77] In terms of economic interest, it was corporations that would be the driving force in exploring, inventing and possibly exploiting. But Pardo also identified governmental interest in the seafloor, and he was in no doubt that this would be mainly of a military nature.[78] He warned of an 'arms race in the sea neighborhood',[79] and stressed that 'vigorous action by the international community is becoming imperative in the interests of all'.[80] Such 'vigorous actions' could include establishing an 'ocean space treaty' that would oversee seabed and sea activities. Pardo designed the 'Draft Ocean Space Treaty' differently from Mann Borgese's 'The Ocean Regime', and it seems reasonable to view his ideas in the light of the beliefs and predictions he set out in his 1968 article. How exactly his own version of holistic ocean governance would look was presented to the Seabed Committee by Pardo himself in 1971.[81]

5 The Maltese 'Draft Ocean Space Treaty'

The treaty was marked as a working paper, and was submitted by Malta. The document had eighty-nine pages, and was separated into five parts. Part one was concerned with 'ocean space', part two with 'coastal state jurisdiction in ocean space', and part three with 'national ocean space'. Part four tackled 'international ocean space', and finally part five dealt with 'the international ocean space institutions'.[82] As with Elisabeth Mann Borgese's draft ocean regime, Arvid Pardo's treaty had undergone development at the *Pacem in Maribus* conferences. In this case it was *Pacem in Maribus* II, which was specifically about 'A Constitution for the Oceans'.[83] Pardo presented his draft to the gathering in Malta, most likely to test and discuss it before putting it forward to the Seabed Committee.[84]

77 Pardo, 'Who Will', 128.
78 *Cf.* Pardo, 'Who Will', 129.
79 Pardo, 'Who Will', 130.
80 Pardo, 'Who Will', 131.
81 *See* A/AC.138/53.
82 *See* A/AC.138/53, 3–4.
83 International Ocean Institute, *Pacem in Maribus.*
84 *See* J. Henry Glazer, 'The Maltese Initiatives within the United Nations – A Blue Planet Blueprint for Trans-National Space', *Ecology Law Quarterly* 4, no. 2 (1974): 291, https://www.jstor.org/stable/24111415.

A contemporary witness, Henry J Glazer, reported on the early PIM convocations[85] in the *Ecology Law Quarterly* in 1974, and he mentioned Pardo and Mann Borgese's draft proposals for ocean regimes. Apart from these documents, drafts from the US, the UK, Tanzania and France were also discussed, each expressing varying standpoints on the freedom of the sea and seabed utilisation.[86] Glazer describes the UK's draft as being on the 'opposing end of the spectrum'[87] to Arvid Pardo's treaty, since it:

> merely provides reinforcement for the proposition that each state on the planet is to be allocated its very own block of seabed [...] to be achieved through a physical division of the entire seabed on a global basis with a parcelling out of wet acreage among states signatory to a type of bizarre treaty which should properly be drafted by private real estate developers.[88]

Looking back at the initial Maltese vision for ocean governance, suggestions like this one from the UK had not been what Arvid Pardo had in mind when he gave his famous 1967 speech. The 'Draft Ocean Space Treaty', on the other hand, was an attempt to propose a form of governance for the ocean as a whole, as one entity – 'hydrospace' – rather than hacking it up into parts. Glazer also recorded some of the responses to Pardo's draft from other participants at PIM II:

> At PIM II Anatoly Kolodkin of the USSR discerned some useful and positive provisions in the ocean space treaty drafts of Pardo and Borgese (see note 58 supra) pointing out, however, as to the Pardo draft, as it then existed, certain conflicts between it and the U.N. charter [...].[89]

'[...] a draft treaty prepared by Arvid Pardo was circulated to participants at PIM II and became the focus of intensive discussion at the conference prior to its formal introduction into the United Nations'.

85 It is somewhat unclear how far the early PIM convocations were strictly about the topics their headlines suggested. Glazer argues that EMB's draft was discussed in PIM II, while I could find EMB's draft already discussed in the *Saturday Review* article, so she must previously have presented it at PIM I. Maybe she discussed an earlier version of it (the 1969 lecture or the 1970 version) and then presented the most recent 1971 version at PIM II.

86 *Cf.* Glazer, 'The Maltese Initiatives', 291.

87 Glazer, 'The Maltese Initiatives', 292.

88 Glazer, 'The Maltese Initiatives', 292.

89 U.N. GAOR Supp. 21, at II, 48 U.N. Doc. A/9021 (1973), quoted in Glazer 'The Maltese Initiatives', 292, footnote 52.

Arvid Pardo's draft was criticised for inflicting change on the UN charter – something Mann Borgese's draft was less likely to do, at least if we believe what she told her audience at the 1969 lecture. In fact, one of her main aims when she presented her own ocean regime was to keep the system flexible without having to change the UN charter.[90]

It is not possible to discuss the entire 'Draft Ocean Space Treaty' at length here. Pardo's draft covered a huge range of matters pertaining to ocean space, from 'navigation' to 'slavery, piracy and narcotic drugs', to 'submarines, pipelines'[91] and so forth. The first two parts of the treaty were 'mainly to update existing law of the sea as incorporated in the 1958 Geneva Convention on the Territorial Sea and in that relating to the High Seas within the framework of a comprehensive approach to ocean space'.[92] The most important parts of the drafted treaty when it came to the principle of the common heritage of mankind were Part 4 (with the common heritage of mankind (CHM)) and Part 5 (regulating freedom of ocean space for the exploitation of natural resources).[93] In these portions, Pardo introduced organisations he called 'International Ocean Space Institutions',[94] which were intended to be overarching transnational institutions with an 'international juridical personality',[95] and would oversee all kinds of activities in ocean space.[96] Among their most important purposes would be to 'Maintain international Law and order in ocean space',[97] to 'safeguard the quality of the marine environment',[98] to 'harmonize the actions of nations',[99] to 'encourage investigation',[100] to 'promote development and practical application of advanced technologies',[101] to 'provide assistance for Contracting Parties'[102] and to 'ensure the equitable sharing by all States in the benefits derived from the development of natural resources'.[103] In the terms of the treaty, every nation state that was part of the Law of the Sea could

90 *See* MS-2-744, Box 139, Folder 16, Lecture on the Ocean Regime by EMB.
91 For an overview of the content of the treaty, *see* A/AC.138/53, 3-4.
92 A/AC.138/53, 6.
93 *Cf.* A/AC.138/53, 46.
94 The International Ocean Space Institutions are not to be mistaken for the future International Ocean Institute.
95 A/AC.138/53, 47.
96 *See* A/AC.138/53, 47.
97 A/AC.138/53, 49.
98 A/AC.138/53, 49.
99 A/AC.138/53, 49.
100 A/AC.138/53, 49.
101 A/AC.138/53, 49.
102 A/AC.138/53, 49.
103 A/AC.138/53, 49.

be a member of these International Ocean Space Institutions, comprised of an assembly, an international maritime court and a secretariat.[104]

Pardo's draft divided the assembly into three member categories that were supposed to meet and discuss certain matters separately before meeting in the assembly. To be in category A, an institution would need to be a coastal state with more than ninety million inhabitants, or to have six out of nine qualities that would qualify them to be a category A member despite having less than ninety million inhabitants. Those qualities included, for instance, having a coastline longer than 5,000 kilometres, or being a state with a strong fishing, marine mineral or cable industry.[105] Category B would be comprised of all other coastal states, and category C of all non-coastal states.[106] Though the members of the different categories had equal rights in the assembly, there was a built-in inequality when it came to the council. All members of category A were supposed to be council members, but while there would be the same number of members from category B, there would only be five members from category C, who were the representatives of the non-coastal states.[107] This hierarchical categorisation reflected an argument Pardo had made back in his 1967 speech, which was that granting more power to coastal and industrial states would be important in securing the willingness of those states to cooperate at an international level.[108]

Henry Glazer wrote that Malta's treaty 'compels the adoption of a completely new and equitable international legal order of a broad institutional character for the whole of hydrospace rather than just a regime and machinery applicable to the seabed beyond national jurisdiction'.[109] Meaning that what made the Maltese treaty special was the fact that Pardo had tried to cover all hydrospace or ocean space within it, not just the seabed. Glazer added that comparisons of drafts similar to the 'Draft Ocean Space Treaty' had been made by others in 1974.[110] According to Glazer, what set the Maltese Treaty apart was that the Maltese idea of a holistic hydrospace was in agreement with 'positions and admonitions of scientists and marine environmentalists who continue to plead their case that no matter what is decided in 1974 at Caracas,

---

104 *Cf.* A/AC.138/53, 51.

105 In more detail, *see* A/AC.138/53, 55–56.

106 *Cf.* A/AC.138/53, 56.

107 *Cf.* A/AC.138/53, 60.

108 *Cf.* Pardo presents this view in the 1967 speech and later in the article. *See* A/C.1/PV.1515; *see also* Arvid Pardo, 'Who Will'.

109 Glazer, 'The Maltese Initiatives', 292.

110 *See* Glazer, 'The Maltese Initiatives', 294.

the entire ecology of the planet will still not arrange itself into neat national compartments'.[111] This comment was directed at other draft treaties that were mainly focused on how to divide the ocean and ocean floor up into different blocks of territory, which could be exploited and utilised under the regime of the respective coastal state. Certainly, not all states taking part in the negotiations were interested in a 'strong operational international machinery'.[112] The United Kingdom, for instance, advocated a minimum of interference from international organs.[113] As a side note, concern about the environment is not entirely absent in Pardo's treaty. Chapter XXV of the draft treaty has a section about 'maintenance of the ecological integrity of International Ocean Space', which is concerned with contamination of ocean space.[114]

Although the tasks of the International Ocean Space Institutions were intricately described in the draft, Pardo's treaty lacked detailed information around the exploitation of natural resources. Elisabeth Mann Borgese argued in 1999 that keeping the draft clear of too many instructions based on estimates and predictions of future inventions had been intentional. She believed that one of the main 'mistakes'[115] later made at UNCLOS III concerning the seafloor provisions had been that they had turned out 'practically inapplicable'[116] because of the 'Over-burdening of the Convention with administrative and even fiscal detail'[117] without knowing the technological realities in which the treaty would be tested in the future. In a footnote to Pardo's 1999 obituary, Elisabeth Mann Borgese quotes the former president of UNCLOS, the late Shirley Amerasinghe, who, according to Mann Borgese, had said shortly before his own death in 1980, 'had we paid attention to Arvid's draft in 1971, we might have spared ourselves ten years of work'.[118]

Both Elisabeth Mann Borgese and Arvid Pardo had prepared draft treaties in 1970 and 1971 that took a 'holistic approach' to ocean governance. What differentiated them from one another was their level of emphasis on the common heritage principle, and the scope of their ambition. While both proposed designing 'international machinery'[119] with the task of overseeing ocean activities, those agencies had different potential across the two drafts. In Mann

111 Glazer, 'The Maltese Initiatives', 293.
112 Glazer, 'The Maltese Initiatives', 291.
113 *Cf.* Glazer, 'The Maltese Initiatives', 292.
114 *Cf.* A/AC.138/53, 71.
115 MS-2-744, Box 345, Folder 4, Arvid Pardo, Retrospect and Prospects, 1999.
116 MS-2-744, Box 345, Folder 4, Arvid Pardo, Retrospect and Prospects, 1999.
117 MS-2-744, Box 345, Folder 4, Arvid Pardo, Retrospect and Prospects, 1999.
118 MS-2-744, Box 345, Folder 4, Arvid Pardo, Retrospect and Prospects, 1999.
119 Like it was asked for in GA Res 2750 (XXV). B. 6.

Borgese's draft, this agency was the Planning Agency. It was designed in a way that would make it easy to develop it further into an agency overseeing world governance, with the potential to broaden the application of the common heritage principle to the high seas, not just the seabed outside national jurisdiction. Arvid Pardo's International Ocean Space Institutions, on the other hand, were only designed to oversee ocean governance. Despite what Pardo said in hindsight, the common heritage principle in the Maltese draft was also applied to what he called 'international ocean space', by which he meant all ocean space outside national jurisdiction. In Pardo's case, though, the question of what exactly lay outside national jurisdiction was not answered, meaning that it would be left to further negotiations to define this. The 'holistic approach' of Arvid Pardo's draft would become a major stumbling block for the Maltese in the lead-up to the UNCLOS negotiations.

CHAPTER 6

Rise and Decline of Headquarters

1 Malta's Struggle for Direction

By the time the Maltese delegation sat down around the negotiating table during the first session in New York in 1973 and the second in Caracas in 1974, Arvid Pardo – their figurehead in ocean matters – was no longer among them.[1] Throughout UNCLOS, he would be present only in a peripheral capacity, since he had lost his political influence on the Maltese government before the convention even started. How had this happened? Arvid Pardo had not planned on being sidelined when he first started to engage in ocean matters on Malta's behalf. On 18 October 1968, Pardo had written to the Secretary of the Ministry of Commonwealth and Foreign Affairs about Malta's role in the new Law of the Sea: 'If Malta is to maintain her leadership in marine matters, it is essential for Government to submit a draft treaty at the U.N.: Seabed Committee session which opens on 19th July'.[2]

At first, it was Pardo's 'Draft Ocean Space Treaty' that the Maltese delegation presented to the Seabed Committee, but this document was quickly set aside.[3] Most likely, Malta was shouted down by other countries that had absolutely no interest in a 'holistic approach' to governing the ocean and establishing 'International Ocean Space Institutions'. The Maltese government would later claim that they could not keep pushing a treaty that had not even attracted the support of developing countries, and that their relationships with these developing countries had started to become 'embarrassing'.[4]

Malta's representatives changed their tune several times over the years between 1971 and 1975. One reason was the change in government, which meant a change in the dominant political personalities when the Labour Party

1 Maltese Delegation *see* A/CONF.62/INF.3/Rev.1, 40: 'H.E. Mr. Joseph Attard Kingswell, Ambassador Extraordinary and Plenipotentiary Permanent Representative to the United Nations (head of Delegation), Mr. Alfred Bellizzi, First Counsellor Deputy Permanent Representative to the United Nations, Mr. Carmel Vella, Second Secretary, Permanent Mission to the United Nations'.

2 PR-Box: Personal Correspondences & Materials, letter from Arvid Pardo to Secretary Ministry of Commonwealth, 18. October 1968, appendix 'C'.

3 *See* Glazer, 'The Maltese Initiatives', 291.

4 MS-2-744, Box 62, Folder 8, Seabed Authority Centre, *Times of Malta*, 29 May 1975.

leader, Dom Mintoff, became Malta's new prime minister in 1971.[5] Another likely factor could have been Malta's changing alliances during the discussions at the United Nations. Though Malta was keen to take a leading role, at the same time it was a tiny nation state that was not prepared to stick its neck out unless it was assured of gathering enough support. Dropping the 'Draft Ocean Space Treaty' was the first demonstration of Malta's indecisiveness.

Ambassador Joseph Attard Kingswell took over from Arvid Pardo as the new head of the Maltese delegation at the United Nations. At first, it seemed like he intended to continue his predecessor's work. In the General Assembly's 1965th Plenary Meeting on Wednesday 13 October 1971, he said of the 'Draft Ocean Space Treaty' that:

> the Government of Malta continues to take a keen and lively interest in the work which the Committee on the Peaceful Uses of the Sea-Bed and the Ocean Floor beyond the Limits of National Jurisdiction is doing in preparation for a conference on the law of the sea, scheduled to take place, we hope, in 1973.[6]

A year later, on 10 October 1972, Kingswell's tone had changed. This time, when he spoke at the General Assembly about Malta's position on the 'Draft Ocean Space Treaty', the Maltese ambassador did so in very different terms:

> One of the items on the agenda of the present session concerns a review of the Charter of the United Nations [item 89]; my delegation is aware of the strong feelings aroused in many quarters by this item, and, to be quite frank, we do not believe that the time is ripe for the Charter to be profitably amended.[7]

Malta had beaten a quick retreat from their bold vision to revolutionise ocean space. Instead, the country would keep a low profile at the ensuing meetings,

5 *Cf. Encyclopaedia Britannica*, s.v. 'Dom Mintoff', accessed 30 September 2021, https://www.britannica.com/biography/Dom-Mintoff.

6 A/PV.1965, 94.

7 A/PV.2061, 242. Malta's hesitation is not broadly discussed in literature about Malta's initiative. *See* Tuerk, 'The Thirtieth Anniversary', 19. However, Borg comments on the Maltese shortcoming in Borg, *Malta and the Law*, 73: 'When his [sic: Pardo's] connection with Malta was discontinued, it was a loss both for Malta and for the U.N. Nobody filled his absence at UNCLOS and one can only conjecture what the final version of the convention would have looked like if he had continued to lead the Malta delegation'.

until the 'international machinery' to oversee activity in the area outside national jurisdiction had been reduced to something that would later be known as the International Seabed Authority.[8] The initial idea of 'International Ocean Space Institutions' – as proposed by Pardo – was discarded. What is more, the idea of gathering together all matters of activity on ocean space under one umbrella (as Mann Borgese had intended with her proposed Planning Agency) had by then been narrowed in scope to the seafloor outside national jurisdiction. It was only then, in autumn 1974, that Malta suddenly came forward wanting to host the International Seabed Authority.[9] The Maltese, represented by the head of their delegation, Alfred Bellizzi,[10] made this announcement in the General Assembly on 9 October 1974:

> my Government feels that it is no longer premature to consider the location of the proposed International Sea-Bed Authority, and it has accordingly made know its decision to offer Malta as the site for the Authority's headquarters. In announcing this offer, my Government believes that many members of the international community would like to associate Malta in the most appropriate way with the tangible and lasting results which will have emerged from the Maltese initiative of 1967.[11]

Playing on the historical importance of Arvid Pardo's speech was a clever move, but it came too late. Jamaica had handed in its application before Malta, and had been able to gather major support from the developing countries.[12] Malta, in contrast, had hesitated too long, and through this delay it had lost both time and momentum. Elisabeth Mann Borgese, who had been working towards establishing an international institution on Malta since 1971, wrote in a telegram to Attard Kingswell in November 1974: 'Our position with regard to the Law of Sea Conference and headquarters rapidly deteriorating immediate action needed I hope you will be able to follow up on suggestions discussed on October 23'.[13] Her

8 The exact date when the authority was called the 'International Seabed Authority' is uncertain. It seems like several proposals were discussed: International Ocean Institutions, Planning Agency.

9 For the statement of the Maltese delegate Mr. Bellizzi, *see* A/PV.2263, 209.

10 *See* delegation A/CONF.62/INF.3/Rev.1, 40.

11 A/PV.2263, 209.

12 *Cf.* MS-2-744, Box 210, Folder 14, Malta and the International Seabed Authority, *The Sunday Times*, 31. May 1981.

13 MS-2-744, Box 94, Folder 1, Telegram EMB to Attard Kingswell, 4 November 1974.

telegram was in vain, however, and in 1981, the International Seabed Authority would finally go to Jamaica.[14]

Years later, the Maltese ambassador Saviour F Borg wrote an article called '30 Years of UNCLOS, Malta's Contribution to the Process: Past and Present'. In it, he touched on Malta's efforts at UNCLOS III, and especially on their ambitions to host the International Seabed Authority.

> The greatest efforts made by the Delegation of Malta during UNCLOS III to obtain the support of the participants for Malta to host the seat of the Authority cannot be underestimated even though at a certain point of time, especially in the first years of the Conference, it relinquished its leadership in this regard.[15]

Malta's seemingly abrupt change of direction in 1971, and its subsequent about-turn in 1975, had a back story. Behind the scenes there had been heated discussions, as Elisabeth Mann Borgese worked intensely to steer Malta one way, while the new prime minister, Dom Mintoff, pulled the wheel in the opposite direction.

2 Dom Mintoff – A Stumbling Block for Elisabeth Mann Borgese and Arvid Pardo?

In a collection of private photographs belonging to Arvid Pardo, there is a picture of a couple of men in black ties and suits posing together. Someone has drawn devil horns on one of the men, and the short, black-haired man in question appears to be Dom Mintoff, Malta's prime minister from 1971–84.[16] On the reverse of the photo, someone has written 'Margot added horns'.[17] Margot was Arvid Pardo's wife, and if she was defacing photos of the Maltese prime minister with devil horns, it was probably because he had caused Arvid Pardo a great deal of trouble in the years between 1971 and 1974. Dom Mintoff engaged

14 Maltese newspaper reports on the loss of the authority: MS-2-744, Box 210, Folder 14, Leo Brincat, Loss of Seabed Authority Site Gross inaccuracies by Opposition, *Daily News*, 25 August 1981; MS-2-744, Box 210, Folder 14, Local reaction to Malta's defeat in vote for I.S.A. site, *Sunday Times*, 23 August 81.

15 Saviour Borg, '30 Years of UNCLOS. Malta's Contribution to the Process: Past and Present', speech at *UNCLOS at 30 Seminar* organised by International Ocean Institute and the University of Malta, 23 November 2012: 3. (copy: courtesy of Saviour Borg).

16 PR-Box: Photographs

17 PR-Box: Photographs

in an intense quarrel with Arvid Pardo and Elisabeth Mann Borgese that would eventually lead to Pardo's dismissal as ambassador.

In a 1972 article from the *New York Times*, Mintoff is described as a 'Loner on a Small Island'.[18] According to the journalist, Paul Hofmann, Mintoff was known to be 'erratic', 'dictatorial, tactless and rude'.[19] Hofmann added that 'Even the Prime Minister's supporters concede that he is secretive and unpredictable, but, an admirer said, "he has charisma" '.[20] In an article in *The Guardian* published in January 1973, the journalist Richard Gott reflected on Mintoff's political achievements after almost two years in office.[21] In the article, Mintoff is described as a 'maverick'[22] who advocated 'Malta for the Maltese'[23] while at the same time having to navigate larger power struggles. At one point, the article quoted Mintoff directly: ' "For a small nation to keep its freedom," Mintoff explains, "it's important to balance the interests of big nations and to see that one neutralizes the other" '.[24] This political style might have kept the government under Mintoff from being too bold in their statements concerning the 'Draft Ocean Space Treaty' and Malta's position in the discussions.

In 1971, when Pardo's services in the Maltese delegation were no longer required, some of those who had followed Malta's initiative closely were rather puzzled, as 'Ironically, the hero-figure of UNCLOS III reforms was left on the touchlines as an observer when the famous conference began officially in December 1973'.[25] For anyone familiar with the Law of the Sea Convention but without in-depth knowledge of the detailed political background, the fact that the person widely referred to as the 'father of the Law of the Sea' was sidelined by their own government would seem odd. The Maltese government's peculiar way of treating the future legend of the convention can be understood either

18 MS-2-744, Box 52, Folder 9, Paul Hofmann, Loner on a Small Island, *The New York Times*, 12 January 1972.

19 MS-2-744, Box 52, Folder 9, Paul Hofmann, Loner on a Small Island, *The New York Times*, 12 January 1972.

20 MS-2-744, Box 52, Folder 9, Paul Hofmann, Loner on a Small Island, *The New York Times*, 12 January 1972.

21 *See* MS-2-744, Box 52, Folder 9, Richard Gott, Mintoff the maverick, *The Guardian*, 27 January 1973.

22 MS-2-744, Box 52, Folder 9, Richard Gott, Mintoff the maverick, *The Guardian*, 27 January 1973.

23 MS-2-744, Box 52, Folder 9, Richard Gott, Mintoff the maverick, *The Guardian*, 27 January 1973.

24 MS-2-744, Box 52, Folder 9, Richard Gott, Mintoff the maverick, *The Guardian*, 27 January 1973.

25 Douglas Johnston, *The Historical Foundations of World Order. The Tower and the Arena* (Boston/Leiden: Martinus Nijhoff, 2007), 58.

as an internal political move or as a necessary expedient to keep Malta on good terms with countries opposed to his holistic approach.

The government considered reintroducing Arvid Pardo in 1975 to help obtain the International Seabed Authority – once the authority had been reduced to a smaller, more specialised institution. Legal historian Douglas Johnston has argued that 'Arvid Pardo refused to sulk in his tent, remaining deeply involved in the great debate on all issues negotiated at UNCLOS III'[26] while also noting that it 'was no secret that he was frustrated by his inability to participate inside the arena, especially when it became clear that much of his vision would be sacrificed to the need for compromises'.[27]

3 Arvid Pardo's Demotion from Ambassador to Seabed Delegate

Arvid Pardo was demoted in two steps. Firstly, with the change of government in 1971, he was removed from his job as head of the Maltese delegation. This did not seem a particularly dramatic development at that time, given that he would keep his position as ambassador in a slightly different form, and would remain involved with the Seabed Committee.[28] Around the time Arvid Pardo's dismissal was being discussed, Elisabeth Mann Borgese met the politician who would later remove Pardo from office, and described him in a letter to her daughter, Nica Borgese. In the letter, dated 14 July 1971, she reported on the 'peaceful revolution' that had taken place in Malta.[29] Mann Borgese seemed content enough with the change of government, reporting that:

> The old Prime Minister was an operetta figure, the new one is a human being, and we got along just fine. […] he opened the Convocation, and it all went very well. […] Financially, it was far less catastrophic than anticipated. We are going to have another Convocation next year, and are setting up the Institute at the University. So, it all is growing, and I cannot complain.[30]

26 Johnston, *Historical Foundations,* 58.

27 Johnston, *Historical Foundations,* 58.

28 Pardo continued to work for a sub-committee at the Seabed Committee until 1973: *See* MS-2-744, Box 108, Folder 1, Permanent Mission of Malta to the United Nations, Statement Delivered by Ambassador Arvid Pardo in Sub-Committee III, 14 March 1973. *See also* PR-Box: Personal Correspondences & Materials, Tony Loftas, Pardo, politics and pollution, *New Scientist and Science Journal*, 8. July 1971.

29 EMB B4 Mann Borgese, 14.07.1971.

30 EMB B4 Mann Borgese, 14.07.1971.

Clearly, she was optimistic despite the change of government. The prime minister had shown willingness to collaborate, and it seemed like the country's new leader did not oppose plans to establish an 'Institute'[31] at the University of Malta that would coordinate further *Pacem in Maribus* convocations.

Interestingly, while Arvid Pardo had been dropped from the Maltese delegation, there were prospects of a new government role. It seemed like Dom Mintoff had no immediate plans to exclude Arvid Pardo completely from all government matters, and this is borne out by a letter to Mintoff that Pardo wrote after *Pacem in Maribus* II on 7 July 1971. In the letter, he discusses his possible role in the new government, and poses the question of how he could 'serve Malta at the United Nations while at the same time not dealing with some political questions, such as the question of China [...]'.[32] This remark about China provides an interesting piece of the puzzle as to why Arvid Pardo had to be removed from the Maltese delegation. Dom Mintoff was keen to forge good relations with the People's Republic of China, in order to distance himself from Malta's former colonial ties with the British government. In 1972, he made an official visit to Peking, where he said in his official speech:

> The people of Malta are just now finding their independence, after many hundreds of years in the service of foreign dominators, after participating in many wars out of which my people won only tears, blood and hunger. The people of Malta, like the people of China, have known at first hand and only recently the bitter humiliations of colonialism and long years of life without dignity. [33]

This was a direct swipe at the British colonial dominance on Malta that had persisted to some extent during the early years of independence. It might be recalled that Arvid Pardo had said in a newspaper article in 1965, right after he came to office, that the Maltese government 'still had ties to Britain'.[34] This might have made it a question of political expediency more than personal

31 The *Pacem in Maribus* Institute was the start of what would later be the International Ocean Institute. It changed its name through the years. First it was conceived as a Mediterranean institute, then as the headquarters of an ocean regime (later reduced to the ISA) all of which was not obtained by EMB and Malta.

32 PR-Box: Personal Correspondences & Materials, Arvid Pardo to the Prime Minister, Appendix 'A', 7 July 1971. Malta and the question of China, *see* Prime Minister Mintoff of Malta Welcomed in China, *Peking Review* 14, April 7, 1972, https://www.marxists.org/subject/china/peking-review/1972/PR1972-14.pdf.

33 Mintoff, *Peking Review*, 8.

34 *Cf.* Daniell, 'Malta Assigns Rare Diplomat', 30.

inclination that Pardo should be removed from the front lines of Mintoff's socialist government. Arvid Pardo's own comment on China in the letter to Mintoff makes it clear that he was aware of this fact. Instead of pleading to stay in the delegation, Pardo asked Mintoff to appoint him as:

> a special adviser (or consultant) to the Government of Malta, with the rank of Ambassador, to deal with such problems as the Governments might wish [...], such as the questions of the Oceans, of the biosphere, of old age, new problems raised by technology, or disarmament matters.[35]

Arvid Pardo concluded his letter by confidently pointing out his expertise in such matters, 'which is not elsewhere available in Malta'.[36] This wish of Pardo's to be appointed as a 'special adviser' to the government on specific issues was granted.

Outside Malta, Arvid Pardo's dismissal from the Maltese delegation to the United Nations gave rise to some astonishment. On 8 July 1971, an article with the headline 'Pardo, politics and pollution' was published in the *New Scientist and Science Journal*, reporting on Pardo's dismissal by Dom Mintoff. 'One of the less publicized actions of Dom Mintoff, Malta's new leader', the article stated, 'has been the dismissal of Dr Arvid Pardo, head of the country's Permanent mission to the United Nations'.[37] The writer in the *New Scientist and Science Journal* added that 'Unfortunately, in the eyes of Malta's socialist eagle, Dr Pardo apparently ranked as a political appointee to be purged with the rest'.[38] This meant that the opening ceremony of *Pacem in Maribus* II, which convened on Malta between 29 June and 5 July 1971, unfolded 'with an air of embarrassment',[39] since Arvid Pardo – who had been one of the key organisers – had suddenly lost some of his official importance as head of the Maltese delegation. The journalist Tony Loftas reported on the atmosphere at the opening ceremony, recounting that:

35 PR-Box: Personal Correspondences & Materials, Arvid Pardo to the Prime Minister, Appendix 'A', 7 July 1971.

36 PR-Box: Personal Correspondences & Materials, Arvid Pardo to the Prime Minister, Appendix 'A', 7 July 1971.

37 PR-Box: Personal Correspondences & Materials, Tony Loftas, Pardo, politics and pollution, *New Scientist and Science Journal*, 8. July 1971.

38 PR-Box: Personal Correspondences & Materials, Tony Loftas, Pardo, politics and pollution, *New Scientist and Science Journal*, 8. July 1971.

39 PR-Box: Personal Correspondences & Materials, Tony Loftas, Pardo, politics and pollution, *New Scientist and Science Journal*, 8. July 1971.

> bold tributes were made and the applause came loud from the attending delegates. But the fact remained that Dr Pardo had been deprived of the forum, the UN, that he treasured most. And Malta had chosen to shun a man who had shown that a small nation can have a positive role in providing vital socially-conscious rallying calls within the UN system.[40]

Regardless of how Tony Loftas felt about Pardo's dismissal as head of the Maltese delegation, it is unlikely that this was a major concern for Elisabeth Mann Borgese or Arvid Pardo himself in July 1971. Pardo had not been 'shunned',[41] rather he had gained a different position – albeit not one with quite the status of being head of the Maltese delegation to the United Nations. That political change would prompt some changes of position was to be expected, especially since Pardo had worked for the previous government. For the time being, Pardo continued as 'Malta's representative in regard to the peaceful uses of the seabed',[42] although he lost his immediate influence at the Maltese delegation in New York.

4 Big Plans for Malta – Establishing the International Ocean Institute

Elisabeth Mann Borgese's campaign to help Malta gain the 'international machinery' that was intended to oversee activities in the area outside national jurisdiction accelerated at *Pacem in Maribus* II in 1971. Now that Pardo had lost his platform, there was some uncertainty about the extent to which the 'Draft Ocean Space Treaty' would be altered by the time Malta presented it at the forthcoming UNCLOS negotiations.[43] Perhaps in an attempt to rescue the initiative, another interesting proposal was made. Loftas reported a discussion about setting up a so-called 'Mediterranean Council'[44] or 'Mediterranean Institute'[45] that would be able to present the treaty in its original form at the United Nations. The plan was to base this enterprise in Malta.

40 PR-Box: Personal Correspondences & Materials, Tony Loftas, Pardo, politics and pollution, *New Scientist and Science Journal*, 8. July 1971.

41 PR-Box: Personal Correspondences & Materials, Tony Loftas, Pardo, politics and pollution, *New Scientist and Science Journal*, 8. July 1971.

42 MS-2-744, Box 52, Folder 9, Governor-General to EMB, 28 July 1971.

43 *Cf.* PR-Box: Personal Correspondences & Materials, Tony Loftas, Pardo, politics and pollution, *New Scientist and Science Journal*, 8. July 1971.

44 *Cf.* PR-Box: Personal Correspondences & Materials, Tony Loftas, Pardo, politics and pollution, *New Scientist and Science Journal*, 8. July 1971.

45 *Cf.* PR-Box: Personal Correspondences & Materials, Tony Loftas, Pardo, politics and pollution, *New Scientist and Science Journal*, 8. July 1971.

It seems likely that this peculiar 'institute' or 'council' was a precursor to the 'international machinery' for the ocean regime that Mann Borgese intended to establish in Malta. It is important to note here that she used various different terms to refer to this organisation. In her letters to the Maltese government, she called it the 'headquarters of the new ocean regime',[46] while if we look at her draft of 'The Ocean Regime', such an organisation would be what she had called the Planning Agency.[47] Loftas mentioned a third name when he reported that 'Elizabeth Mann Borgese, chief architect of the *Pacem in Maribus* meetings, claims that she has found three major institutions interested in helping the Mediterranean Institute during its formative years'.[48] The reason differing terms were in circulation might have been that this 'international machinery' was still evolving, and was being designed and adapted along the way. Perhaps Mann Borgese did not yet have a clear understanding of why exactly the institute should be established, other than some sort of wider vision that it could potentially become an 'international machinery' for governing the ocean regime as a whole.

A letter from Elisabeth Mann Borgese to Dom Mintoff dated 14 August 1971 demonstrates how she attempted to lobby for the establishment of such an organisation.[49] In the letter, she described a chance meeting with a journalist from the *New York Times*. The journalist, it seemed, had become extremely interested in Malta's case for hosting the 'headquarters of the new ocean regime'.[50] For all we know, this 'accidental' meeting might have been completely fabricated, but on the other hand, it could easily have been true. It was perfectly possible that Elisabeth Mann Borgese could have provoked the journalist's interest in the story with her infectious enthusiasm, and the exact circumstances of the meeting do not really matter in the grand scheme of things. The main point here is the way Mann Borgese presented this meeting to the prime minister. Her goals, it seems, were twofold. First, if a publication like the *New York Times* was going to report on Malta's potential interest in providing the 'headquarters of the new ocean regime', a necessary first step would be for Malta to publicly broadcast its interest in such an undertaking. Second, the spectre of an investigating journalist could put some pressure on the indecisive prime minister to take a stance one way or the other, forcing him to signal

46 *See* MS-2-744, Box 52, Folder 9, EMB to Mintoff, 14 August 1971.

47 *Cf.* MS-2-744, Box 132, Folder 1, The Ocean Regime Draft Statute (Revised February 1971).

48 PR-Box: Personal Correspondences & Materials, Tony Loftas, Pardo, politics and pollution, *New Scientist and Science Journal*, 8. July 1971.

49 *See* MS-2-744, Box 52, Folder 9, EMB to Mintoff, 14 August 1971.

50 MS-2-744, Box 52, Folder 9, EMB to Mintoff, 14 August 1971.

to the world whether Malta was interested or not. In this way, Elisabeth Mann Borgese could find out what the government actually wanted, and could pressure Mintoff into taking a public position.[51]

The 'Ocean Regime Headquarters' discussions also marked another important beginning, as Elisabeth Mann Borgese started to seek funding to set this institute up. She had a financing plan all prepared, which she presented to the prime minister in a letter in October 1971. The plan involved the Maltese government making an application for a United Nations Development Programme (UNDP) grant, which would then finance the initial years of a pilot project that would be 'carried out by the *Pacem in Maribus* Institute at the University of Malta'.[52] In this funding document, Mann Borgese had casually introduced another name for her organisation: the '*Pacem in Maribus* Institute'.[53] Though the names varied, Elisabeth Mann Borgese's ambitious plans for the institute were clear: 'The Institute has a tremendous potential for expansion and development. If Malta should become the Headquarters of the international ocean regime, here is a precise and concrete beginning'.[54] This comment proves the scale of her ambition. These plans she had to establish an institute on Malta were ultimately intended to mark the starting point for an international institution or headquarters overseeing the 'international ocean regime'.

Unfortunately, the prime minister was hesitant to seize the day, in spite of Mann Borgese's exhortations to make a 'precise and concrete beginning'. It fell on deaf ears when she argued that 'The world owes Malta a great deal for having initiated the U.N. quest for an international ocean regime. We are working hard to get the international community to pay this debt to Malta by making it the headquarters of the new regime'.[55] It is likely that she enclosed the '*Pacem in Maribus* Institute Draft Budget 1972–1974'[56] when she wrote to Mintoff, and this shows just how far her plans for the institute had already evolved even in 1971. In autumn 1971, several letters flew back and forth between Elisabeth Mann Borgese and the prime minister on the issue of establishing the institute and finding funding, without anything ever becoming more concrete. Mann Borgese referred to governmental interest in the issue when she wrote that 'Both you yourself, Mr. Prime Minister, and Mr. Buttigieg indicated to me your

51 *See* the letter MS-2-744, Box 52, Folder 9, EMB to Mintoff, 14 August 1971.MS 52-9 (p 27) EMB letter to Mintoff August 14, 1971.

52 MS-2-744, Box 52, Folder 9, EMB to Mintoff, 13 October 1971.

53 MS-2-744, Box 52, Folder 9, EMB to Mintoff, 13 October 1971.

54 MS-2-744, Box 52, Folder 9, EMB to Mintoff, 13 October 1971.

55 MS-2-744, Box 52, Folder 9, EMB to Mintoff, 13 October 1971.

56 MS-2-744, Box 52, Folder 9, EMB to Mintoff, 13 October 1971.

strong interest in having a U.N. Specialized Agency or equivalent established in Malta as early as possible'.[57] Apparently, Malta was interested in hosting an institution, but unfortunately we do not know in what form it hoped to do this, or why the government was hesitant to support Mann Borgese's attempts to establish it. At first, the tangible financial plans[58] that she had provided were met with some interest. Mintoff replied in an undated telegram about the funding issue saying: 'Hope you will agree that the maximum we can do is to finance a director some equipment and other small items'.[59] But by the time Mintoff's next telegram turned up, things had already gone downhill: 'Worried about turn of events regarding the setting up of oceanographic institute[60] [...] funds over and above what Malta gets for the other activities regret not to forward proposal stop please inform Pardo Hoffmann accordingly'.[61]

Despite the Maltese government's hesitation to help fund the indefinitely named institute,[62] in 1972 Mann Borgese succeeded in founding an 'independent, international, nongovernmental, nonprofit organization headquartered at the University of Malta'.[63] The organisation was called the International Ocean Institute (IOI).[64] While the name should not be confused with the 'International Ocean Space Institutions' from Arvid Pardo's 'Draft Ocean Space Treaty', we can speculate that the final decision on the institute's title was perhaps influenced by Pardo's proposal. This becomes increasingly plausible when we consider the ambitious plans Mann Borgese had for the institute. It is likely that Mann Borgese managed to get some funding from the Maltese government after all. In a newspaper article in 1973, Mintoff was reported to have said that his government had aided the International Ocean Institute, and had set

57 MS-2-744, Box 52, Folder 9, EMB to Mintoff, 20 October 1971.

58 *See* letter about UNDP and government: MS-2-744, Box 52, Folder 9, EMB to Mintoff, 8 November 1971.

59 MS-2-744, Box 52, Folder 9, Telegram Mintoff to EMB, undated. It was likely the answer to the letter of 8 November 1971.

60 Mintoff meant the IOI idea – we know this because Pardo and Hoffman were those who EMB had been discussing the funding question with. Hoffman had made EMB aware of the fact that she could apply for funds.

61 MS-2-744, Box 52, Folder 9, Telegram Mintoff to EMB, undated.

62 Mintoff introduces the name 'oceanographic institute' – there was most likely confusion not only about the name but also about the function of such an institution. We can see this in MS-2-744, Box 210, Folder 14, Impact, Translation from IN-Nazzjon Taghna, 18 March 1975. After having lost the ISA, EMB had said: 'The most important thing however that Malta could do would be to promote the setting up of the "Ocean Space Authority" since this is even better than the "International Seabed Authority"'.

63 MS-2-744, Box 398, Folder 15, International Ocean Institute – Past, Present and Future.

64 *Cf.* MS-2-744, Box 398, Folder 15, International Ocean Institute – Past, Present and Future.

aside funds to help it organise research in the region.[65] From Mintoff's statement, we learn that Mann Borgese had managed to achieve at least part of her ambition for the institute on Malta. The government had helped establish the institute, but in the official version of events, it had been set up to aid research in the region, not to become the headquarters of a future ocean regime.

Mann Borgese and Mintoff used different terms to refer to the institute in their letters. Names like '*Pacem in Maribus* Institute', 'Mediterranean institute', 'headquarters of the ocean regime' and even 'oceanographic institute' were used interchangeably. Although it is very likely that this confusion over names was due to the fact that there was some disagreement over the form and function of the institution, we cannot completely rule out the possibility that some of the ideas discussed were intended to be separate from one another. However, it is likely that Mann Borgese saw the institute as the 'precise and concrete beginning' of an institute based in Malta with the long-term goal of becoming the 'headquarters of the international ocean regime' – regardless of its eventual name.

5 Dreaming about the Headquarters of the Ocean Regime on Malta

With the International Ocean Institute in place, Elisabeth Mann Borgese had established her own personal headquarters on Malta, from which she could work towards her mission of transforming the IOI into a central organisation in the Law of the Sea. The discussions of how and whether the Maltese government should engage politically with the process of turning the IOI into the 'headquarters of the new ocean regime' continued throughout 1972 and 1973. The issue became more pressing the closer it got to the second UNCLOS session at Caracas, which was scheduled for December 1973. Mann Borgese had foreseen that other countries might show interest in hosting such a prestigious United Nations institution, and she wanted Malta to have it.

Mann Borgese was not alone in her efforts. In fact, Pardo – who in 1972 was still engaged in the Seabed Committee on behalf of the Maltese government – had sent out a memorandum to the Maltese government and ambassador Attard Kingswell. We learn this in a letter from Mann Borgese to the prime minister, sent in early 1973, where she writes that:

65 *Cf.* MS-2-744, Box 94, Folder 1, Borg Olivier, Malta's interest in Caracas conference on Law of the Sea, *Times of Malta*, 23 July 1973.

> In this memorandum he [sic: Pardo] set forth proposals and recommendations which, although we developed our thinking on this subject independently from each other, are remarkably close to those I made to you and the Governor General.[66]

The discussions had now turned from establishing a starting point for the ocean regime headquarters – in the form of the IOI – to how the official headquarters themselves could be obtained. Of course, it was not up to the Maltese government or Elisabeth Mann Borgese to decide whether Malta would be chosen to host the 'international machinery' for the ocean regime. Their application, if they were to present one, had to be approved by all parties to the Law of the Sea Convention, and in order to obtain this approval, detailed plans had to put forward.

Elisabeth Mann Borgese had worked up detailed and practical drafts of how to design such headquarters. In the letter presenting her proposal to Dom Mintoff, she spoke in specific terms, talking about the form of the organisation, the arguments that could be put forward to gain it for Malta, and the strategies the Maltese government should use to achieve this goal.[67] Regarding the form of the institution, Mann Borgese presented two possible options. It could end up being a small institution dealing only with seabed matters, or a larger one responsible for all ocean space. Of these, she believed the latter to be the more likely outcome in 1973, at least if we trust her judgement. She reported that 'Current discussions at the U.N. [...] seem to indicate quite clearly a shift from a narrow concept to a far wider concept of ocean space institutions. This trend was triggered off by the introduction of the Maltese Ocean-space Draft Treaty in August, 1971'.[68]

Clearly, between 1971 and 1973 the scope of the institute Mann Borgese had in mind had changed. It had gone well beyond the concept of a kind of collaborative Mediterranean institute that would be able to present Pardo's 'Draft Ocean Space Treaty' at the United Nations, and Mann Borgese was now presenting practical ideas of how 'ocean space institutions' should be organised. In her letter to Mintoff in 1973, Mann Borgese laid out a proposed structure for the larger version of the institute, and detailed the requirements for the host country. She mentioned secretariats for: 'oceanic mining',[69] 'management

---

66 MS-2-744. Box 84, Folder 12, EMB to Mintoff, 17 January 1973.

67 *Cf.* MS-2-744. Box 84, Folder 12, EMB to Mintoff, 17 January 1973.

68 MS-2-744. Box 84, Folder 12, EMB to Mintoff, 17 January 1973. EMB was probably exaggerating to convince Mintoff.

69 MS-2-744. Box 84, Folder 12, EMB to Mintoff, 17 January 1973.

of living resources',[70] 'shipping and communication',[71] and 'management for international scientific research',[72] all of which were very similar to the ideas for organising a potential international regime into different chambers that she had proposed back in her draft of 'The Ocean Regime' in 1970. Concerning the geographical location, Mann Borgese presented arguments as to why Malta would be well-suited, noting that 'the institutions must be located in a maritime site offering port and dock facilities. Among maritime sites, the Mediterranean offers the most concentrated confluence of communications and cultures [...]'[73] Regarding the island state's political standing, Mann Borgese argued that 'Malta is, politically as well as economically and culturally, a natural mediator between developed and developing nations'.[74] Another argument was the 'historical consideration', in which she emphasised the role of ambassador Pardo and his address at the United Nations in 1967.[75]

Elisabeth Mann Borgese also outlined the financial advantages for Malta of hosting the institutes: '(1) direct inflow of currency and (2) a considerable impulse toward development'.[76] At the same time, she was aware of the fact that hosting a United Nations institution could become a financial burden for smaller countries. Therefore, she presented another solution: 'In the case of a small and developing nation such as Malta (or Kenya) agreements should be such that there is a direct financial benefit. Thus the institutions should pay a rental'.[77] She also attached a detailed plan for 'immediate and long-range steps'[78] that would help Malta achieve the goal of hosting the institute, This included participating in all kinds of conferences and gatherings, and appointing a 'Secretary for Ocean Affairs'[79] along with a group of experts. Finally, she did her best to include the IOI – which by then had been established with United Nations Development Programme funds and money from the Ford Foundation – in the process, stating that 'The Secretary for Ocean Affairs should work in close cooperation with the International Ocean Institute and avail himself of its documentation and files'.[80] In effect, Mann Borgese had

70 MS-2-744. Box 84, Folder 12, EMB to Mintoff, 17 January 1973.
71 MS-2-744. Box 84, Folder 12, EMB to Mintoff, 17 January 1973.
72 MS-2-744. Box 84, Folder 12, EMB to Mintoff, 17 January 1973.
73 MS-2-744. Box 84, Folder 12, EMB to Mintoff, 17 January 1973.
74 MS-2-744. Box 84, Folder 12, EMB to Mintoff, 17 January 1973.
75 *See* MS-2-744. Box 84, Folder 12, EMB to Mintoff, 17 January 1973.
76 MS-2-744. Box 84, Folder 12, EMB to Mintoff, 17 January 1973.
77 MS-2-744. Box 84, Folder 12, EMB to Mintoff, 17 January 1973.
78 MS-2-744. Box 84, Folder 12, EMB to Mintoff, 17 January 1973.
79 MS-2-744. Box 84, Folder 12, EMB to Mintoff, 17 January 1973.
80 MS-2-744. Box 84, Folder 12, EMB to Mintoff, 17 January 1973.

drawn up a detailed formula for 'how to obtain a United Nations institution for the government of Malta',[81] and had basically done the Maltese government's job for them. In theory, all the government had to do was follow her step-by-step guide. Yet even with the master-plan in hand, and the justifications and arguments gathered together for them, they refused to do so. In fact, quite the opposite was about to occur. Over the course of 1973 and *Pacem in Maribus* III and IV, the plan for a Maltese HQ crumbled, together with the goodwill for Arvid Pardo's work on the Seabed Committee.

In summer 1973, the Maltese government publicly admitted its reluctance to host an international authority. In a newspaper article in the *Times of Malta*, the prime minister was asked by a parliamentary representative about Malta's plans for the international authority. Mintoff answered that:

> no decision has yet been taken in Caracas about the setting up of an international authority on the sea-bed. [...] I can state that the Maltese Government has long ago noted that these developments are a long way away. So much so that efforts were made to have in Malta at least an Institute of Marine Research for this region. To achieve this aim Malta dedicated a substantial part of the aid for two years received from the United Nations Development Programme to help the International Ocean Institute – responsible for the coordination of work by all the members of Pacem in Maribus so that this regional research may be carried out in Malta.[82]

Mintoff's newspaper statement suggested that the government had funded the IOI just to 'coordinate' issues, and not to be the seed of something that would later be transformed into the future seabed authority. The IOI was left hanging in thin air. Instead of putting all their efforts into preparing for the International Ocean Institute to be transformed into the headquarters of the ocean regime, the Maltese government wavered. Either the Maltese thought they still had plenty of time since 'developments were a long way away',[83] or they felt they needed to test the waters at the United Nations further, since not all developing nations were agreed on the matter.

81 MS-2-744. Box 84, Folder 12, EMB to Mintoff, 17 January 1973.

82 MS-2-744, Box 94, Folder 1, Borg Olivier, Malta's interest in Caracas conference on Law of the Sea, *Times of Malta*, 23 July 1973.

83 MS-2-744, Box 94, Folder 1, Borg Olivier, Malta's interest in Caracas conference on Law of the Sea, *Times of Malta*, 23 July 1973.

In an exchange of letters between Mann Borgese and Mintoff (undated but most likely from the second half of 1973)[84] we can sense a sudden shift in tone. Instead of promoting practical plans for Malta's next steps in obtaining the ocean regime headquarters, Mann Borgese wrote to Mintoff, 'What I am REALLY concerned about is Malta which I love as much as you do and whose achievements during these last few years have filled me with pride, as though I were a Maltese'.[85] It seems likely that political considerations – probably tensions between developed and developing nations and some clashes of interest – lay at the root of the Maltese government's caution, and Mann Borgese's attempts to persuade the prime minister point towards this interpretation. She wrote, 'Contrary to the impression you may have had, the developing nations have a vital interest in the establishment of a new type of international system for the ocean [...]'.[86] She claimed that the problem was with the superpowers rather than the developing nations, since they were 'blocking progress with their surrealist dreams of annexing half the world's oceans'.[87] To try and convince the Maltese government to take a strong stance on ocean governance issues, she argued that 'they all – and that includes China![88] – want a strong international machinery: strong enough so that it cannot be dominated by the big powers'.[89]

The 'strong international machinery' she spoke of would be located in the headquarters of the ocean regime, and Elisabeth Mann Borgese was still keen to pursue the goal of bringing this to Malta, despite the fact that the prime minister had put the brakes on. The situation must have been enormously frustrating for her, especially since it seemed like the time would soon be ripe to achieve her aim:

> And now that under Malta's leadership we have won the first round, and the Conference is actually going to start, you want to pull out? If you really do, it is a tragedy of the first magnitude. Not so much for the world (although it is a sad loss for the world) as for Malta itself which, at the very last moment, is forfeiting its hard earned first place in this struggle.[90]

---

84 We find this in a handwritten draft with a note that says it is addressed to Mintoff. We cannot know if he read it. *See* MS-2-744, Box 84, Folder 12, EMB draft Mintoff, undated (likely 1973).

85 MS-2-744, Box 84, Folder 12, EMB draft Mintoff, undated.

86 MS-2-744, Box 84, Folder 12, EMB draft Mintoff, undated.

87 MS-2-744, Box 84, Folder 12, EMB draft Mintoff, undated.

88 China was politically very important for the socialist government of Malta. EMB wanted to emphasise that China was on their side.

89 MS-2-744, Box 84, Folder 12, EMB draft Mintoff, undated.

90 MS-2-744, Box 84, Folder 12, EMB draft Mintoff, undated.

Along with the Maltese government's desire to 'pull out', it seemed that the island state's leading figure, Arvid Pardo, was going to be pulled out too. Having already lost his seat in the Maltese delegation in 1971, he was now about to lose his involvement in the Seabed Committee as well, and Mann Borgese was harshly critical of this decision in her letter: 'The price you have to pay for keeping Dr. Pardo in the Seabed Committee (whose work during the next eight weeks in Geneva is of crucial importance) and in the Law of the Sea Conference is really piddling'.[91]

6 Review of Networks and Re-Grouping to Face UNCLOS III

As Elisabeth Mann Borgese became increasingly frustrated with the Maltese government, her home base at the Center for the Study of Democratic Institutions in Santa Barbara was beginning to fall apart. She had not been successful in mobilising general support for her ocean project, beyond getting some support with the first *Pacem in Maribus* conference. The centre's official involvement with *Pacem in Maribus* had finished back in 1970 after PIM I. In the 'Summary Remarks' of the convocation in Malta in July 1970, Harry Ashmore wrote that the centre's 'primary role'[92] in *Pacem in Maribus* ended with the first convocation, and that they stood 'ready to pass on the title'.[93] He also promised to provide the 'considerable body of material [...], to a continuing international group' and that the Center for the Study of Democratic Institutions would be 'available to assist in the effort to locate acceptable financial support for such an undertaking, and to use our offices to guarantee its independence of any national, private or ideological interest'.[94] This statement closed the book on Mann Borgese's vision for the centre. Making the deep sea and the oceans the main topic for the research fellows in Santa Barbara was no longer an option. A year earlier, in 1969, the fellows had already discussed the issue, and one fellow had stated in a memorandum:

91 MS-2-744, Box 84, Folder 12, EMB draft Mintoff, undated.
92 MS-2-744, Box 120, Folder 25, Summary Remarks *Pacem in Maribus* Convocation, 3 July 1970.
93 MS-2-744, Box 120, Folder 25, Summary Remarks *Pacem in Maribus* Convocation, 3 July 1970.
94 MS-2-744, Box 120, Folder 25, Summary Remarks *Pacem in Maribus* Convocation, 3 July 1970.

> I think the Deep Seas is an important subject and problem. I do not think that the deep seas is either sufficiently important or inherently rich in the problematic sense to warrant the imperialist claims now being advanced for it so far as other important Center studies are concerned.[95]

Thus, Elisabeth Mann Borgese's 'imperialistic claims'[96] were sidelined. This meant she had to move on and find another platform from which she could engage in the development of ocean governance. As we have seen, she continued working with Pardo and carried on with the PIM conferences, raising money independently[97] and successfully founding the IOI on Malta – with the purpose of contributing to the Seabed Committee's ongoing discussions, and in an attempt to lay the cornerstone for a future 'international authority' overseeing the ocean regime. Although the Center for the Study of Democratic Institutions at large was not involved in any major way in the subsequent PIM conferences, Mann Borgese continued to be employed by it until 1978.[98] Even in 1974, however, the future of the centre in Santa Barbara was already looking bleak.

In June 1974, The *New York Times* published an article about the centre with the headline: 'Center for Study of Democratic Institutions Has a New Chief and a Fiscal Crisis'.[99] The article was prompted by the fact that Malcom C Moos had taken over Robert M Hutchins's position that same year.[100] Hutchins had been battling ill-health for a while and was finally unable to continue his work. The change in leadership and Hutchins's health issues meant the *New York Times* saw fit to report on the uncertain future of the centre, stating that 'While seeking immortality, the center is running out of money, and intimations of mortality contend with the hope that something may turn up'.[101] The article quoted several fellows who had been asked about their thoughts on the matter. One fellow, John Wilkinson said: '"We've been drifting. […] Everybody made an

---

95 MS-2-733, Box 43, Folder 46, Center Memorandum, 12 February 1969.

96 MS-2-733, Box 43, Folder 46, Center Memorandum, 12 February 1969.

97 How exactly EMB funded and organized PIM is almost as complex as the question of IOI foundation or any kind of funding. The issue is difficult to research because there was private money and EMB's use of connections involved.

98 *See* MS-2-744, Box 16, Folder 19, EMB CV.

99 MS-2-744, Box 85, Folder 17, Israel Shenker, The Center for the Study of Democratic Institutions Has New Chief and a Fiscal Crisis, *The New York Times*, 5 June 1974.

100 MS-2-744, Box 85, Folder 17, Israel Shenker, The Center for the Study of Democratic Institutions Has New Chief and a Fiscal Crisis, *The New York Times*, 5 June 1974.

101 MS-2-744, Box 85, Folder 17, Israel Shenker, The Center for the Study of Democratic Institutions Has New Chief and a Fiscal Crisis, *The New York Times*, 5 June 1974.

itinerary taking him away for long periods, and found a focus and locus outside the center. How could people think when they were above a cloud?" '[102] Another fellow, Harvey Wheeler, who had worked on *Pacem in Maribus*, suggested that Hutchins's style of leadership might have been behind their recent struggles, explaining that the centre was 'a bureaucratization of Hutchinson [sic], an extension of his personality – and he's a strong and compelling person with a piercing mind and an alarming ability to see behind social facades'.[103] Harvey Wheeler told the newspaper, 'It's Hutchin's [sic] Center'.[104] Alexander King told the *New York Times*, 'I am very disappointed with the dialogue. It's too inbred ... incestuous'.[105] He was probably hinting at the ivory tower style of research at the centre, where fellows did not make much of an effort to reach a wider audience with their publications and findings.

Elisabeth Mann Borgese, too, was interviewed for the article. Her verdict was fairly damning: 'The group is pretty polarized [...] There are those who are trying to do something – not just be intelligent, and those who feel they have to be cynical and revel in destructiveness and pessimism and get a kick out of it'.[106] Perhaps her comment was a jab at those who had opposed her ambitious ideas, but in some respects she may have been right. With her plans to engage with the Seabed Committee and questions of ocean governance, she had tried to step outside what King had called the 'incestuous'[107] atmosphere of the centre, and those fellows who had been reluctant to support her may well have been as destructive and pessimistic as she claimed. Ultimately, it is possible that the Center for the Study of Democratic Institutions really had missed out on a chance to gain and retain importance when it decided to drop the ocean question. However, there was also the separate issue of funding, and this had been problematic even when Hutchins still worked there. If it truly was 'Hutchins's Center', then it was going to be even harder to keep it going

102 MS-2-744, Box 85, Folder 17, Israel Shenker, The Center for the Study of Democratic Institutions Has New Chief and a Fiscal Crisis, *The New York Times*, 5 June 1974.

103 MS-2-744, Box 85, Folder 17, Israel Shenker, The Center for the Study of Democratic Institutions Has New Chief and a Fiscal Crisis, *The New York Times*, 5 June 1974.

104 MS-2-744, Box 85, Folder 17, Israel Shenker, The Center for the Study of Democratic Institutions Has New Chief and a Fiscal Crisis, *The New York Times*, 5 June 1974.

105 MS-2-744, Box 85, Folder 17, Israel Shenker, The Center for the Study of Democratic Institutions Has New Chief and a Fiscal Crisis, *The New York Times*, 5 June 1974.

106 MS-2-744, Box 85, Folder 17, Israel Shenker, The Center for the Study of Democratic Institutions Has New Chief and a Fiscal Crisis, *The New York Times*, 5 June 1974.

107 MS-2-744, Box 85, Folder 17, Israel Shenker, The Center for the Study of Democratic Institutions Has New Chief and a Fiscal Crisis, *The New York Times*, 5 June 1974.

without him at the helm.[108] When it came to the centre's reluctance to commit resources to further *Pacem in Maribus* conferences, we also have to bear in mind that it still had two more *Pacem in Terris* convocations to organise – one in 1973 and the last one in 1975 – with up to 3,000 participants attending each gathering.[109] Therefore, it is not surprising that the fellows were disinclined to take on the organisation of another mammoth project on top of the *Pacem in Terris* conferences.

In 1974, Mann Borgese wrote to one of her daughters about the situation at the centre. 'Life is hectic as always. I love the new house. The dogs are fine. The Center is going to hell in a bucket. The oceans are very much alive and keep me on my toes [...]'.[110] In a letter to her mother, Katia Mann, we learn how busy she must have been at the time. Mann Borgese reported travelling to Washington to meet 'the father of the oceans',[111] journeying to New York to attend an energy conference, and that she planned to go straight on from there to Malta to attend a meeting of the Board of Trustees of the International Ocean Institute.[112] She was proud to tell her mother that the IOI – her own project – had been referred to by the media as 'the most influential nongovernmental institute on ocean affairs'.[113]

Because of her 'most influential' institute, Elisabeth Mann Borgese had become one of those fellows in Santa Barbara that existed mostly 'above the clouds'.[114] Instead of relying on the centre in Santa Barbara for support in organising subsequent conferences on ocean governance, she had established the International Ocean Institute on Malta in 1972 and was busy developing it into an operational centre for her work towards a new Law of the Sea. Despite her frustrations with the Center for the Study of Democratic Institutions in

108 Milton Mayer writes about Hutchins's reduced capacity due to illness and refers to the same article in Mayer, *Robert Maynard Hutchins,* 492–493.

109 *See* Mayer, *Robert Maynard Hutchins,* 482: 'Two more *Pacem* convocations were held. One took place in October of 1973 in Washington, attended by three thousand people, who heard Henry Kissinger and William Fulbright in a knock-down, drag-out debate on American foreign policy. The concluding *Pacem in Terris IV* in Washington in December of 1975, was attended by two thousand people. The four conferences, while they produced both notice and income, also produced additional dissatisfaction among the Fellows of the Center, many of whom felt that the Hutchins-Ashmore impresario ventures, successful as they were, were diverting the Center from its appointed task: the dialogue'.

110 EMB B4 Mann Borgese, 15 November 1974.

111 B.III.17-Mann-126, 15.11.1974. 'Vater der Ozeane'

112 *Cf.* B.III.17-Mann-126, 15.11.1974.

113 B.III.17-Mann-126, 15.11.1974.

114 MS-2-744, Box 85, Folder 17, Israel Shenker, The Center for the Study of Democratic Institutions Has New Chief and a Fiscal Crisis, *The New York Times,* 5 June 1974.

1974, the fact remained that since 1967 it had served her well. It had been a platform from which she could organise the *Pacem in Maribus* I conference and a place where important people could meet and exchange ideas. As a centre fellow, Elisabeth Mann Borgese had the necessary official recognition and institutional backing to be taken seriously, and without the centre behind her, it is questionable whether Arvid Pardo would ever have got involved with her work.

From her first engagement with ocean governance in 1967, as she moved through the successful preparation conferences and towards the foundation of the IOI in 1972, Mann Borgese had been establishing a wide network of contacts. Her work organising successive PIM convocations and establishing the IOI on Malta put her in touch with important policy-makers, many of whom were involved in high-level discussions on ocean governance and the Seabed Committee. All of this was achieved with the backing of the centre, and in this regard it was very valuable to her. Through her fellowship in Santa Barbara, Mann Borgese also became involved with the Club of Rome, an international think tank which she was invited to join around 1970 (the exact date and circumstances are a matter of debate).[115] According to Mann Borgese's own recollections, the club's founder, Aurelio Peccei, had visited Santa Barbara to present his plans for establishing the Club of Rome, and it was here that he met Elisabeth Mann Borgese and she introduced him to ocean questions.[116] Apparently, they had realised that their missions were related. The Club of Rome published its most famous report, *The Limits to Growth*[117] in 1972, and this dealt primarily with the increasing scarcity of resources in the face of human expansion. The issue of resource scarcity was tied in with the seabed question, though when Mann Borgese was later asked about her assessment of the report, she stated that she had not considered resource scarcity as the most pressing issue at that time.[118] The Club of Rome's mission was closely related to that of Mann Borgese and her allies in the run-up to UNCLOS III. The club was enquiring into questions that troubled the world, exploring future challenges and possible solutions. Thus, it was not surprising that Mann Borgese was already in contact with the Club of Rome even in the early years of her engagement with the oceans. How important her membership of this organisation

115 Wolfgang Clemens, 'Meereskundliche Weltliteratur. Elisabeth Mann Borgese und der Club of Rome', in *Elisabeth Mann Borgese und das Drama der Meere*, exhibition catalogue, eds. Holger Pils and Karolina Kühn (Hamburg: mareverlag, 2012), 100.

116 *Cf.* Hermann, ed., *Die Meer Frau*, 34.

117 Donella H. Meadows, Dennis L. Meadows, Jørgen Randers and William W. Behrends III, *The Limits to Growth* (New York: Universe Books, 1972).

118 *Cf.* Clemens, 'Meereskundliche Weltliteratur', 100.

was in terms of her ocean engagement is hard to assess. Her first and only report to the Club of Rome would not be published until 1984,[119] when 'The Future of the Oceans' would discuss future challenges of ocean governance in the light of the new Law of the Sea.[120]

In 1973, however, Mann Borgese was mostly interested in bringing the Maltese government's ideas of the role it would play during UNCLOS III into line with her own plans for the country's involvement. While she had been able to establish a useful network of contacts through Santa Barbara, the PIM conferences and the IOI on Malta, she would struggle to influence the negotiations at the United Nations without the full support of the Maltese government for a holistic ocean regime. As the first UNCLOS session in New York approached in 1973, the suspense mounted. The Maltese were hesitant about diving head-first into the conference with Arvid Pardo leading the way, and on this occasion it was not due to Dom Mintoff's 'maverick' attitudes. In fact, it reflected a much bigger international conflict

119 Clemens, 'Meereskundliche Weltliteratur', 100.

120 More about EMB's work with the Club of Rome in Clemens, 'Meereskundliche Weltliteratur', 100.

PART 3

Negotiating the Law of the Sea 1973–82

CHAPTER 7

UNCLOS III – Haves against Have-Nots

1 The World Order Complicates Ocean Governance Negotiations

Some have branded the Law of the Sea negotiations at the United Nations an affair of 'haves against have-nots'.[1] Others have used milder language by calling the discussion 'polarized'.[2] When the negotiations finally started in 1973,[3] no one anticipated that ahead lay nearly a decade of laborious discussion, negotiation, bickering, shifts in direction, risky trade-offs, disputes, deadlocks, alliances, secret group meetings and endless scheming. We must not forget that the United Nations in the 1970s was a microcosm of world politics. Apart from the disagreements on ocean matters, there were larger political animosities to overcome or at least consider. Casting the longest shadow of all was the Cold War, a conflict which represented not just the division between east and west but also an atomic threat that loomed over the whole world. It would be a challenge to negotiate a common ocean governance policy involving the US and the USSR without poking that bear, but surprisingly enough, it was not impossible. In fact, the Cold War backdrop may even have helped the UNCLOS negotiations sidestep some of the larger potential obstacles, since states were more willing to seek compromise rather than risk sparking a conflict that could easily blow up into an atomic world crisis.

There were other issues in play at the negotiations, some even bigger than the conflict between east and west. Ironically, industrialised coastal states in the geographical north often had similar interests concerning the Law of the Sea, whichever side of the ideological divide they lay on. For instance, both

1 MS-2-744, Box 125, Folder 2, Brucan Save the Seas and the Oceans for Mankind.

2 Mahmoudi calls the discussion at UNCLOS until 1976 'polarized'. *Cf.* Mahmoudi, *The Law of*, 180–181.

3 'Procedural History', United Nations Audiovisual Library of International Law, accessed 30 September 2021, http://legal.un.org/avl/ha/uncls/uncls.html. *See* 'On 18 December 1972, having considered the report on the Committee's work during its 1972 sessions (A/8721 and Corr.1), the General Assembly requested the Secretary-General to convene the first session of the Third United Nations Conference on the Law of the Sea in 1973 to deal with organizational matters, and a second session in 1974, as well as subsequent sessions if necessary, to deal with substantive work (resolution 3029 (XXVII)). The Committee submitted its final report to the General Assembly at its twenty-eighth session, in 1973 (A/9021 and Corr.1 and 3)'.

the United States and the Soviet Union wanted a narrow territorial zone, ever mindful of the mysterious underwater vehicles with which they might be able to spy on one another. There were other nations, though, who posed fresh challenges: the newly independent colonies of the so-called 'third world'.[4] Many former colonies had gained independence after World War II. These young states were eager to shape world politics, and the United Nations was the only arena in which they could do so. The reason was simple: at the UN, majority was power. Though the United States and the former European colonists had a unique standing in world affairs, the sheer quantity of new states meant they could simply outnumber them. If these new states were able to form alliances and close ranks, they could have a chance of overruling the former imperial states.[5]

The industrial states feared the rise of the developing countries, and with good reason. These nations had already started working together, and were formulating their own take on the common heritage principle. When the First United Nations Conference on Trade and Development[6] (UNCTAD I) convened in 1964, there was an informal interest group, comprised of seventy-five member states, that was working for the interest of developing countries. It had been established in the previous year to prepare for UNCTAD, and had worked on a resolution called 'Joint Declaration of the Developing Countries'.[7] During UNCTAD I, three states joined the group, New Zealand left it, and the group was henceforth known as the Group of 77.[8] Nations in the group had differing interests, there were some unstable governments on board and the group

4 During the Cold War, the term 'third world' was used widely. Today the term is outdated and its use is inappropriate. It promotes a hierarchy that has its roots in colonial times. In the 1960s the term stood for all countries that were former colonies, most of them in the global south, many of which joined the Group of 77. The terms 'third world' and 'developing country' were used interchangeably, and this is also reflected in the archival material.

5 *Cf.* Edward L. Miles, 'The Structure and Effects of the Decision Process in the Seabed Committee and the Third United Nations Conference on the Law of the Sea', International Organization 31, no. 2 (1977): 177, https://www.jstor.org/stable/2706403.

6 For an overview article about UNCTAD I, II and III (1964 – 1972) *see* Bernardo P. Nun, 'UNCTAD', Lawyer of the Americas 4, no 3 (October 1972): 449–459, http://www.jstor.org/stable/40175626.

7 Carol Geldart and Peter Lyon, 'The Group of 77: A Perspective View', *International Affairs (Royal Institute of International Affairs 1944-)* 57, no. 1 (1980–1981): 85, http://www.jstor.org/stable/2619360. For more UNCTAD documents Geldart and Lyon refer to A.G. Moss and Harry N.M. Winton compilers, *A New International Economic Order. Selected Documents 1945–1975* (New York: UNITAR Document Service No. 1, 1976): 16–19.

8 *Cf.* Geldart and Lyon, 'Group of 77', 85.

lacked coordination skills,[9] but it had the potential to tip the scales based on sheer numbers alone.

The developing nations had also started to use the principle of the common heritage of mankind applied to the seafloor to try and promote the so-called New International Economic Order (NIEO).[10] This was based on the argument that decolonisation had not truly released the former colonies from their one-time masters. Although the developing countries were now politically independent, the former colonists still possessed all the economic and technological advantages.[11] Advocates of the NIEO argued that the principles the international community was built on promoted injustice in the world.[12] They called for cooperation through the exchange of technological knowledge and a new, international law that could help close the gap between developed and developing countries.[13] These ambitions to revolutionise not only ocean governance but also the world economic order were clearly on a collision course with the private, industrial interests of the developed nations, and tensions began to bubble up right from the start of UNCLOS III, as the nations discussed how to shape the decision-making process.

Originally, the first session in New York on 3–5 December 1973 was supposed to draw up the rules of procedure, but the potential for discord soon became apparent. The gathering could not reach an agreement and had to carry the issue over into the second session that gathered in Caracas in the summer of 1974.[14] However, participants at the first session did at least succeed in electing a president – Hamilton Shirley Amerasinghe from Sri Lanka, who had served as president of the Seabed Committee.[15] The Canadian journalist and contemporary witness Clyde Sanger described the first president of UNCLOS III in glowing terms as a well-respected man of integrity and impartiality.[16] Sanger reported of Amerasinghe's leadership style that he:

---

9 For some of the Group of 77 issues during UNCLOS, *see* Miles, 'Preparations for UNCLOS IV?', 427.

10 Monica Allen discusses this in Allen, 'An Intellectual History'. 64. Allen refers to Jagdish N. Bhagwati, ed, *The New international Economic Order: The North south debate* (Cambridge MA: The MIT Press, 1977), 4.

11 *See* Chircop, 'Elisabeth Mann Borgese's humanist conception', 114: 'It is virtually impossible to understand the development of the international law of the sea [...] without an appreciation of the technological forces that shaped and re-shaped ocean policy'.

12 *See* U.N. G.A., Res. 3201, quoted in Allen, 'An Intellectual History', 65.

13 *Cf.* Allen, 'An Intellectual History', 64–65.

14 *See* Miles, 'Structure and Effects', 183.

15 A/CONF.62/SR.1. 1st plenary meeting, Monday, 3 December 1973, at 4.15 p.m.

16 *Cf.* Sanger, *Ordering the Oceans*, 41–42.

> never tried to be an expert on all subjects, but instead concentrated on the broad picture and tried to bring pressure at a high level. He was not afraid of taking personal initiatives. When he thought it necessary, he would call delegates, whether from the big powers or the Group of 77, into his office to rap knuckles or to knock heads together.[17]

Amerasinghe's appointment was good news for Elisabeth Mann Borgese and her involvement with UNCLOS. Not only was he the former president of the Seabed Committee, he was also the president of the board of trustees for the International Ocean Institute on Malta[18] and had participated in several PIM conferences. He and Mann Borgese were on first-name terms,[19] and now he was president of the convention – a role he would occupy until his sudden death in 1980.[20] Apparently, Mann Borgese had managed to mix with the right people prior to the conference.[21]

The first and second sessions discussed the rules of procedure for the negotiation process, and the outcome was 'convention breaking'.[22] This was because, after a long struggle, it was decreed that the Law of the Sea would be negotiated by consensus, not voting.[23] The rules of procedure were later referred to as a 'Gentlemen's Agreement'.[24] This meant that the participating states had to agree on everything, paragraph by paragraph.[25] Only if no consensus could be reached were the delegates allowed to vote. Even the question of the necessary majority in the case of such severe disagreements was a source of discord. The president, Hamilton Shirley Amerasinghe, got his first chance to prove his consensus-seeking skills when he proposed a new rule for these sorts of cases in Caracas in 1974. Rule 64 stated that 'decisions of the Conference on all matters of substance, including adoption of the final Convention, would be by two-thirds of those present and voting provided this amounted to at least

17 Sanger, *Ordering the Oceans,* 41–42.

18 MS-2-744, Box 398, Folder 15, International Ocean Institute – Past, Present and Future.

19 *Cf.* MS-2-744, Box 114, Folder 8, Karl Wolf to EMB, 4 December 1980.

20 *See* MS-2-744, Box 114, Folder 8, Karl Wolf to EMB, 4 December 1980.

21 Baker also refers to this in 'Uncommon Heritage'.

22 Miles, 'Structure and Effects', 180.

23 *Cf.* Miles, 'Structure and Effects', 183. The rules were adopted 27 June. For a discussion on the relevance of consensus seeking and its role during UNCLOS, *see* Barry Buzan, 'Negotiating by Consensus: Developments in Technique at the United Nations Conference on the Law of the sea', The American Journal of International Law 75, no. 2 (April 1981): 324–348, http://www.jstor.org/stable/2201255.

24 Bernaerts, *Bernaerts' Guide,* 8.

25 For more details on the discussion on how to reach an agreement, *see* Miles, 'Structure and Effects', 181–183.

a majority of Conference participants'.[26] If the participants of the convention had agreed on a voting system – as had been the case for both UNCLOS I and II – decision-making would have been speedier.[27]

Delegates would have been able to bring their drafts to the negotiation table and the assembly would simply vote for or against them. In such a scenario, though, the Group of 77 would have had a clear advantage, with 77 members (a number which grew during UNCLOS) out of a total of 160 participating states.[28] Agreement by consensus would be more time-consuming, but would also tip the balance once again in favour of the developed states.

That the consensus system ended up being used was, of course, no coincidence. The developed states were not willing to let up-and-coming ex-colonies take hold of the power by outnumbering them. To prevent this from happening, the developed states made it clear that they would never commit to even discussing a convention that was built on a voting system.[29] The Group of 77 could have dug their heels in and insisted on a voting system, but the outcome would have been devastating. This would have been a 'Pyrrhic victory for the Group of 77'.[30] No developed state would have ratified the convention, and many would probably not even have been willing to sit down at the negotiating table. Since participation in the convention was not compulsory, the only way to get the entire international community on board was to change the procedure. In fact, the developed states displayed a distinct sense of cynicism towards the former colonies and their eagerness to shape decision-making in the international arena. At the time, the general attitude of industrial states towards developing states was that:

---

26 Miles, 'Structure and Effects', 183.

27 On the decision-making process, *see* Harrison, *Making the Law,* 40–41: 'Attended by 86 States, the Conference organized itself in five main committees and a plenary, and followed rules of procedure similar to those of the United Nations General Assembly, so that while provisions could be adopted in one of the committees by simple majority, a two-thirds majority was required when the provision reached the plenary. This procedural rule made it impossible to agree on the breadth of the territorial sea'. *See also* Treves, '1958 Geneva Conventions'.

28 *Cf.* Harrison, *Making the Law*, 39. Full list in the Final Act.

29 On the issue of consensus seeking, *see* Sanger, *Ordering the Oceans*, 36–37. *See also* Buzan, 'Negotiating by Consensus', 329: 'The most likely source of resistance to consensus procedure comes from those states who see advantage in the present form of majority voting. Under present conditions, this logic points towards the Group of 77, many of whose members are weak states reliant on combined voting power as one of their principal sources of influence'.

30 Miles, 'Structure and Effects', 183.

> developing states' behavior has caused Western observers to question whether the developing [sic: nations] are more concerned with image or ideology than with substance, since they have repeatedly rejected developed states' initiatives which might well have made a measurable improvement in the welfare of their peoples.[31]

This implies that some industrial states found it downright ungrateful that the developing states wanted to have a say in what was best for them, and perhaps it was easier to label their ambitions 'ideological' than to admit that many of their suggestions had a realistic, political core. The discussion was an unsettling reminder of a dread that some Americans had harboured as far back as 1949. It was fear of just such internationalism and 'rabbit systems'[32] that had rung in the paranoia of the McCarthy era and had prompted Ely Culbertson to condemn the Chicago committee's draft world constitution, arguing in 1949 that the 'disease of internationalism, such as the Communist internationalism, can be as monstrous as the disease of nationalism'.[33]

What no one could have predicted was that there was another twist to the issue. The biggest obstacle would not be the east-west Cold War or even the north-south tension between developed and developing states, but rather the issues that would arise between coastal and non-coastal states. This completely disrupted the axes of agreement and disagreement,[34] and even led to conflict within the Group of 77 itself – further hampering the group's efforts to coordinate its own interests and actions. As an aside, this also makes it questionable whether a voting system would truly have been so disastrous for the industrial states, since many developing states were coastal states and in fact ended up having similar interests to the superpowers.

The rule of decision-making by consensus – paired with interests that aligned depending on the existence and length of each state's coastline – complicated the negotiation process. Since there were no clear camps, the effectiveness of the convention was very much dependent on good draft papers that

31 Robert L. Friedheim and William J. Durch, 'The International Seabed Resources Agency Negotiations and the New International Economic Order', *International Organization* 32, no. 2 (1977): 330.

32 Culbertson, 'The preliminary Draft', 481.

33 Culbertson, 'The preliminary Draft', 474.

34 *See* Miles, 'Structure and Effects', 184: 'Ironically no one at that time foresaw that having produced a treaty primarily representing the interests of states with long coastlines, the conflict over acceptance […] would be shaped by a burgeoning confrontation between coastal states on the one hand and the Landlocked and Geographically Disadvantaged States Group on the other'.

were often prepared by loosely gathered interest groups. Never mind the fact that the whole enterprise took nine years to conclude, it is remarkable that the Law of the Sea Treaty was ever actually agreed upon at all.

2 The Structure of the Negotiations – Solving a Giant Jigsaw Puzzle through Consensus

It was not just the decision-making process at the convention that was problematic. The content, too, presented the participants with some obstacles to grapple with. The scope of the convention – which was originally intended only to deal with unresolved issues from UNCLOS I and II, like navigation and the area outside of national jurisdiction[35] – had widened considerably. In November 1973, the General Assembly decided that the conference would deal with 'all matters relating to the Law of the Sea'.[36] Which resulted in 'a package of such a size and complexity as almost to be beyond human control'.[37] The issues up for negotiation ranged from the territorial sea to the deep oceans. Some of the most important items included: the breadth of the territorial sea, transit passage, archipelagic baselines, the exclusive economic zone,[38] the limits of the continental shelf, governance of the area outside national jurisdiction, the protection of the marine environment and marine scientific research.[39] All these issues had not only to be defined and discussed, but also to be agreed upon, since voting was not an option.

Another quirk of the convention that complicated negotiations further was that the delegates had no drafted treaty text before the Caracas session in 1974.[40] This was unusual, and might have compounded the issues presented by the consensus system in drawing out the negotiations.[41] Apart from the 'Gentlemen's Agreement' on consensus-seeking, the general structure of the negotiation process still had to be decided on. For that reason, three Main Committees[42] were set up to discuss packages of related issues separately.

35 *Cf.* Miles, 'Structure and Effects', 168.

36 GA RES 3067 (XXVIII), 16 November 1973.

37 Miles, 'Structure and Effects', 173.

38 *See* Francisco Orrego Vicuña, *The exclusive economic zone. Regime and legal nature under international law* (Cambridge: Cambridge University Press, 1989).

39 For all terms and principles *see* Bernaerts, *Bernaerts' Guide,* 26–99.

40 *Cf.* Sanger, *Ordering the Oceans,* 43.

41 *Cf.* Mahmoudi, *The Law of,* 45.

42 *See* Bernaerts, *Bernaerts' Guide,* 8. A/CONF.62/SR.2. The committee under second plenary meeting.

Additionally, the participants agreed to set up a General Committee, a Drafting Committee and a Credentials Committee.[43] All of which meant that the inherent structure of the negotiation process was already fragmented into different areas even before the main discussions began. This might have contributed to what Elisabeth Mann Borgese later called a 'fractured'[44] approach towards the Law of the Sea, complicating efforts to deal with the issue in a holistic way.

The General Committee was set up to be the conference bureau, while the Drafting Committee had the important task of collecting the differing drafts for the treaty text that had been prepared by the various delegates. The Drafting Committee would then assemble the drafts into manageable texts that could be discussed. The committee was necessary because there was no single draft treaty to negotiate.[45] The Drafting Committee was not supposed to re-open discussions, instead it was supposed to resolve drafting issues and be a kind of information-assembling and advice-giving body. Delegates could turn to it for advice on how to formulate their own drafts.[46] The Drafting Committee's job was to try and bring order to the chaotic process of drafting a treaty collaboratively and by consensus. In the beginning, to single out each applicable suggestion that might later form part of a draft treaty, the delegates at Caracas were faced with semi-organised mountains of paper that they were obliged to sift through and discuss. This meant that from the outset, drafting the treaty was like solving an enormous jigsaw puzzle – one with an indefinite number of pieces that could appear, disappear and reappear, depending on the outcome of discussions in the committees. Even if they could get hold of all the right pieces, there was still the task of putting them together into a single treaty.

Clearly, things were already getting complicated before they had even started, despite all the preparation work that the Seabed Committee had done. Prior to the gatherings in New York and Caracas, the Seabed Committee had handed in six volumes of papers for the three Main Committees. [47] The

43 'Procedural History', United Nations Audiovisual Library of International Law, accessed 30 September 2021, http://legal.un.org/avl/ha/uncls/uncls.html. *See also* Bernaerts, *Bernaerts' Guide*, 8–9.

44 MS-2-744, Box 139, Folder 16, Lecture on the Ocean Regime by EMB. EMB states that the approach 'cannot be partial or fractional'.

45 *Cf.* Sanger, *Ordering the Oceans*, 41.

46 *Cf.* Bernaerts, *Bernaerts' Guide*, 8.

47 *Cf.* Sanger, *Ordering the Oceans*, 43. *See also* 'Procedural History', United Nations Audiovisual Library of International Law, 30 September 2021, http://legal.un.org/avl/ha/uncls/uncls.html: '[…]the Convention's main bodies (the three main committees, dealing respectively with the deep-seabed regime, the traditional law of the sea, the protection of the marine environment, marine scientific research and transfer of technology and the informal plenary dealing with the settlement of disputes and general and final clauses)'.

First Committee would deal with the seabed regime, the Second Committee would oversee negotiations around the traditional law of the sea, marine environment protection and technology and research, and the Third Committee would concern itself with dispute resolution and final clauses.[48] Since the Seabed Committee had been set up in 1971 to discuss issues of how the seabed should be governed, most of their material had focused on the area outside national jurisdiction, also called 'the Area' for short.[49] Therefore, this material was mostly only useful for the First Committee, while the other committees had to draw from the outcomes of UNCLOS I and II. In addition, there were some inherent problems with the Seabed Committee's work, since the committee had mainly focused on how the seabed should be governed from an organisational point of view.

The General Assembly had given the Seabed Committee a brief to work to in preparation for the conference, and it was now up to the First Committee to elaborate on this. The first direction from the General Assembly was that the concept of common heritage should be applied to the seabed outside national jurisdiction. Second, they desired that some sort of 'international machinery' should be established to govern this area.[50] What the Seabed Committee had done as they sought to achieve these aims was to look at: '(1) the nature and scope of the Authority [sic: the international machinery]';[51] '(2) the functions and powers of the Assembly';[52] '(3) the compositions of the Council'; and '(4) the functions and powers of the Enterprises'.[53]

What was lacking in this mass of paper from the Seabed Committee was the question of how to govern activity on the seabed – like mining, exploitation and exploration.[54] This was a serious issue, since international interest in the seabed was largely based on how it might be utilised in the future. Some activities were more divisive than others, and Sanger noted that 'seabed mining issues [...] proved the most intractable in the conference'.[55] That the First Committee – which was supposed to discuss the deep seabed regime and mining issues – had the most extensive collection of papers might not have played out in its favour either.[56] According to Sanger, this fact could have been a

48 *Cf.* Sanger, *Ordering the Oceans*, 43.
49 *See* Miles, 'Structure and Effects', 178.
50 *Cf.* GA RES 2750 (XXV). B.
51 Miles, 'Structure and Effects', 178.
52 Miles, 'Structure and Effects', 178.
53 Miles, 'Structure and Effects', 178.
54 *Cf.* Miles, 'Structure and Effects',178.
55 Sanger, *Ordering the Oceans,* 43.
56 *Cf.* Sanger, *Ordering the Oceans,* 43.

disadvantage 'because there was a feeling in Committee I that it could afford to spend time in broad debate, while waiting for the others to catch up'.[57] Sanger argued that this was why the committee working on the seabed regime was more divided than the other committees, though this is questionable.

There were more complicated reasons behind this division than a simple over-abundance of time for debate. Unlike other issues, no progress had been made at UNCLOS I and II on the question of the area outside national jurisdiction and its governance.[58] So while delegates on the other two committees could draw on discussions and decisions from the previous conferences, the First Committee grappled with fresh problems. Many of the core decisions and definitions around what ocean space actually comprised of were already made,[59] but the seabed issue still had to go through the whole process. On top of that, the seabed outside national jurisdiction was the area that evoked most interest among participants at UNCLOS III. While many of the issues discussed – like the limits of the territorial or economic zones – were only of interest to states that actually had a coastline, the area outside national jurisdiction held interest for every last nation state on Earth, including landlocked states. If this area were to be governed under the 'concept of common heritage of mankind' – whatever that meant for those interested in it at the time – they had to make sure that they would get a say in attaching meaning to the concept.

3 Navigating Interests – Groups as the Unofficial Structure of UNCLOS III

Despite the teething troubles of the first session in 1973, the rules of procedure were adopted on 27 June 1974 in Caracas.[60] Finally, the participants could dive into discussing what a treaty for the oceans should actually contain. With so many interest groups and drafts to draw up and so much groundwork to lay, the negotiation process was carried out in an unusual way through informal working groups. International law professor Said Mahmoudi called these groups the 'inofficial structure'[61] of the conference. Mahmoudi further explained that 'A

57 Sanger, *Ordering the Oceans*, 43.

58 Apart from what the 1958 Convention on the High Seas says about the freedom of the seas.

59 1958 Conventions on Fishing and Conservation of the Living Resources of the High Seas; 1958 Convention on the Territorial Sea;1958 Convention on the Continental Shelf.

60 Miles, 'Structure and Effects', 183. The rules were adopted in 27 June 1974 (A/Conf. 62/SR.16, 27 June 1974).

61 Mahmoudi, *The Law of*, 40.

major part of the work of the Main Committees was carried out by these working groups which generally held informal meetings without records'.[62]

The lack of even a draft treaty, coupled with differing interests that were usually dictated by geographical circumstances, led to a string of more or less tightly knit negotiation groups and alliances that were forged and broken during UNCLOS III. Some had quite creative names like the 'Leopard Group'[63] (US delegates and Yankov from Bulgaria, named after a restaurant they met in), and the 'Gang of Five'[64] (US, USSR, Britain, France and Japan). These groups discussed matters in smaller circles, then brought their thoughts to the table when the timing was right.[65] Mahmoudi argued that 'The emergence of special interest groups was a spontaneous response to the demand which could not be fulfilled by the traditional groupings inside the United Nations system such as the regional groups'.[66] Regional grouping was not a viable solution, because the issues at the convention affected states in ways that transcended the general north-south or east-west axes. Therefore, new alliances were brokered in place of the regional system. The states in these groups generally shared interests that were often connected to their respective proximity to the oceans.[67] One of the first groups to form along geographical lines was the 'Coastal States',[68] which was founded as early as

62 Mahmoudi, *The Law of*, 41. Mahmoudi explained further that the informal groups that ' were established to assist the First Committee included: A working group of 50 States in 1974 under the chairmanship of C. W. Pinto (Sri Lanka); a workshop which was an open-ended working group in 1976; an informal working group of the whole on the system of exploitation under Jens Evensen (Norway) in 1977; three negotiating groups were established by the Conference in 1978 as a part of an effort to tackle hard-core issues before the Conference [...]'.

63 Sanger, *Ordering the Oceans*, 32.

64 Sanger, *Ordering the Oceans*, 32. *See also* Beesley, 'Negotiating Strategy', 187–188: 'There were still other important East/West groups. The most interesting, I always thought, was the Group of Five, which I once mistakenly called the Gang of Five in a slip of the tongue, and of course the name stuck [...]'.

65 It would be interesting to study back-room discussions and alliances together with the official UNCLOS proceedings and discussions at sessions. Alan Beesley (Ambassador of Canada to UNCLOS III) has examined the negotiation structure of UNCLOS in Alan Beesley, 'The Negotiating Strategy of UNCLOS III: Developing and Developed Countries as Partners – A Pattern for Future Multilateral International Conferences?', *Law and Contemporary Problems* 46, no. 2 (1983): 132–194.

66 Mahmoudi, *The Law of*, 41.

67 Some were political too. Not everything was decided based on geographical location. Malta, for instance, had been in limbo for a long time and could not decide whether to join the developing nations or the non-aligned group.

68 Sanger, *Ordering the Oceans*, 31. More about the coastal group, *see* Beesley, 'Negotiating Strategy', 186–187.

1973.[69] It grew over the years and eventually consisted of seventy-five delegations, which was almost half of all conference participants. Its aim was to 'outmatch the increasing numbers of the Land Locked group'.[70]

The Group of 'Land Locked States and Geographically Disadvantaged States' (LL/GDS)[71] was the antagonist of the 'Coastals'.[72] 'The LL/GDS group was chaired by Austria and Singapore, and was led by Karl Wolf and Tommy Koh during its most active period'.[73] This group was mostly interested in the seafloor outside national jurisdiction, and among its members it boasted some powerful countries with keen strategic instincts. In particular, the Austrian delegation and its leader, ambassador Karl Wolf, would later become important allies for Mann Borgese. Another group was that of the 'broad-margin states or Margineers'.[74] Members of this small but greedy group were known to be secretive, and some of them kept their affiliation with the group quiet for a long time. The reason was that these delegations were working towards setting the limits of national jurisdiction beyond 200 nautical miles. According to Sanger, 'Early members included Australia, New Zealand, Norway, Brazil, Argentina and Ireland, which took over the leadership from Canada. India, Sri Lanka, Uruguay and Britain joined later'.[75] The 'Land Based Producers',[76] meaning delegations from countries with land-based mineral production, also gathered together, most likely to keep an eye on the possibility of competition from future seabed mining by coastal states. All these groups aimed to draft paragraphs that could be brought to the respective committees for discussion. The groups were loosely knit in order to be able to rearrange themselves depending on different topics. Since a vast variety of issues were covered, not all states in the same group always agreed with one another, and membership was sometimes interchangeable.[77]

---

69 *Cf.* Sanger, *Ordering the Oceans,* 31.

70 Sanger, *Ordering the Oceans,* 31. For groups and alliances, *see also* Mahmoudi, *The Law of,* 40–42.

71 Sanger, *Ordering the Oceans,* 32: '29 of them took part in UNCLOS-3, of whom 14 were from Africa, five from Asia, two from Latin America and the rest from Europe'.

72 *Cf.* Beesley, 'Negotiating Strategy', 187: '[...] it is fair to say that creation of the coastal group led directly to the creation of another very important interest group called the "land-locked and geographically disadvantaged group" '.

73 Sanger, *Ordering the Oceans,* 32.

74 Sanger, *Ordering the Oceans,* 31.

75 Sanger, *Ordering the Oceans,* 31.

76 Sanger, *Ordering the Oceans,* 32.

77 *See* Mahmoudi, *The Law of,* 40.

One example of a fairly influential group that was central in drafting a single negotiating text was the so-called 'Evensen Group'.[78] It was named after the Norwegian delegate, Jens Evensen – another delegate who had participated in the *Pacem in Maribus* gatherings prior to UNCLOS III.[79] The group started forming as early as 1973, and Sanger called the Evensen Group 'semi-official'.[80] Sanger reported an interview in which Evensen told him how the group had first been established back in Geneva in 1973.

> I was approached, strangely enough, by the representatives of the two superpowers – Jack Stevenson of the United States, Alex Yankov from Bulgaria and others – who said we will never be able to succeed without a drafting group; would you be willing to form a very informal drafting group consisting of heads of delegations and experienced international lawyers, and we could work as private persons in order to prepare a legal, political document?[81]

Evensen took on the challenge, and according to Sanger, the group rose to play an important role in the convention. As with several other groups, membership in the Evensen Group was not static. Instead, Evensen invited different delegates to the meetings depending on the topic. Then various drafts were discussed, and Evensen assembled the findings in informal reports and papers. These papers he finally handed to the president, signed as 'anonymous documents from "Friends of the President" '.[82] Evensen told Sanger that he always invited the delegates in a personal capacity, not as representatives or delegates for their country. Over time, Evensen reported that 'It [sic: the group] became so influential that we had some difficulties because people felt insulted if they were not invited. But that would defeat its purpose'.[83] Sanger wrote that the Evensen Group was also used as 'cover group'[84] by other delegations. Which

78 Ingolf Vislie about Evensen Group in Vislie, *Jens Evensen*, 467–468.

79 Evensen took part in PIM. *See* MS MS-2-744, Box 125, Folder 2, Participants in the *Pacem in Maribus* Convocation.

80 Sanger, *Ordering the Oceans*, 29.

81 Sanger, *Ordering the Oceans*, 29–30.

82 Sanger, *Ordering the Oceans*, 30. The group's importance has been underlined by Beesley, *see* Beesley, 'Negotiating Strategy', 191: 'Several of the major Conference concepts were developed into agreed treaty language in the Evenson [sic: Evensen] group and Castenada group. This might not have happened but for the existence of these informal groups'. *See also* Buzan, 'Negotiating by Consensus', 336.

83 Sanger, *Ordering the Oceans*, 30.

84 Sanger, *Ordering the Oceans*, 30.

meant that Evensen put his group's signature – 'Friends of the President' – under documents that had in fact been prepared by state delegations or groups of delegations.[85] Perhaps his intention in doing this was to de-politicise the documents and to remove national conflicts from the equation.

It would be interesting to speculate why the Norwegian delegate, Jens Evensen, was singled out by the United States and Bulgaria to develop draft proposals. Was it because Norway was a 'Margineer'? Or because Norway was a small but significant coastal state? Maybe it was easier and less obvious for the United States to give this task to a seemingly 'harmless' small state with an extensive coastline than to play the role of the drafter themselves? Did they perhaps hope Norway would have the same interests as them, but would be easier to influence than other states?[86]

The system of using groups made the complex negotiations of the Law of the Sea Treaty just about manageable, but it might have contributed to how fragmented the different topics for agreement became. This was partly since a lot of the discussion was not retractable due to missing records in the unofficial groups, but also because ideas occurred over and over again in different settings without being discussed in a bigger arena. How would the international community navigate these issues? And would Elisabeth Mann Borgese be able to find a place for herself and her ideas in this complicated structure of official and unofficial meetings, drafts and proposals?

4 Entering the Conferences – The International Ocean Institute Gains Non-Governmental Organisation Status

Now that the Law of the Sea Treaty negotiations were under way, Elisabeth Mann Borgese had to find a way in. By 1973, she was not affiliated with any national delegation, and the Seabed Committee, with which she had enjoyed close ties through Arvid Pardo, had completed its mission and was dissolving. This was going to be a challenge. Puzzling out a Law of the Sea Treaty – with the endless process of viewing, revising and formulating drafts – was hard enough without having to navigate the complicated unofficial group structure. After all, there was a good possibility that sitting with 'Coastal States' or the 'Leopard Group' on a Friday afternoon could change the course of the convention.

85 Sanger, *Ordering the Oceans*, 30.

86 It is unclear how long the Evensen Group was active. Perhaps until a single negotiation text was agreed on. According to Vislie that would have been in 1976. *Cf.* Vislie, *Jens Evensen*, 468.

Which groups to participate in had to be chosen wisely, and Elisabeth Mann Borgese was eager to jump into the fray and make her own contribution to solving the puzzle.

Her big problem was that she still had no affiliation with any nation state delegation, despite her history of close relations with the Maltese government. Arvid Pardo had been dropped from the Maltese delegation, so neither of them could expect to have automatic direct access to the delegates and their policy-making at the conference. Luckily, the fact that Mann Borgese had established the International Ocean Institute on Malta opened up another possibility. The IOI obtained the status of a non-governmental organisation (NGO)[87] and thereby gained the right to participate in UNCLOS III.[88] Elisabeth Mann Borgese and Arvid Pardo no longer needed to court the goodwill of mercurial governments, and Pardo was appointed 'special consultant'[89] to the president Shirley Hamilton Amerasinghe.[90]

The networks Arvid Pardo and Elisabeth Mann Borgese had built up during the preparation period with the Seabed Committee had obviously paid off. Pardo's appointment was proof that Amerasinghe – and most likely other former members of the Seabed Committee – valued his insights and his contribution to the discussions, regardless of whether or not he was affiliated with a delegation. This appreciation of Arvid Pardo's merits was quite at odds with the manner in which Malta had dismissed its former ambassador. In the aftermath of Caracas in 1974, Mann Borgese reported that Amerasinghe spoke highly of Arvid Pardo. In an undated draft written about how the Maltese government had fallen out with its former key man, she pointed out 'that Ambassador Amerasinghe, President of the Conference on the Law of the Sea, in his closing address in Caracas, had hailed Dr. Pardo as "the father and founder of the whole enterprise" '.[91]

Elisabeth Mann Borgese herself did not have the status of a former ambassador or Pardo's symbolic role as father of the enterprise, and it must have been rather more difficult to keep herself close to the negotiation processes. Therefore, from 1974–6, Elisabeth Mann Borgese used the International Ocean Institute to coordinate NGO activity at UNCLOS III. In a December

87 *See* MS-2-744, Box 398, Folder 15, International Ocean Institute – Past, Present and Future.

88 NGOs at UNCLOS are discussed in Schmidt, *Common Heritage,* 63–66. *See also* Levering and Levering, *Citizen Action*. Hannigan, *Geopolitics of Deep, 65–68.*

89 A/CONF.62/INF.3/Rev.1

90 *See* A/CONF.62/INF.3/Rev.1

91 MS-2-744, Box 62, Folder 8, EMB undated draft. Most likely written shortly after 22. April 1975.

1974 exchange with M René Wadlow from 'The World Association of World Federalists',[92] she discussed the possible directions and alliances for the NGOs.[93] In his own letter, Wadlow asked Mann Borgese what the 'permanently based NGO lobby'[94] should concentrate on, adding that 'I would appreciate your views on what topics will be worth stressing'.[95] Elisabeth Mann Borgese's reply came in January 1975, in which she explained how she thought the NGOs present at UNCLOS III could influence the convention. She had some suggestions about the issue that interested her most: the common heritage principle. She advised Wadlow that:

> the NGOs ought to concentrate on getting the real issue, that is, the common heritage of mankind and the establishment of a new type of international organization, to manage it, back into focus at the Conference.[96]

This correspondence demonstrates that Elisabeth Mann Borgese would take any chance to further her idea of common heritage and a new ocean regime. She made steady efforts to get other NGOs on board and the world federalists were clearly a suitable target. Her past affiliation with the Committee to Frame a World Constitution in Chicago meant she might have had contacts – even some degree of recognition – in such circles, not just because they shared the same interest in the common heritage principle, but also because they came from the same background as Mann Borgese in drafting a world constitution.[97] With the International Ocean Institute, Elisabeth Mann Borgese had not only established a vehicle that would gain her independent entry into political discussions and forums, but also a place from which she could organise and gather her ideas before they were presented to the world. Despite this, up until 1975 Mann Borgese still tried doggedly to become a member of the Maltese

---

92 *See* MS-2-744, Box 101, Folder 1, Wadlow to EMB, 13 December 1974.
93 *Cf.* MS-2-744, Box 101, Folder 1, Wadlow to EMB, 13 December 1974.
94 MS-2-744, Box 101, Folder 1, Wadlow to EMB, 13 December 1974.
95 MS-2-744, Box 101, Folder 1, Wadlow to EMB, 13 December 1974.
96 MS-2-744, Box 101, Folder 1, EMB to Wadlow, 29 January 1975.
97 According to Miriam Levering, EMB also contacted the Neptune Group, but did not find the will to cooperate there. *See* Levering and Levering, *Citizen Action*, 33: 'She [sic: EMB] also amused and spurred on members of the Neptune Group at early conference sessions by telling us that, compared with her, we were amateurs. Although partly true at the time, such comments – as well as her long, prescriptive speech at a plenary meeting in Caracas – were tactless. Having lost much of her effectiveness as an NGO representative by 1975, she sought to influence the negotiation by becoming a delegate from Austria and by asking to publish articles in our publication, *Neptune*'.

delegation, since this would allow her to take part in the discussions in one of the three Main Committees and several of the groups. Her natural place, considering her interest in the common heritage principle and the deep seabed, was the First Committee.

5 A Piece for the Ocean Puzzle – How to Design an International Machinery to Govern the Ocean Floor?

The First Committee's task was to discuss the governance of the seafloor outside national jurisdiction, continuing the work of the Seabed Committee. Many states that had delegates on the Seabed Committee moved over to the First Committee at the start of UNCLOS III.[98] The aim of the committee was to define the function of the 'international machinery' responsible for the governance of the Area. Henceforth, this would be called the International Seabed Authority.

AO Adede, a former delegate for Kenya, has examined the early years of the First Committee's work from 1973–5.[99] According to Adede, the first question the delegates had to tackle was 'Who may exploit the area',[100] and to do this, they used the so-called draft Article 9 as a basis of discussion.[101] The committee started out with four different alternatives for how to shape the International Seabed Authority (A, B, C and D),[102] and their first goal was to reduce these to a single solution that everyone could agree on.[103] No one knew at the time, but agreement was a very long way off, and before we examine the four proposals more closely, we need to understand where the delegates were coming from when they sat down at the discussion table.

Adede paints an interesting picture when he describes the standpoints of the different delegation members. He argues that the four alternatives for how the International Seabed Authority should operate – specifically the

98 *Cf.* Beesley, 'Negotiating Strategy', 189: 'By this time we had not only set up the three separate committees, as in the Seabed Committee, but also we had carried them forward into the Conference – from the time it began'. *See also* A/CONF.62/C.1/SR.1.

99 For the work and tasks of the First Committee, *see* Andronico O. Adede, 'The System of Exploitation of the "Common Heritage of Mankind" at the Caracas Conference', *The American Journal of International Law* 69, no. 1 (January 1975): 31–49, http://www.jstor.org/stable/2200190.

100 *Cf.* Adede, 'System of Exploitation', 32.

101 *Cf.* Adede, 'System of Exploitation', 32.

102 *See* Adede, 'System of Exploitation', 32–33.

103 *Cf.* Adede, 'System of Exploitation', 33.

rules and regulations regarding exploration or exploitation of the seafloor – could be grouped into two conflicting categories. In general, the developed states wanted to put the International Seabed Authority in a 'straight jacket [sic: straitjacket]',[104] while the developing states hoped it could become a 'respectable business partner'.[105] In this example, Adede personifies the international machinery that was supposed to overlook activity in the Area. The International Seabed Authority as a personified entity was either to be restricted and put into a 'straitjacket' – as if it were a force that had to be controlled in order not to create chaos the moment it was set free – or it was to be treated as a 'respectable business partner' with economic interests and the freedom to play with the rules of the free market economy. Essentially, delegates either wanted the International Seabed Authority to be 'weak' or 'strong'.

The developed states, among them many of the coastal states, argued for inscribing very detailed rules and regulations into the Law of the Sea Treaty rather than leaving the International Seabed Authority to devise them, so that the future International Seabed Authority would have limited powers by the time it was established. The reason for this was simple. With their highly advanced technological knowledge and experience, developed states were most likely to conduct exploration and exploitation ventures. For them, leaving the seafloor outside national jurisdiction as open as possible for this was favourable. Although all 'mankind' was theoretically supposed to be able to conduct activity in the Area, it was the industrialised states who could hope for the biggest piece of the pie – so long as the treaty allowed all state parties to just get on with their own business within the limits of the treaty. In their ideal scenario, the International Seabed Authority would just dole out contracts or licence agreements, and would thereafter work with a so-called 'single system'[106] of exploration. Apart from that, the authority would not meddle with exploration and exploitation or make any further rules.

Those who envisioned the authority as a 'business partner' were states that did not have the capacity to conduct activity on the seafloor outside national jurisdiction by themselves. Many of the states belonging to the Group of 77 fell into this category. For them, it was essential to give the International Seabed Authority a flexible mandate to make rules and regulations according to the

104 Adede, 'System of Exploitation', 47. For the US view on the 'straitjacket', *see* Leigh S. Ratiner, 'The Cost of American Rigidity', in Bernhard H. Oxman, David D. Caron and Charles L.O: Buderi, eds., *Law of the Sea U.S. Policy Dilemma* (San Francisco: ICS Press, 1983), 33–38.

105 Adede, 'System of Exploitation', 47.

106 Adede, 'System of Exploitation', 34.

needs that might arise over time. Since the developing states possessed neither sufficient technological expertise nor the financial capacity to gain it on their own, they wanted the International Seabed Authority to become a business partner with which they could form coalitions in order to compete with the industrialised states. The developing states argued for the so-called 'multiple system'[107] that would open up 'joint-venture'[108] exploration. Joint-venture meant that developed states could club together with the authority to conduct activity in areas specifically designated for that purpose. In this scenario, the International Seabed Authority would be equipped with the expertise of the developed states that were applying for exploration or exploitation rights. The developing states argued that only in this way could 'technology transfer'[109] – meaning the obligation of industrialised states to share technological knowledge with developing states – be secured and the common heritage principle put into action. If the authority ended up being a restricted administrative organ, the whole purpose of reserving the seafloor would be undermined. According to Adede, the first step the committee took towards solving these issues was to agree on changing the name of draft Article 9 from 'Who may exploit the Area?'[110] to 'How is the Area to be exploited?'[111] This overarching question was then broken down into several sub-questions that included the following issues: '(1) Who may explore and exploit the area; (2) conditions of exploration and exploitation of the area; and (3) economic aspects of exploration and exploitation in the area'.[112] To manage the three sub-issues, delegates reached a compromise to take up each issue separately, while allowing discussions to draw upon the other issues in cases where there was a close relationship between them.[113]

By 1974, the main disagreements in the First Committee revolved around how to design the power of the International Seabed Authority. As mentioned above, the different camps were divided between a 'single system' (developed

107 Adede, 'System of Exploitation', 34.

108 Alan G. Kirton and Stephen C. Vasciannie, 'Deep Seabed Mining under the Law of the Sea Convention and the Implementation Agreement: Developing Country Perspectives', *Social and Economic Studies* 51, no. 2 (June 2002): 92, http://www.jstor.org/stable/27865277.

109 Beesley, 'Negotiating Strategy', 198. For a discussion about the idea of technology transfer in connection to EMB's initiatives, *see* Chircop, 'Elisabeth Mann Borgese's humanist conception', 116.

110 Adede, 'System of Exploitation', 35.

111 *Cf.* Adede, 'System of Exploitation', 35.

112 Adede, 'System of Exploitation', 37.

113 *Cf.* Adede, 'System of Exploitation', 37

countries) and a 'multiple system' (Group of 77) and they also disagreed over whether the rules and regulations should be written in convention (developed countries) or developed by the ISA itself (Group of 77).[114] This was the First Committee's contribution to the first two sessions. The results were incorporated into the 'major trends' paper that was finished by August 1974. The paper laid the groundwork for further discussions on the Law of the Sea, being 'both a reference text to the work done at Caracas and a point of departure for future work'.[115] Together with the uncertainty surrounding the functions, form and rights of the International Seabed Authority, there was also the question of which state should host it. As Elisabeth Mann Borgese had predicted in her various letters to the Maltese prime minister, Dom Mintoff, it was not long until other states apart from Malta announced their interest.

6 Malta's Failed Attempt to Regain Importance

Elisabeth Mann Borgese tried to mobilise Malta throughout 1974. In a letter to Mintoff, she reported directly from the second session in Caracas:

> Jamaica has put forward its candidacy as host to the headquarters for the ocean authority that should be established by this Conference. Jamaica has already designated land for this purpose, and prepared plans for the buildings. It has already secured the support of the Latin American countries for its candidacy, and is now trying to gain that of the Africans.[116]

The fact that Jamaica was putting itself forward even in 1974 may have alerted the prime minister that time was more limited than he had thought – especially after the impression he had given in the newspaper article of summer 1973, when he had said that 'the Maltese Government has long ago noted that these developments [sic: about the setting up of a Seabed Authority] are a long way away'.[117] Mann Borgese's report underlined the urgency of taking a stance. She also used the episode to point out, once again, the importance of obtaining such headquarters for Malta.[118] She was adamant about which country

114 *Cf.* Adede, 'System of Exploitation', 38, 45.
115 Sanger, *Ordering the Oceans*, 43.
116 MS-2-744, Box 84, Folder 12, EMB to Mintoff, 8 July 1974.
117 MS-2-744, Box 94, Folder 1, Borg Olivier, Malta's interest in Caracas conference on Law of the Sea, *Times of Malta*, 23 July 1973.
118 *See* MS-2-744, Box 84, Folder 12, EMB to Mintoff, 8 July 1974.

deserved the seat: 'There is only one country that is predestined to play this historical role, and that is Malta'.[119] She pleaded that 'If you put forward your candidacy now, the situation can still be saved'.[120] Again, Mann Borgese offered her help and a fully formulated plan of action when she wrote, 'What we can do here is to try to postpone a decision – it might be taken next year – and to mobilize the support of the Non-Aligned Nations of which Malta is now one'.[121]

Elisabeth Mann Borgese was on the case, and in fact she had already started mobilising support for the Maltese application. She mentioned her first lobbying effort in the same letter, where she reported talking with the vice prime minister Vratuša of the Yugoslav delegation. Seemingly concerned about relations between the two countries, she wrote, 'I understand that he is not at all satisfied with the state in which Yugoslav-Maltese relations were left after your visit to Yugoslavia'.[122] Mann Borgese tried to make sure that this piece of information would stay between her and Mintoff, pointing out, 'what I am writing is strictly confidential. I know, however, that if you extended an invitation to Dr. Vratuša for a return visit to Malta, he would gladly accept'.[123] This deft piece of confidential diplomacy was an apparent attempt to reconcile Yugoslavian-Maltese relations and secure Yugoslavian support for the Maltese application to host the International Seabed Authority.

It seems that Elisabeth Mann Borgese's appeal to action, paired with the realisation that Jamaica was already ahead in the race, finally prompted the Maltese to reconsider their hesitant stance. In September 1974,[124] we find a telegram from Elisabeth Mann Borgese to the deputy prime minister of Malta, Jean Buttigieg, in which she was already discussing the speaking slot in the General Assembly in October where Malta was supposed to announce its application for the International Seabed Authority.[125] Once again, Elisabeth Mann Borgese had managed to insert herself into the decision-making process. Apart from having reserved the slot, she also wanted to have a say in who would make the announcement, since 'Malta's cause would be much strengthened by

119 MS-2-744, Box 84, Folder 12, EMB to Mintoff, 8 July 1974.

120 MS-2-744, Box 84, Folder 12, EMB to Mintoff, 8 July 1974.

121 MS-2-744, Box 84, Folder 12, EMB to Mintoff, 8 July 1974. The decision of where to place the ISA postponed until 1981. *See* MS-2-744, Box 210, Folder 14, Malta and the International Seabed Authority, *The Sunday Times*, 31. May 1981. *See also* MS-2-744, Box 210, Folder 14, Local reaction to Malta's defeat in vote for I.S.A. site, *Sunday Times*, 23 August 81.

122 MS-2-744, Box 84, Folder 12, EMB to Mintoff, 8 July 1974.

123 MS-2-744, Box 84, Folder 12, EMB to Mintoff, 8 July 1974.

124 The year 1974 is likely because this was the year when Malta spoke at the UN in October.

125 *Cf.* MS-2-744, Box 94, Folder 1, Telegram EMB to Jean Buttigieg, 25 September.

presentation by deputy prime minister. If your decision were positive, consultation with Pardo as indicated in my last cable would be essential'.[126]

In the end, it was another representative who made the announcement in the General Assembly in October 1974 that the Maltese were interested in hosting the International Seabed Authority.[127] Shortly after Malta had announced this interest, Elisabeth Mann Borgese criticised stridently the manner in which the application had been put forward. She wrote: 'In all frankness, the race got off to a late and bad start. Had the presentation at the U.N. on October 10 been made by a Minister, perhaps it would have gotten more attention. So far, international reactions are very uncertain'.[128] The criticism was followed by a list of strategies and initiatives that Mann Borgese had drafted, starting with the recommendation that the 'Government should stand more visibly behind the efforts of the International Ocean Institute'.[129] This note was perhaps not entirely free of personal interest. Since the International Ocean Institute was the only channel through which Mann Borgese could participate in the UNCLOS negotiations, some backing from the Maltese government would be most welcome, and not just with regard to hosting the International Seabed Authority. Mann Borgese reported that a representative at UNCLOS had said of the Maltese initiative, 'Why, they don't even stand behind the IOI. What do they want the headquarters of the Seabed Authority for?'[130]

To change this perception, Mann Borgese urged that 'The Maltese Missions in New York and elsewhere must engage in an intensive lobbying campaign'.[131] She was clear that 'High-level political activity is needed between now and March',[132] and that the Maltese government needed to engage in this directly, rather than relying on missions. She finished with the important point that 'Malta has got to offer something Jamaica has not got'.[133] In Mann Borgese's opinion, the one advantage that made Malta stand out from the other applicants was the symbolic figure of Arvid Pardo from the Maltese initiative of 1967. Once again, Mann Borgese tried to get Pardo back in the picture. She argued:

126 MS-2-744, Box 94, Folder 1, Telegram EMB to Jean Buttigieg, 25 September.

127 *See* A/PV.2263. Speech by Mr. Bellizzi, 9 October 1974.

128 MS-2-744, Box 84, Folder 12, Memo EMB to Mintoff, 3 October 1974.

129 MS-2-744, Box 84, Folder 12, Memo EMB to Mintoff, 3 October 1974.

130 MS-2-744, Box 84, Folder 12, Memo EMB to Mintoff, 3 October 1974. The representative was Maurice Strong, who pointed out how strange it was that Malta was so keen on the authority but at the same time not too interested in the IOI.

131 MS-2-744, Box 84, Folder 12, Memo EMB to Mintoff, 3 October 1974.

132 MS-2-744, Box 84, Folder 12, Memo EMB to Mintoff, 3 October 1974.

133 MS-2-744, Box 84, Folder 12, Memo EMB to Mintoff, 3 October 1974.

> You have one great expert, who happens to be recognized universally as the greatest expert in the world on ocean affairs. It seems to be awfully wasteful not to use him, at a moment when we have to use everything we have got. Make him the Head of your Delegation to the Conference next March in Geneva.[134]

She also pointed out that it 'would cost the government very little'[135] to reinstate Arvid Pardo, but her initiative was ultimately in vain. It is hard to know exactly why, partly because we have no record of Pardo's side of the story beyond the fact that he was not given the job. Either he was not interested and declined the role, or the government did not want to call him back. It could have been that they failed to grasp his symbolic importance, or perhaps political differences made it impossible for Pardo to be invited back into the Maltese delegation. In the course of the years between 1971 and 1974, Malta's reticence had sown the seeds of doubt about its government's motives and done irreparable damage to its image as an initiator in the international community.[136] Perhaps the last concerted attempt to re-establish Malta's importance was made by Mann Borgese in January 1975, when the International Ocean Institute launched a 'Planning Council Seminar' in Oaxtepec – a small town in Mexico[137] – with the aim of developing a 'new strategy'[138] to put Malta back on the map.[139]

The outcome of the meeting was 'The Declaration of Oaxtepec',[140] a three-page document that attempted to refine the concept of the International Seabed Authority and summarised the differing positions at UNCLOS. The participants in the strategy meeting added a 'Diagram of Boundaries' to illustrate the status quo at the conference. The declaration stated, 'The new strategy

134 MS-2-744, Box 84, Folder 12, Memo EMB to Mintoff, 3 October 1974.

135 MS-2-744, Box 84, Folder 12, Memo EMB to Mintoff, 3 October 1974.

136 *See* Saviour Borg, '30 Years of UNCLOS. Malta's Contribution to the Process: Past and Present', speech at *UNCLOS at 30 Seminar* organised by International Ocean Institute and the University of Malta, 23 November 2012. (copy: courtesy of Saviour Borg): 'Yet, perhaps, one of the major issues which Malta also gave the highest priorities during UNCLOS III was the choice of the seat of the International Seabed Authority. The great efforts made by the Delegation of Malta during UNCLOS III to obtain support of the participants for Malta to host the seat of the Authority cannot be underestimated even though at a certain point of time, especially the first years of the Conference, it relinquished its leadership in this regard'.

137 EMB could be referring to gathering at Oaxtepec. *See* The Law of the Sea, The Declaration of Oaxtepec, *Water International* 1, no.2. (1976): 4–6, https://doi.org/10.1080/02508060768685704.

138 *See* MS-2-744, Box 84, Folder 12, EMB to Mintoff, 16 January 1975.

139 *See* MS-2-744, Box 84, Folder 12, EMB to Mintoff, 16 January 1975.

140 *See* 1976 Declaration of Oaxtepec.

would be based upon the assumption that international management of ocean space beyond national jurisdiction is a necessary complement to the exercise of comprehensive powers by coastal states in wide areas'.[141] At the same time, the declaration also stated that the International Seabed Authority should be 'supplemented by other organizational mechanisms dealing with the management and regulation of other uses of international space'.[142]

The participants at Oaxtepec attempted to support the claims that some developing nations with coastlines were making for extensive coastal margins under national jurisdiction, while at the same time calling for a collaborative international administration. Clearly they were trying to reconcile Malta's – or rather, Pardo's – early ambitions for a holistic ocean space administration with the political realities of developing nations. These were the states upon which Malta had to pin its hopes if it wanted to host the International Seabed Authority, and Elisabeth Mann Borgese must thus have seen that gaining supporters meant rephrasing the Maltese 'vision'. In this regard, in fact, Dom Mintoff might have been more clear-sighted than Mann Borgese in his previous strategy. He had understood that there was no support for a holistic approach and had tried to lay low. It was not until 1975 that Mann Borgese first understood that not all Group of 77 states were eager for a holistic approach to ocean governance. In the aegis of the International Ocean Institute, she took action to redefine Malta's claims. Reporting all this to Dom Mintoff, Mann Borgese wrote:

> Before coming to Mexico, I discussed the Draft of the declaration with Ambassador Attard Kingswell, Mr. Bellizzi, and Mr. Vella. I explained to them that the 'new strategy' was conceived as part of the strategy to restore to Malta its place of leadership at the Conference on the Law of the Sea, to introduce the element of novelty that is needed to change the position of a number of nations on the question of the headquarters, and to underline the advantage Malta has over Jamaica through the vicinity of the FAO, IOC, and IMCO headquarters, since all of these organizations are going to play an important role in the 'new strategy'.[143]

She also explained that the group intended to distribute the Oaxtepec declaration to gain support from the Group of 77, the Afro-Asian Foreign Minister Meeting and the Evensen Group.[144] She could not help pointing out the

141 1976 Declaration of Oaxtepec, 5.
142 1976 Declaration of Oaxtepec, 5
143 MS-2-744, Box 84, Folder 12, EMB to Mintoff, 16 January 1975.
144 *Cf.* MS-2-744, Box 84, Folder 12, EMB to Mintoff, 16 January 1975.

origins and intellectual ownership of the 'new strategy' developed at Oaxtepec, writing that 'the whole plan is the International Ocean Institute's, and the International Ocean Institute is Malta's'.[145]

7 Final Fall-Out with Malta over the International Seabed Authority

With the Declaration of Oaxtepec, Elisabeth Mann Borgese and the other participants of the workshop made a last respectable effort to reintegrate the Maltese initiative into the conference. At the same time, Mann Borgese had seized the opportunity to point out the importance of the International Ocean Institute for Malta and had once again tried to re-establish Arvid Pardo. Interestingly, no-one in the Maltese government had ever appointed Elisabeth Mann Borgese to the task of defending Malta's symbolic key role in the United Nations. Nor did that same government show much interest in inviting Arvid Pardo back into the delegation. On the contrary, by mid-1975 they were publicly opposing him. The fact was that the government had been reticent and inconsistent on the matter since Elisabeth Mann Borgese had first mentioned establishing an authority on Malta.

Although Elisabeth Mann Borgese emphasised her love for Malta in many of her letters to the prime minister,[146] we can assume that she had other reasons for her constant lobbying campaign. Ultimately, she and Pardo needed a way to present and elaborate the ideas they had developed in 'The Ocean Regime' and the 'Draft Ocean Space Treaty' in the United Nations. The Maltese government was a practical vehicle, not because the country was particularly close to Mann Borgese or Pardo's hearts, but because Arvid Pardo's 1967 speech had a symbolic significance that was directly connected with Malta. The issue was that Malta had proved rather stubborn – and in fact the prime minister, Dom Mintoff, had his own ideas about Malta's role in the conference. The issue finally came to a head in the spring of 1975. In April, Elisabeth Mann Borgese asked to be part of the Maltese delegation, but the government politely declined.[147] We do not have Mintoff's rejection letter, but we can read Mann Borgese's reply. Apparently, apart from rejecting her membership, the prime minister had also criticised an introductory piece she had written for a book by Arvid Pardo called *The Common Heritage*. In her letter, Mann Borgese referred to the unwelcome passage in order to explain and defend herself:

---

145 MS-2-744, Box 84, Folder 12, EMB to Mintoff, 16 January 1975.

146 *See* MS-2-744, Box 84, Folder 12, EMB draft Mintoff, undated.

147 *Cf.* MS-2-744, Box 62, Folder 8, EMB to Mintoff, 19 April 1975.

> The sentence in question reads: 'Thus, when the Law of the Sea Conference opened in December 1973, Pardo was not a member of the Malta delegation which has played no further active role in the law of the sea matters'.[148]

Clearly, to state that the delegation had 'played no further active role' was problematic for the government. Not because it was untrue, but because the Maltese were about to try and re-establish themselves and were not pleased to see Elisabeth Mann Borgese pointing out their shortcomings in public. She reassured them that 'what I wanted to say was that the Delegation of Malta did no longer play a leading role. Certainly, no criticism of your Delegation was intended'.[149] We also learn the real reason why Mann Borgese was not considered as a prospective delegation member. She was too closely connected to Pardo and his philosophies: 'Mr. Bellizzi explained to me, your Government now finds it difficult to include me in the Delegation because of a letter Dr. Pardo just published in the Bulletin'.[150] Apparently, Arvid Pardo had criticised the government of Malta, and because of their collaboration, Mann Borgese had been tainted by his statements. Mann Borgese felt she had to correct the Maltese government's impressions about her ties to Arvid Pardo, adding, 'I sincerely hope [...] that you will not condemn me on the basis of guilt by association [...]'.[151] What followed presents an interesting record of Mann Borgese's diplomatic strategies. By 1975 it had become obvious that the Maltese government was no longer advocating Arvid Pardo's initial idea. On the contrary, it seems Pardo had already started a campaign of his own, criticising the Maltese for the way they had mishandled the situation and sold out to further international relations.[152] This made it crucial for Mann Borgese, who apparently had not given up on supporting the Maltese just yet, to get back in favour with the government by distancing herself from Arvid Pardo. She did by this making some strategic insinuations in her letter to Mintoff:

> In other occasions you made some dark allusions to matters in Dr. Pardo's life which you know about but which you would rather not disclose. Could you, as a personal favor, disclose these facts to me so that we can dispose of them one way or another once for all? Since I consider myself

148 MS-2-744, Box 62, Folder 8, EMB to Mintoff, 19 April 1975.
149 MS-2-744, Box 62, Folder 8, EMB to Mintoff, 19 April 1975.
150 MS-2-744, Box 62, Folder 8, EMB to Mintoff, 19 April 1975.
151 MS-2-744, Box 62, Folder 8, EMB to Mintoff, 19 April 1975.
152 Perhaps the government disliked the Common Heritage publication.

> an expert on the Maltese contribution to the Law of the Sea and, therefore, on Dr. Pardo's work and career, I should like to have all my facts straight.[153]

With this statement, Mann Borgese implied that she took the prime minister's reservations concerning Arvid Pardo seriously. She made it seem like she was taking Mintoff's side, but at the same time she offered to clarify the situation by 'disposing' of the 'facts' one way or the other, which created an impression of camaraderie. Unfortunately, her letter came too late. A few days later, we can read in a written draft article by Mann Borgese that the prime minister had published a statement in the *Times of Malta* on 22 April.[154] In this statement, he held Mann Borgese and the International Ocean Institute responsible for the Maltese failure to obtain the International Seabed Authority. Mann Borgese defended herself against these accusations in the draft article, arguing that 'for no apparent reason I have been drawn into a controversy to which I am not a party […]'[155] and stating that she was 'shocked'.[156] She further explained the background to the International Ocean Institute, and how it had been established to obtain the International Seabed Authority for Malta:

> The Prime Minister does not mention that, since 1971, I consistently urged him, with a number of letters and detailed memoranda, to put forward Malta's candidacy for this authority (which I have advocated publicly since 1968). Had he taken these recommendations into consideration and placed his candidacy before Jamaica did, Malta would have had the near-unanimous support of the members of the United Nations.[157]

Shortly after her reaction was published – apparently in a smaller Maltese newspaper – the *Times of Malta* printed a press release from the Department of Information, regarding letters from Arvid Pardo and Elisabeth Mann Borgese in 'some daily newspaper'[158] in which they had referred to the prime minister's statement. The aim of the article was to correct some of their allegations.

---

153 MS-2-744, Box 62, Folder 8, EMB to Mintoff, 19 April 1975.

154 EMB only refers to a speech that was not available at the archive.

155 MS-2-744, Box 62, Folder 8, EMB undated draft. (Most likely shortly after 22. April 1975).

156 MS-2-744, Box 62, Folder 8, EMB undated draft.

157 MS-2-744, Box 62, Folder 8, EMB undated draft.

158 MS-2-744, Box 62, Folder 8, Seabed Authority Centre, *Times of Malta*, 29 May 1975. Unfortunately, we do not know in which local newspaper EMB published the draft.

> Mrs. Borgese alleges in her article that she had written to the Prime Minister as far back as 1971 to promote Malta's candidature for the Seabed Authority. There is no truth in this allegation. No record exists that at any time between 1971 and mid-1974 Mrs. Borgese, verbally, in writing, or in any other way ever put forward this proposal to the Prime Minister.[159]

Finally, the 'maverick' Dom Mintoff had lashed out. Stating that 'no record exists'[160] of the proposal for hosting the authority was simply not true. On the contrary, the Prime Minister had been inundated with letters and telegrams full of pleas from Elisabeth Mann Borgese to start the application process – some of them from as early as 1971.[161] Mintoff's accusations were most likely an attempt to dodge responsibility for having missed out on such an important opportunity.

Although this was an irritating episode for Elisabeth Mann Borgese, it also proved that Malta understood hosting the International Seabed Authority would have been desirable. Otherwise, the prime minister would not have felt the urge to defend himself with outright falsehoods. The government also made clear its attitude towards Arvid Pardo once and for all. Malta would not support Pardo any further. The government stated, 'The Draft Treaty Article put forward by Dr. Pardo does not represent the position of the Government of Malta and this Dr. Pardo himself admitted in his article [...]'.[162] They further undermined his work by letting the newspaper know that 'Dr. Pardo's articles are not corroborated by facts but are merely speculative and politically motivated. Whatever Dr. Pardo might say the Maltese Government's policy will not be changed'.[163] At the same time, the government set forth its own position, stating:

> Fortunately, the Maltese Government changed in the nick of time Dr. Pardo's policy who had hoped to obtain for Malta the Seabed Authority and chose instead to adopt more positive and more realistic measures from which Malta might benefit.[164]

---

159 MS-2-744, Box 62, Folder 8, Seabed Authority Centre, *Times of Malta*, 29 May 1975.

160 MS-2-744, Box 62, Folder 8, Seabed Authority Centre, *Times of Malta*, 29 May 1975.

161 *See* for the records: MS-2-744, Box 84, Folder 12, EMB to Mintoff, 17 January 1973. In the same letter EMB mentions that Pardo had presented a proposal to Kingswell in 1972. She had probably talked to Mintoff before 1973. The government's allegations were false and perhaps a whitewash strategy. *See also* MS-2-744, Box 52, Folder 9, EMB to Mintoff, 13 October 1971.

162 MS-2-744, Box 62, Folder 8, Seabed Authority Centre, *Times of Malta*, 29 May 1975.

163 MS-2-744, Box 62, Folder 8, Seabed Authority Centre, *Times of Malta*, 29 May 1975.

164 MS-2-744, Box 62, Folder 8, Seabed Authority Centre, *Times of Malta*, 29 May 1975.

It remains unclear what this talk of 'more realistic measures' referred to. In fact, the government had not given up on hosting the International Seabed Authority, although they had rejected the specific design for that body favoured by Pardo. To state that the Maltese government had no more interest in gaining the authority was not true, since we know that they began lobbying to obtain it in 1974 and continued until they lost the race against Jamaica in 1981.[165]

These peculiar developments did not end there. In May 1975, the very next day after the article impugning Pardo and Mann Borgese's motives was published in the *Times of Malta* the Maltese lawyer V E Ragonesi wrote a letter to Arvid Pardo.[166] In the letter, Ragonesi referred to a conversation with Elisabeth Mann Borgese concerning the conflict with the prime minister. Apparently, Mintoff had said to her, 'a) there will be no more recriminations; b) the government would like to acquire again your services and those of Elizabeth'.[167] In the letter, Ragonesi had attached the newspaper article from the day before. Based on this, he offered the following advice to Pardo:

> I opined to Elizabeth that you should take time to think it over, that perhaps it would not be in your interest to accept to become again under the services of the Government, and that I was not so sure that the Government meant well. Yesterday the papers carried a reply from the Department of Information, hereto attached, which I consider scurrilous and shows that the Government will not change either its attitude or its policies. How can you form part of its delegation or even help it?[168]

Indeed, it seemed unlikely that 'the Government meant well',[169] considering its libellous comments in the newspaper. With this in mind, Arvid Pardo finally detached himself from Malta and went onto other projects at Woodrow Wilson College.[170] Nevertheless, he always kept an eye on Malta and the Law of the Sea negotiations, and he would be invited several times to join meetings and official gatherings. He would keep up with happenings at the United Nations through the International Ocean Institute and his collaboration with

165 *See* MS-2-744, Box 210, Folder 14, Leo Brincat, Loss of Seabed Authority Site Gross inaccuracies by Opposition, *Daily News*, 25 August 1981. More material on ISA loss and lobbying in the same folder.

166 MS-2-744, Box 62, Folder 8, Ragonesi to Arvid Pardo, 30 May 1975.

167 MS-2-744, Box 62, Folder 8, Ragonesi to Arvid Pardo, 30 May 1975.

168 MS-2-744, Box 62, Folder 8, Ragonesi to Arvid Pardo, 30 May 1975.

169 MS-2-744, Box 62, Folder 8, Ragonesi to Arvid Pardo, 30 May 1975.

170 *See* MS-2-744, Box 108, Folder 1, Curriculum Vitae of Dr. Arvid Pardo.

Elisabeth Mann Borgese.[171] Occasionally, he would attend the gatherings of UNCLOS, and from time to time he published an article about developments in ocean affairs.[172]

For Elisabeth Mann Borgese, things were worse. With Malta in retreat, it became clear that she had planted her seed for the ocean regime headquarters – in the form of the International Ocean Institute – on the wrong island. According to its own statute, the purpose of the International Ocean Institute when it was established in 1972 was: 'to "promote research on the peaceful uses of ocean space and its resources, including the regulation of such uses" '.[173] Mann Borgese's initial idea had been to make the International Ocean Institute the nucleus of the future ocean regime.[174] But as those dreams crumbled with Pardo's withdrawal from the front line and the Maltese government's indecision turned to hostility, it became ever clearer that the International Ocean Institute's purpose would not stretch beyond the description in the statute: to promote research on the peaceful use of the seabed. If Malta had become the host of the International Seabed Authority, maybe there would have been a chance for the International Ocean Institute to morph into the authority. But in 1975, that dream vanished into the ether, along with Mann Borgese's friendly relationship with the Maltese government.

171 *See* A/CONF.62/INF.3/Add.1, 11 July 1974. In the second session in Caracas he was listed under 'Office of the Special Representative' as 'Special Consultant'.

172 *See* Arvid Pardo, 'An opportunity Lost', in Bernhard H. Oxman, David D. Caron and Charles L.O: Buderi, eds., *Law of the Sea U.S. Policy Dilemma* (San Francisco: ICS Press, 1983), 13–26. *See also* Arvid Pardo, 'Before and After', *Law and Contemporary Problems* 46, no. 2, *The Law of the Sea: Where now?* (1983): 95–105, http://www.jstore.org/stable/1191516.

173 Baker, 'Uncommon heritage', 38, 40. Baker refers to: PIM Statute, Ch. X International Ocean Institute. EMB MS-2-744, Folder 38, Box 40.

174 *See* MS-2-744, Box 52, Folder 9, EMB to Mintoff, 14 August 1971.

CHAPTER 8

A Strong International Machinery for the Seabed Outside National Jurisdiction?

1 Non-Governmental Organisations Struggle at the Convention

Having broken with the Maltese government, Elisabeth Mann Borgese now had to fend for herself. Mann Borgese, Pardo and the Maltese government had parted ways over the question of how the International Seabed Authority should be organised, and the conference at large was struggling with the same issue. While agreement on many of the issues in the other two committees was progressing steadily, the First Committee vacillated back and forth between the 'straitjacket' or 'business partner' concepts of organising the International Seabed Authority. Developments between 1974 and 1976 indicated that the balance was edging in favour of an authority with more restricted powers.[1]

The 1975[2] Declaration of Oaxtepec[3] – which Mann Borgese took ownership of by calling it 'the International Ocean Institute's'[4] – illustrated this issue nicely. The strategic meeting at Oaxtepec was not just an (ultimately failed) attempt to find a middle road between Pardo's ideas and those of the Maltese government, but also to reconcile differing opinions among the developing states, in the hopes of fighting back against the unified front presented by the developed states, all of whom favoured a weak International Seabed Authority. And it was not just the proposed authority that was being sapped of its power. Elisabeth Mann Borgese's own 'most influential' institution, the International Ocean Institute, was struggling at UNCLOS too. This was partly because it lacked governmental support (despite Mann Borgese's concerted efforts to remedy this),[5] and after the very public spat with Mintoff in 1975, any further help from Malta was very unlikely. But apart from this, the conference itself presented some difficulties for NGOs in general.

1 *See* Sanger, *Ordering the Oceans,* 45–46.

2 Interim between Caracas and Geneva in 1975. EMB reports to Evensen about Oaxtepec, *see* MS-2-744, Box 89, Folder 18, EMB to Evensen, 25 January 1975.

3 1976 Declaration of Oaxtepec.

4 MS-2-744, Box 84, Folder 12, EMB to Mintoff, 16 January 1975.

5 Most letters on these efforts can be found in MS-2-744, Box 84, Folder 12.

International lawyer Betsy Baker has singled out an event in a 1974 session that might have marked a turning point in the role of NGOs at UNCLOS, including that of the International Ocean Institute. Baker refers to a written statement that Mann Borgese presented on behalf of the International Ocean Institute before the First Committee in August 1974. In the statement, Mann Borgese argued for the preservation of the International Seabed Authority, stating that 'an ocean space authority is an indispensable outcome of this conference'.[6] The Soviet delegation's reaction to this was to demand that 'matters not relevant to the subject'[7] were taken off the record, and that NGOs should be forced to hand in their statements to the chairman, who would then decide whether they were to be considered for further distribution or not.[8] Elisabeth Mann Borgese's efforts to advocate for 'an ocean space authority' were clearly not very popular among some of the delegations. The incident with the Soviet Union suggests that Mann Borgese's self-built vessel for entering UNCLOS – namely the International Ocean Institute – was already starting to heel in 1974. The International Ocean Institute did succeed in presenting four statements at UNCLOS – three in the early period between 1974 and 1976, and a last one in 1983[9] – but Mann Borgese knew she would be much more influential if she could get herself affiliated with a national delegation. In that respect, the 1974 strategic meeting in Oaxtepec was perhaps the International Ocean Institute's last notable effort to directly influence decision-making at UNCLOS. The new strategy for handling 'troublesome' NGOs, as suggested by the Soviet Union, had made it much more difficult to speak to the delegates.[10]

Further problems would arise for the NGOs during the course of UNCLOS. One issue was the unusual structure of informal committee meetings without official records. This made it difficult for NGO delegates to participate

6 Baker, 'Uncommon Heritage', 29–39.

7 *See* Baker, 'Uncommon Heritage', 29. Baker refers to the record in A/CONF.62/C.1/SR.12., 12 August 1974, 12th meeting, 7 August, paras. 31–37, p. 63.

8 *Cf.* Baker, 'Uncommon Heritage', 30.

9 *Cf.* Baker, 'Uncommon Heritage', 29: 'A/CONF.62/C.1/SR.3, 12 July 1974, pp.12–13, Statements on the international regime and machinery (continued); and A/CONF.62/C.1/SR.12, 12 August 1974, 12th meeting, Economic implications of sea-bed mineral development (continued). A/CONF.62/SR.63, 12 April 1976, pp. 7, 45–47. A/CONF.62/WS/36'.

10 *See* Levering and Levering, *Citizen Action,* 30: '[...] partly because of the behaviour of some NGO representatives during the sessions in Caracas in 1974 and at Geneva in 1975, many UN officials and delegates disliked NGO representatives as a whole and wanted to limit their participation in the conference'.

in the negotiations, since they were effectively excluded from parts of the decision-making process. In fact, in April 1976, a collective of NGO representatives[11] – three of them from the International Ocean Institute, including Elisabeth Mann Borgese – made a request to change the rules. The initiator claimed that the practice of informal meetings without records did not 'appear to be in conformity with the rules of procedure adopted by the Conference on the Law of the Sea',[12] and that this situation set a 'unique and highly unfortunate precedent for the conference'.[13] The reply from the under-secretary general was short. He noted that some signatures were missing on the letter, which was true, since only two out of seven had actually signed it. He further argued that, after having conferred with the president of the convention and the chairmen of the committees, 'they do not agree with your interpretation of the Rules of Procedure'.[14] Finally, he added:

> The Conference has decided that the three Main Committees will conduct informal consultation and negotiations, obviously without summary records, and the Secretariat cannot but comply with this decision taken by Sovereign States, in accordance with the relevant Rules of Procedure.[15]

This unambiguous reply highlighted the importance of becoming part of a national delegation. Since Malta had proven tricky to deal with over the International Seabed Authority question, and the prime minister's scheming had made it difficult to foresee what role – if any – the Maltese would take in the Law of the Sea Convention going forward, Elisabeth Mann Borgese was once again on the lookout for a new ally. This time, she turned to one of the leaders of the Group of Landlocked and Geographically Disadvantaged States: Karl Wolf from Austria.

11 MS-2-744, Box 114, Folder 19, NGOs to Ambassador Bernardo Zuleta, 21 April 1976. The names were: Margaret Mead, world Society for Ekistics; Elizabeth Borgese, International Ocean Institute, Arvid Pardo, International Ocean Institute, Harrison Brown, International Council of Scientific Unions, David Poindexter, Population Institute, Lord Richie-Calder, International Ocean Institute, Luther Evans, World Association of World Federalists.

12 MS-2-744, Box 114, Folder 19, NGOs to Ambassador Bernardo Zuleta, 21 April 1976.

13 MS-2-744, Box 114, Folder 19, NGOs to Ambassador Bernardo Zuleta, 21 April 1976.

14 MS-2-744, Box 114, Folder 19, Zuleta to NGOs, 25 April 1976.

15 MS-2-744, Box 114, Folder 19, Zuleta to NGOs, 25 April 1976.

2 Moving over to the Austrian Delegation

In her Curriculum Vitae, Elisabeth Mann Borgese noted that she had joined the Austrian delegation in 1976.[16] Austria was a good fit for several reasons. It was a landlocked state, and was a member of the First Committee that was working on the seabed outside national jurisdiction. Also, the head of the delegation from 1975 onwards was ambassador Karl Wolf, who worked for the Austrian embassy in Oslo, giving him close ties to Norwegian delegate Jens Evensen who led the influential Evensen Group. It is unclear how exactly Elisabeth Mann Borgese ended up in the Austrian delegation. In an interview given in 1993, she was asked why she had joined the Austrian rather than the US delegation, since she still had an American passport at the time. She replied that she was not right for the US delegation, because they were 'on the other side of the spectra'[17] politically. She also felt that she would have to abide by too many restrictions if she threw in her lot with the United States. Of the Austrian delegation, she said:

> The Austrians were colossally generous. I had imagined that I would have to sit quietly and be happy to listen. But that's not how it happened. Instead, a very nice working group had been established. I have been able to work very constructively with the delegation.[18]

Hugh Williamson, who later worked with Elisabeth Mann Borgese in Halifax, suggested that her warm welcome from the Austrians might have had something to do with her German origins. The German-speaking delegates were familiar with one another, and they would certainly have known of Elisabeth Mann Borgese as the daughter of Thomas Mann – who was very much idolised in German-speaking countries. Williamson also suggested that she might have been a welcome representative for the Austrian delegation because she did not carry the stigma of World War II. She could speak with an authority about justice and order that other German-speaking delegates could not.[19]

Also, Austria was spot-on for Mann Borgese in terms of their priorities and attitudes. The Austrian delegation was known to play a 'key role'[20] in the Group

16 *Cf.* MS-2-744, Box 16, Folder 19, EMB CV. *See also* for her further involvement: In 1977 in the fifth session she was listed as an adviser to the Austrian Delegation in the Conference records. *See* A/CONF.62/INF.6/Corr.1.

17 Hermann, ed., *Die Meer Frau,* 87.

18 Hermann, ed., *Die Meer Frau,* 87.

19 In conversation with Hugh Williamson, 29 April 2016.

20 Baker, 'Uncommon Heritage', 31.

of Landlocked and Geographically Disadvantaged States. In addition to this high status in one of the most important alliances of countries interested in the area outside national jurisdiction, they also had no problem letting a quarreller into their ranks – especially since Elisabeth Mann Borgese was fighting for the common heritage principle and common heritage was just about the only way in which a landlocked state could profit from the convention. All of this made the Austrian delegation a much better fit for Mann Borgese than Malta, which had never taken her participation seriously.

Another option for Mann Borgese could have been to join a landlocked developing country. We have no records of any attempts on her part to do this, although she was in contact with many delegates from developing countries. Perhaps she thought advocating for the rights of developing landlocked countries would be easier to achieve by joining a 'respectable' industrial nation. We must remember that the increasing desire of post-colonial developing countries to partake in international decision-making was regarded with considerable suspicion by some industrial nations.[21] Austria had key roles in important committees, coupled with a level of international prestige that meant its delegation could speak with more authority than those of developing countries. It was part of the informal working group that had been established in the First Committee in 1974 to devise the functions of the International Seabed Authority,[22] and this influential role made the Austrian delegation even more attractive to Elisabeth Mann Borgese. Even before she entered the delegation, the Austrians had already been working on proposals that were similar to Mann Borgese's own. For example, the first leader of the delegation, Ambassador Franz Weidinger, had handed in a draft Article on 'participation on exploration and exploitation of the living and non-living resources in the area beyond the territorial sea'.[23]

The year Elisabeth Mann Borgese joined the Austrian delegation was also the year in which UNCLOS held two more sessions, the fourth session in spring 1976 and the fifth in autumn of that same year. Mann Borgese was actively working towards shaping the International Seabed Authority in a way that would make it possible to implement the common heritage principle, and she was dissatisfied with the developments at the fourth session. In spring 1976, she wrote to her daughter Nica: 'Time is passing rapidly. The Conference is quite lousy'.[24] The conference was 'lousy' because there had been no agreement on

21 *See* Friedheim and Durch, 'International Seabed Resources', 350.

22 *Cf.* Adede, 'System of Exploitation', 47. Adede lists all countries in the informal working group.

23 *Cf.* Baker, 'Uncommon Heritage', 31.

24 EMB B4 Mann Borgese, Easter Sunday 1976.

how to organise the functions of the International Seabed Authority without discarding the common heritage principle entirely.

3 How to Exploit the Seabed?

After Caracas, the First Committee had singled out three key issues that they could not agree on concerning the seabed outside national jurisdiction: 'The system, of exploration and exploitation, [...] the condition of exploration and exploitation, and the economic implications of sea-bed mining'.[25] Consequently, when the third session convened in Geneva in 1975, the situation in the First Committee was still overshadowed by the same old contradictory positions on how the International Seabed Authority should be organised.

Sanger wrote about the status of the negotiation process in 1975:

> The Caracas session in 1974 had shown there would be no support from the industrialized countries for the ISA as sole operator, and no support either for the original US idea of the Authority as a 'vehicle license' body with minimal powers.[26]

This approach, that either gave the International Seabed Authority total power or virtually none at all, was called a 'single system' approach. This meant the authority would have one single function: it would either hand out licences/contracts to companies or nation states wishing to conduct seabed activity; or it would conduct all such activity by itself. The negotiations at Caracas had made it abundantly clear that neither of these two contradicting proposals for a 'weak' or 'strong' International Seabed Authority could ever hope to meet with unanimous approval from the various delegations, so the participants had to come up with a compromise.

Back in 1971, the Latin American states had made a proposal to introduce something called 'the Enterprise' to the International Seabed Authority's design.[27] The initial idea was that the Enterprise should be a kind of international cooperative venture, with the sole purpose of conducting activity in the Area on behalf of all mankind.[28] Such a vision of the International Seabed

---

25 *See* 1976 Declaration of Oaxtepec, 4.

26 Sanger, *Ordering the Oceans*, 174.

27 *Cf.* Yuwen Li, *Transfer of Technology for Deep Sea-Bed Mining. The 1982 Law of the Sea Convention and Beyond* (Dordrecht: Martinus Nijhoff, 1994), 81. Li refers to A/8421, 93–101.

28 *See* Li, *Transfer of Technology*, 81. *See also* MS-2-744, Box 121, Folder 18.

Authority was clearly right at the far end of the spectrum of a 'strong' authority in a 'single system', since it would be the only entity with the right to operate in the area outside national jurisdiction. The new idea for a middle ground was to find a way of incorporating both functions: a version of the Enterprise that would carry out activity on behalf of 'all mankind', embedded in an authority that would also allocate contracts or licences for companies or states to conduct exploitation independently.

To help the delegates flesh out this idea, the concept of the Enterprise was rejuvenated in 1975. This time, the Enterprise was not intended to become a sole operator, but an 'operational arm' of the International Seabed Authority.[29] The question now was what kind of company it should be, how much power it should have and how it should operate. To incorporate the Enterprise as an operational arm of the International Seabed Authority meant introducing something called a 'parallel system'.[30] It was called 'parallel' because it would allow deep sea mining activity in the Area to be conducted in two ways. A nation state or company could apply to the ISA for a contract or a licence to conduct activity in a specific place, or the authority itself could conduct activity in a designated area through its operational arm, the Enterprise. Employing a 'parallel system' would mean that states with the technological means and expertise to conduct deep sea mining could do so by applying for contracts or licences from the authority. If the application was granted, then an area of the same size would be reserved for exploitation by developing states or by the International Seabed Authority itself through the Enterprise. In the area that was designated to the applicant, states would be free to conduct their activities under their own national laws. In this way, the companies or private entities involved would be entirely free of International Seabed Authority regulation.[31]

---

29 *See* Sanger, *Ordering the Oceans*, 167–169.

30 *Cf.* Mahmoudi, *The Law of*, 47: 'In 1976 the idea of a parallel system was considered by the Conference. The gist of the idea was to establish [a system] in which both the Authority, through its operational arm – the Enterprise – and the States Parties to the Convention and public or private entities would engage in the activities of exploration for and exploitation of the deep sea-bed resources'.

31 *See* Mahmoudi, *The Law of*, 183: 'The salient character of this 'parallel' system was that those activities which were carried out by the States and private entities in their own areas were regulated by the national law, and the Authority had no control over them. The parallel system was meant to give ultimate control to the Authority over the activities in that area which belonged to it, and provide on the other hand, for the unhampered access of other entities to other parts of the area only subject to the legislations of their respective States'.

The developing states opposed the 'parallel system', since they feared it would allow the industrialised states to conduct exploration and exploitation, while they themselves would have 'symbolic' reserved areas without any means to utilise them. How was the Enterprise going to be able to conduct activity without either the knowledge or the finances to do so? What was the point? Instead, delegates from developing states worked on several proposals that leaned back towards a 'single system' by proposing 'joint venture'. This meant that industrial states and developed states would be forced to cooperate in activities in the Area, making opportunities to conduct exploration and exploitation much more equal.[32]

By 1976, it became clear that developed states had settled on the idea of a parallel system with the Enterprise as an 'operational arm' of an authority that would otherwise interfere with their activities as little as possible.[33] The developing countries, especially the Group of 77, were still very sceptical towards the 'parallel system'.[34] For some developed states, agreement on the function of the future International Seabed Authority was so important that they were prepared to go to great lengths to convince the Group of 77 to give up on their 'joint venture' proposal that would force industrial states to share expertise and profit, to the extent that in 1976 the United States attempted to smooth over the differences by sending statesman Henry Kissinger to UNCLOS.[35] In 1975, Kissinger was reported to have said that 'the US would be "prepared to explore ways of sharing deep seabed technology with other nations" '.[36] When he came to the United Nations in 1976, he proposed an arrangement in which the United States would 'make a financial contribution to the Enterprise'[37] so that it could conduct some activity in order to get started. He also proposed a trial period of twenty-five years, after which the 'parallel system' could be reassessed and changed if necessary.[38]

---

32 *Cf.* Sanger, *Ordering the Oceans,* 171. *See also* Li, *Transfer of Technology* 63: 'The Enterprise was to either carry out these functions on its own or through joint ventures with companies sponsored by States'. *See also* Mahmoudi, *The Law of,* 256.

33 *Cf.* Sanger, *Ordering the Oceans,* 171.

34 Li, *Transfer of Technology,* 72.

35 *Cf.* Sanger, *Ordering the Oceans,* 173. *See also* Li, *Transfer of Technology* 72.

36 Li, *Transfer of Technology* 72. *See also* Schmidt, Schmidt, *Common Heritage,* 85. Apparently, the *New York Times* had reported this on 9 April 1976.

37 Li, *Transfer of Technology,* 72.

38 *Cf.* Li, *Transfer of Technology,* 72. Li refers to the Yearbook of the United Nations, 1976, 87, and the Statement by the US representative, in OFF. Rec., Vol. VI, 73–74. *See also* Sanger, *Ordering the Oceans,* 173.

The Kissinger proposal must have been reasonably effective, since Elisabeth Mann Borgese later said of Kissinger's visit to the conference: 'The big, strong United States prevailed. The lure of dollars carried more conviction than a good idea. The perceived short-term advantage defeated the long-term rational solution'.[39] However, at first it seemed like the participants managed to agree on a solution that favoured Mann Borgese's vision. In the 1976 session, the 'Informal Single Negotiation Text' (ISNT)[40] was revised and turned into the 'Revised Single Negotiating Text' (RSNT).[41] This new RSNT introduced the 'parallel system' to the International Seabed Authority. Though Kissinger might have swayed some delegations, most of the Group of 77 still opposed the implementation of the 'parallel system' as set out in the Revised Single Negotiating Text, and by the end of 1976 the conference 'faced a stalemate'.[42] Sanger wrote that while the 'parallel system was gaining ground [...] the proponents of joint ventures were resorting to ingenious, and sometimes frankly odd, proposals to reconcile the two types of scheme'.[43]

4 Preparing for the Sixth Session in 1977

For Elisabeth Mann Borgese, the 'long-term rational solution' was still a 'joint venture' system. Mann Borgese held the view that the operational arm of the International Seabed Authority should not have to compete with the industrial states, but should rather work hand-in-hand with them. If we look at the Austrian delegation's preparations for the sixth session in July 1977, we can see that they were on the same page as Mann Borgese. She had been invited by Jens Evensen to the 'Intersessional consultation in Geneva, 28 February – 11 March 1977',[44] and invitations like these gave her the chance to influence discussion in meetings that she would have been excluded from as an NGO representative. The topic of the meeting was how the International Seabed Authority should be organised.

39 Sanger, *Ordering the Oceans*, 173, in a reference to EMB. The conversation likely happened after it was clear that there would only be a parallel system. In 1976 there was still the possibility of creating something that was closer to EMB's joint venture proposal.

40 For a detailed review of the ISNT, *see* Miles, 'Structure and Effects', 167. Harrison also discusses the various proposals, *see* Harrison, *Making the Law*, 45–46.

41 For a detailed review of the RSNT, *see* Miles, 'Structure and Effects', 225.

42 Mahmoudi, *The Law of*, 187.

43 Sanger, *Ordering the Oceans*, 171.

44 MS-2-744, Box 89, Folder 18, Fostervoll to EMB, 5 December 1977.

Since official records were not kept of what went on at these intersessional meetings, to understand some of the work Mann Borgese did in them we have to rely on the papers that were circulated in advance of the meetings. In this case, along with the invitation to the meeting, Jens Evensen had enclosed his own proposal for how to find a compromise for the authority, along with background papers that explained the four competing positions at UNCLOS. The papers were from the US, USSR, The Revised Single Negotiation Text and the Group of 77.[45] The Evensen invitation and its attachments are a great illustration of how these intersessional meetings potentially influenced consensus-seeking at UNCLOS III. The four different papers were all roughly one page long and concentrated on one Article – Article 22 – which consisted of three to four bullet points. The differences between the proposals were minor, and sometimes only a couple of words were changed. As an example, Evensen proposed that point 1 of Article 22 (which defined the extent of the ISA's power) should read, 'Activities in the Area shall be organized and controlled by the Authority […]',[46] while the Group of 77's working paper proposal read, 'Activities in the Area shall be conducted exclusively by the Authority'.[47] The difference might seem minor, but actually the impact of the words 'conducted exclusively' compared to 'organized and controlled' is tremendous. While Evensen's proposal would have given the International Seabed Authority a limited amount of influence, the Group of 77's wording would have given it total power. This example shows the huge ramifications of wording in legal texts, and the difficulties the participants had to overcome at the conference. We have to keep in mind that every single paragraph of the Law of the Sea Convention was discussed in this manner.

Ambassador Wolf submitted a new paper on 9 March 1977[48] in which he revisited Article 22, the 'joint venture' system and the Austrian view on it. Although the proposal is not specifically addressed to the intersessional meeting, it is very likely that the Austrians presented it there, since it was dated around the same time as the meeting took place and Austria was invited. In contrast to the main proposals that Evensen had sent out prior to the meeting

---

45 MS-2-744, Box 89, Folder 18, Fostervoll to EMB, 5 December 1977. MS-2-744, Box 89, Folder 18, Evensen, 14. February 1977.

For information on these different proposals *see* Evensen attachment to the different articles in folder 18.

46 MS-2-744, Box 89, Folder 18, Evensen, 14. February 1977. Suggested compromise formula.

47 MS-2-744, Box 89, Folder 18, Evensen, 14. February 1977. G 77 suggestion.

48 *See* MS-2-744, Box 87, Folder 4, paper submitted by ambassador Wolf, 9 March 1977.

as a basis for discussion, Austria stubbornly insisted on returning to the 'single system' and the 'joint venture' concept. Wolf stated that:

> Activities in the area shall be conducted by the Enterprises established by the Authority in joint venture with States Parties or States Enterprises, or persons natural or juridical which possess the nationality of States Parties [...].[49]

By this, he was advocating for 'a conceptually unified system of exploitation in which the authority would have a central and indispensable role in all activities as the Trustee of the Common Heritage'.[50] According to Wolf's proposal, the authority was 'meant to provide a framework for cooperation rather than competition with established industry'.[51] The gist of the Austrian proposal was that the International Seabed Authority should always be involved in activity on the seabed outside national jurisdiction, without any exceptions. This would be ensured by establishing enterprises, which would be formed through collaborations with active companies or other actors conducting mining in the Area. In the Austrian proposal, there was no room for activity on the seabed without cooperating with the International Seabed Authority. This was, in essence, a return to the 'single system' approach that had been rejected in 1976. The Austrian proposal was similar to the working paper presented in advance by the Group of 77, but even they had moved on from the 'joint venture' idea and had started to make concessions towards designing a parallel system. In their proposal, activity in the Area was controlled by the International Seabed Authority, but the authority was not the sole executor of activities in the Area.[52]

Why was Austria attempting to re-introduce the 'joint venture' and 'single system' approaches to the International Seabed Authority? Wolf emphasised that the draft paper was 'intended as an illustration, not as a basis for discussion'.[53] The draft did not dictate any strict rules for the authority, but rather kept things flexible so that the authority could adapt to changing technology and other circumstances.[54] This was what the developing states envisioned for the 'international machinery' that would govern the Area: it should be flexible in order to shape the rules that would evolve over time depending on

49 MS-2-744, Box 87, Folder 4, paper submitted by ambassador Wolf, 9 March 1977.
50 MS-2-744, Box 87, Folder 4, paper submitted by ambassador Wolf, 9 March 1977.
51 MS-2-744, Box 87, Folder 4, paper submitted by ambassador Wolf, 9 March 1977.
52 *See* MS-2-744, Box 89, Folder 18, Evensen, 14. February 1977. G 77 proposal.
53 MS-2-744, Box 87, Folder 4, paper submitted by ambassador Wolf, 9 March 1977.
54 *Cf.* MS-2-744, Box 87, Folder 4, paper submitted by ambassador Wolf, 9 March 1977.

new developments and technology. The Austrian contribution to the intersessional meeting in 1976 seems to have been an attempt to travel back in time to the discussions about a New International Economic Order and the early days of the Seabed Committee. By the time these discussions were happening, there was little hope for the Group of 77 of turning the International Seabed Authority into effectively 'their' institution in order to effect some measure of justice in an economically imbalanced world.[55] The conference at large had moved on by this point in 1976, and was busy developing a compromise within the framework of the 'parallel system' instead of re-opening the 'single system' discussion. Was the Austrian delegation behind the times? Was Elisabeth Mann Borgese holding on to an ideal that would have to be scaled back sooner or later?

5 Reviving a Corpse? – Attempts to Reintroduce Rejected Concepts

In order to understand the Austrian proposal, we should examine its origins. In fact, the proposal was closely related to a draft that Elisabeth Mann Borgese and Arvid Pardo had worked on called 'the Enterprises'.[56] Mann Borgese sent this draft to Karl Wolf in May 1977.[57] Although the 'single system' approach and the 'joint venture' idea had been seriously undermined in 1976 by Kissinger's offer of financial aid and seemed like they might have had their day, Elisabeth Mann Borgese was still eager to present her Enterprises draft at the sixth UNCLOS session in July 1977.[58]

Karl Wolf was concerned, and replied that he had no hopes of getting any agreement in the session in question. It is likely that he had tested the waters at the intersessional meeting, and presumably the reaction to the Austrian proposal had not been very positive. Perhaps this was why he was reluctant to circulate Mann Borgese's 'Enterprises' draft, seeking to avoid prolonging the discussion and the risk of manoeuvring the conference into a 'deadlock'.[59] Instead, Wolf suggested publishing the draft under Mann Borgese's own name and distributing it within the Group of Landlocked and Geographically

55 *See* Allen, 'An Intellectual History'. 64. Allen refers to Jagdish N. Bhagwati, ed, *The New international Economic Order: The North south debate* (Cambridge MA: The MIT Press, 1977), 4.
56 *See* MS-2-744, Box 87, Folder 4, EMB to Wolf, 9 May 1977.
57 *See* MS-2-744, Box 87, Folder 4, EMB to Wolf, 9 May 1977.
58 *See* MS-2-744, Box 87, Folder 4, EMB to Wolf, 9 May 1977.
59 MS-2-744, Box 87, Folder 4, Wolf to EMB, 19 April 1977.

Disadvantaged States.[60] It is unclear what effect Wolf thought it would have to distribute a paper under Mann Borgese's name. Did he hope it might re-mobilise the group to consider taking up the 'joint venture' idea and the 'single system' once again? Was he looking to sound out potential interest? Or did he just want to placate Mann Borgese by allowing her to distribute a paper that he knew was a dead-end? We do not know.

What we do know is that Mann Borgese and Pardo's 'Enterprises' draft was a detailed and well-thought-through attempt to revive a concept that was pretty much dead in the water. By 1976, no industrialised state wanted a 'strong' International Seabed Authority, and since consensus on an agreement was so imminent, there was no real chance of backtracking. The 'parallel system' was pretty much a fact, and the main point of discussion now was how that parallel system would be designed. The main assertion of the Pardo-Borgese draft was that whatever principle was introduced at the start would most likely become a permanent foundation. They felt that 'by first admitting, and then proceeding to undo, a parallel system, one does not, and cannot, obtain a unitary system. A unitary system has to be set up as such from the beginning'.[61] This remark was an allusion to the Kissinger proposal to test the 'parallel system' and then to review it after twenty-five years. Mann Borgese and Pardo considered that a change of system at that stage would be unlikely, and also questioned whether Kissinger's offer of start-up funding for the Enterprise would translate into long-term support from the industrialised nations, writing that 'it is difficult to imagine that the U.S. proposal for financing a first project of the Enterprise be matched by other countries'.[62] Therefore, they argued that 'the proposed parallel system be discarded and replaced by a single unitary system'.[63]

The idea was that state parties, companies or other entities[64] could apply to the ISA for permission to conduct resource exploitation. The authority would then direct this entity to form an enterprise 'controlled by the Authority'.[65]

60 MS-2-744, Box 87, Folder 4, Wolf to EMB, 19 April 1977: 'Meiner Meinung nach sollte die Arbeit unter Ihrem Namen veröffentlich werden und sie könnte wahrscheinlich auch an alle Mitglieder unsere Gruppe zur Verteilung gelangen'. Her proposal was published in 1978. *See* Elisabeth Mann Borgese, 'The Enterprises: A proposal to reconceptualise the operational arm of the International Seabed Authority to manage the common heritage of mankind', *I.O.I Occasional Papers*, no. 6 (November 1978).

61 Mann Borgese, 'The Enterprises', iv.

62 Mann Borgese, 'The Enterprises', v.

63 Mann Borgese, 'The Enterprises', vi.

64 EMB writes: 'State Party or public or private entity designated by a state party or any combination thereof'. *Cf.* Mann Borgese, 'The Enterprises', vi.

65 Mann Borgese, 'The Enterprises', vi.

Which meant that for every single activity, a new enterprise would be formed in cooperation with the authority. For instance, if the US wanted to conduct deep sea mining in the Area, it would have to send in an application to the International Seabed Authority. If the application were approved, the US would then be obliged to form an enterprise that would be controlled by the authority. The specific investment on the part of each entity was broken down as such:

> The Authority must provide 52% of the investment capital, including the value of the nodules in situ, which are the common heritage of mankind. The remaining capital, technology, and managerial skills are to be provided by the participating entities.[66]

Among the proposals set out by Mann Borgese and Pardo, 'One was the direct association of companies from developing countries with enterprises in industrial countries that possessed the necessary technology'.[67] In practice, no country in possession of such technology would be interested in this kind of system. Why would they be? In most 'parallel system' proposals, once the application had been approved, activity in the Area would be conducted under the law of the state that the company or state entity was part of.[68] Returning to a single unitary system was no longer a viable option in 1976. For industrial states, an acceptable compromise was already on the table in the form of the 'parallel system', in which the International Seabed Authority's common heritage activities were limited to designated parts of the Area. Where was the compromise in the Mann Borgese-Pardo proposal that would appeal to the industrial states? There was none.

6 Secret Changes to the Draft Treaty in Favour of the Developing Countries

Developments during the sixth session provided further proof that the convention was on shaky ground where the International Seabed Authority was concerned. It was reported that Jens Evensen, through laborious discussions,

---

66 Mann Borgese, 'The Enterprises', vii.

67 Sanger, *Ordering the Oceans*, 171. Sanger did not say this in connection with EMB's proposal but joint venture proposals in general.

68 *See* Sanger, *Ordering the Oceans*,172: 'By 1976 the idea of the 'parallel system' was gaining ground, pushed by the industrial countries[..]'.

had finally managed to broker a quasi-compromise that allowed delegates to see an end to the discussion of seabed issues.[69] According to an American delegate, 'Minister Evensen offered real prospect that the impasse on seabed mining issues could be resolved on terms acceptable to both developed and developing nations'.[70] Evensen's informal working group had finally presented the possibility of 'bridging the gap'[71] between the interests of developed and developing countries.

By the end of the 1977 session, the convention had made a breakthrough. Finally, a draft treaty 'with 17 parts'[72] was produced, called the 'Informal Composite Negotiating Text (ICNT)'.[73] In the ICNT, the part about the area outside national jurisdiction was given its final name: Part XI. From then on, Part XI incorporated everything that had been discussed as Article 22, and was concerned with the International Seabed Authority and seabed regime.[74] Surprisingly, though, Part XI of the ICNT did not include the Evensen compromise.[75] How could this have happened, after the tremendous amount of work that had gone into compromise-seeking in the Evensen Group? According to Sanger and Mahmoudi, there had been some scheming behind closed doors that had led to a last-minute revision of the draft. The final draft of Article 22, soon to be incorporated in the ICNT, had been drawn up by the leader of the First Committee, Paul Engo of Cameroon. Apparently, he had changed the provisions of Article 22 'secretly'[76] to suit the interests of the developing states. Even the 'joint venture' idea was partly reintroduced,[77] and this radical change resulted in the US stating that the new Part XI was 'now fundamentally unacceptable'.[78]

Two things are interesting here. First, there is the fact that Wolf had been quite right when he warned that re-introducing the 'joint venture' idea could lead to a 'deadlock' in the Evensen Group. Second, Elisabeth Mann Borgese and Arvid Pardo had apparently not been alone in their attempts to re-introduce

69 *See* Sanger, *Ordering the Oceans*, 44–45. Schmidt writes about the difficulty of agreement that was finally solved by Evensen, *see* Schmidt, *Common Heritage*, 195.

70 *See* Mahmoudi, *The Law of*, 188. Mahmoudi quotes E.L. Richardson, chief of American delegation.

71 Mahmoudi, *The Law of*, 188.

72 Sanger, *Ordering the Oceans*, 45.

73 Sanger, *Ordering the Oceans*, 45.

74 *Cf.* Mahmoudi, *The Law of*, 189. Numbers 133–192 – A/CONF.62/WP.10.

75 Mahmoudi, *The Law of*, 189. *See also* Sanger, *Ordering the Oceans*, 45.

76 Sanger, *Ordering the Oceans*, 45

77 *See* Mahmoudi, *The Law of*, 188, 189, 190.

78 Mahmoudi, *The Law of*, Mahmoudi, 189.

the 'joint venture' idea. It would be intriguing to know whether Mann Borgese took any part or had any influence in the 'secret changes' to Part XI that were made under Paul Engo's supervision.[79] Regardless of the precise circumstances in which the changes were applied to the final draft, the incident showed that some developing states were not content with the Evensen compromise – otherwise it would have been approved by the First Committee and incorporated in the ICNT without the leader of that same committee incorporating a raft of secret changes. In order to convince these developing states to accept the 'parallel system', a new compromise had to be found.

7 New Strategies and Alliances for Landlocked and Geographically Disadvantaged States

The Paul Engo incident shone a spotlight on the role of groups, alliances and back-room negotiations at the conference. On the one hand, the groups were a necessary tool for producing drafts and shaping opinions that could be brought to the session meetings for discussion. Conversely, they made decision processes blurry, and facilitated secret changes and scheming. For the Austrian delegation, the Group of Landlocked and Geographically Disadvantaged States was their most important alliance. In October 1977, Elisabeth Mann Borgese wrote a letter to Wolf with a new draft of a working paper about the 'Composite Text',[80] in order to improve the first flawed draft of the ICNT. The letter addressed the question of how the Group of Landlocked and Geographically Disadvantaged States should position themselves in the next UNCLOS session. Mann Borgese reported that Tommy Koh, the head of delegation for Singapore and a key figure in the group, had pointed out that alliances should be formed within the three committees to 'strengthen'[81] positions. With this in mind, she emphasised that:

> we [sic: The group of Land Locked and Geographically Disadvantaged States] can safeguard our interests in the oceans only through international organizations; therefore the better organized and the more comprehensive such organizations are, the better it will be for the States of our group. Since, in this respect, the economically disadvantaged States have the same interests as the geographically disadvantaged States[…].[82]

79 Relevant correspondence might be available in MS-2-744, Box 54, Folder 25.
80 MS-2-744, Box 87, Folder 4, EMB to Wolf, 17 October 1977.
81 MS-2-744, Box 87, Folder 4, EMB to Wolf, 17 October 1977.
82 MS-2-744, Box 87, Folder 4, EMB to Wolf, 17 October 1977.

After the disagreements over Part XI, Elisabeth Mann Borgese was once again ready to adapt to the situation. Regardless of whether or not she had taken any active part in pushing through the reintroduction of 'joint venture' into the ICNT, the reaction from the industrialised states had made one thing clear: they would never submit to an overtly strong international machinery governing the Area. So what options were left to those nations wanting to secure meaningful implementation of the common heritage principle?

In the letter to Wolf, Mann Borgese suggested, 'If our group could decide to endorse the joint-venture alternative to the "parallel system" our group could assume some leadership which would pay back in other areas'.[83] This was a clever, diplomatic move. Mann Borgese's strategy was to look for ways in which a 'joint venture' solution could be incorporated into the 'parallel system'. After the somewhat unrealistic attempts to re-introduce the 'single system' with the Mann Borgese-Pardo draft, she had finally understood that the industrial countries would never approve a 'single system', and that other alternatives had to be found:

> perhaps the strongest arguments now are (a) that we NEED an alternative proposal to break the deadlock on the Evenseon [sic: Evensen] compromise; (b) that the LL and GDS need an effective and operational Seabed Authority; (c) that, to be effective, the operational system must be such that it can be applied to the international area as well as to areas under national jurisdiction.: that is, it must be flexible.[84]

Elisabeth Mann Borgese had adjusted to the realisation that the 'parallel system' was inevitable. Instead of discarding the 'joint venture' proposal on the grounds that it had initially been tailored to a 'single system', she now proposed to apply it to the 'parallel system'. Interestingly, point (c) of her proposal was effectively a loophole. By proposing to design the 'operational system' in such a way that it could be applied to both the international area and 'areas under national jurisdiction',[85] she was creating the future possibility to apply the functions of the 'machinery' to all ocean space. This was not a new strategy. In fact, Mann Borgese had proposed a similar approach in her draft of 'The Ocean Regime', in which she had designed the chambers of the Planning Agency in a way that would allow the ocean regime to expand into a world regime. It is questionable whether Mann Borgese ever truly expected that these in-built

83 MS-2-744, Box 87, Folder 4, EMB to Wolf, 17 October 1977.

84 MS-2-744, Box 87, Folder 4, EMB to Wolf, 17 October 1977.

85 MS-2-744, Box 87, Folder 4, EMB to Wolf, 17 October 1977.

possibilities for expansion would eventually be used. Perhaps the approach is more an expression of her long-term, functional and solution-oriented way of thinking – a sort of 'just in case' optimism.[86]

8 Austria Loses Faith – An Era of Instability

In the course of 1977, the discussions at the sixth session had revealed the 'hard core issues'[87] of the convention. Three of these seven issues were related to the seabed mining propositions. Apart from that, Sanger could report a degree of optimism: 'By 1978 UNCLOS-3 appeared to be nearing the home stretch. Canadian Officials had been reporting that it might take two more sessions to overcome difficulties over seabed mining'.[88] The Canadian officials had made a grave miscalculation. In February 1978, the *Washington Post* published an article about the United States' position in the conference: 'U.S. Seeks Seabed Mining Showdown'.[89] Journalist William Claiborne wrote that 'The United States [...] has begun playing the diplomatic equivalent of "chicken" in the long-running United Nations Law of the Sea Conference'.[90]

The US strategy, according to the article, was to take a 'hard-line posture',[91] and the essence of this was to question whether the treaty was even needed at all. The journalist pointed out that this was an interesting argument, considering that nearly ten years of hard work lay behind the conference participants.[92] Instead of negotiating international compromise, Congress was about to pass a bill that would 'authorize and encourage U.S. mining companies to unilaterally begin to mine the trillions of dollars of cobalt, nickel, manganese and copper on the bottom of the oceans'.[93] Claiborne also mentioned that US officials were opposed to a 'treaty that was secretly rewritten by a handful of Third

86 Kerstin Holzer characterized EMB as short-term pessimist, long-term optimist, *see* Holzer, ' "Short-term pessimist" ', 180.

87 Sanger, *Ordering the Oceans*, 46.

88 Sanger, *Ordering the Oceans*, 46.

89 MS-2-744, Box 87, Folder 4, William Claiborne, U.S. Seeks Seabed Mining Showdown, *Washington Post*, 13 February 1978.

90 MS-2-744, Box 87, Folder 4, William Claiborne, U.S. Seeks Seabed Mining Showdown, *Washington Post*, 13 February 1978.

91 MS-2-744, Box 87, Folder 4, William Claiborne, U.S. Seeks Seabed Mining Showdown, *Washington Post*, 13 February 1978.

92 MS-2-744, Box 87, Folder 4, William Claiborne, U.S. Seeks Seabed Mining Showdown, *Washington Post*, 13 February 1978.

93 MS-2-744, Box 87, Folder 4, William Claiborne, U.S. Seeks Seabed Mining Showdown, *Washington Post*, 13 February 1978.

World delegates',[94] and this was obviously a reference to Paul Engo's problematic excision of the Evensen compromise in 1977. If this was true, then Engo's actions had complicated international relations and had a negative influence on US willingness to cooperate.

The United States' negative attitude towards the conference in general did not pass unnoticed. Mann Borgese attached the article to a letter she sent to Karl Wolf, in which she reported back to him on the general mood and tone of a session she had attended without him (probably a working group). Apparently, the situation was complicated, the end of the session 'a funeral'[95] and the 'Latinos, more persistent, aggressive and angry than ever'.[96] On the bright side, she could report that the United States had been very 'mild, seductive and auspicious',[97] but that she still had the impression that they would never drop the 'parallel approach', regardless of what compromises were offered.[98] Elisabeth Mann Borgese assumed that the US's strategy was to play for time by disrupting efforts to reach a consensus until the conference fell apart. She wrote, 'That is how time goes by, [...] and then there is no Part XI'.[99] To do something about the 'desperate'[100] situation, she suggested distributing a working paper at the upcoming seventh session in Geneva.[101]

Elisabeth Mann Borgese was not ready to give in, but Karl Wolf, on the other hand, reported that his government was starting to scale back their involvement.[102] In July 1978, he informed Mann Borgese that he was the only delegate who would be attending the resumed seventh session from August to September in New York.[103] This also complicated Mann Borgese's own role in

94 MS-2-744, Box 87, Folder 4, William Claiborne, U.S. Seeks Seabed Mining Showdown, *Washington Post,* 13 February 1978.

95 MS-2-744, Box 87, Folder 4, EMB to Wolf, 28 February 1978. ‚ein Begräbnis'.

96 MS-2-744, Box 87, Folder 4, EMB to Wolf, 28 February 1978. ‚Die Latinos hartnäckiger, aggressiver, und böser als jeh'.

97 MS-2-744, Box 87, Folder 4, EMB to Wolf, 28 February 1978. ‚mild, verführerisch, vielversprechend'.

98 MS-2-744, Box 87, Folder 4, EMB to Wolf, 28 February 1978. ‚Wie sie aus meinem beiliegenden Bericht sehen werden, waren die Amerikaner auf dieser letzten Arbeitssitzung besonders mild, verführerisch, und vielversprechend. Sie werden den parallel approach nie fallen lassen, aber auch nie zu einem wirklichen Kompromiss kommen[...]'.

99 MS-2-744, Box 87, Folder 4, EMB to Wolf, 28 February 1978. ‚[...] und so vergeht die Zeit, und das ist wohl auch die Absicht, und dann ist eben kein Part XI da ...'.

100 MS-2-744, Box 87, Folder 4, EMB to Wolf, 28 February 1978.

101 *See* MS-2-744, Box 87, Folder 4, EMB to Wolf, 28 February 1978.

102 MS-2-744, Box 87, Folder 4, Wolf to EMB, 6 June 1978. 'Der wachsende Widerstand in Regierungskreisen gegen die UN-Seerechtskonferenz hat nunmehr auch Wien erreicht'.

103 MS-2-744, Box 87, Folder 4, Wolf to EMB, 6 June 1978.

the Austrian delegation. If Wolf was the only person being sent to New York, would she still be part of the delegation? For the Geneva session in spring, the Austrians had sent a six-strong delegation with Elisabeth Mann Borgese as an adviser.[104] Attendance was drastically reduced for the resumed seventh session in New York, with the government sending only Karl Wolf and two advisers. Mann Borgese was not listed in the document.[105] It is hard to know for sure why the Austrian government had cut down its number of delegates. It may simply have been a cost-cutting measure to avoid flying in delegates to a United Nations gathering in New York that seemed unlikely to hold any potential benefit for Austria. Whatever the case, Karl Wolf did not want Mann Borgese excluded from the delegation. In July 1978, he asked her, in confidentiality, to join the session regardless in an attempt 'To rescue what is left to rescue'.[106]

104 He was perhaps worried about being the only one to travel to the conference. Still, in 1978, six people were listed for the Austrian delegation to UNCLOS. *Cf.* S-0571-0013.

105 *See* S-0571-0013. She would be reinstated as adviser in 1979, *see* A/CONF.62/INF.11, 4, 14 August 1979. And in 1980, *see* A/CONF.62/INF.13, 3, 20. August 1980.

106 MS-2-744, Box 87, Folder 4, Wolf to EMB, 6 June 1978. 'Unter diesen Umständen hoffe ich, dass es Ihnen möglich sein wird, an der New Yorker-Tagung teilzunehmen, um zu retten, was noch zu retten ist'.

CHAPTER 9

To Rescue What Is Left to Rescue

1 A New Headquarters in Halifax

While the Austrian ambassador was feeling lonely with his reduced delegation at the resumed seventh session in New York, Elisabeth Mann Borgese was going through some upheavals in her private life. In the autumn of 1978, she left her position as a fellow at the Center for the Study of Democratic Institutions in Santa Barbara. Since the foundation of the International Ocean Institute on Malta, Mann Borgese had used the initials of the institute in most of her UNCLOS correspondence. It is questionable to what extent she was still involved in the day-to-day business at the crumbling centre, taking into account her hectic itinerary and her commitments to the Austrian delegation and Law of the Sea projects. In 1978, however, a fresh home base appeared on the horizon. Her new position would be a fellowship at Dalhousie University in Halifax, Canada.

During a memorial lecture held in June 2010, the man who employed her, Gilbert Winham, told the story of how she came to Halifax. It began when the university received a letter from Elisabeth Mann Borgese, who Winham knew 'not by person but by reputation'.[1] The political science department had been contacting other institutions in search of a 'mid-level research-associate',[2] and they had asked the Center for the Study of Democratic Institutions whether they had anyone suitable. Elisabeth Mann Borgese replied saying that she did not have any candidates to propose, but 'would we consider her [own] candidacy?'[3] Later, Winham found out that the centre in Santa Barbara was 'a dying institution'.[4] As with so many accounts featuring Elisabeth Mann Borgese, Winham's lecture mentioned her eccentric lifestyle. In the case of Dalhousie University, this became apparent more or less as soon as she got the position, when she asked whether the university could help her find a house with space for her famous English setter kennel, which at the time consisted of about six dogs.[5] The university found a house in Sambro Head, a fishing village some

---

1 Gilbert Winham, introductory remarks, 2010.

2 Gilbert Winham, introductory remarks, 2010.

3 Gilbert Winham, introductory remarks, 2010.

4 Gilbert Winham, introductory remarks, 2010.

5 *Cf.* Gilbert Winham, introductory remarks, 2010.

FIGURE 4 Elisabeth Mann Borgese's house by the sea
MONACENSIA LITERATURARCHIV UND BIBLIOTHEK MÜNCHEN, EMB F 22
PHOTO: NICA BORGESE

miles outside of Halifax, and Mann Borgese was able to move to Canada in autumn 1978.[6] She would spend the rest of her life there.

1978 was also the year in which the first volume of *The Ocean Yearbook* was published. The publication was branded 'a flagship IOI publication',[7] and was produced out of the International Ocean Institute in Malta. Elisabeth Mann Borgese described the purpose of the yearbook in the preface of the first volume: 'Besides assembling economic and ecological data related to the exploration and exploitation of the oceans, the Ocean Yearbook attempts to analyse trends and to present them in their interaction'.[8] The first issue was very much concerned with recent UNCLOS issues, and Arvid Pardo contributed to the publication with a commentary of the Informal Composite Negotiating Text (ICNT) that had been developed by the participants at the conference.[9] The headquarters of the International Ocean Institute would remain on Malta,

6 *Cf.* B-III.17-MANN-144, 09.10.1978.
7 Sunli M. Shastri, 'Elisabeth Mann Borgese: A Life Dedicated to Pacem in Maribus', Ocean Yearbook, 18 (Brill 2004): 81.
8 Elisabeth Mann Borgese, 'Man and the Oceans', *Ocean Yearbook* 1 (Brill 1978): 1.
9 *See* Elisabeth Mann Borgese, et al, eds, *Ocean Yearbook* 1 (Brill 1978).

despite Mann Borgese's fall-out with the Maltese government, and she used the institute to actively promote her ocean governance ideas. The International Ocean Institute continued to organise the *Pacem in Maribus* conferences, focusing on relevant topics and issues from UNCLOS. In 1976, for instance, the PIM topic was 'The Law of the Sea and Latin America' (Mexico), in 1977 it was 'The Law of the Sea and the New International and Economic Order' (Algeria), and in 1978 the topic of the convocation was 'Africa and the Law of the Sea' (Cameroon).[10]

From 1978 onwards, though, Mann Borgese's own home base would be Halifax. Many years later, she was asked how she had decided to end up in Halifax. She answered pragmatically that she had not made the decision herself, but that it had been chance or fate that had brought her there. And she had stayed because she liked it.[11]

There were, perhaps, certain things that made Dalhousie University attractive. The campus was small and the university was relatively unknown, but it had all the facilities a university needed. Maybe she hoped she could create something there that had not been possible in Santa Barbara. Then again, perhaps she was just looking for a job and the position suited her. In addition, Halifax was largely anglophone, and it was closer to New York and Europe than the west coast of the United States had been. A position in Canada was also Mann Borgese's chance to leave the United States. She had been vocal about her disdain for much of the United States' politics, and was perhaps happy to get away from it.[12] While Mann Borgese began to settle into life in Halifax, preparations for the eighth UNCLOS session scheduled for March 1979 were taking shape.

2 Austria's Report on Jens Evensen's Intersessional Meeting – Visions Falling Apart

Though Elisabeth Mann Borgese was reinstalled as adviser for Austria in 1979, we learn from the letters she and Karl Wolf exchanged in the last four years of

10 *See* the full list of PIM conference at: International Ocean Institute, *Pacem in Maribus*, https://www.ioinst.org/about-1/ioi-story/pacem-in-maribus-pim-conferences/.

11 *Cf.* Elisabeth Mann Borgese and Eberhard Görner, '"Für mich ist Politik, an eine bessere Zukunft zu denken"'- Ein Gespräch', in *Elisabeth Mann Borgese und das Drama der Meere*, exhibition catalogue, eds. Holger Pils and Karolina Kühn (Hamburg: mareverlag, 2012), 226.

12 *See* Hermann, ed., *Die Meer Frau*, 87: 'The US was "on the other side of the political spectra"'.

the conference that she did not attend all the intersessional meetings.[13] Wolf often mentioned the reduced Austrian delegation, but also informed Mann Borgese about important intersessional meetings in order to invite her.[14] Her exact official role in the increasingly pessimistic Austrian delegation during the last four years of the conference is not quite clear and would need further investigation. She was invited to several intersessional meetings organised by Jens Evensen, though this may have been in a personal capacity.[15] In her own Curriculum Vitae from 1982, she continued to list herself as 'Member of Austrian Delegation'.[16] Perhaps, while the delegation was reduced on paper in 1978, Mann Borgese was still a member in practice and continued her work for Austria until she was reinstalled officially in 1979. The fact that she was very active during the last years of the conference support this view.[17]

The letters that passed between Wolf and Mann Borgese during this period show that she was well informed about UNCLOS, and that she attended meetings and wrote reports. Her detailed overviews, reviews and reports on several core issues of the negotiations are testament to her in-depth knowledge on the matters in question,[18] and she was clearly able to attend the 'backroom meetings' in which a lot of the decision-making happened. Meanwhile, Austria's downbeat attitude became increasingly pronounced. In January 1979, Wolf wrote a letter to Mann Borgese from Oslo – where he was serving in the Austrian embassy – in which he voiced his concerns about Austria's further participation in UNCLOS, recounting that 'The mood in Vienna is still not the best'.[19] It seemed that several other members of the Group of Landlocked and Geographically Disadvantaged States were beginning to retreat too. Even on a personal level, Karl Wolf admitted that he was starting to doubt whether the outcome of the convention could be favourable for states without a coastline.[20]

By the end of 1979, the conference still faced the same fundamental problems as it had in 1977 and 1978.[21] The whole issue could be boiled down to the

13 EMB back as adviser, *see* A/CONF.62/INF.11, 4, 14 August 1979.

14 MS-2-744, Box 114, Folder 7, Wolf to EMB, 16 January 1979.

15 MS-2-744, Box 114, Folder 7, Wolf to EMB, 16 January 1979.

16 MS-2-744, Box 16, Folder 19, EMB CV.

17 She would be a member of the Prep Com Seabed Authority with Austria from 1982 onwards, *see* MS-2-744, Box 16, Folder 19, EMB CV.

18 We will come back to various proposals in this chapter.

19 MS-2-744, Box 114, Folder 7, Wolf to EMB, 16 January 1979. 'Die Stimmung in Wien für die Seerechtskonferenz ist nach wie vor nicht die beste'.

20 MS-2-744, Box 114, Folder 7, Wolf to EMB, 16 January 1979. 'Man ist auch in Wien mehr und mehr der Ansicht, dass für uns, also die LL-GDS überhaupt nichts herausschauen wird und es fällt mir selbst immer schwerer, nicht dieser Auffassung zu sein'.

21 *See* Sanger, *Ordering the Oceans*, 45–46.

conflict between developing and developed countries. Karl Wolf forwarded a report about an 'intersessional meeting'[22] in Geneva, in which this interpretation was reflected in a summary of outstanding issues by the Norwegian delegate Jens Evensen. The report outlined the difficulties in coming to an agreement, despite the 'factual atmosphere'[23] and the 'obviously maximal will'[24] to reach a consensus. This desire for final resolution is hardly surprising, since after so many years most delegates must have been keen to see an end to the convention. The biggest issue remained the divide between the developing and industrial states, especially the USA.[25] The developing countries were still eager to create a strong International Seabed Authority that they could influence,[26] while the US was clear that Congress would never ratify such a system.[27] At least the intersessional meeting succeeded in illuminating some crucial points of discussion. There was disagreement over how far amendments could or should be made to the convention – meaning whether it should be permissible to change parts of the Law of the Sea after it came into force, or whether the treaty should be treated like constitutional law that could not be amended.[28] Directly related to the issue of potential amendments was the worry from developing countries that the main Law of the Sea Treaty might be detached from the disputed Part XI dealing with seafloor issues. This would make the International Seabed Authority ineffective, and would render redundant the whole idea of reserving the seafloor for the common heritage of mankind, since the industrial countries could then pick

22 MS-2-744, Box 114, Folder 7, Wolf to EMB, 12 December 1979. '3. UN-Seerechtskonferenz: Bericht über das Intersessionelle Meeting über die Schlussklauseln (Genf, 19.-28. November 1979) vom 31. Oktober 1979'.

23 MS-2-744, Box 114, Folder 7, Wolf to EMB, 12 December 1979.

24 MS-2-744, Box 114, Folder 7, Wolf to EMB, 12 December 1979.

25 MS-2-744, Box 114, Folder 7, Wolf to EMB, 12 December 1979. 'Trotz des sehr sachlichen Klimas und des offensichtlichen maximalen Bemühens der Teilnehmer, zu Ergebnissen zu kommen, liess sich doch nicht verbergen, welche grundsätzlichen Schwierigkeiten noch vor allem zwischen den Entwicklungsländern und den Industriestaaten und hier vor allem den USA bestehen'.

26 MS-2-744, Box 114, Folder 7, Wolf to EMB, 12 December 1979. ‚[…] bemüht, ein System der International Seabed Authority zu erreichen, welches aufgrund der Mehrheitsverhältnisse in den Vereinten Nationen dann von ihnen gehandhabt werden kann […]'.

27 MS-2-744, Box 114, Folder 7, Wolf to EMB, 12 December 1979. ‚[…] die USA betont nach wie vor, dass ein so organisiertes System nicht die leiseste Chance habe, vom Kongress ratifiziert zu werden'.

28 MS-2-744, Box 114, Folder 7, Wolf to EMB, 12 December 1979. 'Points of discussions were: „Amendment (Art. B)", "Zusätzlich zur Revisonskonferenz nach 20 oder 25 Jahren, möchten die Entwicklungsländer eine Möglichkeit schaffen, ihre diesbezüglichen Wünsche schon vorher durch amendments durchsetzen zu können" '.

and choose which paragraphs they wanted to obey.[29] Another issue was the fear that some industrial countries would reject the convention.[30] At least one issue was agreed upon: the convention would be put into force if at least sixty states ratified it.[31]

The intersessional meeting in autumn 1979 reflected the overarching mood at the conference. Although there was a strong will among the delegates to finalise the convention, certain issues were proving difficult to agree on, and the United States delegation was particularly stubborn in its demands about how the International Seabed Authority would function. These were the issues that burdened the negotiation process.

That the report was sent to Elisabeth Mann Borgese is an indication of how heavily she was still involved in the discussion and negotiations at UNCLOS, despite the new commitments that accompanied her move to Halifax. She had to get used to a new work environment, teach courses and carve out a position for herself in the department. By the time she had been in her position in Halifax a year, she had already managed to establish a branch of the International Ocean Institute at Dalhousie University[32] and had also started to develop and organise an 'International Ocean Institute Training Programme for Third World Participants'.[33] In January 1980, Mann Borgese replied to Wolf's report about the intersessional meeting. She wrote that she had heard about a 'Russian proposal'[34] to make 'accession to Part XI optional',[35] which she found 'somewhat alarming'.[36] Taken as a whole, her letter reflected Wolf's earlier pessimism. She even wrote that she had no hope there would be any progress made at the next meeting – which was scheduled for March and April

---

29 MS-2-744, Box 114, Folder 7, Wolf to EMB, 12 December 1979. ‚Relation to Part XI (art. D) In der Debatte zu diesem Punkt zeigt sich das unterschwellige Befürchten der Entwicklungsländer, es könne zu einer Trennung zwischen der Kovention und ihres Teiles XI (International Seabed Authority) kommen'.

30 MS-2-744, Box 114, Folder 7, Wolf to EMB, 12 December 1979. 'Denunciation (Art. G) [...] Die Hauptsorge ist offenbar, dass ein grosser Industriestaat die Konvention aufkündigt und dann unilateral an die Ausbeutung des Meeresbodens schreitet. Nach Darstellung des US-Vertreters ist jedoch eine relativ einfache Aufkündigung Grundlage für die Ratifikation des Vertragswerkes durch den Kongress'.

31 MS-2-744, Box 114, Folder 7, Wolf to EMB, 12 December 1979. ‚Inkrafttreten der Konvention (Art. 301 des ICNT) 60 Ratifikationen'.

32 *Cf.* Shastri, 'Elisabeth Mann Borgese', 81.

33 MS-2-744, Box 16, Folder 19, EMB CV.

34 MS-2-744, Box 114, Folder 7, EMB to Wolf, 15 January 1980.

35 MS-2-744, Box 114, Folder 7, EMB to Wolf, 15 January 1980.

36 MS-2-744, Box 114, Folder 7, EMB to Wolf, 15 January 1980.

of 1980 – especially when she considered what she called the 'devastating'[37] state of the world.

The state of the world was that Soviet Russia had invaded Afghanistan in December 1979, and antagonism between the United States and the Soviet Union was heating up. Although Elisabeth Mann Borgese did not mention the conflict directly, this must have been the 'devastating' situation she referred to. It seemed possible that the deteriorating international relations between the two superpowers might threaten the progress of the convention. Wolf replied in January 1980, confirming Mann Borgese's worries. He wrote that 'The proceeding of the Law of the Sea Conference and how it will be influenced in a negative way by the currently prevailing frosty climate is a completely open question'.[38]

3 Losing the President of the Law of the Sea Convention Causes a Crisis

Over the course of 1980–1, several incidents would prove Elisabeth Mann Borgese and Karl Wolf correct in their concerns about the progress of the Law of the Sea Convention. The reasons, however, were rather more complex than the Soviet-US conflict and the deteriorating political world situation that surrounded it. First of all, though, came a breakthrough and some positive developments that were in stark contrast to Mann Borgese and Wolf's dire predictions. By 1980, the delegates had managed to move past the informal negotiation text and to agree on a so-called 'draft convention'.[39] This breakthrough occurred in the ninth session of UNCLOS in 1980[40] and it left the delegates hopeful for the future. It seemed like the end of the interminable discussions

37 MS-2-744, Box 114, Folder 7, EMB to Wolf, 15 January 1980. ‚Nun bin ich wieder zuhause in Halifax, und find hier Deinen hoch interessanten Bericht. Ich hatte schon von einem Russischen Vorschlag, accession to Part XI optional zu machen, gehört, und das ist natürlich einigermassen besorgniserregend. Im übrigen ist die Weltlage nun dermassen verheerend, dass man sich kaum vorstellen kann, dass irgendwelche Fortschritte gemacht werden können, auf unserer nächsten Sitzung'.

38 MS-2-744, Box 114, Folder 7, Wolf to EMB, 25 January 1980. 'Wie es mit unserer Seerechtskonferenz weitergehen wird und inwieweit sie durch das derzeit herrschende frostige Klima im negativen Sinn beeinflusst werden wird, ist eine vollkommen offene Frage'.

39 Sanger, *Ordering the Oceans*, 48.

40 Sanger, *Ordering the Oceans*, 48.

might just be within reach. In a review of the draft convention,[41] Mann Borgese wrote, 'the world wide optimism at the end of the Ninth Session appeared justified. All major issues that had defied the skills and will of the diplomats for years, had been solved'.[42] Sanger wrote about the outcome of the ninth session that:

> it was still a negotiating text, and the hope was to turn it into an official draft in time for adoption by consensus, if possible rather than by vote – 1981. In fact, delegations had unanimously agreed in Geneva in August 1980 that, after nearly seven years of negotiations, they would make the New York meeting in March-April the last negotiating round.[43]

The New York meeting in March–April 1981 would be the tenth session. But before the new year rolled around, there was a tragic development that threatened to destabilise the optimistically scheduled 'last' negotiation round. On 4 December, Wolf wrote to Mann Borgese bearing sad news. Shirley H Amerasinghe – the universally popular president of the convention – had suffered a stroke and died.[44] This sudden death of a friend and ally was not just a personal shock for the two members of the Austrian delegation, but the tragedy also raised a new issue: who would lead the tenth session? Wolf proposed discussing this in an intersessional meeting.[45] He was concerned that Amerasinghe's death could delay – or even prevent – the convention from reaching the finish line. Elisabeth Mann Borgese replied to Wolf's letter on 26 December 1980:

> This was a bad shock. Poor Shirley. In Vienna he was still so funny and literally sang and danced. He was an old good faithful friend. Anyone who

41 *See* MS-2-744, Box 176, Folder 13, EMB, The Draft Convention on the Law of the Sea: An Appeal for action now. Harrison about the draft convention, see Harrison, *Making the Law*, 46:

'At the close of the ninth session in 1980, the title of the document was changed to "draft convention," although its status as a negotiating text remained unaffected until its final adoption in 1982'.

42 MS-2-744, Box 176, Folder 13, EMB, The Draft Convention on the Law of the Sea: An Appeal for action now. Concerning the remaining issues, *see* '[…] the question of the delimination between States with adjacent or opposite coasts and the settlement of dispute thereon; an American proposal for a provision regarding preparatory investment protection; and details concerning the preparatory Commission'.

43 Sanger, *Ordering the Oceans*, 48.

44 *Cf.* MS-2-744, Box 114, Folder 8, Wolf to EMB, 4 December 1980.

45 *Cf.* MS-2-744, Box 114, Folder 8, Wolf to EMB, 4 December 1980.

> does not want the convention to be finished will seize the opportunity to take advantage of this tragedy.[46]

She then quickly moved on to damage limitation. If the convention were to be finalised, a replacement for the lost president had to be found, and fast. Mann Borgese outlined two available options: either they could elect a new president or they could appoint the current vice-president. Mann Borgese favoured the 'vice-president solution',[47] because it would avoid wasting time on the procedures necessary to elect a new president.[48] The disadvantage was that there would be no leader in 'difficult moments'.[49] According to Elisabeth Mann Borgese, the two candidates who came to mind for the new president role were Tommy Koh of Singapore and Chris Pinto of Sri Lanka. Mann Borgese weighed up the advantages and disadvantages of Koh and concluded, 'Tommy has gained great prestige through his excellent work and has the trust of the US. Singapore is not popular with the 77'.[50] As it turned out, the delegates at the convention decided that the deceased president should be replaced by a new candidate, and Tommy Koh from Singapore was picked for the job.[51] Appointing a new president so late in the convention was a challenge for the president himself, but it also caused some more general changes. The delegate who would take over Amerasinghe's position was different in both character and diplomatic style. Clyde Sanger compared Tommy Koh's presidential style at the convention with that of Amerasinghe, noting that Koh was 'of a quite different temperament, eager to master the detailed subject and quick to plunge into issues with articulate argument'.[52]

Tommy Koh stepped up to become president at a difficult moment. He was soon faced with trying to sort out a dramatic US withdrawal, alongside finding compromises to resolve the outstanding seabed issues. For the few remaining

---

46 MS-2-744, Box 114, Folder 8, EMB to Wolf, 26 December 1980. 'Das war ein arger Schock, mit dem armen Shirley. In Wien war er noch so lustig und hat, buchstäblich gesunden und getanzt. Er war auch ein alter guter treuer Freund. Wer nun nicht will, dass die Convention fertig wird, wird diese tragische Gelegenheit schön ausnutzen '.

47 MS-2-744, Box 114, Folder 8, EMB to Wolf, 26 December 1980. ‚Die Vice-President Lösung hätte den Vorteil von weniger Prozedur-Quälerei und Zeitverlust'.

48 MS-2-744, Box 114, Folder 8, EMB to Wolf, 26 December 1980.

49 MS-2-744, Box 114, Folder 8, EMB to Wolf, 26 December 1980. ‚[…] und den Nachteil, dass in schwierigen Momenten, die sicherlich bevorstehen, keine Führung da ist'.

50 MS-2-744, Box 114, Folder 8, EMB to Wolf, 26 December 1980. 'Tommy hat sich durch seine ausgezeichnete Arbeit grosses Prestige erworben, und hat das Vertrauen der US. Singapore ist aber bei den 77 nicht beliebt'.

51 *Cf.* Sanger, *Ordering the Oceans*, 42. *See also* Sebenius and Green, *Tommy Koh.*

52 *Cf.* Sanger, *Ordering the Oceans*, 42.

years of the convention, it was Koh's job to reconcile the differing opinions and find practical solutions that were acceptable for every delegation, in the face of dwindling time and motivation.

4 United States' Retreat Stalls the Negotiations

This was not the only change in presidency to put a strain on the conference. Shortly after the delegates had settled down to continue the negotiations, Ronald Reagan was elected as the next president of the United States. With his election in 1981, the US's attitude towards the Law of the Sea Treaty changed for the worse.[53]

Among the vast heaps of Elisabeth Mann Borgese's documents at the Dalhousie University Archives, there is a little collage that perfectly represents Mann Borgese's view of the Reagan administration. In a folder labelled 'Arvid Pardo',[54] three photographs are glued to a yellowed piece of card. On the left-hand side are two polaroid pictures of Arvid Pardo. From the collection of books in the background, he is perhaps in a library or study of some sort. He looks friendly behind his enormous, black-framed glasses, with his hands in his pockets and his tie loose around his neck. On the right hand side of the card, there is a picture of Ronald Reagan saluting in an open aeroplane door. Above the pictures, an anonymous hand has written in crooked letters, 'Which man do you trust with the future??'[55]

Perhaps the collage was an inside joke, made by one of Mann Borgese's students on an ocean governance course and stuck on a wall somewhere. Whatever its origins, it is a neat illustration of how Mann Borgese and probably other participants at the conference saw Reagan as a disruptive force. Instead of holding a steady course – like Arvid Pardo, who remained true to his common heritage principles – Reagan radically changed the tack of US policy. He swapped out his whole delegation and took a policy line that was almost hostile towards everything the convention had achieved. By openly questioning the whole endeavour, Reagan was taking the 'hard-line posture' that the *Washington Post* journalist, Claiborne, had reported on in 1978.[56]

53 For US problematique, *see* Ratiner, 'American Rigidity', 27.

54 MS-2-744, Box 235, Folder 4, Which man do you trust with the future?

55 MS-2-744, Box 235, Folder 4, Which man do you trust with the future?

56 *See* Sanger, *Ordering the Oceans,* 49: 'As a result of the virtual withdrawal of the United states, negotiations at UNCLOS-3 during 1981'. EMB said in her appeal that the US left the convention, *see* MS-2-744, Box 176, Folder 13, EMB, The Draft Convention on the Law of the Sea: An Appeal for action now.

FIGURE 5 'Which man do you trust with the future??'
DALHOUSIE UNIVERSITY ARCHIVES MS-2-744 BOX 235 FOLDER 4
CREATOR: UNKNOWN

In 1980, the former leader of the delegation for the US, Elliot Richardson,[57] had announced that, as far as the US was concerned, there were just three points of contention left:

> participating in the treaty by entities that were not sovereign states (including regional organizations, like the EEC, and liberation movements); the power of the Preparatory Commission in writing the rules and regulations for the Seabed Authority; and – a newly raised concern of the United States. 'preparatory investment protection' (or PIP) for those private enterprises that had already invested millions in the exploration of manganese nodule deposits […].[58]

Fast-forward to 1981, and Malone, the new delegation leader under Reagan, turned the negotiation draft upside down.[59] Clyde Sanger reported on the new course of the US during the tenth session:

> Malone told the tenth session that the US Government had 'serious problems' with the negotiating text and in August, at the 'resumed tenth' session in Geneva, he named eight particular concerns to do with seabed mining but did not mention any other article.[60]

According to Sanger, Malone's actions at the tenth session brought the negotiations to a 'crawl'.[61] The US was essential to the convention, and without its cooperation, there was a serious risk that the Law of the Sea Treaty would turn into an ineffectual, symbolic international convention on the oceans. Additionally, the US withdrawal in 1981 could 'inspire' other industrial states to re-consider their willingness to collaborate. When the US announced that it would not attend any more meetings in 1981, the outcome of the convention was suddenly thrown into doubt.[62]

---

57 Richardson left in October 1980. *See* Sanger, *Ordering the Oceans,* 49.

58 Sanger, *Ordering the Oceans,* 49.

59 Reagan administration sets up a new delegation to UNCLOS. *See* Schmidt, *Common Heritage,* 218–219.

60 Sanger, *Ordering the Oceans,* 49.

61 Sanger, *Ordering the Oceans,* 49.

62 *See* MS-2-744, Box 176, Folder 13, EMB, The Draft Convention on the Law of the Sea: An Appeal for action now.

5 Elisabeth Mann Borgese's Appeal to Act without the United States

The situation must have inspired Mann Borgese and others to throw themselves into damage limitation efforts. Various reports, appeals and speeches from among Elisabeth Mann Borgese's papers demonstrate that she had detailed knowledge and insight into the various ongoing conflicts at UNCLOS, both small and large, and this was especially true of the tenth session in 1981, at which the US under Reagan and Malone announced they would have to review the draft treaty.

Elisabeth Mann Borgese addressed this issue in a document with the title 'The Draft Convention on the Law of the Sea – An Appeal for Action Now'.[63] The date of the document is uncertain, but since it addresses the incidents at the tenth session in April 1981, we can assume it must have been written sometime after that. Unfortunately, we also do not know where or even if it was published, making it difficult to gauge her influence through this kind of document. Nevertheless, it gives us valuable insights into Mann Borgese's view on the crisis with the US and her ideas about how to overcome the issues and proceed with the negotiations.

Mann Borgese started her appeal for action by saying that the conference's tenth session had 'marked a most regrettable set-back'[64] because it had been 'paralysed by the U.S. announcement that the Reagan Administration was undertaking an extensive, comprehensive review of the Draft Convention and would not be in a position to negotiate this year'.[65] She then reported on the four different options that the new president of UNCLOS, Tommy Koh, had presented on how the conference might unfold in the light of the United States' withdrawal. Case one: the US would change their mind and return to the bargaining table speedily. The convention might then be able to close in 1981. Case two: the US would ask for changes that were insignificant enough to be incorporated into the convention without major negotiation. In this case too, finalising things in 1981 would still be possible. Case three: the US would demand extensive changes, which would delay the negotiations significantly and make it impossible to see an end to the convention in the upcoming years. And the

63 MS-2-744, Box 176, Folder 13, EMB, The Draft Convention on the Law of the Sea: An Appeal for action now.

64 MS-2-744, Box 176, Folder 13, EMB, The Draft Convention on the Law of the Sea: An Appeal for action now.

65 MS-2-744, Box 176, Folder 13, EMB, The Draft Convention on the Law of the Sea: An Appeal for action now.

fourth and worst case: the US would decide to refuse the treaty, meaning that the remaining countries would have to try and finish the treaty without it.[66]

These, then, were the possible scenarios for the future. Mann Borgese feared that the US would choose the third option, and would demand major changes to the convention – especially the seabed mining sections in Part XI. She worried that the US would exert serious influence on the fate of the convention because its eventual participation in the treaty was of major importance for many states. Therefore, the US was effectively in a position to demand such sweeping changes to the paragraphs on seabed mining that the common heritage principle could end up being practically removed.[67]

For Mann Borgese, the future looked bleak. She predicted that 'unless the Convention is adopted this year it will not be adopted at all'.[68] In her view, any re-negotiation of basic issues would 'break up the Conference'.[69] To prevent this from happening, she proposed to resort to voting for the adoption of the convention, instead of seeking consensus.[70] As we might recall, this was a last-resort option and only the president of the convention could approve it. It was also a favourable option for those states who found themselves in diplomatically difficult positions, but who would outnumber rival industrial states in certain cases. The danger with this strategy would be the effect it might have on those who lost out in the voting, and whether they would end up adopting the convention or not. In essence, to introduce voting was to risk losing the support of important industrial states, and the consensus model had been followed precisely to prevent this from happening. Why would Mann Borgese want to re-consider the fundamental processes at this late stage?

Naturally, Elisabeth Mann Borgese had thought of this too. In her appeal to action, she argued as to why voting might be a decent last resort solution, even though 'the losses, already now, would be heavy'.[71] The losses would be the US, Japan and many of the European states. Mann Borgese still hoped that pushing

66 MS-2-744, Box 176, Folder 13, EMB, The Draft Convention on the Law of the Sea: An Appeal for action now.

67 *Cf.* MS-2-744, Box 176, Folder 13, EMB, The Draft Convention on the Law of the Sea: An Appeal for action now.

68 MS-2-744, Box 176, Folder 13, EMB, The Draft Convention on the Law of the Sea: An Appeal for action now.

69 MS-2-744, Box 176, Folder 13, EMB, The Draft Convention on the Law of the Sea: An Appeal for action now.

70 *Cf.* MS-2-744, Box 176, Folder 13, EMB, The Draft Convention on the Law of the Sea: An Appeal for action now.

71 MS-2-744, Box 176, Folder 13, EMB, The Draft Convention on the Law of the Sea: An Appeal for action now.

through the adoption without the US could put pressure on its government – given that the US was still, in principle, interested in a functioning Law of the Sea. If enough other states demonstrated that they would see the convention through with or without the US, Mann Borgese even saw the possibility that the US might return to the negotiating table, since 'The strong posture adopted now pays only so long as it appears to reach results'.[72]

Apparently, Tommy Koh's assessment of the situation was not so different from Mann Borgese's. According to her, he had said that he was willing to go through with the convention in the absence of the US, but the difference between their two proposed approaches was in the timing. Koh wanted to wait and see whether the US delegation would return to the bargaining table, and what demands they might bring with them. Mann Borgese, on the other hand, urged that time was short and they had to act. Therefore, the 'appeal [was] to act now'.[73]

'Acting now', in Elisabeth Mann Borgese's plan, would mean voting to adopt the Draft Convention that had been revised in the ninth session the year before and that had fuelled so many hopes. Mann Borgese was positive that 'all socialist states and China',[74] along with a reasonable proportion of the Group of 77, would vote for the treaty.[75] For this to happen, Mann Borgese pointed out three crucial things that had to be in place prior to the voting. In essence, it was important to ensure that Part XI would not be abolished or damaged by renegotiations and amendments. She suggested a 'Preparatory Commission' would first have to be established, which would be responsible for shaping and organising 'The Authority' after the Treaty was adopted.[76] Mann Borgese argued that such a commission was essential, otherwise the International Seabed Authority would turn into an ethereal institution that only existed on paper.[77] She explained this as such:

72 MS-2-744, Box 176, Folder 13, EMB, The Draft Convention on the Law of the Sea: An Appeal for action now.

73 *Cf.* MS-2-744, Box 176, Folder 13, EMB, The Draft Convention on the Law of the Sea: An Appeal for action now.

74 *Cf.* MS-2-744, Box 176, Folder 13, EMB, The Draft Convention on the Law of the Sea: An Appeal for action now.

75 *Cf.* MS-2-744, Box 176, Folder 13, EMB, The Draft Convention on the Law of the Sea: An Appeal for action now.

76 *Cf.* MS-2-744, Box 176, Folder 13, EMB, The Draft Convention on the Law of the Sea: An Appeal for action now.

77 *Cf.* MS-2-744, Box 176, Folder 13, EMB, The Draft Convention on the Law of the Sea: An Appeal for action now.

> To be functional, the Authority has to adjust its activities to the reality that is emerging in the 80s, which is very different from the perceptions of the 70s. This can be done without changing the Convention. The Preparatory Commission is the body most suited to this task.[78]

This lead to the second point she found necessary to agree on prior to voting: that no amendments should be allowed to the convention once it was adopted.[79] This would prevent opening up new discussions around core issues that had been agreed upon in laborious discussion over the course of many years. We have to remember that during the negotiations, participants had worried on several occasions that re-opening issues could cause a kind of chain reaction of new negotiations that would aggravate all kinds of old conflicts and feuds. If amending the convention was forbidden, then they could avoid opening 'Pandora's box' or – to return to an old metaphor – destroying the jigsaw puzzle. The US's announcement that it wanted to review several parts of the draft text concerning the seabed had already proven how re-opening issues could threaten the whole convention. Third, since changes over time were unavoidable, Mann Borgese proposed that there should be a 'Review Conference'[80] five or ten years after the convention was adopted, to discuss disputed Articles.[81] Elisabeth Mann Borgese closed her appeal for action by stating that: 'If we force action now, we may, or we may not, succeed. If we accept US pressure for stalling, the cause is lost. We may get a Convention now. We certainly will not get one in 1982 or later'.[82]

Obviously Mann Borgese preferred to try and pass the Draft Negotiation Treaty without the US, rather than risking serious changes to it. What made this version of the draft treaty so important to Elisabeth Mann Borgese and her allies that they would risk pushing it through without US support?

---

78 MS-2-744, Box 176, Folder 13, EMB, The Draft Convention on the Law of the Sea: An Appeal for action now.

79 *Cf.* MS-2-744, Box 176, Folder 13, EMB, The Draft Convention on the Law of the Sea: An Appeal for action now.

80 MS-2-744, Box 176, Folder 13, EMB, The Draft Convention on the Law of the Sea: An Appeal for action now.

81 *Cf.* MS-2-744, Box 176, Folder 13, EMB, The Draft Convention on the Law of the Sea: An Appeal for action now.

82 MS-2-744, Box 176, Folder 13, EMB, The Draft Convention on the Law of the Sea: An Appeal for action now.

6 Why the Rush to Finalise the Convention in 1980?

There are two possible interpretations of Elisabeth Mann Borgese's appeal to save the treaty through immediate and drastic action. The first one is the explanation she herself laid out in the 'appeal to act now'. Namely that there would either be a treaty passed through by voting – without the US – or there would be no treaty at all. If we take this to be the genuine reason, then the motivation was that of necessity. It was an all-or-nothing approach, in which Mann Borgese was willing to face whatever losses needed to be incurred to rescue what was left. However, another interpretation is possible. Namely, that the draft treaty that was agreed upon in 1980 favoured Mann Borgese's aims for Part XI. It contained provisions for a reasonably strong and flexible International Seabed Authority, it was set up to prevent amendments (and thereby preserve the common heritage principle), and it involved the establishment of a preparatory commission (prep com)[83] that would be responsible for breathing life into the International Seabed Authority after the treaty was finished.

The folder with the 'Appeal to Act Now' contains another document: 'The Draft Convention by Elisabeth Mann Borgese'.[84] Perhaps this document was presented together with 'the appeal to act now', since it discusses the draft convention in the light of the 'failed' tenth session. In the document, we learn what Mann Borgese thought of the 1980 draft treaty. It quickly becomes clear that Elisabeth Mann Borgese was content with many of the compromises that had been reached on Part XI's core problems during the eighth and ninth sessions. The issue of voting in the council of the International Seabed Authority had been resolved, and this particular dispute had been a reflection of the problems in the conference at large, since how the authority council was organised presented yet another potential power struggle. The delegates had also deliberated at length about how much power the International Seabed Authority should get, and in the draft treaty from 1980, its council was to have substantial decision-making powers.[85] Mann Borgese was also content with the decision that amendments to Part XI would 'require consensus'[86] and that there could be 'no amendments to the basic principle relating to the Common

83 MS-2-744, Box 176, Folder 13, EMB, The Draft Convention on the Law of the Sea: An Appeal for action now.

84 MS-2-744, Box 176, Folder 13, The Draft Convention by Elisabeth Mann Borgese.

85 *See* MS-2-744, Box 176, Folder 13, The Draft Convention by Elisabeth Mann Borgese.

86 MS MS-2-744, Box 176, Folder 13, The Draft Convention by Elisabeth Mann Borgese.

Heritage of Mankind'.[87] Finally, she praised the 'Preamble to the Convention', that had been written by the late president Amerasinghe. She explained that the preamble:

> sets the new Law of the Sea into its full historic context. [...] It recognizes the unity of ocean space; it highlights the importance of U.N. Resolution 2749 (XXV) which declares the seabed and its resources to be a Common Heritage of Mankind; and it inserts the making of the new Law of the Sea into the broader U.N. effort to create a more equitable international economic order.[88]

All in all, Mann Borgese expressed hope that the convention, with the 1980 draft intact, could be finalised without the US and still be effective. Her hope was that enough states would ratify it that they would eventually pressure hesitant industrial countries into becoming treaty parties. It seemed that Mann Borgese would rather accept a possibly ineffective treaty with Part XI intact, than an effective treaty with a non-existent Part XI.

Although the draft convention in many ways carried through the ideas that the Austrian delegation, together with many of the landlocked and geographically disadvantaged states, had fought for, Karl Wolf did not share Mann Borgese's cautious optimism. He wrote in a letter to her in July 1981, 'Unfortunately, I do not share your hope that single states could decide to finalize the convention without the US'.[89] He pointed out several reasons for his pessimism to Mann Borgese. For instance, even though the Norwegians were obviously interested in finalising the convention due to their 'enormous gains',[90] they would 'be wary of'[91] pushing through the convention unilaterally.[92] Wolf based his gloomy outlook not only on the difficult negotiation situation caused by the US, but also on general developments in the world.

87 MS MS-2-744, Box 176, Folder 13, The Draft Convention by Elisabeth Mann Borgese. 'As set forth in article 136'.

88 MS MS-2-744, Box 176, Folder 13, The Draft Convention by Elisabeth Mann Borgese.

89 MS-2-744, Box 87, Folder 4, MS 87-4 Wolf to EMB, 4 July 1981. 'Deine Hoffnungen, dass die einzelnen Länder sich auch ohne die USA entschliessen könnten, die Konvention abzuschliessen und dann auch zu signieren, teile ich leider nicht'.

90 MS-2-744, Box 87, Folder 4, MS 87-4 Wolf to EMB, 4 July 1981. 'enormen Gewinne'.

91 MS-2-744, Box 87, Folder 4, MS 87-4 Wolf to EMB, 4 July 1981. 'sich hüten'.

92 *Cf.* MS-2-744, Box 87, Folder 4, MS 87-4 Wolf to EMB, 4 July 1981. ‚So gerne beispielsweise die Norweger die Konvention hätten, um ihre enormen Gewinne auch in einem internationalen Papier festzuschreiben, so sehr werden sie sich hüten es im Alleingang zu versuche'.

> For even if we had concluded the convention, nothing would have happened for years, since the economic world situation does not require marine mining, because the raw materials are cheaper on land and initially for the next decades the 200 miles zone and then the Continental shelf share of the individual coastal states will be sufficient. No one needs the area.[93]

The last sentence is a harsh statement. The original term he used in German is even harsher: 'Kein Mensch, braucht die Area', which means that no human being needs the Area. This is interesting in that Part XI was the part of the Law of the Sea that Elisabeth Mann Borgese and Wolf had shaped in the course of their work for Austrian delegation. Why was Wolf being so negative about the situation? Why would he dismiss a part of the treaty – concerned with the seabed outside national jurisdiction – that had essentially been the whole reason the Austrian delegation were interested in negotiations on ocean governance in the first place?

In many ways, Wolf's statement is self-explanatory. The world's parameters had changed. The confident predictions of rapidly advancing technology that could bring the harvesting of deep sea minerals within reach had proved overly optimistic. This meant the anticipated 'race to the seafloor', had slowed down to a 'crawl', much like the pace of the negotiations. What had seemed extremely likely in the 60s and 70s, when the core principle of the common heritage had kicked off negotiations, seemed much further off by the start of the 80s. Instead, other political considerations had gained ground that were much more future-oriented, capitalist and market-driven. For instance, the US and other industrial states wanted to make sure that the future regime for the Area would be set up in a way that allowed them to exploit it without much regard for the principle of common heritage, rather than the way delegates had looked to shape the regime in the 60s and 70s. Wolf closed his bleak prediction by writing:

> And when the Americans come with their change requests, that will be the end. Everyone will then shed crocodile tears, especially the big states

93 MS-2-744, Box 87, Folder 4, MS 87-4 Wolf to EMB, 4 July 1981. ‚Denn auch wenn wir die Konvention abgeschlossen hätten, wäre ja zunächst auf Jahre hinaus überhaupt nichts passiert, da die ökonomische Weltlage keinen Meeresbergbau benötigt, da die Rohstoffe an Land gefördert billiger kommen und zunächst ja auf die nächsten Jahrzehnte die 200 Meilen Zone und dann noch der Kontinentalsockelanteil der einzelnen Küstenstaaten vollkommen ausreichen wird. Kein Mensch braucht die Area'.

> of the 77, but secretly they will be very happy that the US pulled these chestnuts out of the fire for them and stained itself with the blame of the whole world.[94]

This final remark was an accurate illustration of how divided the developing countries were over Part XI of the convention. By 1981, not all of the Group of 77 were in agreement on Part XI and the common heritage approach. Wolf's assessment of the situation within the Group of 77 proves that the conflict clearly transcended the north-south axis, and that it had come to revolve mainly around the opposing interests of coastal and landlocked states. A number of developing states had large coastlines and thus had an inherent interest in an extensive continental shelf. Since any kind of deep sea activity remained far out of reach, for those countries the shallow waters of the continental shelf held much more promise of wealth than some far-off deep seabed that had crippled negotiations and had morphed from being a beacon of hope for developing world economies into a stumbling block that threatened the very existence of the convention.

There was not much the delegates could do other than bide their time and see whether the Reagan administration would return to the negotiations. Elisabeth Mann Borgese's plea to go ahead and agree on the Law of the Sea without the US went unheard. Instead, the international community waited for the US to come back with their list of proposed changes.

7 Moving on in Halifax – The Second International Ocean Institute

While things looked grave at the United Nations, at least Elisabeth Mann Borgese's work at the university and with the International Ocean Institute was going well. In November 1981, she wrote a letter to Wolf about her day-to-day life in Halifax. She could report that she had just finished a book on ocean mining[95] and that she already had too much 'to be lumbered with'.[96] She had

94 MS-2-744, Box 87, Folder 4, MS 87-4 Wolf to EMB, 4 July 1981. ‚Und wenn dann die Amerikaner mit ihren Änderungswünschen kommen, wird erst recht alles zu Ende sein. Jeder wird dann Krokodilstränen vergiessen, insbesondere die grossen Staaten der 77, aber insgeheim werden sie sehr froh sein, dass ihnen die USA diese Kastanien aus dem Feure geholt und sich dafür noch mit dem Tadel der ganzen Welt belastet haben'.

95 Wolfgang Graf Vitzthum, ed., *Die Plünderung der Meere. Ein gemeinsames Erbe wird zerstückelt* (Frankfurt am Main: Fischer Taschenbuch Verlag, 1981).

96 MS-2-744, Box 87, Folder 4, EMB to Wolf, 2 November 1981. 'Nun ist mein ocean mining Buch fertig – und ich hab schon wieder viel zu viel anderes auf dem Hals. Erstens ist es nun wirklich ernst mit der Universität – ich habe 28 Studenten, mit Doktoranden und

twenty-eight students, 'pretty much work',[97] and she had started doing consultancy for the United Nations Industrial Development Organization (UNIDO) and the world bank.[98] This last job was 'Mostly to get money for our training programs'.[99] The training programmes were courses that Elisabeth Mann Borgese had started holding in 1979. They probably started out as short courses on ocean governance, along with things that were relevant to Mann Borgese's work with the United Nations but that could also be interesting for students in her department. They were organised by the International Ocean Institute and the courses were most likely held in both Malta and Halifax.[100] To finance them, Elisabeth Mann Borgese had to find funding.

She also told Wolf about her plans to turn the International Ocean Institute into a United Nations University Campus so that it would be 'easier financially. If it is at all possible to make plans in this crazy world'.[101] Though Mann Borgese seemed somewhat sobered by the developments – or lack of them – in the Law of the Sea negotiations, she was still very much involved. She told Wolf that she had recently been at a meeting at the International Law Academy in the Hague with people like Yankov, Warioba, Njenga, Pinto and Arvid Pardo – all key figures in the negotiations and all on the side of the developing countries. She reported that in general one heard a lot of criticism towards the draft convention, but that she 'came away with the feeling that it must be signed'.[102] She did, however, recommend that there should be an overall revision Article, since 'it makes no sense that only Part XI should be revised, and the rest should last for eternity'.[103] She also chimed in on a worry that Wolf had expressed early in 1981, namely that 'there was a broad consensus that the Seabed Authority

Master Thesis Kandidaten: hübsch viel Arbeit. Dazu bin ich jetzt auch noch consultant für UNIDO und für die Weltbank – alles hauptsächlich, um Geld für unser Training Programme aufzutreiben'.

97 MS-2-744, Box 87, Folder 4, EMB to Wolf, 2 November 1981.

98 *Cf.* MS 87-4 MS-2-744, Box 87, Folder 4, EMB to Wolf, 2 November 1981.

99 MS-2-744, Box 87, Folder 4, EMB to Wolf, 2 November 1981.

100 *See* Chircop, 'Elisabeth Mann Borgese's humanist conception', 216–217.

101 MS-2-744, Box 87, Folder 4, EMB to Wolf, 2 November 1981. 'Ausserdem werden wir die IOI in einen Campus der United Nations University umwandeln – dann wird auch finanziell alles etwas leichter gehen – wenn man überhaupt Pläne machen kann, in dieser verrückten Welt'.

102 MS-2-744, Box 87, Folder 4, EMB to Wolf, 2 November 1981. 'Alles in allem, hört man sehr viel Kritik an der Draft Convention, kam aber trotzdem mit dem Gefühl weg, sie muss unterzeichnet werden. Nur sollte man wirklich einen Revisions Artikel einfügen: es hat keinen Sinn, dass nur Part XI revidiert werden soll, und der Rest soll für die Ewigkeit bestehen'.

103 MS-2-744, Box 87, Folder 4, EMB to Wolf, 2 November 1981.

would have nothing to do'[104] because there was little likelihood that seabed mining would be conducted before the turn of the century, and even when it was, it would happen in the exclusive economic zones of coastal states.[105]

Despite the unpromising outlook, Mann Borgese was positive that the International Seabed Authority could be saved, since it was an 'ingenious idea'.[106] Within the parameters of a revised draft convention, she still saw the chance to 'rethink its functions'.[107] Mann Borgese was obviously not going to give up on her vision for the International Seabed Authority, although she could tell that the new head of the US delegation, Leigh Ratiner, was 'up to mischief'.[108] Elisabeth Mann Borgese predicted that the US would hold off until spring 1982, then would submit some points of change, 'pro forma'.[109] Maybe it would not even do that. Instead, she suspected that the US might prolong its silence so as to sow confusion among the other delegations. Therefore, in her view the main question remained whether the participating states were willing to finalise the treaty without the US or not.[110]

8 Shedding Crocodile Tears? A Law of the Sea without the United States

Eventually, those crocodile tears had to be shed. Contrary to Mann Borgese's predictions, Reagan returned to the bargaining table in January 1982 with a

---

104 MS-2-744, Box 87, Folder 4, EMB to Wolf, 2 November 1981.

105 *Cf.* MS-2-744, Box 87, Folder 4, EMB to Wolf, 2 November 1981. '[…] auch darüber, dass die Seabed Authority nichts zu tun haben wird, war man sich weitgehend einig: erstens, weil es kein seabed mining geben wird vor Ende des Jahrhunderts, und zweitens, wenn es kommt, kommt es in EEZ's'.

106 MS-2-744, Box 87, Folder 4, EMB to Wolf, 2 November 1981. 'Da wir sie aber nicht verloren gehen lassen wollen, die Seabed Authority – es war doch eine geniale Idee – so müssen wir eben ihre Funktionen umdenken lernen: Das lässt sich machen, im Rahmen der Convention'.

107 MS-2-744, Box 87, Folder 4, EMB to Wolf, 2 November 1981.

108 MS-2-744, Box 87, Folder 4, EMB to Wolf, 2 November 1981. 'Unwesen'.

109 MS-2-744, Box 87, Folder 4, EMB to Wolf, 2 November 1981.

110 MS-2-744, Box 87, Folder 4, EMB to Wolf, 2 November 1981. ,Das Pentagon will den Vertrag. Was ich für das Wahrscheinlichste halte ist, dass bis Frühjahr gar nichts geschieht. Dann werden vielleicht, wenn überhaupt, pro forma ein paar Punkte eingereicht, von denen man genau weiss, dass die 77 sie ablehnen. Im übrigen, halte ich es für einen Fehler, solche Punkte einzureichen, da dies die Entschlossenheit der 77, die nicht so sehr stark ist, stärken würde. Viel besser, aus amerikanischer Sicht, weiter zu zaudern und zu zögern, und damit Konfusion anrichten. Wie dem auch sei, die Frage bleibt: werden die anderen Länder nun ohne USA abschliessen'.

six-point programme in hand.[111] Not surprisingly, all six points concerned Part XI of the convention, meaning the seafloor and its resources outside national jurisdiction. Others have discussed the US policy regarding the Law of the Sea negotiation in detail.[112] Two things were important for Elisabeth Mann Borgese and the overall outcome of the convention. Firstly, the US claims were concerned with the powers of the International Seabed Authority and especially its council, which would hold the decision-making power. The US wanted this power to be as limited as possible. And secondly, as a consequence of the first point, the US wanted the future seabed mining industry to be restricted by as few rules and regulations made by the council as possible.[113]

The head of the US delegation, Leigh Ratiner, handed in these points first in January and again in March as part of a larger document called the 'Green Book', and this strategy caused several delegates to question the United States' overall aims.[114] Mann Borgese had predicted that the US would submit claims 'pro forma',[115] which implied that she doubted the US's objections were aimed at actually finding solutions to problems within the draft convention. After perusing the 'Green Book', several other delegates uttered similar concerns. According to Sanger:

> Alvaro de Soto of Peru, who had often led the Group of 77 in negotiations, said that the US opposition 'was more of an ideological than a practical nature [...] there was no way to make the ends meet – time would not have helped the United States scale down its demands'.[116]

Sanger also reported assessments from other delegates. The Australian delegate Keith Brennan noted that:

> It [sic: the Green Book] is an intolerably burdensome document'; while on behalf of the Group of 77 Iman Ul Haque of Pakistan declared that the US proposals 'would set the negotiations back to the early seventies'.[117]

---

111 *Cf.* Sanger, *Ordering the Oceans,* 51. *See also* MS-2-744, Box 87, Folder 4, Wolf to EMB, 10 February 1982.

112 Schmidt, *Common Heritage;* Ratiner, 'American Rigidity'.

113 Sanger, *Ordering the Oceans,* 52.

114 Sanger, *Ordering the Oceans,* 52.

115 MS-2-744, Box 87, Folder 4, EMB to Wolf, 2 November 1981.

116 Sanger, *Ordering the Oceans,* 53.

117 Sanger, *Ordering the Oceans,* 52.

Despite the negative reception of the 'Green Book', several attempts were made to reconcile the US with Part XI by making concessions to some of their claims. A working group called 'The Good Samaritans'[118] (the name speaks for itself) was set up. It was officially called the 'Group of 12', because it consisted of twelve delegation leaders who worked in a personal capacity for a feasible solution.[119] The group worked through the six-point criticism from the Reagan administration to see whether concessions could be made, for instance as regarded the power of the council of the International Seabed Authority, or on the question of seabed mining provisions.[120] Although some of the Samaritans' proposals were incorporated as amendments, the attempts to satisfy the US regime ultimately failed.[121]

In the end, despite opposition from the president, Tommy Koh, the US delegates called for a vote, likely aiming to close all future discussions for good and to see whether there was still enough support for the convention at all. A hundred and thirty delegates voted for the draft convention.[122] Among them were many of the Group of 77, along with Canada, France, Japan, the Nordic countries and New Zealand.[123] The US, Israel, Venezuela and Turkey voted against, and 17 countries abstained from the vote, which were: Britain, West Germany, Belgium, the Netherlands, Luxembourg, Italy, Spain, Thailand, and nine socialist countries.[124]

---

118 Sanger, *Ordering the Oceans*, 52.

119 *Cf.* Beesley, 'Negotiating Strategy', 190: 'Initially, the Group of 12 consisted of heads of delegations acting in their purely personal capacity. We were all interested in the Convention. We had put a lot into it. […] We failed, and we deeply regret it, but we still remain convinced that we were very near success, in spite of the differences'.

120 The proposal can be found in A/CONF.62/L.104 and Add.1, 13 April 1982.

121 *Cf.* Sanger, *Ordering the Oceans*, 52. *See also* Beesley, 'Negotiating Strategy', 190.

122 *Cf.* Sanger, *Ordering the Oceans*, 53: 'And the conference president, Tommy Koh, refused various pleas […] to extend the session beyond 29 April when he learnt word that, apparently unknown to Ratiner, other US diplomats, led by Ken Adleman (then deputy head of the US Mission to the United Nations) were busy throughout the last week lobbying Western European countries with mining interests – and even Thailand – to vote against the convention, or at least to abstain. So, although both Koh and Beesley appealed to Malone not to insist on a vote […] the United States called for a vote on the whole draft Convention'.

123 *Cf.* Sanger, *Ordering the Oceans*, 53.

124 *Cf.* Sanger, *Ordering the Oceans*, 53. *See also* Harrison, *Making the Law*, 47 (102): 'The principle objection of the USA was to the provisions of the International Seabed Area in Part IX of the Convention. Turkey, Israel and Venezuela also voted against the Convention, albeit for different reasons. Turkey and Venezuela both objected to the methods outlined in the Convention for delimiting the continental shelf and the EEZ. Israel, on the other hand, principally opposed the provisions on straits contained in Part II of the Convention'.

Although Elisabeth Mann Borgese's words about the United States' unwillingness to participate had been prophetic, at least she was wrong about the prediction made in her 1981 'Appeal to Act Now'[125] document that the convention would be lost unless it was voted for in that same year. In December 1982, the final act was opened for signature and signed by 140 states.[126] 'The convention now took on a life of its own, waiting for the acceptance of all states in order to become an unrivalled and comprehensive Law of the Sea for the international community'.[127] Elisabeth Mann Borgese's work, however, did not end there. Together with the final act, the conference also passed a resolution[128] to set up the 'Preparatory Commission' for the International Seabed Authority.[129] The so called 'Prep Com' had a very clear mandate to breathe life into an otherwise hollow international institution for the governance of the seafloor outside national jurisdiction, within the parameters set out by the convention. Mann Borgese hoped for enough room to shape the institution in a way that would best serve her own wish (and that of her allies) to incorporate the concept of common heritage of mankind, within the limits of the treaty.[130]

Several Articles of Part XI of the 1982 Law of the Sea Convention represented victories for Mann Borgese and her allies. Article 136 declared, 'The Area and its resources are the common heritage of mankind'.[131] In Article 140, meanwhile, the International Seabed Authority was given the mandate to govern the Area according to principle of benefit-sharing. The Article runs: 'Benefit of mankind: The Authority shall provide for the equitable sharing of financial and other economic benefits derived from activities in the Area through an appropriate mechanism, on a non-discriminator basis [...]'.[132] Also, the power of the authority in connection with underprivileged treaty parties was taken care of in Article 152, 1 and 2: 'The Authority shall avoid discrimination in the

125 *See* MS-2-744, Box 176, Folder 13, EMB, The Draft Convention on the Law of the Sea: An Appeal for action now.

126 *United Nations Convention on the Law of the Sea (with annexes, final act and procès-verbeaux of rectification of the final act dated 3 March 1986 and 26 July 1993)*, Montego Bay, 10 December 1982, *United Nations Treaty Series*, vol 1833. No. 31363, p.3, available at https://treaties.un.org/Pages/showDetails.aspx?objid=080000028004 3ad5.

127 Bernaerts, *Bernaerts' Guide,* 9.

128 Three resolutions were passed, *see* Bernaerts, *Bernaerts' Guide,* 9.

129 *Cf.* Bernaerts, *Bernaerts' Guide,* 9: 'Resolution I: Establishment of a Preparatory Commission for the International Sea-Bed Authority and for the International Tribunal for the Law of the Sea [...]'.

130 MS-2-744, Box 176, Folder 12, EMB, the Law of the Sea: Ratification, Implementation, and Progressive Development.

131 Article 136, printed in *Bernaerts' Guide,* 194.

132 Article 140, printed in *Bernaerts' Guide,* 195.

exercise of its powers and functions including the granting of opportunities for activity in the Area. 2. Nevertheless, special consideration for developing states [...] shall be permitted'.[133] The system of an enterprise within the authority was set out in Article 153,[134] which granted developing countries a degree of participation in future seabed ventures. Finally, a review conference 'fifteen years from now'[135] was put in place to renegotiate or revise the system of exploration and exploitation (laid out in Article 153) if necessary.[136]

From 1982 onwards, the convention 'took on a life of its own'.[137] This ethereal 'life' was, of course, not entirely unsupervised by further discussions at the United Nations. The Prep Com – of which Elisabeth Mann Borgese was a member on behalf of the Austrian delegation[138] – played a role in this future life of the convention, as did other committees. Opening for signatures was just the start. It would take another twelve years until the required sixty ratifications were reached and the treaty could come into force. In the meantime, the life of the convention continued to unfold with Elisabeth Mann Borgese in the midst of it.

133 Article 152, 1.2., printed in *Bernaerts' Guide*, 202.
134 *See* Article 152, printed in *Bernaerts' Guide*, 202.
135 Article 155 printed in *Bernaerts' Guide*, 203.
136 Article 155 printed in *Bernaerts' Guide*, 203.
137 Bernaerts, *Bernaerts' Guide*, 9.
138 *See* MS-2-744, Box 16, Folder 19, EMB CV.

PART 4

Can the Common Heritage of Mankind Be Rescued? 1982–94

CHAPTER 10

1994 Agreement and the Boat Paper Crisis

1 The Life of the Convention after 1982

The most fascinating aspect of the life of the Law of the Sea Convention is that, although it formally reached the finish line in 1982, in reality the work was nowhere near complete. In the immediate aftermath of UNCLOS, the Preparatory Commission started its work on organising the International Seabed Authority as per the specifications of the treaty.[1] Elisabeth Mann Borgese was deeply involved with the work in the Prep Com. In order to understand how committed Mann Borgese was to applying her internationalist ideas to UNCLOS through Part XI, it is worth providing an overview of the last twelve years of her work with the convention.[2]

There is a vast amount of material in Mann Borgese's archive that could be used to illustrate what exactly happened during the Prep Com period, but above all, one document will be central to reviewing the last twelve years of her work with the convention. In the document, Mann Borgese explained to a wider audience the work of the Prep Com and the problems the committee had encountered. The document is dated 4 June 1991 and has the title 'The Law of the Sea: Ratification, Implementation, and Progressive Development'.[3] It is a speech, likely delivered to Canadian government officials at a 'symposium'[4] that is not more clearly defined. We learn that Mann Borgese was the first speaker at the symposium, because she began her speech by apologising

1 *Cf.* Bernaerts, *Bernaerts' Guide*, 9: 'Resolution I: Establishment of a Preparatory Commission for the International Sea-Bed Authority and for the International Tribunal for the Law of the Sea; […]'.

2 For an overview of the first years, *see* Elisabeth Mann Borgese, 'Notes on the Work of the Preparatory Commission', *Ocean Yearbook* 5 (Brill 1985): 1–9, https://doi.org/10.1163/22116008 5X00023. *See also* Lee Kimball, 'Conference reports- Heated exchange in Geneva', *Marine Policy* 10, no. 1 (January 1986): 60–62. For archive materials, *see* MS-2-744, Box 208, Folder 2, The preparatory commission: [report]. MS-2-744, Box 132, Folder 32, The Preparatory Commission for the International Sea-bed Authority (ISBA) and the International Tribunal for the Law of the Sea (ITLS).

3 MS-2-744, Box 176, Folder 12, EMB, the Law of the Sea: Ratification, Implementation, and Progressive Development.

4 MS-2-744, Box 176, Folder 12,
EMB, the Law of the Sea: Ratification, Implementation, and Progressive Development.

for setting a tone that was 'going to be somewhat shrill'.[5] She continued by saying that her 'position on the future Law of the Sea [...] is quite controversial'.[6] Mann Borgese then proceeded to lay out this controversial position, along with an assessment of the previous nine years.

When the fate of the draft convention was at stake in 1981, Mann Borgese had taken action in the form of her 'appeal to act now'. Now, ten years later, she would do something quite similar. The purpose of the speech was to give the audience 'Ten reasons why this Convention is so important and why it is important to bring it into force now: this year'.[7] There is no need to go into detail about why Mann Borgese was convinced that the convention was important. Ten years after the convention had opened for signature, her reasons for supporting it were the same as they had been during the storm of voting in 1982. The convention had preserved the common heritage of mankind, and would provide the opportunity for developing countries to gain wealth and partake in important industrial operations through the establishment of the International Seabed Authority in Part XI.[8] The interesting aspect of the speech is that Mann Borgese went on to assess the work of the Prep Com, which had been holding annual meetings since 1983.[9] According to Mann Borgese, the Prep Com had two official written mandates and one unofficial mandate.[10] The first mandate (resolution I)[11] was to establish 'the Commission and task it with paper work, the drafting of rules and regulations headquarter agreements, studies etc'.[12] In other words, the Prep Com was to take care of the administrative side of establishing international institutions. According to Mann Borgese, this task had gone fairly well. The second mandate (resolution II)[13] was to create 'an interim regime for deep-seabed mining, to protect the

---

5 MS-2-744, Box 176, Folder 12, EMB, the Law of the Sea: Ratification, Implementation, and Progressive Development.

6 MS-2-744, Box 176, Folder 12, EMB, the Law of the Sea: Ratification, Implementation, and Progressive Development.

7 MS-2-744, Box 176, Folder 12, EMB, the Law of the Sea: Ratification, Implementation, and Progressive Development.

8 *Cf.* MS-2-744, Box 176, Folder 12, EMB, the Law of the Sea: Ratification, Implementation, and Progressive Development.

9 *Cf.* MS-2-744, Box 176, Folder 12, EMB, the Law of the Sea: Ratification, Implementation, and Progressive Development.

10 *Cf.* MS-2-744, Box 176, Folder 12, EMB, the Law of the Sea: Ratification, Implementation, and Progressive Development.

11 *See*, Article 308, 4&5, in *Bernaerts' Guide*, 258.

12 MS-2-744, Box 176, Folder 12, EMB, the Law of the Sea: Ratification, Implementation, and Progressive Development.

13 *See*, Article 308, 4&5, in *Bernaerts' Guide*, 258.

interest of those States which have made considerable investments in seabed mining technology and exploration'.[14] This task was of a practical nature: to create rules and parameters for future deep seabed mining ventures and to reach agreement with 'Pioneer investors'.[15] According to Mann Borgese, this part too was going well. She could report to her audience that 'amazing developments have taken place',[16] and that she was hopeful seabed mining would occur 'under the Convention regime'.[17]

The real head-scratcher was the 'unwritten' mandate. In Mann Borgese's words this was, 'to adjust and adapt the ideas and ideals of the Seventies to the economic and political realities of the Nineties [...]'.[18] And Mann Borgese feared that this element of the Prep Com's work had not gone well at all. There are several possible explanations as to why this was the case – at least in Mann Borgese's view. The most obvious explanation would be that the 'unwritten mandate' was not actually a mandate at all. To 'adjust and adapt' was not one of the Prep Com's designated tasks.[19] While it was clearly something Mann Borgese wished to allocate to the Prep Com (and it is likely that other Prep Com participants supported and shared her view), officially the Prep Com had no such mandate. So why did Mann Borgese single it out at the symposium?

Most likely, the work of the Prep Com had shown that the International Seabed Authority – along with its various purposes and tasks – was no longer a feasible entity in the light of technological but also political developments that had taken place by the beginning of the 90s. In Mann Borgese's own words, the United Nations Secretariat had called for:

> 'dialogue', 'to make the Convention universally acceptable', which frustrates and invalidates the work of the Preparatory Commission, manifestly paralyses the ratification process and leads us headlong towards the

14 MS-2-744, Box 176, Folder 12, EMB, the Law of the Sea: Ratification, Implementation, and Progressive Development.

15 MS-2-744, Box 176, Folder 12, EMB, the Law of the Sea: Ratification, Implementation, and Progressive Development.

16 MS-2-744, Box 176, Folder 12, EMB, the Law of the Sea: Ratification, Implementation, and Progressive Development.

17 MS-2-744, Box 176, Folder 12, EMB, the Law of the Sea: Ratification, Implementation, and Progressive Development.

18 MS-2-744, Box 176, Folder 12, EMB, the Law of the Sea: Ratification, Implementation, and Progressive Development.

19 MS-2-744, Box 176, Folder 12, EMB, the Law of the Sea: Ratification, Implementation, and Progressive Development.

> disintegration of the Convention and the calling for a Fourth Conference on the Law of the Sea […].[20]

What Mann Borgese meant by this was that she feared Part XI of the convention – the part that the Prep Com was working with because it contained all the provisions on the International Seabed Authority and the seafloor – was going to be renegotiated. Elisabeth Mann Borgese felt that the Prep Com was becoming superfluous or even meaningless thanks to the Secretariat's desire to engage in a new dialogue.[21] She predicted that this would lead to the 'pick and choose'[22] approach that the participants of the convention had worked so hard to avoid.

The underlying issue was the US's persistent refusal to sign the convention. Other industrialised states had followed its lead, and unless these major industrialised countries became state parties to the treaty, the consensus strategy that had made the convention such a laborious undertaking would not have paid off. Only if the majority of states joined would the consensus model have been worth the effort – otherwise the convention would end up being a symbolic treaty, binding developing nations to a contract that did not make sense without the backing of the developed states. Since Part XI remained the largest obstacle, the international community had tried to find a way through – hence the Secretariat's action in engaging in dialogue.

In principle, Elisabeth Mann Borgese agreed with the Secretariat that something had to be done. However, she disagreed with the form of action they had suggested. She wanted the Prep Com to have the power to adapt the convention to the changing situation. In essence, Mann Borgese wanted more definitive power over rules and regulations for the Prep Com. She proposed a three-point plan of action, which she believed could rescue Part XI and prevent it from floundering in re-opened discussions. First, she proposed freezing all Articles that were concerned with finances and any specific provisions on how deep sea mining was to be conducted, since they were 'totally meaningless and unreal in the present situation'.[23] Instead, Mann Borgese proposed renegotiating

20 MS-2-744, Box 176, Folder 12, EMB, the Law of the Sea: Ratification, Implementation, and Progressive Development.

21 *Cf.* MS-2-744, Box 176, Folder 12, EMB, the Law of the Sea: Ratification, Implementation, and Progressive Development.

22 MS-2-744, Box 176, Folder 12, EMB, the Law of the Sea: Ratification, Implementation, and Progressive Development.

23 MS-2-744, Box 176, Folder 12, EMB, the Law of the Sea: Ratification, Implementation, and Progressive Development.

these provisions in ten to fifteen years.[24] Second, she recommended encouraging ratification, stating that she was 'dedicating all my energy to mobilizing the needed 15 ratifications […]'.[25] Third, she proposed that the Enterprise – meaning the operational arm of the International Seabed Authority – should be 'merged with what now is called "the nuclear enterprise" which is quite unrealistic'.[26] The 'nuclear enterprise' was what was left of the original idea of Enterprises through 'joint ventures', which consisted of an administration that did not have any technical expertise to conduct activity.

What officials had observed in the development of the convention during the years running up to 1991 was that it was those same core issues in Part XI that were still stopping states from ratifying it. Therefore, United Nations officials were looking for other solutions. Clearly, the convention itself could not be re-written, but parts of it could. Elisabeth Mann Borgese was opposed to this solution, and with good reason. She probably suspected that if the United States and other industrial states got their way with Part XI of the convention, the common heritage principle would be in real danger. The US strategy in the 'Green Book' from 1982 had shown that US officials were mostly interested in a free market approach to the area outside national jurisdiction, and many of the other industrial states felt the same way. As long as the provisions of Part XI were frozen, they were still in existence and could not be changed. Freezing the provisions could have two other advantages. First, the freezing period would enable developing countries to catch up to the industrial states in the technological sphere. Second, technological progress (and thereby the possibility and form of future seabed mining) would be easier to assess the closer that development came to actual mining activity. All those rules and regulations formulated in the 70s and 80s had been developed without any clear idea of the future realities of such technological activity. Perhaps Mann Borgese hoped that freezing the provisions of Part XI would give her more time to prepare a defence of the common heritage elements, while also giving the international community time to make more accurate predictions about future technological progress. We must remember that Arvid Pardo's speech in 1967 had accelerated negotiations because he had emphasised the imminent possibility of mining seabed minerals on the seafloor outside national jurisdiction.

---

24 *Cf.* MS-2-744, Box 176, Folder 12, EMB, the Law of the Sea: Ratification, Implementation, and Progressive Development.

25 MS-2-744, Box 176, Folder 12, EMB, the Law of the Sea: Ratification, Implementation, and Progressive Development.

26 MS-2-744, Box 176, Folder 12, EMB, the Law of the Sea: Ratification, Implementation, and Progressive Development.

When it began to dawn on developing states that this abundance of minerals would be out of reach for the foreseeable future, they had lost interest. Even Karl Wolf had said 'no one needs the Area'.[27]

Elisabeth Mann Borgese argued for keeping the mandate of adapting Part XI within the Prep Com for one simple reason: it would ensure that the committee retained its decision-making power for the future form of the International Seabed Authority. Unfortunately, since this particular mandate was 'unwritten', others had different plans.

2 The Boat Paper – A Betrayal of the Task?

Developments between 1991 and 1994 showed that Elisabeth Mann Borgese faced a number of obstacles as she attempted to convince others of her plan. Her initial actions were twofold: she engaged in an active ratification campaign[28] and sent out letters to key figures in the Law of the Sea negotiations who were rooting for adapting the convention. Various examples of these proposed adaptations could be studied. We will focus on one case that would prove an almighty headache for Elisabeth Mann Borgese: The 'Boat Paper'[29] incident.

The Boat Paper was an anonymous document (although many knew who was behind it)[30] that put forward a number of changes to Part XI of the convention, essentially to make it acceptable to the United States. The paper first surfaced at the start of the 90s, and a revised version was submitted in 1993.[31] Its content flew in the face of everything Elisabeth Mann Borgese had worked for since 1967. The Boat Paper case would lead to a full-on quarrel between Elisabeth Mann Borgese and Satya Nandan of Fiji[32] – one of the officials responsible for the Boat Paper and a man who would later become the first secretary-general of the International Seabed Authority.[33] Nandan had initiated the 'dialogue' proposed by the secretary general, a course of action that would ring in the creation of the 1994 Implementation Agreement.[34]

---

27 *See* MS-2-744, Box 87, Folder 4, MS 87-4 Wolf to EMB, 4 July 1981.

28 For ratification efforts, *see* MS-2-744, Box 276, Folder 1.

29 For the 1993 version of the Boat Paper, *see* MS-2-744, Box 323, Folder 18, Boat Paper. Draft Resolution for Adoption by the General Assembly, 3 August 1993.

30 MS-2-744, Box 276, Folder 1, EMB to Colombo, 30 December 1993.

31 Boat paper version 1993

32 *See* MS-2-744, Box 236, Folder 11, Satya Nandan, biographical note.

33 EMB commented on this in a letter to Wolf. *See* MS-2-744- Box 355, Folder 24, EMB to Wolf, 7 May 1994.

34 *See* MS-2-744, Box 236, Folder 11, Satya Nandan, biographical note.

The conflict started rather tentatively with a letter Elisabeth Mann Borgese wrote to her colleague in June 1991.[35] She opened her letter to Nandan very cordially by stating that she was writing to him in 'a very personal way'[36] and that she hoped he would 'receive it in a spirit of friendship'.[37] The mysterious 'it' was the critique Mann Borgese was about to deliver to Nandan concerning his strategy to adapt and even change the Law of the Sea. She started by saying she had been 'very sceptical' towards his 'idea of "making the Convention universally acceptable" '.[38] And further, that 'I see in this a sort of betrayal of our task, which is to get the Convention ratified and into force'.[39]

To others, she spoke much more plainly. Back in January 1990, she had already written to another colleague, Frank Njenga of Kenya, about Nandan's new strategy: 'You may be interested in seeing my letter to Jean-Pierre Levy. I really think what he and Nandan are doing is totally unacceptable from every point of view'.[40] Njenga answered in February 1990, and was very much in agreement with Mann Borgese's assessment. He replied that it seemed like 'Mr. Nandan and Dr. Levy are continuing their pet project of destroying the Convention to please the big powers'.[41] And further that it was 'necessary that all efforts be made to unmask this conspiracy [...]'.[42] He even aired the suggestion that some of the leaders of the Secretariat should be shifted out to 'prevent the perpetration of irreparable damage by individuals who seem to have become partisans for the point of view of some powerful nations at the expense of common heritage of mankind'.[43] Needless to say, as the Kenyan representative, Frank Njenga[44] was very much on the side of the developing countries, and therefore on Mann Borgese's too. Together with Njenga, Elisabeth Mann Borgese embarked on a ratification campaign, in which she contacted many state officials and encouraged Njenga to reach out to others to collect the missing ratifications needed for the convention to come into force.[45] In January 1991, she wrote in a frank letter to her former Austrian colleague and friend Karl Wolf (with whom she had kept up a steady correspondence since

35 MS-2-744, Box 236, Folder 11, EMB to Satya, 13 June 1991.
36 MS-2-744, Box 236, Folder 11, EMB to Satya, 13 June 1991.
37 MS-2-744, Box 236, Folder 11, EMB to Satya, 13 June 1991.
38 MS-2-744, Box 236, Folder 11, EMB to Satya, 13 June 1991.
39 MS-2-744, Box 236, Folder 11, EMB to Satya, 13 June 1991.
40 MS-2-744, Box 276, Folder 1 EMB to Njenga, 31 January 1990.
41 MS-2-744, Box 276, Folder 1, Njenga to EMB, 19 February 1990.
42 MS-2-744, Box 276, Folder 1, Njenga to EMB, 19 February 1990.
43 MS-2-744, Box 276, Folder 1, Njenga to EMB, 19 February 1990.
44 MS-2-744, Box 276, Folder 1, Biography Njenga.
45 Ratification efforts with Njenga in MS-2-744, Box 276, Folder 1.

their collaboration in the Austrian delegation)[46] about her frustration with the Fijian delegate:

> I am very angry with Nandan, who wants to change our convention before it comes into force. He has no right to do that. Aside from that, it's stupid, and Baker has already made it very clear that the US is not interested in amendments, and still wants nothing to do with the convention.[47]

In July 1994 she wrote to Gianni De Michelis of Italy about the ratification progress, most likely in order to update the Italian government on the situation. But her report also had a more subtle agenda:

> The Seychelles have just ratified, and thus we have reached 48. All we need is 12 more. I have started very active campaigns in India, and in Germany, whose accession is merely a question of time; I have reasons to hope that Bulgaria may ratify very soon. Portugal may ratify after the elections this fall. Even Canada is beginning to change its mind. I hope and pray that Italy will be a leader in Europe.[48]

The letter to Italy shows that Mann Borgese was strategic with her ratification campaign. She knew that if she could get one European nation on board, others might follow. Hence this plea to Italy in 1991, heavy with claims about the state of ratification plans in other European nations – which were likely exaggerated in an attempt to get Italy to take the bait.

The strategy did not really pay off. Come 1993, she was still working on Italy. This time the recipient of her appeal was Umberto Colombo, who she knew in person and addressed by his first name. The letter was sent in December 1993, in the wake of the 'Boat Paper' crisis.[49] In the letter she urged Colombo to convince the Italian government to ratify the convention. She also voiced her concern about the fate of the convention, saying that 'The "Consultations" are at a cross-roads'.[50] She wrote about the 'infamous, anonymous "Boat Paper"

46 *See* folder Ms 355-24.

47 MS-2-744- Box 355, Folder 24, EMB to Wolf, 13 January 1991. ‚Ich bin sehr zornig auf Nandan, der da unsere Convention ändern will noch eh sie in Kraft tritt. Dazu hat er kein Recht. Abgesehen davon ist es dumm, und Baker hat bereits ganz klar gesagt, die USA ist an amendments nicht interessiert, und will nach wie vor von der Konvention nichts wissen'.

48 MS-2-744, Box 276, Folder 1, EMB to Michelis, 4 July 1991.

49 MS-2-744, Box 276, Folder 1, EMB to Colombo, 30 December 1993.

50 MS-2-744, Box 276, Folder 1, EMB to Colombo, 30 December 1993.

(called "Boat Paper" because it has a boat on the front cover)'.[51] She was very clear about her view of this paper, which she called a 'gratuitous humiliation of the developing countries [...]'.[52] Without going too deep into a detailed review of the actual document, Mann Borgese's letter to Colombo gives us a good summary of everything that was problematic with the Boat Paper: '[..] No Enterprise; no money for it; and it is the Council that is to decide if and when the Enterprise is to be established'.[53] Apparently, the power of the council was weakened too, since 'the voting system has been so rigged ("Chamber voting") as to give a veto to the industrialised countries; no technology transfer, no production control. Everything the developing countries had achieved at UNCLOS III is gone'.[54] Elisabeth Mann Borgese did not hold back on naming those she held responsible for the 'infamous' paper: 'Satya Nanda of Fiji; Anderson of the U.K., Scholtz of the State Department, and French of Australia'.[55] Unfortunately, Colombo could not help. When he replied in January 1994, he wrote that he had not seen the 'Boat Paper', adding 'I do note, however, that though you describe it as "anonymous" on page one, on page two of the letter you cite the names of the four reputed authors'.[56] Of these, he noted that 'at least, they do seem representative of key players'.[57] Although he shared Mann Borgese's assessment of the situation to some degree, he also noted that the current US government under Clinton could be the one most inclined to renegotiate Part XI.[58] During the course of 1994, others obviously felt the same way, and not long after this exchange with Colombo, moves were made to pass the 'Boat Paper' through the General Assembly as a resolution.[59]

In May 1994, Elisabeth Mann Borgese wrote a pessimistic letter to her old friend and former ally, Karl Wolf. Wolf was no longer involved in the Law of the Sea Convention and its aftermath, having resigned in 1986.[60] For a long time, he and Mann Borgese had fought side-by-side for the same cause, but he was now outside the negotiation processes at the United Nations. Therefore, her

51 MS-2-744, Box 276, Folder 1, EMB to Colombo, 30 December 1993.
52 MS-2-744, Box 276, Folder 1, EMB to Colombo, 30 December 1993.
53 MS-2-744, Box 276, Folder 1, EMB to Colombo, 30 December 1993.
54 MS-2-744, Box 276, Folder 1, EMB to Colombo, 30 December 1993.
55 MS-2-744, Box 276, Folder 1, EMB to Colombo, 30 December 1993.
56 MS-2-744, Box 276, Folder 1, Colombo to EMB, 21 January 1994.
57 MS-2-744, Box 276, Folder 1, Colombo to EMB, 21 January 1994.
58 *Cf.* MS-2-744, Box 276, Folder 1, Colombo to EMB, 21 January 1994.
59 *Cf.* MS-2-744, Box 355, Folder 24, EMB to Wolf, 7 May 1994.
60 MS-2-744, Box 355, Folder 24, Wolf to EMB, 5 February 1989. 'Die schönen Tage von Aranjuez sind vorüber – mit anderen Worten, meine Tätigkeit als österreichischer Delegierter zur Seerechts- nunmehr Vorbereitungskonferenz sind zu Ende gegangen'.

letter to him about the deconstruction of Part XI that had started with the Boat Paper initiative is perhaps the most honest and frank assessment available.

> I am very worried about our convention because it is in the process of dissolution. The so-called Secretary-General's Consultations are first-class racquets [sic: rackets]. Nandan has done this to us. He is paid for it by the Australians. Five villains did all the damage: Nandan, Scholtz (USA), Anderson (UK), French (Australia), and Rattray. The latter because he wants the Authority so badly in Jamaica that he does not care if he gets it alive or dead. Well, he gets it dead.
>
> The so-called "Boat Paper", which is now to pass as a resolution by the General Assembly, is a real shame. The Authority and our poor Enterprie [sic: Enterprise] are just there to do NOTHING. Nandan will be appointed Secretary General of the Authority, he too, to do NOTHING, but becomes the highest paid official in the U.N. System. Worse than the content is the procedure that scoffs description, slaps the Vienna Convention on Treaties in the face and generally does not concern itself with international law. A bad precedent case.[61]

The not-so-anonymous Boat Paper finally passed through the General Assembly and morphed into the 'Agreement relating to the Implementation of Part XI'.[62] While Mann Borgese called it a slap in the face for the Vienna Convention on the Law of Treaties, others have described it as a triumph of international law-making.[63] We cannot go into detail on why exactly the

61 MS-2-744, Box 355, Folder 24, EMB to Wolf, 7 May 1994. ‚Über unsere Konvention mache ich mir grösste Sorgen, denn sie ist in der Auflösung. Die so-genannten Secretary-General's Consultations sind ein Racket erster Klasse. Das hat uns der Nandan angetan, der dafür von den Australiern bezahlt wird. Fünf Gauner haben den ganzen Schaden angerichtet: Nandan, Scholtz (USA), Anderson (UK), French (Australia), und Rattray. Der letztere, weil er die Authority so dringend in Jamaica haben will, dass es ihm egal ist, ob er sie lebendig oder tot bekommt. Nun, er bekommt sie tot. Das so genannte "Boat Paper", das nun als Resolution durch die General Assembly passieren soll, ist eine wirkliche Schande. Die Authority und unser armes Enterprie [sic: Enterprise] sind nur dazu da, NICHTS tun zu können. Nandan wird Secretary-General der Authority, auch er, um NICHTS zu tun, wird aber der höchst bezahlte Beamte im U.N. System. Schlimmer noch als die Substanz ist die Procedure, die jeder Beschreibung spottet, der Vienna Convention on Treaties ins Gesicht schlägt und sich im Allgemeinen um Völkerrecht nicht bekümmert. Ein arger Precedenzfall'.

62 *See* A/RES/48/263, 17 August 1994.

63 Discussed in E.D. Brown, 'The 1994 Agreement on the Implementation of Part XI of the UN Convention on the Law of the Sea: breakthrough to universality?', *Marine Policy* 19, no. 1 (January 1995): 5–20, https://doi.org/10.1016/0308-597X(95)92569-S. For the US

process with which the Boat Paper passed through the United Nations system could have been problematic. In fact, it was not very different from the general practice of working in semi-official groups that had been used during the negotiation period between 1973 and 1982. Perhaps it was perceived as a personal 'slap in the face' for Mann Borgese because it had such a devastating impact on the provisions of Part XI.

What had the 'villains' changed? What 'damage' had they inflicted upon Part XI and thus upon the core of what Elisabeth Mann Borgese had worked for at the United Nations? Elisabeth Mann Borgese was very clear about the effect of the changes to Part XI through the Boat Paper. At the end of May 1994, she wrote to Njenga: 'Our poor Law of the Sea Convention has been kidnapped!'[64]

3 The Law of the Sea Kidnapped by Villains in 1994

On 22 July 1994, 'The 1994 Agreement on Implementation of the Seabed Provisions of the Convention on the Law of the Sea'[65] was voted for and adopted in the General Assembly. 121 voted in favour, 7 abstained and no one voted against it.[66] The purpose of the agreement was exactly as Nandan and his entourage had advertised, which was to:

> enhance the prospect for widespread ratification of the Convention by responding to problems with the deep seabed mining regime in Part XI, particularly those that troubled industrial states, including the United States.[67]

The initiative was effective. The United States, together with almost all other industrial states, signed the agreement the next day.[68] However, the US still did not sign the convention itself, and other industrialised states remained reluctant. Some have discussed whether the agreement did indeed realise its

position, *see* Louis B. Sohn, 'International Law Implications of the 1994 Agreement', *The American Journal of International Law* 88, no. 4 (October 1994): 696–705, http://www.jstor.org/stable/2204137.

64 MS-2-744, Box 276, Folder 1, EMB to Njenga, 26 May 1994.

65 GA Res 48/263, July 28, 1994.

66 *Cf.* Bernhard H. Oxman, 'The 1994 Agreement and the Convention', *The American Journal of International Law* 88, no. 4 (October 1994): 687, http://www.jstor.org/stable/2204136.

67 Oxman, '1994 Agreement', 688.

68 Oxman, '1994 Agreement', 687.

promise of more widespread support from industrialised states,[69] but what is most important in connection to Elisabeth Mann Borgese's work are the changes it inflicted on Part XI.

If Mann Borgese's assessment is to be believed, these changes so drastically altered the core of the common heritage principle that it was more or less dead in the water, together with the authority that was supposed to safeguard and govern it.[70] Working through the whole agreement point-by-point would exceed the scope of this book, but we can look into some of the core elements of the mining provisions and the International Seabed Authority to see what was changed and how. To do this, we will go through the concerns Elisabeth Mann Borgese had expressed in her letter to Colombo in 1993, when she had feared the impact that the Boat Paper would have on Part XI. Had these things genuinely become reality in 1994?

Elisabeth Mann Borgese had reported that the Boat Paper proposal planned to weaken the council of the International Seabed Authority. This was true in that the agreement provided for a seat on the council for 'the State, on the day of entry into forces of the Convention, having the largest economy in terms of gross domestic product'.[71] This was obviously the United States.[72] Furthermore, the 'one nation, one-vote assembly' was also changed to a chamber system. This meant that the developing states could not use their superior numbers to overpower the industrialised states when it came to important decision-making.[73] Another point of Part XI that had been of the utmost importance for Mann Borgese's idea of a more just distribution of opportunity and wealth was the provision for technology transfer. In the 1982 convention, it was inscribed that 'Private deep seabed miners would be subject to a mandatory requirement for the transfer of technology to the Enterprise and to developing countries'.[74] This technology transfer was of paramount importance for a well-functioning future Enterprise under the International Seabed Authority that would mine on behalf of the developing countries. Without technology transfer, the

69 *Cf.* D. H. Anderson, 'Resolution and Agreement Relating to the Implementation of Part XI of the UN Convention on the Law of the Sea: a General Assessment', *ZaöRV* 55 (1995): 275–289. https://www.sciencedirect.com/science/article/pii/0308597X9592569S?via%3Dihub

70 In fairness, not everyone holds Nandan's work to be a 'first class racket'. *See* Michael J. Lodge, 'Satya Nandan's Legacy for the Common Heritage of Mankind', in *Peaceful Order in the World's Oceans. Essay in Honor of Satya* N. Nandan edited by Michael W. Lodge and Myron H. Nordquist, 282–300. (Leiden/Boston: Brill Nijhoff, 2014).

71 Oxman, '1994 Agreement', 690: Agreement, annex, sec. 3, para. 15.

72 *Cf.* Oxman, '1994 Agreement', 690.

73 *Cf.* Oxman, '1994 Agreement', 689.

74 *Cf.* Oxman, '1994 Agreement', 689. Oxman refers to White House Fact Sheet Jan. 29, 1982.

Enterprise would be in danger of becoming a hollow institution, lacking the necessary knowledge to be active in exploration or exploitation operations on behalf of 'mankind'. The Implementation Agreement abolished the mandatory transfer of technology, saying it 'shall not apply'.[75]

The agreement also weakened the overall ability of the Enterprise to enter into joint ventures with private investors, since any investor could now prevent themselves from being drawn into a joint venture arrangement. The investor or miner also had 'priority rights to the reserved area if the Enterprise itself does not apply for exploration or exploitation rights to the reserved area within a specified period'.[76] Concerning access to mining sites outside national jurisdiction, the agreement granted the US so-called 'grandfather rights', and decreed that general access to promising mining sites would be 'on a first-come, first-served basis'.[77] This tore down the idea of equal chances for access, since industrial states like the US with the necessary technology could easily reach these promising sites faster than developing countries who would have to acquire the technological knowledge and skills first. Finally, the review conference was abolished,[78] since it could 'impose treaty amendments on the United States without its consent'.[79]

The bottom line was that the Implementation Agreement pretty much destroyed everything Elisabeth Mann Borgese and her allies had worked for during the UNCLOS negotiations. It is hardly surprising, then, that she was furious when the Boat Paper surfaced and disrupted the promising provisions of Part XI as set out in the 1982 convention. However, in theory, the common heritage of mankind is permanently written into the Law of the Sea Convention, since the delegates had agreed that the Law of the Sea Treaty should not be amended. The Implementation Agreement is a paper outside of the convention that gives instructions on how to read Part XI, but it does not change or amend what is written in the 1982 convention. This means that the principle of common heritage of mankind remains inscribed in the convention, although its practical implications for activity in the Area are questionable. Some would argue that it has in effect been abolished altogether,[80] while others maintain

75 Agreement, annex, sec. 5 para 2, quoted in Oxman, '1994 Agreement', 689.

76 Agreement, annex, sec. 2, para. 5, quoted in Oxman, '1994 Agreement', 693.

77 Oxman, '1994 Agreement', 692.

78 Oxman, '1994 Agreement', 695.

79 Oxman, '1994 Agreement', 695.

80 *See* Taylor, 'The Common Heritage'. Taylor illuminates the shortcomings of the principle. *See also* Sabine Höhler, 'Exterritoriale Ressourcen: Die Diskussion um die Tiefsee, die Pole und das Weltall um 1970', *Jahrbuch für Europäische Geschichte* 15, (2014): 53–82. Höhler argues that the CHM principle introduced to UNCLOS did not revolutionise territorial thinking through introducing global commons.

that it is still an important part of the convention with a reasonable amount of influence on the Law of the Sea.[81] Whatever the case, in 1994, one of the main advocates of the common heritage principle, Elisabeth Mann Borgese, wrote to her old ally Karl Wolf that the International Seabed Authority was practically 'dead'[82] and that the common heritage was 'a joke'. 'What was left?'[83] she asked. The villains had kidnapped the convention, but Elisabeth Mann Borgese still did not give up on her bigger mission to achieve some tiny portion of her ideal of internationalism. She closed the letter to Karl Wolf by stating, 'We will have to pick up the pieces and see what we can do with them'.[84]

Her career did not end until her death in 2002. Right to the last, she continued working for the Law of the Sea. She held annual training programmes at the International Ocean Institute in Halifax and in the other institutes around the world, to which she invited scholars, entrepreneurs and government officials from developing countries to educate them in ocean governance and share technological expertise. On a small scale, Elisabeth Mann Borgese achieved one of her ambitions for the Law of the Sea Convention, in the form of technology transfer through education. The International Ocean Institute – though downscaled and slightly differently governed than in its heyday – is still running, putting on at least one training class each year and continuing Mann Borgese's work.

---

81 Payoyo discusses the possibilities for developing states in connection with the CHM applied to the Area. *See* Payoyo, *Cries of the Sea*, 237. *See also* Annica Carlsson, 'The US and UNCLOS III – The Death of the Common Heritage of Humankind Concept?', *Maritime Studies* 95 (1997): 27–35, https://doi.org/10.1080/07266472.1997.10878492.

82 MS-2-744, Box 355, Folder 24, EMB to Wolf, 7 May 1994.

83 MS-2-744, Box 355, Folder 24, EMB to Wolf, 7 May 1994. ‚Also, Teil XI (man muss ja zugeben, dass er nicht besonders gut war!) ist hin. [...] Wenn die EEZ weg ist, und das Common Heritage, ein Spott – was bleibt?'

84 MS-2-744, Box 355, Folder 24, EMB to Wolf, 7 May 1994.

Conclusion

1 Elisabeth Mann Borgese as the 'realist of tomorrow'

The Third United Nations Law of the Sea Convention was finalised in 1994, when the Law of the Sea Treaty together with the 1994 Implementation Agreement gained the required sixty ratifications. By then, Elisabeth Mann Borgese had spent twenty-seven years of her life working to influence the Law of the Sea.

The origins of her internationalist ideals, however, went back much further than that. Early influences were her marriage aged twenty-one and her husband's involvement with the Committee to Frame a World Constitution in Chicago. This laid the intellectual groundwork for her subsequent interest in seabed governance and also put her in contact with an important academic, Robert Maynard Hutchins, who some years later offered her a fellowship at the Center for the Study of Democratic Institutions in Santa Barbara.

The centre in Santa Barbara (where she worked from 1964–78) not only provided a platform from which she could deepen her academic training and develop proposals for world and ocean governance, but it also showed her how research institutions could be organised as think tanks to influence decision-makers. Inspired by Arvid Pardo's speech at the United Nations in 1967, she began to focus increasingly on how her ideas could be applied to ocean governance. From 1967–73, Mann Borgese attempted to involve herself in the preparation phase of UNCLOS III, collaborating with Pardo to organise the first of many *Pacem in Maribus* conferences that directly targeted diplomats and key actors at the United Nations. She also developed a detailed draft of a holistic ocean treaty called 'The Ocean Regime' that applied the common heritage of mankind principle to ocean governance. These ideas became the thread that would run through all her future proposals at the United Nations.

In 1972, Elisabeth Mann Borgese founded the International Ocean Institute on Malta – an institution that would evolve over the years. It started out as a think tank and the administrative engine behind the *Pacem in Maribus* conferences, but later obtained the status of a non-governmental organisation (NGO) so that Elisabeth Mann Borgese could access the negotiations during the early years of UNCLOS III from 1973–5. She hoped that the International Ocean Institute might eventually morph into the International Seabed Authority (ISA) – the 'international machinery' that would govern the seabed – but unfortunately the Maltese government mismanaged its bid to host the authority and this ambition was never realised.

© TIRZA MEYER, 2022 | DOI:10.1163/9789004511446_013

By 1975, non-governmental organisations were banned from speaking in UNCLOS meetings, so Mann Borgese kept herself involved in the negotiations by arranging to join the Austrian delegation, which led the group of Landlocked and Geographically Disadvantaged States at UNCLOS III. By then, it was already clear that the principle of common heritage would be restricted to the seafloor outside national jurisdiction and that a great majority of states did not want a holistic approach to ocean governance.

During the last phase of the negotiations from 1975–82, Elisabeth Mann Borgese worked on proposals for how the International Seabed Authority could administer the seafloor outside national jurisdiction. Together with the Austrian Ambassador Karl Wolf, Mann Borgese made several suggestions for shaping the operational arm of the authority – the Enterprise – in a way that would enable developing states to partake in seabed activity.

In 1982, the Law of the Sea Treaty was voted for and adopted by the United Nations. This included Part XI that was concerned with the seafloor outside national jurisdiction and the application of the common heritage principle. The functions of the Enterprise were designed to help developing nations undertake exploration and exploitation activities, and through this, the treaty partly secured the common heritage principle in connection to the seabed.

The treaty still needed ratifying, and this process got off to a slow start. Between 1982 and 1994, Elisabeth Mann Borgese contacted politicians and state leaders to try and collect the sixty ratifications necessary to secure the treaty. However, the United States and other industrialised states remained set against it, and eventually a small number of states developed the 1994 'Implementation Agreement' to get them on board. Mann Borgese warned that this agreement would unpick many of the principles that were embedded in Part XI, and would adversely affect the power, rights and design of the International Seabed Authority. Despite this, however, the Implementation Agreement was voted through on 22 July 1994. It destroyed much of what Elisabeth Mann Borgese and her allies had worked for, though the common heritage principle remains inscribed in the original convention to this day.

2 The Origins of Mann Borgese's Internationalist Ideals

Elisabeth Mann Borgese's route into academia was unusual and her position as a woman working alongside men in the 1950s was even more so. As a newlywed housewife, secretarial work was one of the few employment avenues open to her, but she saw that it could be her way into the academic world. As her daughter, Nica Borgese, told me in November 2015, 'I think she was just quick to learn and ambitious and idealistic [...], she was not going to remain a secretary'.[1]

We must also acknowledge the importance of her relationships with older men, which she repeatedly described as having had an enormous impact on her. One of these men was her husband, Giuseppe Antonio Borgese, whose influence lasted long beyond his own death in 1952. In a letter to him, she once wrote: 'Concerning Lehr- und Wanderjahre I am *not yet* content. My opinion is one has to lernen und zu wander all one's life'. And Elisabeth Mann Borgese did indeed go on to learn and wander for the rest of her days. Self-confidence in her own abilities was a vital ingredient for Mann Borgese's success, though almost as important were the opportunities she got to demonstrate these capabilities. As a case in point, Mann Borgese's work with the Committee to Frame a World Constitution in Chicago proved that her abilities went far beyond secretarial work and opened the door for her future career.

The Chicago committee also played a vital role in introducing her to the internationalist ideals that she later attempted to apply to ocean governance. As early as 1948, the committee stated that 'the four elements of life – earth, water, air, energy – are the common property of the human race'. The potential link between water and the common heritage principle was already there, and Mann Borgese would go on to translate the Chicago committee's ideas into practical proposals at the United Nations

The connections Mann Borgese had made in Chicago would ultimately lead to her fellowship at the Center for the Study of Democratic Institutions in Santa Barbara. Robert M Hutchins's discussion-based style of working and the centre's huge *Pacem in Terris* conferences inspired Mann Borgese to organise her own International Ocean Institute in a similar fashion. Some fellows said of Santa Barbara that it was 'Hutchins's Center'. The same could be said about the institution Mann Borgese built in 1972. The International Ocean Institute was Borgese's institute. Hutchins's work was motivated by a deep-rooted belief in international cooperation, and Mann Borgese transferred this ideal to the sphere of ocean governance. But to make the leap from world governance to ocean governance, Mann Borgese first had to be introduced to the oceans.

1 Interview with the author, 26 October 2015.

3 Arvid Pardo and a Meeting of Ideals

In the narrative about the starting point of UNCLOS III, Arvid Pardo is usually referred to as 'the Father of the Law of the Sea', while the significant part Elisabeth Mann Borgese played in their collaboration is sometimes overlooked. In this and other ways, Pardo's role in UNCLOS and the nature of his ideals can make him an interesting comparison to Mann Borgese.

Where Mann Borgese was more of an activist, Pardo was a career diplomat. His official status as the Maltese ambassador gave him wide recognition and a level of access to the political arena that Mann Borgese would never have, but his influence dwindled after he lost his position. While Mann Borgese worked unstintingly to keep herself engaged with the convention, their correspondence suggests that Pardo did not make particularly concerted efforts to get reinstated, and in fact it seems like Mann Borgese tried harder to re-affiliate Pardo with a delegation or NGO than he did himself.

Though he had iconic status as the man who had 'kick-started' the Law of the Sea negotiations by giving the right speech at the right point in time, Arvid Pardo was unhappy with the convention's eventual outcome. He remained vocally opinionated about the Law of the Sea in later years, but he does not appear to have taken much direct action after the Seabed Committee's work commenced in 1973. The limited source material available about Pardo makes it difficult to assess his participation accurately, but the research suggests that his ongoing role in UNCLOS III was more symbolic than proactive. This withdrawal might be explained by a reluctance to adapt. The outcome of the Law of the Sea Convention was not what Arvid Pardo had envisioned and perhaps he was less willing than Mann Borgese to adjust his vision to the changing political circumstances. So although he is widely recognised as the 'Father of the Law of the Sea', this is not really true, since he ultimately disliked and possibly even abandoned his 'child'.

Others, though, saw the possibilities in Arvid Pardo's iconic status, and the United Nations invited him to speak at the closing ceremony in 1982 after the convention had been voted for – underlining the sense of finality by letting the 'kick-starter' of the whole endeavour close it. Mann Borgese, too, tried to capitalise on his symbolic value several times during the course of the negotiations – for example when she tried to convince Dom Mintoff to invite Arvid Pardo into the Maltese delegation (and her along with him), or when she sited the International Ocean Institute on Malta in the hopes that it might evolve into the International Seabed Authority. Mann Borgese understood that Pardo's symbolic role made Malta a likely candidate to host a United Nations institution for ocean governance, and her eye for an opportunity was much better than that of the Maltese government, who hesitated too long to make their pitch and missed out.

Apart from comparing Pardo's role in the convention to that of Mann Borgese, other aspects of his biography are essential to understanding his idealistic goals, and this too makes him an interesting parallel to Mann Borgese. In Pardo's case, he had been directly involved in World War II and it had affected him deeply. Pardo's idealism was best summed up in a small biographical note about him, where the author stated, 'The diverse experiences of Arvid Pardo has been his willingness to act upon his opposition to war in the pursuit of peace'.[2]

While Mann Borgese had left Europe before the outbreak of war, the rise of fascism had forced both her own family and many people she knew (including her future husband) into exile. For both Elisabeth Mann Borgese and Arvid Pardo, their personal backgrounds played a part in their visions for ocean governance. Both wanted to incorporate a new approach to international justice and resource distribution, and this was rooted in the conviction that collaboration was better than conflict, and that justice was necessary to prevent war.

4 The Time Was Ripe – Political and Technological Development in the Mid-Twentieth Century

With its enthusiasm for new technologies, progress and the possibilities of the uncharted territory on the seafloor, the mid-twentieth century was a breeding ground for ideas around different forms of governance. In 1991, Mann Borgese wrote about the role of technology in society and politics: 'Technology is a tool which simply reinforces and magnifies the consequences of the existing social and economic order'.[3] This is an accurate description of how UNCLOS III came about, though the notion is not absolutely correct – since the relationship between technological progress and society goes both ways. Technology shapes society but society also shapes technology.

The 1960s were characterised by a strong, sometimes overestimated belief in technological progress, and this was especially true of deep sea mining technology. Discussions about the governance of the seabed outside national jurisdiction were fuelled largely by the notion that imminent developments in underwater mining would soon bring inaccessible spaces within reach, and

2 MS-2-744, Box 186, Folder 4, Ambassador Arvid Pardo.

3 Chircop, 'Elisabeth Mann Borgese's humanist conception', 114.

this also drove enthusiasm for applying the common heritage principle to the seafloor. Clearly, the industrialised countries (which were also the former colonial powers) would develop the relevant technology first and the idea of sharing it with developing nations became a stumbling block for agreement at UNCLOS III. However, when it became apparent in the 1970s that underwater mining technology for the deep seabed was more futuristic than realistic, interest in the seafloor and the common heritage principle declined, leading Karl Wolf to write to Mann Borgese 'Kein Mensch interessiert sich für die Area'.

Another factor that drove the UNCLOS negotiations was the general re-establishment of world orders. After World War II, the world in general began to rethink governance on a grand scale. None of the people involved with the radical developments in ocean or world governance at that time possessed an unusual amount of visionary power, it was just that the discussions they were involved in had sprung out of the extraordinary social and political developments during the first half of the twentieth century. This is especially apparent when we consider some of the attempts to re-shape world governance that emerged in the post-war years, such as the World Federalist Movement, for example. We might recall that one of Mann Borgese's tasks during her early years in Chicago was to review all kinds of proposals for world constitutions. These initiatives emerged independently of one another, but all had a similar goal: to propose a new order for a world that obviously needed one, especially in the light of humanity's latest and most deadly technological development. The Chicago Committee to Frame a World Constitution itself had been founded as a direct response to the atomic threat and was the brainchild of someone who had helped create that threat in the first place. Humanity's ability to split the atom made the need for a more united world abundantly apparent, and the existence of such a weapon made it necessary to rethink conflict and conflict management on a global scale.

The atomic threat was also responsible for the seemingly sudden need in 1967 to reserve the seafloor for peaceful purposes. While Pardo's speech is often pinpointed as a starting point for a completely new way of dealing with international law-making (because he introduced the principle of the common heritage of mankind), in reality the codification of the Law of the Sea had been a long and creeping process that was tightly bound up with the fact that humanity had started to travel further and deeper into the sea than ever before. With this continuing exploration, weaponry stations on the seafloor were beginning to become a potential tool of warfare, and many in the international community were keen to prevent this.

In this atmosphere of future possibilities and a growing need for legislation, the Maltese ambassador's speech was more like another step along the way towards the Law of the Sea, as opposed to the start of the journey. His suggestion was a response to the need to define governance of an area that could become important in the future. Even the principle Pardo introduced to the discussion was not inherently new. The Outer Space Treaty of 1967 had already coined the term 'province of mankind', and although the term is different, the principle behind it is comparable to that of 'common heritage'. It states that 'exploration' should be 'carried out for the benefit and in the interests of all countries [...]'. Likewise, the Chicago committee had introduced a similar idea in their draft for a world constitution, where they wrote that 'The four elements of life – earth, water, air, energy – are the common property of the human race'. Though the terms varied between 'property', 'province' and 'heritage', their meanings were closely related.

Developments in real-world politics also underlined the need to rethink world governance. In the case of the Law of the Sea, one such event was the Truman declaration in September 1945. It showed that while Elisabeth Mann Borgese and the Chicago committee were grappling with world governance at a conceptual level, ocean governance on the other hand was already up for discussion. The United States' attempts to secure claims offshore with the Truman declaration triggered other nation states to follow their lead, and the international community had to act before individual states ended up taking the matter entirely into their own hands. These developments showed that clarifying maritime boundaries would be vital to maintaining a stable world order, while the shadow of the Cold War and the ever-present atomic threat made the need even more pressing. Since the international community was not overtly interested in open conflict, these issues had to be solved through diplomacy.

Fluctuations in the balance of world power further complicated the negotiations. The decolonisation process had divided the world into developed and developing countries. For an increasing number of post-colonial developing states, UNCLOS III was the first time they could enter the international arena, and the Group of 77 is an excellent example of the rising power of developing states through necessary collaboration. In his speech, Arvid Pardo had mentioned the possibility of a 'race into the deep' – in which industrialised countries would grab seabed resources for themselves before developing states had the chance to invent the requisite technology – and this highlighted the inherent unfairness embedded in the whole system. It is no surprise that nations in the Group of 77 favoured applying the common heritage principle to the seafloor outside national jurisdiction, since this system of ocean governance would help them catch up in terms of development and balance out some of the injustice. However, the developing countries suffered an important defeat right in the very first session in 1973, when the decision to work with a consensus system instead of a voting system negated their power in numbers. Instead, compromises had to be found, but Elisabeth Mann Borgese and her allies still hoped to level out the technological superiority of the industrialised states by implementing the principle of common heritage of mankind.

5 Common Heritage or Common Property

Elisabeth Mann Borgese entered the negotiations on ocean governance with concrete suggestions that she hoped would help her seed a little piece of internationalism into the Law of the Sea. Her aim was to fill out the common heritage principle with detailed meaning and then to find ways of applying it to the real-life political situation. The principle itself went through an interesting transformation during UNCLOS. In the 1970s, the way Mann Borgese intended to apply it brought the principle closer to what the Chicago committee had called the 'common property' of mankind. This was because she wanted it to level out the economic injustice in the world order, and in order to do this, the area outside national jurisdiction had to generate revenue that could be distributed.

Mann Borgese's drafts for ocean governance show that the word 'heritage' was used rather loosely in relation to the common heritage principle. This is unsurprising when we consider why the seabed was reserved for the common heritage of mankind in the first place. Discussions on the subject had arisen because people in the 1960s believed geologist John Mero's optimistic predictions that the resources on the seafloor could soon be exploited, and so the international community was mostly interested in the question of 'rights of access' and 'means of utilisation'. For Mann Borgese too, her view of the seafloor revolved primarily around how to utilise such a store of resources that had no 'natural' owner, and how access to these riches could be shared out fairly. According to Mann Borgese's way of thinking, this meant giving every human on Earth the chance to benefit from the resources of the seabed.

In practice, the question of 'rights' and 'means' was about which states would appropriate or utilise the resources and how they would do it. Would the industrialised states be able to keep these resources all to themselves, or would the developing nations get to benefit from them too? With this in mind, Mann Borgese allied herself with those states who had the greatest interest in a very broad application of the common heritage concept – those without any expertise in utilising marine minerals who were interested in making rules that would secure access for them despite the fact they lacked the necessary technology. In a strict reading of Mann Borgese's suggestion to solve the issue of unequal access to resources, she proposed compelling industrialised states to go into partnership with developing countries if they wanted to carry out deep sea mining activities in the area outside national jurisdiction. Through this, developing countries could gain technological knowledge through cooperation.

Less in focus during the early discussions about the common heritage principle was the question of what the term 'heritage' meant in terms of reserving and protecting areas for future generations. This was barely discussed at the convention. Articles 192–237 deal with issues of pollution, but the section is vague on exact rules or regulations. While Mann Borgese discussed the environmental aspects of UNCLOS with her students at Dalhousie University, this perspective was mostly absent from the convention itself – and particularly from Part XI.[4] A future study of this aspect of UNCLOS would be interesting, and a good starting point might be one of the treaty's opening statements, in which the parties state that the convention shall 'recognize [...] the equitable and efficient utilization of their resources, the conservation of their living resources, and the study, protection and preservation of the marine environment'.[5]

Elisabeth Mann Borgese's ambitions for the area outside national jurisdiction in the 1970s were mainly driven by a fascination with what might be technologically possible when it came to exploiting underwater resources. This attitude corresponded with Arvid Pardo's futuristic vision as laid out in his 1967 speech. For the pioneers of the common heritage concept, at the core of ocean governance was peace, justice and an opportunity to help level out economic injustice in the world. They could do this by favouring developing states through an International Seabed Authority that would redistribute revenue and force industrialised states to collaborate on seabed exploitation. In Mann Borgese's case, this went right back to the concept of 'common property of the human race' that she had worked with on the Chicago committee.

6 The Idea in Action through Institution-Building

During UNCLOS, Mann Borgese's work was characterised by her constant ability to change course and find new solutions if necessary. She was not afraid to downsize her ideal in line with changing political realities that made it

4 The Ocean Yearbook publications 11 and onwards would address the issue of the protection of the environment.

5 Bernaerts, *Bernaerts' Guide, 153 – Preamble to the United Nations Convention on the Law of the Sea.*

increasingly apparent how unrealistic her dreams of a holistic ocean regime really were. Mann Borgese adapted her methods and the ideal itself – which was to insert internationalism into ocean governance – to the challenges that arose during the negotiation process. The outcome was not what she had hoped for, and Mann Borgese had to cut her losses to some extent, but a fraction of her ideal survived all the same.

Throughout UNCLOS, Elisabeth Mann Borgese used several different institutions (or attempted to use them) to try and influence decision-making processes at the negotiations. She used existing channels into the convention in the form of the Maltese and Austrian delegations, but also established new platforms and institutions – like the *Pacem in Maribus* convocations and the International Ocean Institute.

Initially, Mann Borgese founded the International Ocean Institute in the hopes that it would evolve into a United Nations institution that would govern the world oceans. In the late 1960s and early 1970s, Mann Borgese could not know the future shape and form of this institution, which at the time was referred to as 'international machinery' to govern the seafloor, but judging from her suggestions in 'The Ocean Regime', she hoped it would be an overarching institution responsible for all activities in the oceans, not just the seafloor. Possibly it could even extend its capabilities to world governance.

We know today that the International Seabed Authority is the real-world version of what Elisabeth Mann Borgese envisioned in 'The Ocean Regime', though on a much smaller scale than she proposed. The International Seabed Authority is not located in Malta and it does not have any overarching functions other than to administer the seafloor outside national jurisdiction. Since Mann Borgese's International Ocean Institute did not end up evolving into the seabed authority as anticipated, its tasks and purpose also changed accordingly over time, and when the negotiations started in 1973, Mann Borgese was quick to give herself a way into the convention by adapting the IOI into a non-governmental organisation.

After it became apparent early on in UNCLOS III that NGOs would struggle to influence the negotiation process, Elisabeth Mann Borgese solved the problem by joining the Austrian delegation. With the Austrians she had a platform from which she could once again directly influence negotiation processes, send in drafts and discuss paragraphs. An additional advantage was that Jens Evensen, who played a prominent role in the drafting committee, and Karl Wolf, the head of the Austrian delegation, were both based in Oslo. Although there is no direct proof that this gave them easier access to an important policy maker in the form of Evensen, we do know that Mann Borgese and Wolf were invited to Evensen's influential intersessional meetings on several occasions.

Even in terms of her own workplace, Mann Borgese made changes during the period of her involvement with the Law of the Sea. The first *Pacem in Maribus* conference was organised by the Center for the Study of Democratic Institutions in Santa Barbara, but her attempts to engage the centre further in the ocean endeavour failed because the other fellows were not willing to follow her lead. When the centre began to fall apart, she actively sought a new position at Dalhousie University in Halifax, spending the rest of her life there and opening another branch of the International Ocean Institute so that she could remain closely involved with the institution that she had founded.

Mann Borgese's various ways into UNCLOS over the years show that she changed location and affiliation when necessary in order to achieve her goal of inserting internationalist ideas into the convention. And she was flexible with respect to her ideals too, downsizing her vision in line with social, political and diplomatic changes. We can see this from the differences in scale between her draft of 'The Ocean Regime' – in which the common heritage principle encompasses the entire ocean space – and its later incarnations. First, it was scaled back and limited to the International Seabed Authority and later to the authority's executive branch – the Enterprise. Even in this smaller form, it would still give developing nations a chance to partake in the exploitation of marine minerals.

Whenever her current strategy did not pay off, or whenever the circumstances shifted, Elisabeth Mann Borgese developed a new plan – a new 'appeal to act now'. She was not and could never be a delegate for any one specific camp or cause, so it is not surprising that she changed affiliations several times during UNCLOS III. Her involvement with the law-making process was never static and neither was her strategy. Only her aim remained fixed – to insert even just a microscopic trace of her internationalist ideals into ocean governance.

7 Elisabeth Mann Borgese's Legacy

What was left after the 1994 Implementation Agreement? The last chapter of this book discussed the amendment period between 1982 and 1994, during which time Mann Borgese tried to keep the provisions of Part XI intact in an effort to protect the common heritage principle. Despite her efforts, she was ultimately overruled by those who felt the convention could only be effective if these provisions were altered in order to get the United States and other industrialised states to sign and ratify the treaty.

Mann Borgese's own assessment directly after the Implementation Agreement had been approved was that in practice the common heritage principle was no longer effective. It is possible that she moderated this position in later years in response to fresh developments, but this remains to be studied more closely. As ever, Elisabeth Mann Borgese adapted to a new situation and pushed on. On the basis of the material examined for this book, we can see that her subsequent efforts to repair the damage included using her own International Ocean Institute's training programmes to implement technology transfer to developing nations.

Indeed, if one were to pinpoint a definitive legacy for Elisabeth Mann Borgese, it would be the International Ocean Institute on Malta, with its sister institutions in Halifax and in other places around the world. Even today, the International Ocean Institute still holds annual training courses for state officials and scholars from developing nations working in fields that are related to ocean or coastal management. In many respects, the evolution of the International Ocean Institute reflects Elisabeth Mann Borgese's own ability to adapt. The institution started out as the 'concrete beginning' of the future International Seabed Authority and the ocean regime, and served as a think tank organising *Pacem in Maribus* during the preparation phase prior to UNCLOS III. It became an NGO to give Mann Borgese a platform at UNCLOS when she was struggling to join a national delegation, and finally it turned into a training facility for scholars from developing nations. In its current incarnation, it fills a gap that was originally supposed to be occupied by the International Seabed Authority before it was compromised due to the 1994 Implementation Agreement, in that it practises technology transfer to developing nations.

It is relatively simple to assess Mann Borgese's legacy in terms of what she did outside of UNCLOS, but more difficult to quantify her direct impact on the negotiations. Without knowing the specifics of how other individuals and groups operated, it is tricky to estimate the extent of Elisabeth Mann Borgese's influence. We know that she was in contact with influential key actors at the convention, but whether her proposals were heard or just resonated with other people's is hard to determine without having studied the ideas set out by other individuals. To investigate her effectiveness more closely would require a case study that aimed to follow one or more specific initiatives through the entire process. One obvious starting point could be to investigate the Paul Engo case, where provisions were secretly changed in favour of developing states. If a closer investigation of this issue were to show that Mann Borgese was involved, this could give us an indication of her influence above and beyond her proposals.

This book has followed her ideals, her proposals and ideas, and the strategies she employed to try and apply her ideal of internationalism to ocean governance. We have seen that she did this through various channels: by founding institutions, organising conferences, joining delegations, writing reports and delivering speeches. We have also seen that she was able to ally herself with key people in the negotiation processes, like Jens Evensen, Shirley Amerasinghe and many others. Dalhousie University Archive holds an abundance of letters to important delegates at the United Nations, many of whom Elisabeth Mann Borgese was on a first-name basis with. These letters provide possible threads that could be followed further to get a more precise picture of her involvement and potential impact on decision-making in the Law of the Sea negotiations.

Today we know that Part XI, together with the Implementation Agreement of the Law of the Sea Convention, did not turn out as Mann Borgese and Pardo had envisioned in the 1970s. To what extent the common heritage principle is still a vital part of the Law of the Sea and whether it has any function or not remains to be seen. Nevertheless, we can only guess at whether common heritage would have been applied in any shape or form to the seafloor outside national jurisdiction without Arvid Pardo and Elisabeth Mann Borgese.

The Leverings from the Neptune Group criticised Mann Borgese for being an ivory tower idealist, but her path through the convention contradicts this argument. An ivory tower idealist would not have adapted and changed course as Mann Borgese did several times during the negotiation process. Perhaps the Leverings were so critical of Mann Borgese's actions because they fought for different causes. The Leverings wanted to aid the consensus-seeking process, while Mann Borgese's aim was to contribute concrete proposals to the negotiation process. In some cases the Leverings may have been justified in objecting to her methods. Her sometimes controversial proposals had the potential to disrupt consensus instead of aiding it, particularly when she re-introduced ideas that had already been rejected – like the proposal of a joint venture compromise that would never be accepted by the United States and eventually caused a stalemate when provisions were secretly changed in favour of developing countries.

Inspired by Arvid Pardo, Mann Borgese was perhaps overly enthusiastic about the abundance of mineral resources on the seafloor, without taking into account that they might be out of reach. However, this was a flaw she shared with many of the delegates at UNCLOS III. Her enthusiasm for the implementation of the common heritage principle and her lobbying efforts to recruit allies were also unrealistic at times. Perhaps she believed that one had to set ambitious goals in order to achieve even a tiny proportion of them, but this strategy can be counterproductive, and it is possible that her overly ambitious proposals sometimes disrupted her cause more than they helped her reach her aims. Nevertheless, she left an impressive record of proposals, papers, speeches, and drafts – not to forget the networks she built with influential people during the negotiations and the institutions she founded to enhance and further her vision of the future of ocean governance.

8 Epilogue – The Future of Ocean Governance – What Is Next?

This final section could easily be the beginning of a new book. 'EMB 2.0 – Elisabeth Mann Borgese's post-mortem role in the future of ocean governance'. Her proposals, especially 'The Ocean Regime', addressed issues that the United Nations is still grappling with today. This has to do with the fact that, decades after it came into force, the Law of the Sea Treaty remains a legal document in progress – not because the law text itself is unfinished, but because the delegates at UNCLOS III wrote many of the Articles based on imagined future developments, so new instruments and agreements are periodically added to address fresh challenges.

Many of the technologies Elisabeth Mann Borgese and others envisioned in the 1960s and 70s have not been realised as they anticipated. This is no surprise, since it is impossible to predict the future. But this in turn means that a number of the Articles that were written so long ago are only now (and only gradually) being filled with meaning. In some cases, their effectiveness is just beginning to be tested, while in other cases this may happen in the future – or perhaps never.

A good example of an area in which the Law of the Sea is still transforming and adapting is the ongoing BBNJ conference at the United Nations. BBNJ is an abbreviation for the 'Intergovernmental Conference on Marine Biodiversity of Areas Beyond National Jurisdiction'.[6] Though this may sound complicated, what it means is that United Nations delegates have called for a conference to create additional rules and to clarify existing provisions for the area outside national jurisdiction.[7] This area includes the deep seabed that was of such great interest for Elisabeth Mann Borgese. The aim of the BBNJ conference is to make rules that will protect the environment in areas outside national jurisdiction and to make additional rules for marine genetic resources – meaning

6 The full title: Intergovernmental Conference on an international legally binding instrument under the United Nations Convention on the Law of the Sea on the conservation and sustainable use of marine biological diversity of areas beyond national jurisdiction (General Assembly resolution 72/249).

7 In UN jargon this is called an 'international legally binding instrument' under UNCLOS.

anything from microbes to other living things in this area. But why were marine genetic resources not included in the Law of the Sea Treaty in the first place? Through this book we have seen that the seafloor and its resources were discussed at length and with vigour during UNCLOS III, but the main focus in the 1970s was on the resources on and under the seafloor. Even the common heritage of mankind proposal was primarily concerned with the just distribution of mining rights and economic benefits. The ecosystem itself and the threat human activity could pose to it were not yet perceived as major issues, and the main concern was to agree on how to use the oceans, not how to protect them.

The Law of the Sea Treaty was the child of a different era – the second half of the twentieth century. 2021 marked the first year of the 'United Nations Decade of Ocean Science for Sustainable Development (2021–2030)'[8] and much has changed. Human activity in the ocean and its consequences – overfishing, over-acidification, coral bleaching and habitat loss to name just a few – have pushed the issue of how to protect the marine environment high up the agenda. At the same time, industrial use of the ocean is increasing. Some of the existing provisions have to be adjusted in order to meet today's challenges and this is what the BBNJ aims to do.

We know that the delegates at UNCLOS III were not blind to the uncertainty of future developments. The International Seabed Authority was set up in a flexible way with the Prep Com as an insurance against an uncertain future. And even back when Elisabeth Mann Borgese wrote 'The Ocean Regime' she already had the possibility of change in mind. Her first visions for ocean governance were much more 'holistic' and internationalist than those that later went into the Law of the Sea Treaty, but she always thought big. In her first draft she intentionally left a kind of loophole, designing the ocean regime in such a way that it could transform into a world regime. She did this firstly because she came from a world governance background and had a deeply rooted conviction that unity was better than nationalism, and secondly because she was convinced that everything in the ocean and also in the world at large was interconnected – and that only a governance system that encompassed the entire planet could meet the challenges the world faced both in her own time and in the future.

These ideas are similar to what today is termed an 'ecosystem approach', which is also being discussed at the BBNJ conferences.[9] Ecosystem approaches

8 '2021–2030 United Nations Decade of Ocean Science for Sustainable Development', Ocean Decade, UNESCO 2019, 30 September 2021, https://www.oceandecade.org/.

9 *See for example* Vito De Lucia, The BBNJ negotiations and ecosystem governance in the arctic, Marine Policy, 2019, https://doi.org/10.1016/j.marpol.2019.103756.

call for a more holistic world governance system to regulate human footprints on our planet in the light of one of the biggest challenges of our time: the climate crisis. This might seem as lofty and unrealistic as 'The Ocean Regime' did in the 1970s, but perhaps elements of the ideal of a unified Earth System Government can be adapted into methods for governing large, international areas like the oceans. This suggests that Elisabeth Mann Borgese's ideas are still relevant today. It might be interesting to return to several of these earlier proposals with the current situation in mind. One could try and assess whether some of the challenges the BBNJ conferences (and future ocean governance negotiations) are trying to solve have already been pondered by their twentieth-century predecessors, and whether we can learn from the ideas, pitfalls, miscalculations and problems of these earlier negotiations.

The Law of the Sea Treaty contains the provisions and ideas that survived the negotiation process, but a lot was lost on the way. I found that many seemingly sound proposals never made it into the law text – often not because the idea was bad, but because they fell victim to political trade-offs or because the timing was not right. Therefore, it is interesting to examine the negotiation process by following the progress of individual ideas such as Mann Borgese's. We can see how the process affected these ideas, illuminating them and prompting adaptations and alternatives. Perhaps some of the ideas that came out of UNCLOS III are a better fit for tackling today's challenges than for those of the time.

Apart from everything else, Elisabeth Mann Borgese's story also proves that one needs a certain degree of persistence and flexibility to stay afloat in an international process like UNCLOS III. Elisabeth Mann Borgese knew that her ideas were often seen as idealistic and even utopian, but she also understood that idealism could be much more nuanced and practical than that. As she stated in 1999, she believed that the idealists of today are the realists of tomorrow. Though she remained a lifelong idealist at heart, her adaptability and her willingness to downsize and rearrange her ideas show that she was a realist in practice.

FIGURE 6 Elisabeth Mann Borgese in Nova Scotia Crystal Crescent Beach, December 25, 2000
MONACENSIA LITERATURARCHIV UND BIBLIOTHEK MÜNCHEN, EMB F 29
PHOTO: NICA BORGESE

Archival Material

Dalhousie University Archive – Elisabeth Mann Borgese Fonds

Elisabeth Mann Borgese Fonds, MS-2-744, Dalhousie University Archives and Special Collections, Halifax, Canada

MS-2-744, Box 16, Folder 19
MS-2-744, Box 43, Folder 17
MS-2-733, Box 43, Folder 46
MS-2-744, Box 43, Folder 48
MS-2-744, Box 43, Folder 49
MS-2-744, Box 43, Folder 54
MS-2-744, Box 47, Folder 6
MS-2-744, Box 52, Folder 9
MS-2-744, Box 62, Folder 8
MS-2-744, Box 63, Folder 1
MS-2-744, Box 84, Folder 12
MS-2-744, Box 85, Folder 17
MS-2-744, Box 87, Folder 4
MS-2-744, Box 89, Folder 18
MS-2-744, Box 94, Folder 1
MS-2-744, Box 101, Folder 1
MS-2-744, Box 108, Folder 1
MS-2-744, Box 114, Folder 7
MS-2-744, Box 114, Folder 8
MS-2-744, Box 114, Folder 19
MS-2-744, Box 120, Folder 25
MS-2-744, Box 121, Folder 18
MS-2-744, Box 125, Folder 2
MS-2-744, Box 125, Folder 3
MS-2-744, Box 132, Folder 1
MS-2-744, Box 132, Folder 32
MS-2-744, Box 135, Folder 22
MS-2-744, Box 139, Folder 16
MS-2-744, Box 145, Folder 11
MS-2-744, Box 147, Folder 1
MS-2-744, Box 175, Folder 21
MS-2-744, Box 176, Folder 12
MS-2-744, Box 176, Folder 13

MS-2-744, Box 186, Folder 4
MS-2-744, Box 208, Folder 2
MS-2-744, Box 210, Folder 4
MS-2-744, Box 210, Folder 14
MS-2-744, Box 218, Folder 33
MS-2-744, Box 235, Folder 4
MS-2-744, Box 236, Folder 11
MS-2-744, Box 276, Folder 1
MS-2-744, Box 323, Folder 18
MS-2-744, Box 345, Folder 4
MS-2-744, Box 355, Folder 24
MS-2-744, Box 398, Folder 15

Harry S. Truman Presidential Library & Museum

Press release by the White House. 'Immediate Release. Statement by the President of the United States'. August 6, 1945, available at: https://www.trumanlibrary.gov/library/research-files/press-release-white-house.

Harry S. Truman. 'Proclamation 2667: Policy Of The United States With Respect To The Natural Resources Of The Subsoil And Sea Bed Of The Continental Shelf (1)'. September 28, 1945, available at: https://www.trumanlibrary.gov/library/proclamations/2667/policy-united-states-respect-natural-resources-subsoil-and-sea-bed.

IMO International Maritime Law Institute – Pardo Archives

Box: Personal Correspondences & Materials

PR-Box: Personal Correspondences & Materials, undated letter from Dr. Arvid Pardo to Salvino Busuttil (handwritten note on the right corner). CC: Joe Friggieri, Fr Peter Serracino Inglott, Freddie Amato Gauci, ~~Victor Gauci~~, Charlie Vella, Elizabeth Mann Borgese, ~~Victor Ragonesi~~

PR-Box: Personal Correspondences & Materials, letter from Arvid Pardo to Secretary Ministry of Commonwealth, 18. October 1968, appendix 'D'

PR-Box: Personal Correspondences & Materials, letter from Arvid Pardo to Secretary Ministry of Commonwealth, 18. October 1968, appendix 'C'

PR-Box: Personal Correspondences & Materials, letter from G George Olivier to Arvid Pardo, 23. November 1964

PR-Box: Personal Correspondences & Materials, letter of appointment, 15. August 1946

PR-Box: Personal Correspondences & Materials, Tony Loftas, Pardo, politics and pollution, *New Scientist and Science Journal*, 8. July 1971

PR-Box: Personal Correspondences & Materials, Arvid Pardo to the Prime Minister, Appendix 'A', 7 July 1971

PR-Box: Tributes

PR-Box: Tributes, Feature, 47, 1990

Monacensia Literaturarchiv, Nachl. Elisabeth Mann Borgese, EMB, München, Germany

EMB B4

EMB B3

Images

EMB F22

EMB F29

EMB F179

EMB F203

Nica Borgese Private Collection Milano

Nica Borgese, Private Collection, Milano, Italy.

NB-Folder 5

Britannica II, Dec, 1963-, May 20, 1964

Thomas Mann Archiv, Zürich, Switzerland

Ergänzter Nachlass Thomas Mann, B-III Briefe von Familienmitgliedern (direkte Nachkommen Thomas und Katia Manns, deren Ehepartner sowie Katia Mann), Thomas-Mann- Archiv, Zürich, Switzerland.

B III Briefe von Familienmitgliedern

B-III.17.EINS-1

B-III.17-KENN-1

B-III.17-MANN-106

B-III.17-MANN-107

B-III.17-MANN-108

B-III.17-MANN-109

B-III.17-MANN-110

B.III.17-MANN-126

B-III.17-MANN-144

United Nations Archive New York City

Office of the Secretary-General Law of the Sea Conference Records 1973–1983, United Nations Archives & Record Management Section, New York City, United States of America.

Office of the Secretary-General Law of the Sea Conference Records 1973–1983.

S-0571-0013

S-0289-0009-36

United Nations Resolutions, Documents, Statements, Treaties

General Assembly Resolutions

United Nations, General Assembly resolution, *International conference of plenipotentiaries to examine the law of the sea*, GA A/RES/1105, 21 February 1957, available at: https://digitallibrary.un.org/record/207865.

United Nations, General Assembly resolution 1307 (XIII), *Convening of a second conference on the Law of the Sea*, GA RES 1307 (XIII), 10 December 1958, available at: https://digitallibrary.un.org/record/207045.

United Nations, General Assembly resolution 2172/XXI, *Resources of the sea*, GA RES 2172 (XXI), 6 December 1966, available at: https://digitallibrary.un.org/record/203184.

United Nations, General Assembly resolution 2340(XXII), *Examination of the question of the reservation exclusively for peaceful purposes of the seabed and the ocean floor, and the subsoil thereof, underlying the high seas beyond the limits of present national jurisdiction, and the use of their resources in the interest of mankind*, GA A/RES/22/2340, 18 December 1967.

United Nations, General Assembly resolution 2750/XXV. B, *Reservation Exclusively for the peaceful Purposes of the sea-bed and the ocean floor, and the subsoil thereof, underlying the high seas beyond the limits of national jurisdiction and use of their resources in the interests of mankind, and convening of the Third United Nations Conference on the Law of the Sea*, GA RES 2750 (XXV). B, 17 December 1970.

United Nations, General Assembly resolution 3067 (XXVIII), *Reservation Exclusively for the peaceful Purposes of the sea-bed and the ocean floor, and the subsoil thereof, underlying the high seas beyond the limits of national jurisdiction and use of their resources in the interests of mankind, and convening of the Third United Nations Conference on the Law of the Sea (A/9278)*, GA RES 3067 (XXVIII), 16 November 1973.

United Nations, General Assembly Resolution, A/RES/48/263, *Agreement relating to the implementation of Part XI of the United Nations Convention on the Law of the Sea of 10 December 1982*, A/RES/48/263, 17 August 1994, available at: http://undocs.org/A/RES/48/263.

United Nations Documents

United Nations, Third Conference on the Law of the Sea, Summary records of meeting of the First Committee 1st meeting, Extract from the *Official Records of the Third United Nations Conference on the Law of the Sea, Volume II*, A/CONF.62/C.1/SR.1, 10. July 1974, available at: http://legal.un.org/docs/?path=../diplomaticconferences/1973_los/docs/english/vol_2/a_conf62_c1_sr1.pdf&lang=E.

United Nations, Third Conference on the Law of the Sea, Delegations to the Third United Nations Conference on the Law of the Sea, A/CONF.62/INF.6/Corr.1, 3 February 1977, available at https://undocs.org/en/A/CONF.62/INF.6/Corr.1.

United Nations, Third Conference on the Law of the Sea, Delegations to the Third United Nations Conference on the Law of the Sea, A/CONF.62/INF.11, 14 August 1979, available at: https://undocs.org/en/A/CONF.62/INF.11.

United Nations, Third Conference on the Law of the Sea, Delegations to the Third United Nations Conference on the Law of the Sea, A/CONF.62/INF.13, 20 August 1980, available at: https://undocs.org/en/A/CONF.62/INF.13.

United Nations, Third Conference on the Law of the Sea, 'Amendments/Australia, Austria, Canada, Denmark, Finland, Iceland, Ireland, New Zealand, Norway and Sweden', Documents of the Conference 219–220, A/CONF.62/L.104 and Add.1, 13 April 1982.

United Nations, Third Conference on the Law of the Sea, 'Delegations to the Third United Nations Conference on the Law of the Sea, Second session', A/CONF.62/INF.3/Rev.1., 19 July 1974, available at: http://undocs.org/A/CONF.62/INF.3/Rev.1.

United Nations, United Nations Conference on the Law of the Sea, Extract from the Official Records of the United Nations Conference on the Law of the Sea, 1958, Volume II (Plenary Meetings), annexes, resolution VIII, document A/CONF.13/L.56, 27 April 1958, available at: https://legal.un.org/diplomaticconferences/1958_los/docs/english/vol_2/a_conf_13_l_56.pdf.

United Nations, General Assembly, Plenary, 22nd Session, 1583rd Meeting, Malta: request for the inclusion of a supplementary item in the agenda of the twenty-second session, A/6695, 18 August 1967, available at: https://undocs.org/A/6695.

United Nations, General Assembly, 'Organization of the Twenty-second Regular Session, Adoption of the Agenda and Allocation of Items, A/6840, 22 September 1967, available at: http://undocs.org/A/6840.

United Nations, General Assembly, 'Examination of the question of the reservation exclusively for peaceful purposes of the seabed and the ocean floor, and the subsoil thereof, underlying the high seas beyond the limits of present national jurisdiction, and the use of their resources in the interest of mankind', A/6964, 12 December 1967, available at: http://undocs.org/A/6964.

United Nations, Committee on the Peaceful uses of the Sea-Bed and the Ocean Floor Beyond the Limits of National Jurisdiction, Draft Ocean Space Treaty: working paper/submitted by Malta, A/AC.138/53, 23 August 1971, available at: https://undocs.org/A/AC.138/53.

United Nations, Commission on International Trade Law, *Yearbook* Volume IX, A/CN.9/SER.A/1978, (New York: United Nations, 1978).

United Nations, General Assembly, Twenty-Second Session, Official Records, A/PV.1528, 6 October 1967, available at: undocs.org/A/PV.1582. https://undocs.org/A/PV.1582.

United Nations, Department of International Economic and Social Affairs, *Sea-Bed Mineral Resource Development,* ST/ESA/107/Add.1 (New York: United Nations, 1982), available at: undocs.org/ST/ESA/107/Add.1. https://undocs.org/ST/ESA/107/Add.1.

Statements and Speeches

United Nations, First Committee, Statement of Arvid Pardo 1515th & 1516th Meeting, A/C.1/PV.1515, A/C.1/PV.1516, 1 November 1967.

United Nations, General Assembly, Speech by Mr. Attard Kingswell, 1965th Plenary Meeting, A/PV.1965 13. October 1971, available at: http://undocs.org/A/PV.1965.

United Nations, General Assembly, Speech by Mr. Attard Kingswell, 2061st Plenary Meeting, A/PV.2061, 10 October 1972, available at: http://undocs.org/A/PV.2061.

United Nations, Statement by Mr. Hamilton Shirley Amerasinghe (Sri Lanka), elected President, Third United Nations Conference on the Law of the Sea, 1st meeting. United Nations Headquarters, New York: Codification Division, Office of Legal Affairs. (3 December 1973), available at: http://legal.un.org/avl/ha/uncls/video01.2.html.

United Nations, General Assembly, Speech by Mr Bellizzi, 2263rd Plenary Meeting, A/PV.2263, 9 October 1974, available at: http://undocs.org/A/PV.2263.

Treaties

1958 Convention on the High Seas, Geneva, 29 April 1958. 450 UNTS 11 (entered into force 30 September 1962). United Nations, *Treaty Series*, vol. 450, p. 11, available at: https://treaties.un.org/doc/Treaties/1964/06/19640610%2002-10%20AM/Ch_XXI_01_2_3_4_5p.pdf.

1958 Conventions on Fishing and Conservation of the Living Resources of the High Seas, Geneva, 29 April 1958. 559 UNTS 285, (entered into force 20 March 1966). United Nations, *Treaty Series*, vol. 559, p. 285, available at: https://www.gc.noaa.gov/documents/8_1_1958_fishing.pdf.

1958 Convention on the Territorial Sea and the Contiguous Zone, Geneva, 29 April 1958. 516 UNTS 205, (entered into force 10 September 1964). United Nations, *Treaty Series*, vol. 516, p. 205, available at: https://treaties.un.org/doc/Treaties/1964/06/19640610%2002-10%20AM/Ch_XXI_01_2_3_4_5p.pdf.

1958 Convention on the Continental Shelf, Geneva, 29 April 1958. 499 UNTS 311, (entered into force 10 June 1964). United Nations, *Treaty Series*, vol. 499, p. 311, available at: https://treaties.un.org/doc/Treaties/1964/06/19640610%2002-10%20AM/Ch_XXI_01_2_3_4_5p.pdf.

Tr*eaty on Principles Governing the Activities of States in the Exploration and Use of Outer Space, including the Moon and Other Celestial Bodies*, Adopted by the General Assembly in its resolution 2222 (XXI), opened for signature on 27 January 1967, entered into force on 10 October 1967.

United Nations Convention on the Law of the Sea (with annexes, final act and procès-verbeaux of rectification of the final act dated 3 March 1986 and 26 July 1993), Montego Bay, 10 December 1982, *United Nations Treaty Series*, vol 1833. No. 31363, p.3, available at: https://treaties.un.org/Pages/showDetails.aspx?objid=0800000280043ad5.

US Congressional Record

113 CONG. REC. H12681 (daily ed. 28 September 1967) (statement of Rep. Hall).

Other Published Sources

'First Report Submitted to the Council by the Preparatory Committee for the Codification Conference'. *The American Journal of International Law* 24, no. 1, Supplement: Official Documents (January 1930): 1–3. http://www.jstor.org/stable/2213295.

Daniell, Raymond. 'Malta Assigns a Rare Diplomat to U.N'. *New York Times*, 24 January 1965. Reprinted in *Commemoration of the 30th Anniversary of the United Nations Convention on the Law of the Sea and the Common Heritage of Mankind* (Malta: Ministry of Foreign Affairs; IMO International Maritime Law Institute), 30.

United Nations, *Disarmament and International Security (first Committee)*, accessed 30 September 2021, http://www.un.org/en/ga/first/.

Oda, Shigeru ed. *The Law of the Sea in our Time – II The United Nations Seabed Committee 1968- 1973*. Leiden: Nijhoff, 1977.

The Law of the Sea. 'The Declaration of Oaxtepec'. *Water International* 1, no.2. (1976): 4–6. 10.1080/02508067608685704. https://doi.org/10.1080/02508067608685704.

'The Chicago University Roundtable – 8/12/45 – Gordon Skene Sound Collection', accessed 30 September 2021, https://pastdaily.com/2015/08/13/the-atomic-bomb-now-what-august-12-1945/.

Wood, Forrest G., Naval Oceans Systems Center San Diego, 'Annotated Bibliography of Publications from the U.S. Navy's Marine Mammal Program'. Update November 1987, available at: https://apps.dtic.mil/sti/citations/ADA188266.

Bibliography

Adede, Andronico O. 'The System of Exploitation of the "Common Heritage of Mankind" at the Caracas Conference'. *The American Journal of International Law* 69, no. 1 (January 1975): 31–49. http://www.jstor.org/stable/2200190.

Allen, Monica. 'An Intellectual History of the Common Heritage of Mankind as Applied to the Oceans'. Master thesis, University of Rhode Island, 1992.

Anderson, David, ed. *Modern Law of the Sea. Selected Essays*, Publications on Ocean Development Volume 59. Leiden/Boston: Martinus Nijhoff Publishers, 2008.

Anderson, D. H. 'Resolution and Agreement Relating to the Implementation of Part XI of the UN Convention on the Law of the Sea: a General Assessment'. ZaöRV 55 (1995): 275–289.

Andert, Karin. *Monika Mann. Eine Biographie.* Hamburg: mareverlag, 2010.

Baker, Betsy. 'Elisabeth Mann Borgese: Making her way'. In *Elisabeth Mann Borgese und das Drama der Meere*, exhibition catalogue, edited by Holger Pils and Karolina Kühn, 88–97. Hamburg: mareverlag, 2012.

Baker, Betsy. 'Uncommon Heritage: Elisabeth Mann Borgese, Pacem in Maribus, the International Ocean Institute and Preparations for UNCLOS III'. *Ocean Yearbook Online*, Vol. 26 (Brill 2012): 11–34. https://doi.org/10.1163/22116001-92600099.

Baratts, Joseph Preston. *The Politics of World Federation: United Nations, UN Reform, Atomic Control.* Westport, Conn.: Praeger Publishing, 2004.

Baslar, Kemal. *The Concept of the Common Heritage of Mankind in International Law.* Dordrecht, The Netherlands: Martinus Nijhoff, 1998.

Beesley, Alan. 'The Negotiating Strategy of UNCLOS III: Developing and Developed Countries as Partners – A Pattern for Future Multilateral International Conferences?'. *Law and Contemporary Problems* 46, no. 2 (1983): 132–194.

Behnam, Awni. 'Whither IOI? (2): Ten Years beyond the Loss of Elisabeth Mann Borgese'. *Ocean Yearbook Online.* Vol. 26 (Brill 2012): 7–9. https://doi.org/10.1163/22116001-92600100.

Bernaerts, Arnd. *Bernaerts' Guide to the 1982 United Nations Convention on the Law of the Sea: Including the Text of the 1982 UN Convention & Agreement Concerning Part XI of 1994.* Oxford: Trafford Publishing, 2006.

Borgese, Dominica. 'Reminiscences of my mother'. In *Elisabeth Mann Borgese und das Drama der Meere*, exhibition catalogue, edited by Holger Pils and Karolina Kühn, 138–141. Hamburg: mareverlag, 2012.

Borgese, Giuseppe Antonio. *Goliath – The March of Fascism.* New York: Viking Press, 1937.

Borg, Saviour F. ed. *Malta and the Law of the Sea. A Vision – An Initiative.* Malta: Ministry of Foreign Affairs, 1996.

Borg, Saviour. '30 Years of UNCLOS. Malta's Contribution to the Process: Past and Present', speech at *UNCLOS at 30 Seminar* organised by International Ocean Institute and the University of Malta, 23 November 2012. (copy: courtesy of Saviour Borg).

Boyle, Alan. 'Law of the Sea Perspective on Climate Change'. In *The 1982 Law of the Sea Convention at 30: Successes, Challenges and New Agendas,* edited by David Freestone, 157–164. Leiden/Boston: Martinus Nijhoff Publishers, 2013.

Bronson, Rachel. 'Statement from the President and CEO'. in 'It is two and a half minutes to midnight – 2017 Doomsday Clock Statement'. *Bulletin of the Atomic Scientists* (2017): 1. https://thebulletin.org/sites/default/files/Final%202017%20Clock%20Statement.pdf.

Brown, E.D. 'The 1994 Agreement on the Implementation of Part XI of the UN Convention on the Law of the Sea: breakthrough to universality?'. *Marine Policy* 19, no. 1 (January 1995): 5–20. https://doi.org/10.1016/0308-597X(95)92569-S.

Brown, Judith M. '"Life Histories" and the History of Modern South Asia'. *The American Historical Review* 114, nr. 3 (June 2009): 587–95. https://doi.org/10.1086/ahr.114.3.587.

Busuttil, Salvino. 'Foreword', in *Common Heritage of Mankind. A Bibliography of Legal Writing,* edited by Prue Taylor and Lucy Stroud, xii. Valetta: Foundation de Malta, 2012.

Busuttil, Salvino. 'Ocean affairs'. *Times of Malta,* November 6, 2007. https://www.timesofmalta.com/articles/view/20071106/opinion/ocean-affairs.181476.

Buttigieg, Jean. 'Arvid Pardo: a diplomat with a mission'. *Symposia Melitensia,* no 12(2016). https://www.um.edu.mt/library/oar//handle/123456789/14918.

Buzan, Barry. 'Negotiating by Consensus: Developments in Technique at the United Nations Conference on the Law of the sea'. The American Journal of International Law 75, no. 2 (April 1981): 324–348. http://www.jstor.org/stable/2201255.

Carlsson, Annica. 'The US and UNCLOS III – The Death of the Common Heritage of Humankind Concept?'. *Maritime Studies* 95 (1997): 27–35. https://doi.org/10.1080/07266472.1997.10878492.

Chircop, Aldo. 'Elisabeth Mann Borgese's humanist conception of marine technology transfer'. In *Elisabeth Mann Borgese und das Drama der Meere,* exhibition catalogue, edited by Holger Pils and Karolina Kühn, 121–221. Hamburg: mareverlag, 2012.

Clemens, Wolfgang. 'Meereskundliche Weltliteratur. Elisabeth Mann Borgese und der Club of Rome'. In *Elisabeth Mann Borgese und das Drama der Meere,* exhibition catalogue, edited by Holger Pils and Karolina Kühn, 98–103. Hamburg: mareverlag, 2012.

Culbertson, Ely. 'The preliminary Draft of a World Constitution, by the Committee to Frame A World Constitution', *Indiana Law Journal* 24, no. 3, (1949): 475–482. http://www.repository.law.indiana.edu/ilj/vol24/iss3/20.

Deese, Richard Samuel. 'From World War to World Law: Elisabeth Mann Borgese and the Law of the Sea'. *World History Bulletin* 32, no. 2, (2016): 5–8. https://www.researchgate.net/publication/311707074_From_World_War_to_World_Law_Elisabeth_Mann_Borgese_and_the_Law_of_the_Sea.

De Lucia, Vito. 'The BBNJ negotiations and ecosystem governance in the arctic'. *Marine Policy* (2019). https://doi.org/10.1016/j.marpol.2019.103756.

Eckert, Wolfgang U. 'Das "Utopia" der Meer-Frau. Elisabeth Mann Borgese und der "Aufstieg der Frau" (1963–1965)'. In *Elisabeth Mann Borgese und das Drama der Meere*, exhibition catalogue, edited by Holger Pils and Karolina Kühn, 64–71. Hamburg: mareverlag, 2012.

Elferink, Alex G. Oude ed. *Stability and Change in the Law of the Sea: The role of the LOS Convention.* Leiden: Martinus Nijhoff Publishers, 2005.

Elias, Ann. *Coral Empires: Underwater oceans, colonial tropics, visual modernity.* Durham: Duke University Press, publication date 15 March 2019.

Freestone, David, ed. *The 1982 Law of the Sea Convention at 30: Successes, Challenges and New Agendas.* Leiden/Boston: Martinus Nijhoff Publishers, 2013.

Friedheim, Robert L. 'A Proper Order for the Oceans: An Agenda for the New Century'. In *Order for the Oceans at the Turn of the Century,* edited by Davor Vidas and Willy Østreng, 537–554. The Hague: Kluwer Law International, 1999.

Friedheim, Robert L., and William J. Durch. 'The International Seabed Resources Agency Negotiations and the New International Economic Order'. *International Organization* 32, no. 2 (1977): 343–384.

Friendly, Jonathan. 'Saturday Review Shuts down'. *New York Times*, August 17, 1982. https://www.nytimes.com/1982/08/17/business/saturday-review-shuts-down.html.

Friggieri, Joe and Salvino Busuttil. 'Preface'. In *Interfaces: essays in philosophy and bordering areas in honour of Peter Serracino Inglott,* edited by Joe Friggieri and Salvino Busuttil, xi–xiv. Malta: University of Malta, 1997.

Friggieri, Joe, and Salvino Busuttil, eds. *Interfaces: essays in philosophy and bordering areas in honour of Peter Serracino Inglott.* Malta: University of Malta, 1997.

Gauci, Victor J. *Genesis of Malta's Foreign Policy: A Personal Account.* Luqa: Agenda, 2005.

Geldart, Carol and Peter Lyon. 'The Group of 77: A Perspective View'. *International Affairs (Royal Institute of International Affairs 1944-)* 57, no. 1 (1980–1981): 79–101. http://www.jstor.org/stable/2619360.

Gelpke, Nikolaus. 'Der Wille hinter dem Kichern'. In *Elisabeth Mann Borgese und das Drama der Meere,* exhibition catalogue, edited by Holger Pils and Karolina Kühn, 176–179. Hamburg: mareverlag, 2012.

Gjerde, Christina M. 'Challenges to Protecting the Marine Environment beyond National Jurisdiction'. In *The 1982 Law of the Sea Convention at 30: Successes, Challenges and New Agendas,* edited by David Freestone, 165–173. Leiden/Boston: Martinus Nijhoff Publishers, 2013.

Glasby, G.P. 'Historical Introduction'. In *Marine Manganese Deposits,* edited by G. G. Glasby, 1–9. New York: Elsevier Oceanography Scientific Publishing Company, 1977.

Glazer, J. Henry. 'The Maltese Initiatives within the United Nations – A Blue Planet Blueprint for Trans-National Space'. *Ecology Law Quarterly* 4, no. 2 (1974): 279–318. https://www.jstor.org/stable/24111415.

Goettsche-Wanli, Gabriele. 'The United Nations Convention on the Law of the Sea: Multilateral Diplomacy at Work'. *Conference Diplomacy 1815–2015, UN Chronicle*, 51, no. 3 (2014). https://www.un.org/en/chronicle/article/united-nations-convention-law-sea-multilateral-diplomacy-work.

Grima, Christopher. 'Special Tribute to the late Ambassador Arvid Pardo of Malta on the occasion of the Thirtieth Anniversary of the United Nations Convention on the Law of the Sea', in *Commemoration of the 30th Anniversary of the United Nations Convention on the Law of the Sea and the Common Heritage of Mankind*, 5–7 (Malta: Ministry of Foreign Affairs; IMO International Maritime Law Institute).

Grotius, Hugo. *The Free Sea, trans. Richard Hakluyt, with William Welwod's Critique and Grotius's Reply*, edited by David Armitage. Indianapolis: Liberty Fund, 2004. http://oll.libertyfund.org/titles/859.

Hannigan, John. *The Geopolitics of Deep Oceans.* Cambridge: Polity Press, 2016.

Harrison, James. *Making the Law of the Sea. A Study in the Development of International Law.* Cambridge: Cambridge University Press, 2011.

Harpprecht, Klaus. *Thomas Mann: Eine Biographie.* Reinbek: Rowohlt, 1995.

Heidbrink, Ingo Klaus. 'The Oceans as the Common Property of Mankind from Early Modern Period to Today'. In *History Compass* 6, no. 2 (February 2008): 659–672, https://doi.org/10.1111/j.1478-0542.2007.00504.x.

Hermann, Ingo ed. *Elisabeth Mann Borgese. Die Meer Frau. Gespräch mit Amadou Seitz in der Rehe "Zeugen des Jahrhunderts"* (Göttingen: Lamuv Verlag GmbH, 1993).

Hollick, Ann. *U.S. Foreign Policy and the Law of the Sea.* Princeton: Princeton University Press, 1981.

Holzer, Kerstin. *Elisabeth Mann Borgese. Ein Lebensporträt.* Frankfurt am Main: Fischer Verlag, 2003.

Holzer, Kerstin. '"Short-term pessimist, long-term optimist!" Meere, Visionen, Scherze: eine Erinnerung an Elisabeth Mann Borgese'. In *Elisabeth Mann Borgese und das Drama der Meere*, exhibition catalogue, edited by Holger Pils and Karolina Kühn, 180–185. Hamburg: mareverlag, 2012.

Hong, Seoung-Yong, and Jon M. Van Dyke, eds. *Maritime Boundary Disputes, Settlement Processes, and the Law of the Sea*, Publications on Ocean Development Volume 65. Leiden/Boston: Martinus Nijhoff Publishers, 2009.

Höhler, Sabine. 'Exterritoriale Ressourcen: Die Diskussion um die Tiefsee, die Pole und das Weltall um 1970'. *Jahrbuch für Europäische Geschichte* 15, (2014): 53–82.

Hutchins, Robert M. et al. 'Preliminary Draft of a World Constitution', *Bulletin of the Atomic Scientists* 4, no. 5 (1948): 145–150.

Hutchins, Robert M. et al. *Preliminary Draft of a World Constitution.* Chicago: The University of Chicago Press, 1947/1948.

Jens, Inge, and Walter Jens. *Frau Thomas Mann: Das Leben der Katharina Pringsheim.* Reinbek: Rowohlt, 2004.

Johnston, Douglas. *The Historical Foundations of World Order. The Tower and the Arena.* Boston/Leiden: Martinus Nijhoff, 2007.

Kimball, Lee. 'Conference reports- Heated exchange in Geneva'. *Marine Policy* 10, no. 1 (January 1986): 60–62.

Kirton, Alan G., and Stephen C. Vasciannie. 'Deep Seabed Mining under the Law of the Sea Convention and the Implementation Agreement: Developing Country Perspectives'. *Social and Economic Studies* 51, no. 2 (June 2002): 63–115. http://www.jstor.org/stable/27865277.

Leaffer, Randall. 'Mare clausum (The Closure of the Sea or The Ownership of the Sea) 1635 John Selden (1584–1654)'. In *The Formation and Transmission of Western Legal Culture. 150 Books that Made the Law in the Age of Printing*, (Studies in the History of Law and Justice 7), edited by Serge Dauchy, Georges Martyn, Anthony Musson, Heikki Pihlajamäki and Alain Wijffels, eds., 190–194. Cham: Springer Verlag, 2016.

Leary, David Kenneth. *International Law and the Genetic Resources of the Deep Sea* Publications on Ocean Development Volume 56. Leiden: Martinus Nijhoff Publishers, 2007.

Levering, Ralph B., and Miriam L. Levering. *Citizen Action for Global Change. The Neptune Group and Law of the Sea.* New York: Syracuse University Press, 1999.

Lodge, Michael W., and Myron H. Nordquist, eds. *Peaceful Order in the World's Oceans. Essays in Honor of Satya N. Nandan.* Leiden/Boston: Brill Nijhoff, 2014.

Lodge, Michael. 'The International Seabed Authority and Deep Seabed Mining'. *UN Chronicle* 54, no. 1&2 (May 2017): 44–46. https://doi.org/10.18356/ea0e574d-en.

Li, Yuwen. *Transfer of Technology for Deep Sea-Bed Mining. The 1982 Law of the Sea Convention and Beyond.* Dordrecht: Martinus Nijhoff, 1994.

Lühe, Irmela von der. '"Ich gehöre doch zu den Kleinen" Elisabeth Mann Borgese als Chronistin ihrer "amazing family"'. In *Elisabeth Mann Borgese und das Drama der Meere*, exhibition catalogue, edited by Holger Pils and Karolina Kühn, 18–33. Hamburg: mareverlag, 2012.

Mann Borgese, Elisabeth. *Ascent of Woman.* New York: George Braziller, 1963.

Mann Borgese, Elisabeth and Eberhard Görner. '"Für mich ist Politik, an eine bessere Zukunft zu denken"'- Ein Gespräch'. In *Elisabeth Mann Borgese und das Drama der Meere*, exhibition catalogue, edited by Holger Pils and Karolina Kühn, 236–245. Hamburg: mareverlag, 2012.

Mann Borgese, Elisabeth. 'Man and the Oceans'. *Ocean Yearbook* 1 (Brill 1978): 1–8.

Mann Borgese, Elisabeth. 'Notes on the Work of the Preparatory Commission'. *Ocean Yearbook* 5 (Brill 1985): 1–9. https://doi.org/10.1163/221160085X00023.

Mann Borgese, Elisabeth. 'The Enterprises: A proposal to reconceptualise the operational arm of the International Seabed Authority to manage the common heritage of mankind'. *I.O.I Occasional Papers*, no. 6 (November 1978).

Mann Borgese, Elisabeth. *To Whom it May Concern.* New York: George Braziller, 1960.

Mccaughey, Robert A. 'Shaking things up in Chicago'. *The New York Times*, 1989. https://www.nytimes.com/1989/09/03/books/shaking-things-up-at-chicago.html.

Meadows, Donella H., and Dennis L. Meadows, Jørgen Randers and William W. Behrends Iii. *The Limits to Growth.* New York: Universe Books, 1972.

Mecklin, John, eds. 'It is a 100 seconds to midnight – 2020 Doomsday Clock Statement'. *Bulletin of the Atomic Scientists* (2020). https://thebulletin.org/wp-content/uploads/2020/01/2020-Doomsday-Clock-statement.pdf.

Mero, John L. 'Economic Aspect of Nodule Mining'. In *Marine Manganese Deposits,* edited by G. G. Glasby, 327–356. New York: Elsevier Oceanography Scientific Publishing Company, 1977.

Mero, John L. *The Mineral Resources of the Sea.* New York: New York: Elsevier Oceanography Scientific Publishing Company, 1964.

Miller, Hunter. 'The Hague Codification Conference'. *The American Journal of International Law* 24, no. 4 (October 1930): 674–693. http://www.jstor.org/stable/2190056.

Noce, Hannibal S. 'Giuseppe Antonio Borgese'. *Modern Philology* 50, no. 4, (May 1953): 217–218. https://www.jstor.org/stable/pdf/434830.pdf?refreqid=excelsior%3A4c09664181508579e876d414c219c14f.

Mahmoudi, Said. *The Law of Deep Sea-Bed Mining. A Study of the Progressive Development of International Law Concerning the Management of the Polymetallic Nodules of the Deep Sea-Bed.* Stockholm: Almqvist & Wiksell International, 1987.

Mallia, Patricia and David Testa. 'Elisabeth Mann Borgese, Gender and the Law of the Sea'. In *Gender and the Law of the Sea*, 106–121. Leiden: Brill | Nijhoff, 2019. https://doi.org/10.1163/9789004375178_005.

Mann Borgese, Elisabeth. 'The Years of my Life. The Nexus Lecture (1999)'. In *Elisabeth Mann Borgese und das Drama der Meere*, exhibition catalogue, edited by Holger Pils and Karolina Kühn, 206–225. Hamburg: mareverlag, 2012.

Mann Borgese, Elisabeth. *The oceanic circle: Governing the seas as a global resource.* Tokyo/New York/Paris: United Nations University Press, 1998.

Mann, Klaus. *Der Wendepunkt. Ein Lebensbericht.* Reinbek: Rowohlt 2006, first edition 1952.

Mann, Monika. *Vergangenes und Gegenwärtiges. Erinnerungen.* München: Kindle Verlag, 1956.

Massa, Daniel. *PSI Kingmaker: Life, Thought and Adventures of Peter Serracino Inglott.* Valetta: Allied Newspapers Ltd, 2013.

Mayer, Milton. *Robert Maynard Hutchins. A Memoir*. Berkley: University California Press, 1993.

Miles, Edward L. 'Preparations for UNCLOS IV?'. *Ocean Development and International Law* 19, no. 5 (1988): 421–430. https://doi.org/10.1080/00908328809545870.

Miles, Edward L. 'The Structure and Effects of the Decision Process in the Seabed Committee and the Third United Nations Conference on the Law of the Sea'. International Organization 31, no. 2 (1977): 159–234. https://www.jstor.org/stable/2706403.

Nun, Bernardo P. 'UNCTAD'. *Lawyer of the Americas* 4, no. 3 (October 1972): 449–459. http://www.jstor.org/stable/40175626.

Oda, Shigeru. *Fifty Years of the Law of the Sea: With a Special Section on the International Courts of Justice*. Leiden/Boston: Martinus Nijhoff, 2003.

Oxman, Bernhard H. 'The 1994 Agreement and the Convention'. *The American Journal of International Law* 88, no. 4 (October 1994): 687–696. http://www.jstor.org/stable/2204136.

Pace, Eric. 'Norman Cousins, 75, Dies; Edited The Saturday Review'. *New York Times*, December 1, 1990. https://www.nytimes.com/1990/12/01/obituaries/norman-cousins-75-dies-edited-the-saturday-review.html.

Pardo, Arvid. 'An opportunity Lost'. In *Law of the Sea U.S. Policy Dilemma,* edited by Bernhard H. Oxman, David D. Caron and Charles L.O: Buderi, 13–26. San Francisco: ICS Press, 1983.

Pardo, Arvid. 'Before and After'. *Law and Contemporary Problems* 46, no. 2, *The Law of the Sea: Where now?* (1983): 95–105. http://www.jstore.org/stable/1191516.

Payoyo, Peter Bautista. *Cries of the Sea World Inequality, Sustainable Development and the Common Heritage of Humanity*, Publication on Ocean Development Volume 33. The Hauge: Martinus Nijhoff Publishers, 1997.

Pils, Holger, and Karolina Kühn, eds. *Elisabeth Mann Borgese und das Drama der Meere*, exhibition catalogue. Hamburg: mareverlag, 2012.

Plessen, Elisabeth, and Michael Mann, eds. *Meine ungeschriebenen Memoiren*. Frankfurt am Main: Fischer Verlag, 1974.

Pörtner, Julia. 'Zwischen utopischem Optimismus und futuristischem Pessimismus. Elisabeth Mann Borgese's politische und literarische Schriften'. In *Elisabeth Mann Borgese und das Drama der Meere*, exhibition catalogue, edited by Holger Pils and Karolina Kühn, 72–85. Hamburg: mareverlag, 2012.

Ranganathan, Surabhi. 'Global Commons'. *European Journal of International Law* 27, no. 3 (August 2016): 693–717. https://doi.org/10.1093/ejil/chw037.

Ratiner, Leigh S. 'The Cost of American Rigidity'. In *Law of the Sea U.S. Policy Dilemma,* edited by Bernhard H. Oxman, David D. Caron and Charles L.O: Buderi, 33–38. San Francisco: ICS Press, 1983.

Robinson, Sam. 'Scientific imaginaries and science diplomacy: The case of ocean exploitation'. *Centaurus* (2020): 1–2. https://doi.org/10.1111/1600-0498.12342.

Rothwell, Donald R., et. al. *The Oxford Handbook of the Law of the Sea.* Oxford/New York: Oxford University Press, 2015.

Rozwadowski, Helen M. *Vast Expanses A History of the Oceans*. London: Reaktion Books, 2018.

Sanger, Clyde. *Ordering the Oceans – The Making of the Law of the Sea*. London: Zed Books Ltd., 1986.

Scharf, Michael P. 'Seizing the Grotian Moment: Accelerated Formation of Customary International Law During Times of Fundamental Change'. *Faculty Publications*, 18 (2010). http://scholarlycommons.law.case.edu/faculty_publications/18.

Schmidt, Markus G. *Common Heritage or Common Burdon? The United States position on the development of a regime for deap [sic: deep] sea-bed mining in the Law of the Sea Convention*. Oxford: Clarendon Press, 1989.

Scott, Joan W. Gender. 'A Useful Category of Historical Analysis'. *American Historical Review* 91, no. 5 (December 1986): 1053–1075.

Scott, Shirley V. 'The LOS Convention as a Constitutional Regime for the Oceans'. In *Stability and Change in the Law of the Sea: The role of the LOS Convention*, edited by Alex G. Oude Elferink, 9–38. Leiden: Martinus Nijhoff Publishers, 2005.

Sebenius, James K., and Laurence A. Green. *Tommy Koh: Background and Major Accomplishments of the "Great Negotiator, 2014"*. Working Paper 14-049, Harvard Business School, 2014.

Shastri, Sunli M. 'Elisabeth Mann Borgese: A Life Dedicated to Pacem in Maribus'. In *Ocean Yearbook*, 18 (2004): 75–85.

Shibata, Akiho. 'International Law-Making Process in the United Nations: Comparative Analysis of UNCED and UNCLOS III'. *California Western International Law Journal*, 24, no.1 (1993): 17–38.

Shils, Edward. 'Robert Maynard Hutchins'. *The American Scholar* 59, no. 2 (1990): 211–35. http://www.jstor.org/stable/41211779.

Sinjela, A. Mpazi. *Land-Locked States and the UNCLOS Regime*. London: Oceana Publications, Inc., 1983.

Sohn, Louis B. 'International Law Implications of the 1994 Agreement'. *The American Journal of International Law* 88, no. 4 (October 1994): 696–705. http://www.jstor.org/stable/2204137.

Sparenberg, Ole. 'A historical perspective on deep-sea mining for manganese nodules, 1965–2019'. *The Extractive Industries and Society* 6, nr. 3 (2019): 842–854. https://doi.org/10.1016/j.exis.2019.04.001.

Sprecher, Thomas. 'Eine Jugend in Zürich. Elisabeth Mann in den Jahren 1933–1938'. In *Elisabeth Mann Borgese und das Drama der Meere*, exhibition catalogue, edited by Holger Pils and Karolina Kühn, 34–45. Hamburg: mareverlag, 2012.

Stefano, Giovanni di. 'Giuseppe Antonio Borgese. Porträt eines unruhigen Weltenbürgers'. In *Elisabeth Mann Borgese und das Drama der Meere*, exhibition catalogue, edited by Holger Pils and Karolina Kühn, 46–63. Hamburg: mareverlag, 2012.

Suy, Erik. Foreword to *Land-Locked States and the UNCLOS Regime.* London: Oceana Publications, Inc., 1983, xi.

Taylor, Prue. 'The Common Heritage of Mankind: A Bold Doctrine Kept Within Strict Boundaries'. In *The Wealth of the Commons. A World Beyond Market & State,* edited by David Bollier and Silke Helfrich. Amherst: Levellers Press, 2013. http://wealthofthecommons.org/essay/common-heritage-mankind-bold-doctrine-kept-within-strict-boundaries.

Testa, Michael. 'An insider's look at foreign policy'. *Times of Malta,* November 13, 2004. https://www.timesofmalta.com/articles/view/20041113/local/an-insiders-look-at-foreign-policy.107258.

Treves, Tullio. '1958 Geneva Conventions on the Law of the Sea'. United Nations Audivisual Library of International Law, (2008). http://legal.un.org/avl/ha/gclos/gclos.html.

Treves, Tullio. 'Historical Development of the Law of the Sea'. In *The Oxford Handbook of the Law of the Sea,* edited by Donald R. Rothwell et. Al, 1–23. Oxford/New York: Oxford University Press, 2015.

Tuerk, Helmut. *Reflections on the Contemporary Law of the Sea.* Boston: Martinus Nijhoff Publishers, 2012.

Tuerk, Helmut. 'The Thirtieth Anniversary of the United Nations Convention on the Law of the Sea and the Common Heritage of Mankind'. In *Commemoration of the 30th Anniversary of the United Nations Convention on the Law of the Sea and the Common Heritage of Mankind,* 17–27. Malta: Ministry of Foreign Affairs; IMO International Maritime Law Institute.

Van Doorn, Rijk. *Legal implications of the 'common heritage' principle for Atlantic bluefin tuna.* (Berlin: Duncker & Humblot, forthcoming).

Van Duzer, Chet. 'Hic sunt dracones: the geography and cartography of monsters'. In *The Ashgate Research Companion to Monsters and the Monstrous,* edited by Asa Simon Mittman and Peter Dendle, 387–435. Oxford: Routledge, 2012.

Vasciannie, Stephen Charles. *Land-Locked and Geographically Disadvantaged States in the International Law of the Sea.* Oxford: Clarendon Press, 1990.

Vicuña, Francisco Orrego. *The exclusive economic zone. Regime and legal nature under international law.* Cambridge: Cambridge University Press, 1989.

Vitzthum, Wolfgang Graf, ed. *Die Plünderung der Meere. Ein gemeinsames Erbe wird zerstückelt.* Frankfurt am Main: Fischer Taschenbuch Verlag, 1981.

Vidas, Davor, ed. *Law, Technology and Science for Oceans in Globalisation. Iuu Fishing, Oil Pollution, Bioprospecting, Outer Continental Shelf.* Leiden: Martinus Nijhoff Publishers, 2010.

Vidas, Davor, and Willy Østreng, eds. *Order for the Oceans at the Turn of the Century.* The Hague: Kluwer Law International, 1999.

Vislie, Ingolf. *Jens Evensen. Havet, oljen og retten.* Stamsund: Orkana forlag as, 2017.

Watt, Donald Cameron. 'First steps in the enclosure of the oceans. The origins of Truman's proclamation on the resources of the continental shelf, 28 September 1945'. *Marine Policy,* 3 (1979): 211–224. Doi: 10.1016/0308-597X(79)90053-8.

Wehrli, Peter K. '"Überall ist alles anders!" Mit Elisabeth auf dem Landweg nach Indien'. In *Elisabeth Mann Borgese und das Drama der Meere*, exhibition catalogue, edited by Holger Pils and Karolina Kühn, 142–175. Hamburg: mareverlag, 2012.

Zangrandi, Ruggero. *A Train to the Brenner.* London: GALLERY PRESS LTD, 1963.

Webpages

Bulletin of the Atomic Scientists. 'Background and Mission: 1945–2018' accessed 30 September 2021, available at: https://thebulletin.org/background-and-mission-1945-2018.

Duve, Thomas, 'Treaty of Tordesillas', *Max Planck Encyclopedia of Public International Law,* January 2013, accessed 30 September 2021, available at: https://opil.ouplaw.com/view/10.1093/law:epil/9780199231690/law-9780199231690-e2088#.

Encyclopaedia Britannica, s.v. 'History of Publishing – The United States – Saturday Review', accessed 30 September 2021, available at: https://www.britannica.com/topic/Saturday-Review-American-magazine.

Johnson, Lyndon B. 'Remarks at the Commissioning of the Research Ship – Oceanographer'. (speech, Washington, DC, 13 July 1966). *The American Presidency Project,* accessed 30 September 2021, available at: http://www.presidency.ucsb.edu/ws/index.php?pid=27711.

METI Ministry of Economy, Trade and Industry. 'World's First Success in Continuous Ore Lifting test for Seafloor Polymetallic Sulphides, Pilot test of excavating and ore lifting conducted for seafloor polymetallic sulphides under the sea area near Okinawa Prefecture'. METI, 2017, accessed 30 September 2021, available at: http://www.meti.go.jp/english/press/2017/0926_004.html.

The Club of Rome. 'Timeline', accessed 30 September 2021, available at: https://www.clubofrome.org/about-us/history/.

The International Ocean Institute. 'Pacem in Maribus (PIM) Conferences – Past Conferences: (1970–2013)', accessed 30 September 2021, available at: https://www.ioinst.org/about-1/pacem-in-maribus-pim-conferences/.

Ocean Decade, UNESCO 2019. '2021–2030 United Nations Decade of Ocean Science for Sustainable Development', accessed 30 September 2021, available at: https://www.oceandecade.org/.

United Nations Audiovisual Library of International Law. 'Procedural History', accessed 30 September 2021, available at: http://legal.un.org/avl/ha/uncls/uncls.html.

Index

Printed in the United States
by Baker & Taylor Publisher Services